UNDERSTANDING CULTURE

UNDERSTANDING CULTURE

JOHN J. HONIGMANN
PROFESSOR of ANTHROPOLOGY
UNIVERSITY of NORTH CAROLINA

HARPER & ROW, PUBLISHERS
NEW YORK, EVANSTON, AND LONDON

Contents

Preface

Science, Charles Péguy said, is perpetually uncertain while, on the contrary, teaching demands imperturbable assurance. I hope that the confidence with which I assert certain ideas, definitions, and viewpoints will be understood as the mask of a teacher.

By including in this book events of our own time I do what Edward B. Tylor, pioneer anthropologist, branded as unwise. Cultural anthropology has changed since Tylor's day. It needs very much to test its strength on things "of high importance" rather than on "dead old history." Anthropology can be of greatest service when it treats issues "alive with intense party feeling," even though such issues invite judgment "biassed by the pressure of personal sympathy."[1]

My indebtedness includes many individuals and groups. To the interest of Cornelius Osgood and a fund established by Mr. and Mrs. William A. Castleton aided by contributions from the Peabody Museum, Yale University, I owe my opportunities to visit the Kaska Indians in 1944 and 1945 for a total of eight months. All references to the Kaska are prior to that date (just as Hopi data are generally pre-1941). A Fulbright research grant for Pakistan enabled me to spend 14 weeks in Swat during the spring and summer of 1958. The Wenner-Gren Foundation for Anthropological Research generously supported other field studies that increased my ability to understand culture. The Research Council of the University of North Carolina Graduate School in many ways furthered my research and to a tremendous extent I have benefited from membership in the Institute for Research in Social Science. The preparation of this book was quite directly aided from that source. I must also acknowledge the benefit derived through a most equitable teach-

[1] Edward B. Tylor, *Primitive Culture,* 3rd ed., 2 vols. (London, 1891), vol. I, p. 158.

vii

ing schedule at the University of North Carolina.

Coming to individuals, Victor Barnouw, Frances Ferguson, Ruth S. Freed, Stanley A. Freed, and Mickey Gibson read parts of the manuscript and offered me the benefit of their criticism. I have been helped by Joffre Coe, John Gulick, Harold M. Hodges, Jr., George Holcomb, Robert J. Braidwood, and Lewis Levine. Less in response to my direct questions many other professional colleagues and graduate students have guided my ideas. Elsewhere I acknowledge individuals and institutions supplying photographs and other art work; here I want to offer them my personal thanks. Photos not otherwise credited are hereby acknowledged as my own, with the exception of page 172 where names are withheld to spare possible embarrassment. Shanta Bhutani checked many references and hunted down obscure quotations. Samuel M. Boone of the Photographic Laboratory, Wilson Library, University of North Carolina, solved several photographic problems for me. The whole library staff proved most generous in its assistance. Finally, Irma Honigmann's unsparing criticism and help contributed greatly to an effort for which I assume full responsibility.

J. J. H.

Chapel Hill
October, 1962

UNDERSTANDING CULTURE

What Is There to Understanding Culture?

The lofty contempt which a civilised people entertains for barbarous neighbours has caused a remarkable negligence in observing them, and this carelessness has been aggravated at times by fear, by religious prejudice, and even by the use of these very terms—civilisation and barbarism—which convey to most persons the impression of a difference not merely in degree but in kind.

Henry Maine (1861)[1]

INTERCULTURAL RELATIONS ABROAD AND AT HOME

Today's world challenges everyone to understand culture. Through radio, television, tourism, foreign relations, and technical assistance programs, we all come up against people whose values, interests, and intentions clash with ours. Despite thoroughgoing differences we must enlist their collaboration. Occasionally, with unusual insight, we do penetrate another culture. It makes sense that Eskimo, who depend on a treeless terrain, willingly eat uncooked meat and fish. We understand why people lacking knowledge of ovum and sperm should accept children as given by gods. We can see that other myths than ours are able to conserve and sanctify the past and boost morale.

On the whole, however, we are inadequately prepared to deal with cultural diversity. Experts who go abroad technically well qualified to cut down infant deaths, improve nutrition, or increase food production are unequipped to understand how the problems with which they must deal are rooted in a foreign way of life. Guidebooks tell tourists precisely what monuments and buildings to visit but stop short of explaining lifeways they will encounter abroad. If we

[1] *Ancient Law,* Everyman's Library edition (London, 1917), p. 71.

1

THERE MUST BE UNDERSTANDING

"If we are to develop the kind of understanding that will avoid the great catastrophe of war, we must know about the cultures of these countries—the history of them. And above all, why do they react to certain actions, certain considerations and circumstances in this world in a different way from which we do. Will we be able to achieve an understanding that shows why they do it, make allowances for it, and then knowing that, go ahead in devising and composing those arrangements in the world that will gradually abolish this terrible scourge?"

Dwight D. Eisenhower

Speech at Trinity College, Hartford, Conn., October 20, 1954. Quoted from a White House release.

want to learn, we must know what questions to ask and how to interpret our observations.

Ours is a closely knit world in which, thanks to efficient communication, powerful transportation, and deadly long-range weapons, time and distance have shriveled. Hence, more than ever before it is hazardous for people of different cultures to live together with inadequate understanding. Don't expect the distributive energies of Hollywood and other arms of American business to submerge international cultural differences. In fact, without ever leaving home, in a U.S. town cultures diverging from one social class or ethnic group to another challenge our understanding. Not only unfamiliar customs but even our own taken-for-granted lifeways frequently benefit from fresh understanding. The aim of this book is to develop skill for the better understanding of any culture.

CULTURE

Two hundred Kaska Indians live in the boreal forest of northwestern British Columbia.[2] Their culture includes substantial log cabins with glass windows and stoves. Though the Indians themselves make only the cabins, buying the windows and stoves, all three elements are traits of Kaska culture. This culture also includes the Indians' techniques of trapping beaver and other fur-bearing animals, catching fish, and hunting moose. It includes their covert beliefs and knowledge that guide these activities and endow their lives with purpose. Traits limited to men or women, like men's pride in hunting or women's ambivalent feelings toward marriage, also comprise Kaska culture.

[2] John J. Honigmann, *The Kaska Indians: An Ethnographic Reconstruction,* Yale University Publications in Anthropology, no. 51, 1954.

Obviously this term culture embraces a great deal. It designates man-made artifacts, activities people perform, and ideas and feelings. When I speak of *a* culture I mean a way of life belonging to a designated aggregate of people, for instance, to the 200 Kaska Indians. Some of a culture's traits may be universally shared and others restricted to one age or sex. Some traits emanated from other cultures, arriving perhaps in trade, to become elements of the culture in question. Every culture is a unique constellation of traits, even though some of the traits are very widespread in human society.

SOCIAL STANDARDIZATION

What do cultural traits like houses, glass, stoves, hunting techniques, pride, and ambivalence share that allows them to be combined in a single concept? In the first place—unlike hair, salivating, or breathing—their existence depends little on biological heredity or maturation but on individuals' membership in society. Cultural traits are natural, yet they are not part of nature like trees, moose, snow, and rivers. Artifacts and both overt and covert behavior become cultural through social standardization.

In any culture a house is what it is because, through communication with others in society, the builder derived his ideas of what a dwelling should be. Furthermore, the house became what it is through the construction skills, tools, and labor available in a particular society. Change these and you change the house. In much the same way every cultural trait is socially standardized, that is, it is shaped or patterned by an individual's interaction with other individuals or by artifacts—tools, navigation aids, and vehicles—that are themselves products of social life. As an individual matures he does practically nothing that is not socially standardized or cultural. A hunter does not look for game simply because he is hungry. He hunts to fulfill his duty as husband or father and to preserve or enhance his reputation with his fellows. He learns his techniques of hunting or he originates new ones to improve on what he sees other men do. His techniques are also influenced by available equipment; the gun's advent led the Kaska to alter their hunting techniques, which in turn led them to modify other elements of their life. Social standardization penetrates even into covert traits of behavior, into a person's dreams, anxieties, and unconscious fantasies.

I am aware that I have offered only a skeleton definition of culture by equating it with artifacts, activities, and thoughts and feelings that are socially standardized. Really all I have done is to delineate phenomena called culture. I have demarcated culture from other parts of the world with which an anthropologist is only secondarily concerned. Actually, this book is an extended characterization of culture. Before going on to this, however, I propose to look at understanding as it applies to culture.

Houses, ornament, carvings, dress, posture, expression, states of feeling, in fact practically everything man does is conditioned through the individual's membership in society. (*New Zealand Embassy, photograph from National Publicity Studios, Wellington.*)

STARTING WITH HISTORY

When we confront an unfamiliar custom most of us ask at once how it came to be. Early anthropologists also occupied themselves zealously trying to account for living customs in terms of the dead past. The trouble is that these nineteenth-century scholars lacked direct historical evidence to back up their conclusions. Here is an example. Seeking the origin of animal sacrifice among Arabs and Biblical Jews, William Robertson Smith sought to trace it back to human society's primogenial times.[3] In those early days, Smith affirms, all kins-

[3] William Robertson Smith, *Lectures on the Religion of the Semites,* 3rd ed., (New York, 1927; first published in 1889).

men on occasion shared a common meal from which they barred nonkin. Because early man ethnocentrically regarded his god as a kinsman, he was included in the party. The animal killed for meat really represented another human kinsman who was being symbolically sacrificed to god. In time, Smith explains, sacrificial rites, although descended from this ancient ceremony, no longer acknowledged the animal to represent a human being. Robertson Smith's great influence reached Vienna where Sigmund Freud incorporated parts of Smith's theory of early sacrifice into his own work. According to Freud, however, the animal sacrificed in Arab and Jewish rites unconsciously symbolized a father slain in earliest times by his rebellious sons.[4] The old man had been

Parts of the body may be socially standardized, like the hair of these boys. (*Government of India Information Services.*)

guilty of monopolizing all women in the horde, arousing his sons' sexual jealousy.

The accounts of Freud and Smith do not correspond, and who can possibly say which one is true because neither is backed by evidence. Most professional anthropologists have abandoned the nineteenth-century method of speculating about how culture began. True history depends on trustworthy, first-hand evidence that has managed to escape ravages of flood, fire, theft, and loss in its persistence from the past. Documents, newspapers, or archeological remains dug from the earth's littered crust constitute acceptable evidence for history. But such evidence of the past is scarce. For many customs we simply lack any evidence of how they became what they are.

Furthermore, if we did know the history of, say, polygamy in an African tribe, Eskimo infanticide, or sodomy in a New Guinea initiation rite, how well would we understand these customs? Is history really what we want? Suppose somebody asks me about the custom of Americans carrying small travel clocks and wrist watches. I research the custom and tell him that small clocks originated in medieval Europe while "wrist clocks" go back to the sixteenth century. How satisfied will he be? If, like many Americans, he has been forced to study history for 8 or 12 years, he may be stunned into silence. He doesn't know what other questions to ask. How much better he would grasp the custom of making timepieces our constant companions if I point out to him two things which at first glance he doesn't connect with the custom:

4 Sigmund Freud, *Totem and Taboo,* trans. A. A. Brill (New York, 1918).

CONTRIBUTION OF THE PAST

(British Information Services)

Make a test for yourself, without prejudice. What contribution does history make to understanding this typical scene of English workingmen drinking beer in a pub?

Six thousand years ago Mesopotamians and Egyptians from cereals brewed a beer fit for the gods. Ancient Germans engaged in boisterous and quarrelsome drinking bouts that lasted up to 24 hours. Note that drinking in boisterous male company, as men in the photograph seem to be doing, is an antique trait of European culture. Not until Christian times did Europeans add hops to beer. Even before the Angles and Saxons left Germany and arrived in Britain (fifth century A.D.), beer had been brewed in Britain. Christian missionaries there tried to check excessive drinking but even monks tippled and besides they brewed excellent beer. In 1400 commercial inns grew up alongside religious hospices to accommodate travelers. These alehouses—forerunners of pubs—formed social centers frequented by local people.

Now, how well do you understand what these men are doing?

Based on Brian Spiller, "The Story of Beer," *The Geographical Magazine*, 28 (1955), 86-94, 143-154, 169-181. Pubs are treated on pp. 178 ff.

Americans' compulsive time-consciousness and the fact that our lives are rigidly ordered. We have a saying, "Time is money." Trains and planes depart (and more miraculously often arrive) precisely on a minute. Anyone late to work or for an appointment inconveniences others. He is trained to feel embarrassed at being late and may have part of his wages docked. Isn't our use of travel clocks and wrist watches understood better in this context of culture than simply in the light of history?

My attitude toward history claims that the best understanding of culture comes when we know about all relevant characteristics present in a situation at a given time. Something that belongs wholly to the past is as irrelevant for understanding the present as something wholly in the future. The American Civil War helps us understand contemporary relations between North and South only to the extent that its bitter traces have survived. These traces must be known for they are relevant to the problem. But note that they are important only because they continue to live in the present and are not wholly a part of the dead past. Having said this, let me admit that tracing a current event back to wholly past events out of which it grew can be useful. Our use of clocks and watches is illumined by knowledge of horological beginnings and the subsequent evolution of timepieces. My complaint is that we too readily substitute historical illumination for another kind of enlightenment—the kind that social science emphasizes.

Some questions about culture are best answered historically. I have in mind questions of cultural transformation, for example, how did civilization evolve in the Near East, eastern Mediterranean, and North America? Also, satisfactory answers to some questions about living cultures demand historical facts. Why does Russia use an alphabet different from the Roman script common in western Europe? Russians, we could say, prefer their script and perpetuate their literature by retaining it. Surely a less hollow answer is that the Cyrillic alphabet is part of the script which ninth-century Greek Christian missionaries created to spread their doctrines.

Unfortunately, the past often delivers no remainders from which to read history. Nonliterate people in particular can't leave written documents. Occasionally ingenious substitutes can be employed to overcome the absence of tangible historical information. A check on the degree to which cultural traits correspond in different parts of the world may show whether they could have come from a single source. Are the pyramids built by ancient Mexicans lineal descendants of ancient Egyptian pyramids? How much do they actually correspond in their construction and use? South of the Rio Grande truncated pyramids provided platforms on which to poise temples. Ancient Egyptians, however, constructed sharp conical pyramids containing sealed tombs. The fact is that forms correspond as little as use. This constitutes reasonable proof that the two traits are historically independent. Other resemblances between these two civilizations when closely examined turn out to be equally superficial, making it fairly clear that no matter how far Egypt's influence reached, it failed to arrive in prehistoric Mexico. Now consider a pair of mosques, one located in West Africa and the other in Lahore, a cosmopolitan city of West

Similarities of form and use between these mosques in West Africa (top) and Pakistan (bottom) attest to their historical relationship. (*French Embassy Press and Information Division; Pakistan Embassy.*)

Pakistan. Despite numerous but unessential differences in architectural style and decoration, each is an Islamic place of prayer. Construction encloses an open place facing a wall niche that orients worshipers toward the Arabian city of Mecca. The conical pillars of the African mosque parallel the stately minarets on the larger Asian structure. Form and use correspond at so many points that the two traits must be connected. In this instance abundant documentary evidence confirms Islam's propagation in these two regions.

CONTEXT IS VITAL

The first rule for understanding any bit of culture is that it must be seen in its fullest possible context—in relationship to all other simultaneously present, relevant factors. This is a big demand. It takes time and intellectual effort to grasp a total culture. And a total culture is the fullest relevant context in which particular aspects—religion, economy, family life, politics—take on meaning and significance. It is for this reason that an anthropologist tries to spend at least a year and often more learning another culture. What he observes may be misinterpreted or seem meaningless unless it can be studied in relation to the total culture.

Take these words which have conveniently been translated into English. What have we here?

> With your strong feet rise up to protect me
> With your healthy mind rise up to protect me.[5]

Navaho Indians speak these lines in a ceremony addressed to a deity. The context, a ceremony, tells us that here we have something religious. In addition to the smaller context, the ceremony, it helps to know more about the larger context, Navaho life as a whole, including the geographical conditions in which the Navaho lives. This knowledge tells us more about the meaning of the lines. Navaho farm in an arid region where crops easily fail. They also raise livestock, but heavy winter snows threaten their herds. Instead of trying to bend the geographical environment to their wills, for example, through mighty feats of irrigation, they aim to live in harmony with nature. To maintain harmony, trained singers mediate between man and forces in his universe, and the words quoted are part of a long liturgy which competent singers have mastered. Now you see how context enriches understanding.

Care is essential in collecting facts of context. Stereotyped presuppositions of what a culture is like won't help understanding and can do serious harm. Each culture must be known in its own terms. Nothing is gained by lumping Navaho Indians with all other American Indians or with so called "primitive people." Cultural context is best mastered by living in it, which means moving among the people and sharing their lives as much as possible. To attain such intimacy anthropologists do field work. Talent for mastering a foreign culture requires humility and willingness to be taught. People who are intolerant and impatient with everything that is unlike their own life can't go far in understanding exotic cultures.

TWO QUESTIONS

Understanding any bit of culture viewed in context means answering two questions: What is the purpose or meaning of this behavior or artifact? What are its functions?

[5] Gladys A. Reichard, *Prayer: The Compulsive Word,* Monographs of the American Ethnological Society, no. 7, 1944, p. 24.

The Ewe (West Africa) school children and the air force couple are both dancing, but the contexts are quite different. (*British Information Services, Crown Copyright Reserved; U.S. Air Force.*)

We discover purpose and meaning by asking people why they have particular artifacts, act in certain ways, or hold given beliefs. If the actor is conscious of his motives he gives us the answer we seek. He describes the goals he is pursuing, explains how he evaluates his situation, or reveals his regard for the invisible realm that ultimately controls the outcome he expects. We learn the assumptions with which he plants, prays, sorcerizes his enemy, or woos his bride. These covert matters constitute the existential, that is, the subjective, side of culture. They tell us how individuals experience their culture and, in fact, the whole world in which they move. Men act in terms of their realm of meanings, goals, values, assumptions, and perceptions. Everything people find to exploit in their environment depends on what that environment means to them. The "same" activity can spring from vastly different frames of meaning. The Navaho singer's words, "rise up to protect me," may be spoken with a covert sense of surrender and helplessness or, as the Navaho in fact speak them, as a charm containing within itself the power to compel automatically some kind of reciprocal return. We can't tell from the song alone; we must know the underlying meaning of the words for the individual.

I shall ignore the fact that intentions are sometimes obvious and need no probing. It is more important to recognize that the aims people confess can simply be collective rationalizations. We note such rationalizations faithfully, even though we suspect that more subtle, implicit purposes and meanings also motivate their behavior. To learn these implicit or even unconscious meanings requires close study of many kinds of behavior and attentive familiarity with the actors. Subtle clues expose the deeper currents of thought.

Whether people reveal aims and meaning straightforwardly or an observer

A HAPPY MEANING

(*C. O'Kane*, Sun in the Sky, *University of Oklahoma Press.*)

This design has an especially happy significance for the Hopi Indians of Arizona. It symbolizes the whirlwind that precedes rain. During the growing season rain promises life and abundance for these desert people.

painstakingly deduces them, the final test of correctness lies in the context of the behavior we seek to understand. Purpose and meaning are always checked against context for consistency. A hundred years ago a traveler would have heard a Kaska Indian describe his menstruating wife as a threat to his hunting powers.[6] The traveler would also have seen the religious care with which menstruating women secluded themselves in the forest away from dwellings and their cautious avoidance of contact with a hunter's snowshoes and weapons. In this behavior the traveler would have found corroboration of what the Indian had told him about menstruation being a threat to hunting. The traveler penetrated still further into the meaning of menstruation when he noted that hunting was vital for Kaska survival. Everything supported the literalness of the hunter's fear.

Meanings and values alter with time, even if the outward form of traits— say, ceremonial observances—remains the same. The Chiricahua Apache Indians retain many traits of a girl's puberty ceremony which their ancestors used long ago when they still lived in the Canadian north, neighbors of the Kaska Indians.[7] A girl at puberty is still forbidden to touch water with her lips; hence she drinks through a tube. She dare not scratch herself with her nails lest they inflict scars; so she uses a stick. She restricts her movements and doesn't wash. She doesn't laugh or talk much. These are old traits in the Indians' culture. But the Apache have endowed a girl's puberty rite with new

---

[6] Honigmann, *op. cit.*, pp. 122-126.
[7] Morris E. Opler, *An Apache Life-Way* (Chicago, 1941), pp. 82-134.

meaning. In the Far North menstruation threatened men because it weakened their hunting ability. The Apache ceremonially rejoice when a girl reaches menstruation because then she embodies a goddess who confers blessing, long life, and health.

THE DIFFERENCE IT MAKES

The function of any item of culture is whatever difference it makes in the whole realm of life being studied. What hinges on it? Even if Kaska Indians today retained their former custom of secluding a menstruating woman (which they don't) we wouldn't expect them to be able to explain fully the difference that seclusion makes. They lack a theory for the task and functional interpretation depends on theory.

Judging from what we know about customs that separate men from women—that is, going by our theory—menstrual seclusion among the Kaska probably reinforced a notion firmly entrenched in many cultures, namely, that men and women constitute very different kinds of human beings. Menstrual seclusion probably served a second function. Purposefully, remember, it sought to protect the hunter's vital ability from mystical contamination. Functionally, it accentuated the hunter's importance and conspicuousness, reminding people that here was a man who contributed heavily to survival. Also, the Indians stood convinced that menstrual sequestration was necessary. The actual practice of seclusion regularly displayed that conviction publicly, the way pledging the flag openly demonstrates our patriotism. As with any conviction shared by a social group, bringing this one out in the open probably promoted social solidarity. That was its third function. Finally, seclusion must have effectively prevented men from having sex relations with a menstruating woman. So presumably it functioned to protect men from infection during this interval in the woman's monthly cycle.

Note how often I used "probable" in explaining this bit of culture functionally. Seldom can we be positive that a functional relationship indeed holds true. Though only probable rather than certain, each relationship I traced between seclusion of women and another concomitant condition is wholly warranted by the theory I used to understand menstrual seclusion. And I have come through this exercise convinced that the underlying theory possesses sufficient plausibility to continue using it in other cultures until a better one comes along.

A theory is clearly a basic instrument for understanding culture functionally. Anyone who explains an act in terms of its likely "consequences" is applying theory. Take, for example, the statement, "Swimming in that dirty river will make people sick." An underlying theory predicts that dirty water is infectious. This much of the theory is popular knowledge in our culture. Further research may explain more clearly why swimming in dirty water injures health. The theory may then become quite technical. Technical theories are restricted to specialists. Because anthropological theory is restricted, everybody doesn't possess requisite knowledge to make functional interpretations about culture. Of course, theory can be learned. To understand culture it is worthwhile to spend some time becoming familiar with cultural anthropological theories.

New theories are likely to be created whenever an observer puzzles over the difference some custom makes. Obviously he is puzzled because he lacks a satisfactory theory to apply. Finally, from his knowledge of the custom's context he essays a functional explanation and then critically examines it to make certain that it fits the facts of the particular situation. If it does, the theory is ready to be tested in other cultures. Should it continue to make cultural facts intelligible then we can bless it as useful, at least for the time being. Scientific theories are not unalterable dogmas. They are tentative statements about how the world is organized. What truth they possess comes from their ability to withstand serious contradiction and their sustained utility.

The function of a cultural trait is very apt to be confused with the task it does. Family life purposefully provides care for children too young to survive by themselves. That is its obvious task. A generator provides power; that constitutes its use. Little theory is needed to discover task and use compared to far less obvious functional relationships.

FUNCTIONS FOR INDIVIDUAL, GROUP, OR CULTURE

Functionalism dominates contemporary anthropology. Most anthropologists prefer to follow this method rather than to understand culture in purely existential terms of purposes and meanings.

The functions anthropologists trace are of different kinds. Following Malinowski we can examine a culture trait to see how it serves or fails to serve individual needs.[8] Does it promote adaptation, that is, does it help the individual to survive? Hunting obviously aids survival; in fact, survival is its major purpose. Or, adjustment may hinge on a practice. A custom is adjustive rather than adaptive when it gratifies some learned but not vital individual need or when it reduces tension. The now widespread coffee break in American business is adjustive when it provides workers with a chance to ventilate their gripes, loosen their accumulated tensions, and boost their prestige by exchanging experiences. In the long run adjustive customs doubtlessly contribute to survival; but taking a shorter view demonstrates their more immediate functions. An item of culture may very well function to pile up stress or tension, at least for some of the people whom it involves. Discrimination directed against Negroes in the United States hinders their adjustment and exposes

[8] Bronislaw Malinowski, *A Scientific Theory of Culture and Other Essays* (Chapel Hill, 1944). Malinowski is also interested in societal "needs."

them to severe stress. Stress is one of the functions of discriminatory practices in this country.

In distinction to Malinowski's individual-centered approach, Radcliffe-Brown[9] taught us to see culture for the difference it makes for an organized aggregate of people. Does the trait help maintain a group intact continuously from one generation to another? The family with its many component customs of child care and socialization contributes to a community's continuity. Does the trait promote social cohesion, group solidarity, or social stability? Shared social values—values for or against anything—further social solidarity. Almost any religion, no matter how pointless an outsider finds it, cements a group and so do emblems, flags, and mascots. Culture traits that function to restrain behavior within approved limits do much to maintain group stability and temporal continuity.

Finally, we may choose to understand culture functionally by asking how any particular item of culture depends on or gives rise to other traits.[10] Plow agriculture makes a difference in many other aspects of culture. The rise of cities, for example, is connected with plow farming. Plow farming can support a large number of people all of whom need not be engaged in agriculture. Nonfarmers aggregate in cities and carry on crafts, administration, and other professions. Note that plows do not act directly on the physical development of cities. Refer back a moment to how periodic seclusion of women creates and maintains the idea that men are important figures. Men's enhancement occurs in the perception of people who experience the act of seclusion and participate in its meaning. So a flag that symbolizes a group cements individuals who rally around the emblem. The relationships between flag and group unity, seclusion and masculine importance, and plow and city life are all mediated through human consciousness. In the case of the flag, people experience an emotional thrill in rallying. This thrill cements their attachments to one another. The relationship of cities to plows is a bit more complex. Before cities can appear people must perceive an advantage in the plow. In one way or another they must choose to produce enough crops to support administrators and craftsmen and the latter must elect to live in cities. The relationship is not direct, causal, or deterministic but a matter of motivation or choice.

Functional relationships are often stated mechanically—this is a function of that—but this is merely a shorthand way of speaking. Abstractions—plow agriculture, cities, enhancement of man's importance—cannot act on one another the way one chemical works on another. Functional relationships that explain culture in terms of the surrounding world (mud walls and small windows in hot, dry lands function as defenses against heat) must also be

[9] A. R. Radcliffe-Brown, *A Natural Science of Society* (Glencoe, Ill., 1957).
[10] E. D. Chapple and C. S. Coon take this position in *Principles of Anthropology* (New York, 1942).

TIME OUT FOR HERRING

(*Caltex*)

Customs in every culture are to a large degree arbitrary. How people will order their lives depends partly on the resources of nature and on their biological demands. Thus, everybody must eat. Food comes from the seas, forests, and fields that people exploit. But *what* people choose to eat, how often they eat daily, or what they deem to be a fitting meal varies from one culture to another.

The coffee break gives Americans a chance to recoup energy and morale. In Holland the herring break serves the same function. This photograph was taken outside an oil refinery near Rotterdam.

conceived of as mediated by choosing, reflective, inventive organisms. Nature doesn't cause us to build thick walls, eat herring, wear clothes, or carry umbrellas. Rather, we experience some feature of the natural world, reflect on it, and discover ways of adapting it for greater human satisfaction.

However, when a functional relationship is traced the other way, from culture to the natural world (erosion of the high plains west of the Mississippi was one function of plow farming), then human consciousness is not as closely involved. True, man has a choice of plowing or not plowing and a latent ability to perceive what follows his choice, but the earth can't choose. Tracing relationships from culture to noncultural phenomena is in the tradition of natural science which, unlike social science, need not be concerned with matters of reflection and decision. A great vogue exists to use natural science methods as completely as possible to solve social science problems. I believe that a substantial distinction exists between the two fields and that in studying man a unique approach, summarized in the last three paragraphs, is desirable.

FURTHER PATHS TO UNDERSTANDING

In addition to assessing purpose, meaning, and function other approaches lead to understanding. Just to see a culture as a whole, to view its political and economic dogmas against a total background toward which the people themselves are oriented, enhances understanding. A view of the whole culture is apt to show the same basic themes—competitiveness, resourcefulness, a sense of life as threat—recurring in several areas of life. Noting these themes enriches our understanding of a culture. The whole extends beyond culture and embraces the environmental situation in which people exist. We gain fuller appreciation of political problems facing a nation in an arid land when we also attend to the geographic fact of aridity. Anthropology ranks as unique among social sciences for the comprehensive way it pursues holistic understanding. It attempts to see poetry, religion, philosophy, class, and politics as interwoven in a total setting.

We profit, too, by noting when exotic customs are analogous to our own, recognizing, for example, that other people, too, practice religion, etiquette, or discrimination; only the forms of the behaviors differ. The aboriginal Kaska Indians abandoned an aged member who could not keep up when the hungry band traveled in pursuit of game and fish. Is this so shocking? To understand their custom consider that the Kaska unwillingly sacrificed one person in hope of reaching food for the others. In much the same reluctant way we expect our fittest young men to die heroically in wartime.

The previous paragraph illustrates still another device for enhancing cultural understanding, that is, to describe behavior with the aid of perceptive concepts that force new sense out of the facts. The Kaska did not simply abandon an oldster and go on looking for life-giving resources. They sacrificed one person, enabling others to survive. The latter phrasing casts the particular act in a new light. Among Hopi Indians brittleness of marriage becomes clearer when seen in terms of "a strong lineage principle."[11] Brothers,

[11] Fred Eggan, *Social Organization of the Western Pueblos* (Chicago, 1950), pp. 113-114.

sisters, and other relatives descended from the same ancestress constitute a solidly unified, property-owning in-group, a lineage. The husband is not part of this descent group. Awareness of lineage strength renders the loose husband-wife tie more understandable.

A measure of cultural understanding comes through technical interpretations of a group's symbols, whether these be graphic signs, acts, or dreams and fantasies. Technical interpretations differ from meanings established directly by asking people or determined indirectly by inferring them from a context in which action takes place. An outsider, technically sophisticated in psychoanalysis or in some other theory which claims it can unlock the meaning of symbols in human culture, perceives, say, a religious rite in which the participants deliberately wash their hands. Without a moment's hesitation he interprets the act as signifying symbolic purification. In another rite commoners bow before a ruler. Again the outsider doesn't need to probe. His knowledge of human gestures and the circumstances in which they are used informs him that the commoners are symbolically expressing their subordination. So, too, dreams may be interpreted on the basis of psychodynamics grounded in European and American clinical practice.[12] Technical interpretations may err. Hence, they should always be formulated tentatively and then checked for consistency in the context of a particular culture. Naturally, people can also be asked for an explicit meaning of the symbol. If this meaning bears little resemblance to the technical interpretation it doesn't automatically deny the latter.

Ability to understand culture grows as we become familiar with more cultures. That's why an anthropologist trains himself to remember facts about a broad range of the world's people. The more cultures he knows, the easier he comes to grips with a new one. He is able to recognize its ground plan, perceive its truly distinctive features, and work out functions for specific customs.

GOOD, GENUINE, OR DECADENT?

Can customs be evaluated, that is in some way more useful than branding them as disgusting, barbaric, low, or high? Such dogmatic, ethnocentric expletives reveal only biases that hinder genuine understanding.

It is difficult to evaluate cultures. Judges rarely agree on what standards to use. What would be useful and also fair evaluative criteria? We can compare hunting and agriculture and measure them in terms of how effectively each produces food over a given period of time. Agriculture will usually come out ahead. But someone is bound to object to this procedure and point out

[12] Clyde Kluckhohn and William Morgan, "Some Notes on Navaho Dreams," in George B. Wilbur and Warner Muensterberger, eds., *Psychoanalysis and Culture* (New York, 1951).

that our comparison is unfair because it ignores other satisfactions afforded by each system. And even if hunting can be compared objectively to agriculture in terms of how many food calories each produces, what standard can possibly measure the effectiveness of Christianity versus orthodox Buddhism? How can two conceptions of God be evaluated? Two puberty ceremonies? Different styles of poetry or painting? Some traits, it seems, can't be measured objectively.

Another kind of evaluation admits to being subjective. It emulates the informed judgment with which a critic appraises a painting or musical composition. Using this approach, we admire the ingenuity with which a people manage to cope with a difficult environment. We commend the talent some African tribal courts show in reconciling disputants. We note the genius with which Indians who hunted and fought on the plains west of the Mississippi accommodated men who wanted to be women rather than warriors and gave scope to women too manly hearted to be content with the culturally ordained, unassertive, feminine role. In an age that expects an uncomfortable degree of conformity, we might even learn something useful from the Plains Indians' attitudes toward social deviants.

Subjective judgment told Edward Sapir that some cultures are genuine and others spurious.[13] The genuine culture is an inherently harmonious, balanced, and self-satisfying way of life; it is a culture relatively free of internal contradictions, one that spares people from a persistent sense of frustration and bewilderment. In contrast, incompatibilities and spiritual discords rend the spurious culture, efficient as it may be when it comes to producing wealth or maintaining far-flung political control.

This raises a question founded on an analogy with the human body. Are there sick cultures? The idea of a culture doing poorly is plausible. Civil wars, economic depressions, political instability, or forcible invasion by a foreign power accompanied by an inevitable clash of values means that people have failed to organize their efforts effectively and so fall short of solving critical problems. As with illness, cultural malaise affects different areas of life unequally. A people beset by unresolved racial tensions that verge on violence nevertheless carry on profitable commerce and produce great art. Therefore, I doubt if much is gained by focusing on dyscrasic phenomena and then labeling a whole way of life sick. Does any culture work perfectly? A surer understanding comes from perceiving what irreconcilable conflicts entangle a community or where people's knowledge falls short of their situation so that they come to grief in war and depression. Perhaps we ought not be so shy of a term, like "sick," but words, major tools of social science, must be chosen with care for their connotations.

[13] Edward Sapir, "Culture, Genuine and Spurious," *American Journal of Sociology,* 29 (1924), 401-429.

Evaluating a civilization as decadent represents another kind of judgment. Applied to culture, decadence denotes sharp, highly refined sensibilities. At least some people in a decadent culture see in life a challenge to extract from each moment as much gratification as possible. Or decadence may be used to express the idea that a culture may decay or that people responsible for a way of life gradually exhaust their potentialities. Energies flag and artists run out of new ideas so that their work grows imitative and breakthroughs in technology and science grow rare.

Evaluative judgments only seem easy to make. When they are well informed and based on a careful study of facts they become quite difficult. Anthropologists generally avoid subjective evaluations, mainly because they fear that such judgments conceal obstinate, ethnocentric prejudices and disparagements. It is a safe rule to make evaluative judgments only when qualified by sympathy, sensitivity, and detachment.

THE LIMITS OF UNDERSTANDING

We overrate understanding if we expect it to solve all intercultural relations. Tell the U.S. executive, angry after having waited 45 minutes for an appointment with a Latin American businessman, that Latin Americans have less respect for time than North Americans and see if he is mollified. As long as our understanding remains primarily intellectual it leaves culture-bound intolerance well entrenched. To attack ethnocentrism successfully requires something more: man-to-man appreciation, sympathy for the people whose customs we study. An anthropologist who lives closely with people he studies and shares their joys and sorrows gains an appreciation of them and their culture which transcends purely intellectual understanding.

Still there remains a difficulty, a perplexing one. I suspect that sooner or later the best efforts at achieving a cross-cultural appreciation must come up against a nearly insurmountable barrier. It is hard, or even impossible, to marshal sympathy and respect for customs that defy deeply ingrained attitudes.

In the realm of physical science the man who understands a phenomenon is often well on the way to controlling it. Understanding social behavior along the lines I have suggested still leaves us nearly impotent to engineer and manipulate culture regardless of people's own desires. Nevertheless, cultural understanding is useful. It serves us like a map, summarizing terrain across which we must travel. It opens our eyes, prevents costly blunders, saves us from risky detours. Understanding enriches even familiar experiences in our own culture that we ordinarily take for granted.

FURTHER READING

Edward T. Hall wrote *The Silent Language* (Garden City, N. Y., 1959) to develop better cultural understanding; note especially Chapters 1 and 2. Numerous, dramatic instances of intercultural misunderstanding are given in Eugene A. Nida, *Customs and Cultures* (New York, 1954). Anthropologists have gotten into sticky difficulties trying to define culture satisfactorily. A. L. Kroeber and Clyde Kluckhohn review many definitions in *Culture: A Critical Review of Concepts and Definitions,* Papers of the Peabody Museum of Archaeology and Ethnology, Harvard University, vol. 47, no. 1, 1952. Bronislaw Malinowski's essay, "Culture," in *Encyclopaedia of the Social Sciences* (New York, 1931), vol. 4, is very helpful introductory reading. Ruth Benedict treats culture vividly in the first two chapters of *Patterns of Culture* (Boston, 1934). She emphasizes that ethnocentrism is incompatible with trying to understand exotic cultures. For the likelihood of social standardization affecting animal behavior see David Roberts, "Imitation and Suggestion in Animals," *The Bulletin of Animal Behavior,* 1 (1941), 11-19.

My attitude toward history is the position taken by fiield theorists in psychology like Kurt Lewin; see his "Defining the 'Field at a Given Time'," *Psychological Review,* 50 (1943), 292-310. What I call importance of context others have named importance of situation. See, for example, Kurt Lewin, *Field Theory in Social Science,* ed. Dorwin Cartwright (New York, 1951); this volume also contains the previously mentioned paper by Lewin. For a short introduction to "The Existential-Phenomenological Foundations for a Science of Persons," see R. D. Laing, *The Divided Self, A Study of Sanity and Madness* (London, 1960), chap. 1. Kenneth L. Pike refers to purpose and meaning in *Language in Relation to a Verified Theory of the Structure of Human Behavior,* 2 vols. (Glendale, Calif., 1954), vol. I, chap. 2. Max Weber emphasized meaning as a key to understanding society in *The Theory of Social and Economic Organization,* trans. A. M. Henderson and Talcott Parsons, ed. T. Parsons (New York, 1947), pp. 87-95. Else Frenkel-Brunswik also dwells on the significance of meanings in her paper, "Interaction of Psychological and Sociological Factors in Political Behavior," *The American Political Science Review,* 46 (1952), 44-65. Literature on functionalism in social science is immense. I recommend Raymond Firth, "Function," in W. L. Thomas, Jr., ed., *Yearbook of Anthropology—1955* (New York, 1955); the first few pages of an essay with the same title by Joseph H. Greenberg in *Essays in Linguistics,* Viking Fund Publications in Anthropology, no. 24, 1957; Talcott Parsons, "Malinowski and the Theory of Social Systems," in Raymond Firth, ed., *Man and Culture, an Evaluation of the Work of Malinowski* (London, 1957); and Dorothy Emmett, *Function, Purpose and Powers* (London, 1958), chaps. 3-4. S. F. Nadel writes on "Explanation" in his book, *The Foundation of Social Anthropology* (London, 1951), chap. 8. In *Coral Gardens and Their Magic,* 2 vols. (New York, 1935), vol. II, pp. 45-62, 214-215, Bronislaw Malinowski shows how even the meaning of words derives from their function. Regarding one type of cultural evaluation see David Bidney, "The Concept of Cultural Crisis," *American Anthropologist,* 48 (1946), 534-552. A. L. Kroeber has written a classic in cultural evaluation, *Configurations of Culture Growth* (Chicago, 1952). He also answers the question "Have Civilizations a Life History?" in *Centennial Collected Papers.*

Presented at the Centennial Celebration, Washington, D. C., September 13-17, 1948 (Washington, 1950).

An easy-to-read survey of anthropology for the newcomer is Clyde Kluckhohn's *Mirror for Man* (New York, 1949). The first seven chapters describe the major specialties and give an adequate idea of results produced in each. The aims of British social anthropologists are given in the first chapter of Raymond Firth's *Elements of Social Organization* (London, 1951). Not many years ago no book dealing with anthropology would have gotten through its first chapter without seriously referring to "primitives." Today such a restriction has practically disappeared. For an analysis of what has happened see Edward P. Dozier, "The Concepts of 'Primitive' and 'Native' in Anthropology," in W. L. Thomas, Jr., ed., *Yearbook of Anthropology—1955* (New York, 1955). Wilton M. Krogman, "Sherlock Holmes as an Anthropologist," *The Scientific Monthly*, 80 (1955), 155-162, provides a lighter introduction to anthropology. William C. Sturtevant has written a pamphlet on *Anthropology as a Career* (Washington, 1958).

2

Coping with the World

Civilized man . . . is always moving, sweating, toiling, and racking his brains to find still more laborious occupations: he goes on in drudgery to his last moment, and even seeks death to put himself in a position to live, or renounces life to acquire immortality.

Jean Jacques Rousseau (1755)[1]

SOCIAL SYSTEMS

Culture extends continuously in space; one culture shades into another from one inhabited part of the earth to the next. Marked cultural differences are apt to occur between groups thrust apart by mountains or large bodies of water that they cannot traverse. Culture also flows continuously through time; each generation inherits an overwhelming share of its way of life from parents and far more remote, anonymous ancestors. Normally we study culture as people live it in specific, organized human aggregates called social systems or communities. A farming village, a band of forest hunters, a tribe of desert pastoral nomads, a teeming metropolis, and even a full-scale nation, all represent relatively integral social systems of a kind visited by inquiring anthropologists. Even a historical period, like the Hellenistic Age, Revolutionary America, Renaissance Italy, or Mughal India, forms a kind of integral social system. Then there are part social systems, cells integrated into larger units, like a New England shoe factory, an air force bomber squadron, or a restaurant.

I have identified a social system as an organized aggregate of people, but it possesses other distinguishing properties. A core of shared interests, including

[1] "A Discourse on the Origin of Inequality," in G. D. H. Cole, trans., *The Social Contract and Discourses* (London, 1913), p. 220.

22

values held with such intensity that people are ready to kill and be killed for them, holds the group together. Equally important are the complementary differences found in every social system. For why would people organize if everyone were precisely alike? There could be no team with only catchers; no market with only buyers, no family without two parents. Then, too, every community makes valiant, if never wholly successful, efforts to draw boundaries between itself and neighbors and forestall excessive interference in its affairs. Rarely, however, is any social system fully independent. Finally, every social system engages in external relations, peaceful or hostile, with other systems in its society.[2] Kaska Indian society, for instance, encompasses the whole network of people of whom Kaska Indians are consciously aware. Nonmembers from the larger society, welcome and unwelcome, penetrate a social system as merchants, tax collectors, public health nurses, tourists, diplomats, and visiting teachers, or else exert their influence impersonally through newspapers, newsreels, books, radio, and imported trade goods. Also the remembered dead might be included within a society's limits. Living members credit the dead with ideas, poetry, and paintings. Among the deceased are the sources of inherited debts and the men who built the irrigation ditches or cleared the fields from which people still prosper. Communities that intercede

Pravda links Chuckchee hunters in northeastern Siberia with a large society. (*Sovfoto.*)

with ancestors for health, rain, and prosperity strikingly show their awareness of the common interests that unite living and dead.

Although society, like culture, extends in space and time, we observe it

[2] Godfrey Wilson and Monica Wilson, *The Analysis of Social Change* (Cambridge, Eng., 1945), chap. 2.

while poised in a specific social system. A social system whose culture is busy with war, trade, or exploration ranges further afield in its societal network than one bound up only with local affairs. The former is large in social scale, the latter relatively small. If a social system cultivates writing and scholarship, then its society penetrates into the past as well. Of course, individuals who belong to the same social system vary in scale depending on their range of awareness. There are large- and small-scale persons just as there are large- and small-scale communities. Since members of a community form part of their total society, as a community's population increases so does the society grow in scale.

CULTURE AS A WAY OF COPING

An advantageous way to start understanding social systems is to observe how they cope with their problems. Man's versatility in solving problems surpasses anything in the animal kingdom. His power of reflection transmutes experience into a cultural repertory of problem-solving techniques that makes him primate of all nature. Observe how men extend their individual strength

Whether hunter, farmer, or manufacturer, man, through his power of reflection transmuted into culture, has attained extraordinary control of nature. (*Hudson's Bay Company, photograph by Richard Harrington.*)

by organizing to carry out big tasks in concert. Look at how man takes raw materials, sometimes imported from many scattered environments, and converts them into cultural artifacts that augment his comfort or safeguard his life. He possesses unusual ability to move goods and people. Kaska Indians use canoes and dog-drawn toboggans; Hopi Indians use horses and donkeys acquired from Spanish conquerors of the New World and automobiles more lately imported into their culture. The modern industrial age through powerful means of transportation and communication has reduced the earth's size.

Mastery begins when man observes his environment. Pondering on what he sees he formulates rules to explain his observations. He explains why plants grow, fire burns, and people collaborate or fight. Applied knowledge augments human power; for example, it brings control over ravaging disease. Man even tries to control his fellows by applying his experience through education, psychiatry, and propaganda.

Man's coping ability waxes as cultures become technically more highly developed, that is, as they increase their ability to cope with the physical world. Technical development means increased use of energy in the form of coal, oil, or electric power, higher output of crops and factory goods, higher food consumption, a longer span of life, and all the enhanced comforts brought about by heated or air-conditioned homes, offices, and cars. All over the world, though not at an equal rate, coping ability is spurting. As an Austrian peasant said to me: "We have never had it so good."

FUEL FOR THE BODY

Subsistence supplies one of the sharpest indicators by which to judge a community's ability to cope. The way food is secured, whether at a low level of technical development by hunting and gathering or at a higher level with a plow drawn by oxen or tractor-powered, also makes a difference in many other items of culture. Much else that man does hinges functionally on his subsistence techniques. It is easy to see why. Food provides human beings with bodily energy and upon this fuel the rest of the culture ultimately depends: manufacturing, transportation, religion, art, government, and family life. Not that food-getting is more important than ideas or organization. Without knowledge stored up from previous learning a hunter could kill nothing and a farmer could not begin to cultivate. Religion and recreation are as important as techniques if they inspire men to work together collaboratively toward a harvest.

Subsistence comes in two fundamentally different ways. In small-scale communities food gatherers pick food off the surface of the earth as they hunt or trap game, fish, and collect fruits, roots, berries, and shellfish. Food gathering as the sole source of subsistence represents a very simple degree of technical

A YUGOSLAV PEASANT OPTIMISTICALLY DESCRIBES DEVELOPMENT

"There is electric current, a room for movies, radio sets, and all this came so suddenly that I hardly can believe everything could change so much in my lifetime. The death rate of children has dropped greatly, and the life of old people is made longer with the help of doctors. There are no whole families who die from contagious diseases, nor epidemics which wipe out entire counties. There still is some backwardness, but this will soon be improved."

Joel M. Halpern, *A Serbian Village* (New York, 1958), p. 302.

development. Such social systems have simple cultures; their lives are marked by limited variety. Undoubtedly our earliest hominid ancestors survived through this form of subsistence after they had become distinct from apes. Only today are food gatherers finally disappearing. Although man formally shares food gathering with the rest of the animal kingdom, great differences separate this human skill from the analogous habits of other creatures. Man endows hunting and fishing with value. He derives prestige from the chase. He augments his bodily resources with extrabodily weapons; traps are clever devices that in effect allow a single hunter to be in several places simultaneously waiting for game. Also man reflects on food gathering. He attributes success or failure to his moral conduct or to extramundane agencies with which he tries to keep on good terms. No other animal elaborates food gathering to such an extent.

Ten thousand years ago food production appeared, the second fundamental mode of subsistence. Food producers plant vegetable foods, tubers, cereals, and legumes. They rear animals like cattle, sheep, goats, and barnyard fowl and either eat their flesh or their other products including milk and eggs. Not all farmers are on the same level of technical development or cultural elaboration. There is a difference between those who carry on agriculture manually, that is, armed with only a digging stick or hoe, and those who benefit from plows.

By comparing three different social systems I shall attempt to demonstrate that subsistence technology—the way food is secured—makes a difference in scale and other aspects of culture. In discussing Kaska Indians, Hopi Indians, and the small Asian principality of Swat I will be comparing food gatherers, hoe farmers (sometimes called horticulturists), and plow farmers (full-fledged agriculturists). Consider the following vignettes as introductory. I shall not try to describe each culture in detail. (The footnotes direct you to more comprehensive accounts.) In later chapters I will refer again and again to Kaska Indians, Hopi Indians, and Swat to illustrate other ideas.

ISOLATED FOOD GATHERERS

Just prior to 1800 the social system of the aboriginal Kaska Indians contained less than 300 persons who scoured an area about 15,000 square miles for game, fish, a few plants, and berries.[3] Their country was ruggedly mountainous and during part of the year so bitterly cold (temperatures at times dropped to —70° F.) that nobody could move far from the house. The Indians lived in five regional groups. In each region people traveled in small bands containing about 30 or 40 related persons.

Over much of the year the bands kept moving. People followed hunters to where they had killed large game like caribou, visited berry patches, or traveled to set fish nets in lakes and build weirs in streams. Because they depended mostly on mobile game and uncertain supplies of fish, the Indians could not afford to settle down in permanent villages. Food was neither abundant nor dependable enough to allow a dense population to thrive. In autumn, when game grew fat, men killed bear, groundhog, and caribou. Preparing for the long, cold season ahead, women dried the meat and stored it in caches to eat during the

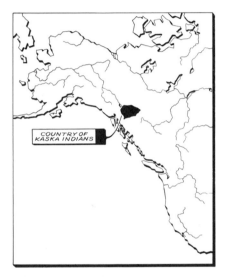

COUNTRY OF KASKA INDIANS

Kaska Indians live in northern British Columbia and the southern Yukon, Canada. In 1943 the newly completed Alaska Highway opened their country, the Cassiar, to motor traffic.

winter. Cold weather found several families camped around a fish lake, their conical dwellings tightly chinked. Young fellows made periodic trips to the meat caches, for when it was very cold men could do no hunting.

This mode of subsistence encouraged a simply organized social system. The Kaska had no opportunity to develop an elaborate social structure, one possessing, say, political leaders, social classes, and associations. The small band remained the largest unit of effective social organization. Of people like this Montesquieu said, they "enjoy great liberty; for as they do not cultivate the earth, they are not fixed: they are wanderers and vagabonds; and if a chief

[3] John J. Honigmann, *The Kaska Indians: An Ethnographic Reconstruction,* Yale University Publications in Anthropology, no. 51, 1954.

should deprive them of their liberty, they would immediately go and seek it under another, or retire into the woods, and there live with their families."[4]

Naturally, people depended on each other. Children depended on parents for care and survival and parents looked to each other for emotional security and cooperation. Members of a band shared food, and on occasion a husband in the same generous spirit loaned his wife to another man. But compared to a larger-scale social system, the Indians relied little on one another for goods and services. The intensity with which people related to each other within the social system was low. How could professional tailors, canoemakers, warriors, or other specialists support themselves in so sparse a population of restless food gatherers? Where would the professional find a big enough market to keep his talents busy and a market rich enough to provide him with food and other goods to support both himself and his family? Kaska Indians maintained equally shallow relations with neighboring social systems. They knew of non-Kaska Indians living at a distance, but just as they ethno-centrically called themselves "dinè" (human beings), they pictured their poorly known neighbors as subhuman and dangerous. Ethnocentrism on this

Scenes of contemporary Kaska Indian life recall their aboriginal culture. These views show a sparsely settled country and strongly self-sufficient families. These people must be resourceful if they are to survive isolated in the forest, as they still are during the winter months.

scale inspired no social visiting. The Indians had no time to make goods for foreign trade. Equally feeble ties linked contemporaries with the past. Apart from keepsakes, the Kaska inherited no wealth from past generations. Illiteracy effectively prevented them from conserving the past in records and their memories were short. Even today a man can't recall the names of all four of his grandparents. True, folk tales dealt with a marvelous past in which animals could speak but the obvious unreliability of such traditions leaves them without true historical significance. The numerically small, physically isolated

[4] Charles de Secondat, Baron de Montesquieu, *The Spirit of Laws,* trans. Thomas Nugent, rev. J. V. Prichard (Chicago, 1952; first published in 1748), pp. 127-128.

Kaska Indian community lived autonomously in a restricted societal network. More accurately, each small, migratory Kaska band lived a largely independent existence and rarely sought aid or sociability from comparable units.

Hunters and fishermen who move around a great deal cannot acquire much in the way of portable wealth. Their community does not become layered into castes or social classes, each purer, richer, and more powerful than the other. Like other small-scale social systems the Kaska possessed a high degree of cultural homogeneity. Apart from inevitable differences of behavior, distinguishing one individual from another or marking off men from women and adults from children, everybody participated in a common culture. Everyone dressed approximately the same and held similar values and beliefs. Religion remained a simple affair; the individual capably mediated his own relationship to the supernatural, though in truly critical circumstances he sought help from a more powerful intercessor.

Early in the nineteenth century, as the Kaska adopted fur trapping for Canadian merchants and ceased to supply all their own needs independently, their society expanded in scale. Their culture rapidly embraced an increased measure of technical development, more variety, and greater comforts. The evolution of their culture followed after white men had opened stores and churches in Kaska territory. Voluntarily or involuntarily the Indians surrendered a measure of their former autonomy for the sake of flour, baking powder, matches, steel axes, and other goods. In some respects, however, wider scale brought the Kaska into conflict with their larger society. They rejected some of its laws and values in an effort, mostly futile, to maintain a substantial degree of autonomy.

MIDDLE-RANGE HOE FARMERS

A hunter harvests the bounties of nature but does nothing deliberate to restore resources on which energy he depends. Farmers, like the Hopi Indians, first plant their food and then eat it.[5] They feed part of their crop to domesticated animals which in turn provide them with meat, milk, and eggs.

The Hopi live in Arizona and are one of the tribes of so-called Pueblo ("village") Indians who are concentrated in the semidesert, southwestern United States. With the Hopi we again encounter a loosely cohering social system but one that diverges sharply in many features from the aboriginal Kaska. On a reservation of about 3900 square miles, over 3,000 Hopi Indians inhabit 13 independent villages. Hereditary chiefs hold some authority in

[5] Mischa Titiev, *Old Oraibi: A Study of the Hopi Indians of Third Mesa*, Papers of the Peabody Museum of American Archaeology and Ethnology, Harvard University, vol. 22, no. 1, 1944; Ernest Beaglehole, *Notes on Hopi Economic Life*, Yale University Publications in Anthropology, no. 15, 1937; Laura Thompson and Alice Joseph, *The Hopi Way* (Chicago, 1944).

Locations of the Hopi and some other southwestern Indians.

A roof-top view of Hotevilla, a Hopi village, with peaches drying in the foreground. (*U.S. Department of Agriculture, Soil Conservation Service Photo by Milton S. Snow.*)

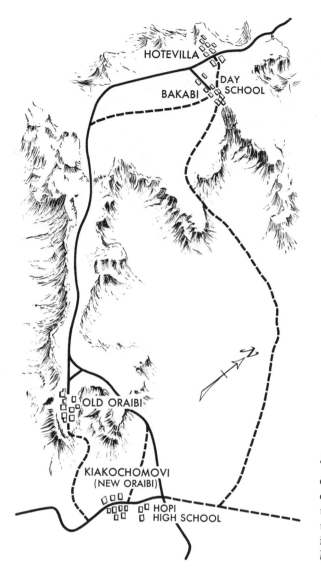

HOTEVILLA

DAY
BAKABI   SCHOOL

OLD ORAIBI

KIAKOCHOMOVI
(NEW ORAIBI)

HOPI
HIGH SCHOOL

This sketch shows the location of older Hopi villages at the edge of the mesa. From the tableland people descend to their fields. (*C. O'Kane,* Sun in the Sky, *University of Oklahoma Press.*)

village affairs but primarily public opinion enforces moral values. Hopi possess little in the way of a police force or government as we know it.

Hopi farmers, using hoes and other manual tools, cultivate mainly maize, squash, beans, and fruit. Because they have more recipes for preparing a greater variety of food, they enjoy a considerably more varied cuisine than the Kaska or other food gatherers. Men do most of the cultivation, wielding their hoes on land that will be inherited by daughters, not sons. Arizona's semiarid locale makes farming difficult but with typical human ingenuity they have learned to cope. For example, in this area of whimsical rainfall a family cultivates land in several different places, sometimes traveling as much

Terraced farm plots belonging to Hotevilla. (*U.S. Department of Agriculture, Soil Conservation Service Photo by Milton S. Snow.*)

as 4 miles from the village and descending 600 feet below the tableland where the village sits. If a shower fails in one place, enough rain may fall in another field. The Hopi also irrigate with flood water, whose sedimentary deposit annually renews the soil's fertility, and store water in tanks from which it is channeled to the terraced fields. Farmers plant deeply in moist soil, at depths that the burning sun cannot reach. Despite these felicitous time-tested techniques for coping with semiarid conditions, the Indians have suffered from famines and still fear them.

Hopi culture, with its blend of traits perpetuated from the past and new elements learned in federal schools or bought from mail order houses, possesses more variety than the culture of the Kaska Indians formerly did. Both social systems lack sharply divergent social classes, some of which parade their wealth and sophistication while others live in poverty and backwardness. However, a Hopi village contains more subgroups than a Kaska band and these subgroups maintain control over religious events from which the whole unit benefits. Also, men and women who excel in weaving, pottery, silver jewelry, and manufacturing religious dolls produce an economic surplus of goods which is sold to other Hopi or marketed elsewhere in their society. Specialist priests officiate in ceremonies, but since they also raise and prepare their own food, they are only part-time specialists. Some men work for non-Indians and draw cash wages to support their families. The volume of internal and external trade has recently grown, but even in former days hoe farming

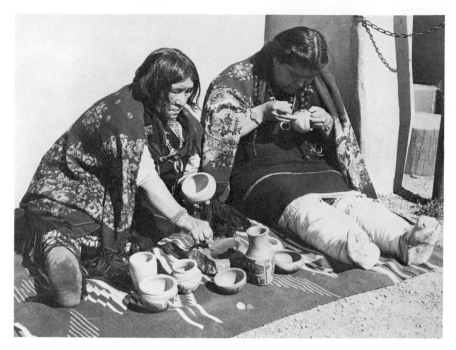

Some Hopi women are part-time specialists who manufacture pottery for sale. (*Santa Fe Railway Photograph.*)

Hopi springs mean life in the desert and are well tended. (*U.S. Department of Agriculture, Soil Conservation Service Photo by Milton S. Snow.*)

sufficed to support a population dense enough to carry on a modest degree of barter.

Within a village large religious ceremonies designed to promote fertility encourage further interdependence. Sparsely distributed Kaska Indian bands could never have managed ceremonies of such magnitude. A common religion, very elaborate in composition, overrides the political separateness of each Hopi village and provides a sense of large-scale unity that knits together all Hopi except a few Christian Indians. Men in a village also cooperate on communal tasks like cleaning springs and hunting rabbits as formerly they worked periodically on the village chief's lands.

Because farmers are spared from the nearly constant pursuit of game they build more substantial houses aggregated in permanent settlements. Hopi villages boast far more social capital than a Kaska encampment. They include ceremonial chambers used for religious rituals, ceremonial paraphernalia, shrines, roads, and well-tended springs.

The Indian's knowledge of his past is shallow except for individuals who have learned to read the white man's books and newspapers. Recently schools and government agents have vastly increased the Indians' awareness of the world beyond the pueblo. Enlistment in the armed forces and jobs taken in nearby cities have had a similar broadening influence. In some ways, though, the Hopi have deliberately kept their social scale from expanding. Just as they resisted Spanish conquerors and missionaries, so each village still guards its autonomy, striving to manage its own affairs without government interference. Their name, which means "good in every respect," betrays a note of small-scale ethnocentrism.[6] Yet Hopi society is undoubtedly larger than aboriginal Kaska society, and with larger scale go a number of cultural correlates, such as heightened technical development and greater cultural elaboration. Agriculture itself indicates more control over nature. In his index of social development, Raoul Naroll gives the Hopi a rating of 36 points. Food gatherers in southernmost South America receive only 12 points (the lowest rating in his list); the West Greenland sea-hunting Eskimo, 23; and the civilized Inca and Aztec (who, however, lacked plows) high scores of 55 and 58 respectively.[7]

LARGE-SCALE PEASANTS

Starting in the Middle East the plow entered the stream of human culture about 6000 years ago. With this tool the same labor force that previously

[6] Charles F. Voegelin and Florence M. Voegelin, *Hopi Domains, A Lexical Approach to the Problem of Selection,* Indiana University Publications in Anthropology and Linguistics, Memoir 14, 1957.

[7] Raoul Naroll, "A Preliminary Index of Social Development," *American Anthropologist,* 58, (1956), 687-715.

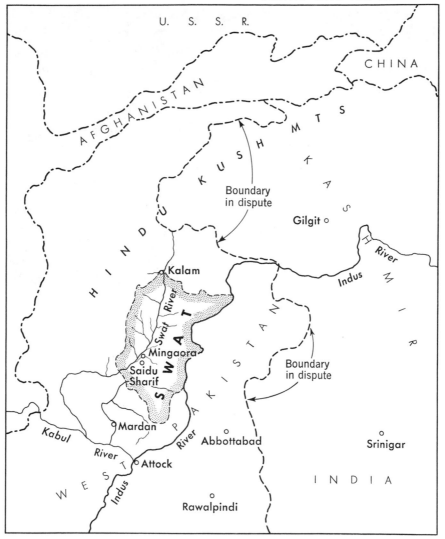

Location of Swat in West Pakistan.

wielded manual implements could now cultivate a significantly larger amount of land in the same period of time. The labor force could provide more crops than it could consume. Exported to cities, the peasants' crop provided nourishment for manufacturers, scholars, merchants, and administrators. All this was possible because the plow harnessed to a powerful, placid ox augments human with animal energy.

Swat lies cradled in the Hindu Kush mountains of northern West Pakistan.[8] It survives as one of the few remaining princely states out of the 500

[8] Fredrik Barth, *Political Leadership Among Swat Pathans*, London School of Economics, Monographs on Social Anthropolgy, no. 19, 1959; Fredrik Barth, *Indus and Swat Kohistan*, Studies Honouring the Centennial of Universitetets Etnografiske Museum, Oslo, 1857-1957, vol. 3, 1956.

The plow harnessed to a powerful ox augments human energy. (*Pakistan Embassy.*)

that Britain recognized in old India. One main, fertile river valley, into which a number of smaller streams debouch, traverses the length of this 4000 square mile nation. Four hundred thousand people crowd the main valley and its tributaries; another 100,000 eke out their existence in the less fertile mountains. Unlike the Hopi and Kaska Indians, who each speak one language and comprise a single ethnic group, Swat with its diversity of people is comparable to heterogeneous modern nations in Europe and America. Pathans, who several hundred years ago invaded the main valley and conquered its former inhabitants, form the bulk of the population. Non-Pathans occupy less desirable parts of the country. Most Swatis are peasant farmers who work with plows rather than, like the Hopi, solely with hoes. The peasant family produces much of its own food, especially in low altitudes where the winter is mild enough to allow two annual harvests. Major crops are rice, wheat, maize, fruit, and animal fodder. To find sufficient arable land in some of the narrow valleys peasants terrace their fields along the sides of steep mountains. Rainfall is neither regular nor dependable enough to assure fertility; hence cultivators irrigate. A village taps the swiftly falling mountain stream and directs the water along stone-lined channels or wooden ducts until it reaches the crops. Technical development also shows up in the way farmers assiduously maintain fertility by use of manure, compost fertilizer, fallowing, and crop rotation. Cheap waterpower operates village grain mills and oxen relieve men of some labor in threshing. Men take charge of agricultural operations while children tend cows, water buffalo, and goats. Social capital exceeds anything in Hopiland for it includes richly ornamented palaces, beautiful mosques,

Terraced fields in a side valley of Swat. (*Pakistan Embassy.*)

Irrigation ditches take off water from mountain streams of Swat. En route to the cultivated fields the water powers grain mills. (*Pakistan Embassy.*)

saints' tombs, constantly groomed roads, substantial houses aggregated into villages and cities, schools, hospitals, dispensaries, and even a college. Some land is reserved for sports and men hunt not out of necessity but for recreation. But poverty, too, exists. Each fall hundreds of poor mountain families migrate on foot to the lower lands of Pakistan in search of jobs and pasture for their cattle and goats. When the mountainsides bloom pink and white with springtime blossoms the transhumants return to their high-altitude farms.

Peasants work hard to produce goods beyond their own needs, and they exchange their economic surplus for the products and services of carpenters, jewelers, bus drivers, barbers, and other full-time specialists. People depend

Buses help tie together the mountainous land of Swat.

on one another for much that they utilize. The bazars of Swat display goods imported from practically the whole world: aluminum cooking ware, cloth, dishes, shoes, sugar, biscuits, jams, and stationery from Pakistan; oil out of the Middle East; razor blades, batteries, tinned food, ink, and condoms with U.S. trademarks; British biscuits; Indonesian spices; and rice, flour, shoes, vegetables, fruit, and cloth produced in Swat itself. Customers are mostly men. Social ranks can be distinguished by the assorted garb: the Punjabi, far from home, by his wrap-around skirt; the mountain Swati by his woolen blanket and leggings; the wealthy landlord and his armed bodyguard by their ballooning, crisp, white, cotton trousers; and the college student by his high-collared, tightly fitting black coat. Occasional European or American tourists are highly conspicuous. Pathans find foreign women's bare legs and arms shockingly immodest.

In return for a share of his income paid as a tax the peasant receives police and other administrative services rendered in the name of the country's powerful ruler. Certain affairs, like coinage, mails, and foreign relations, are managed by Pakistan. Thus, Swatis are not only highly dependent on each other for goods, professional services, and government, but they are also deeply involved in more far-reaching social ties. The fact that Swatis nearly all profess Islam and therefore identify with other Muslims in Pakistan, the Middle East, and elsewhere knits them into a still larger social network. The sacred literature of Islam keeps them aware of the past. Genealogies kept by some Pathans go back many generations and validate the power and prestige of landlords.

Kaska Indians hunted over a broad territory and recognized no private ownership of land. Among Hopi Indians arable land, the most important source of wealth, is controlled by kin groups but tends to be fairly evenly distributed between families. In Swat land is even scarcer and more valuable, and it is the basis of social stratification. Invading Pathans captured and have

House types illustrate cultural heterogeneity. The dwellings to the left belong to relatively poor Pathan tenant farmers. In the two-story single house to the right lives a family belonging to the Gawrii, an autochthonous ethnic group restricted to the mountains by the invading Pathans.

retained the best land. The country is divided into social strata, rich and poor. Each class aspires to maintain its own standard of living and follows a somewhat different style of life. Some upper-rank men emulate western customs; poorer folk retain traditional customs and are highly circumscribed in outlook. The country's several ethnic groups possess their own languages and distinctive customs. The relative cultural homogeneity of the Kaska and Hopi has been replaced by intensive heterogeneity that affects even religion. Although practically everybody is Muslim, there are divergent ways of interpreting Islam and individuals differ in sincerity of belief, rigor of fasting, and diligence of devotion. A few men are so secular that they question most of the tenets of religion; they are atheists.

In many respects Swat resembles other modern nations that produce crops with help from animal- or tractor-drawn plows. However, the culture of the United States, Great Britain, or France cannot be understood solely in terms of plow farming. The dominant mode of manufacturing which uses machines powered by tremendous amounts of energy must also be considered. The combination of plow and power machinery insures great wealth, entails highly refined occupational specialization and heavy trade, and encourages complex forms of social organization, including a busy government. These correlates have not fully appeared in Swat where much manufacturing is still carried on by hand.

In northern Canada man's coping ability spurted with the arrival of gasoline engines on canoes and aircraft. Eskimo and Indians benefit when critically ill patients can be rushed to government hospitals on aircraft like this. (*Top, National Film Board of Canada.*)

VARIETY AND THE CLASH OF VALUES

Considered in terms of evolution, food gathering, horticulture, and plow agriculture are three steps which man took while increasing his control over nature. With industrial manufacturing he took one more gigantic developmental stride. Each of these achievements in human coping supports a larger social system and encourages—or even demands—more far-flung relations in larger societies. Each brings longer and surer memories of the past. In other words, social scale keeps pace with technical development. Traveling from the hunting and fishing Kaska to Hopi and Swati farmers we have also observed social organization grow more complex. More people capable of being nourished mean more types of groups and groups are more elaborately organized, culminating in the intricate bureaucracies of modern nations. The cultures of food producers further contrast with those of food gatherers because the former possess greater heterogeneity in dress, housing, transportation, sport, food, philosophy, religion, literature, language, child rearing, and even entertainment. In large-scale social systems ways of life vary between families of different rank, between ethnic groups, and from one region of a nation to another. Some of this prodigious variety is allocated among specialists. Everybody in Swat no longer knows everything about his religion; theologians ponder erudite matters that fall outside of the laymen's ken. Professional goldsmiths, shoemakers, mechanics, physicians, and weavers ply skills that have ceased to be common property. No individual has time, energy, or sufficient resourcefulness to take in more than a restricted segment of a highly variegated culture.

Whence comes so much variety? It would be too simple to ascribe it solely to the fact that more people are living together free of the need to hunt or grow their own food and hence able to devote time to creating culture. Up to a point that is true. A large-scale social system also conserves an ever-increasing number of traits from the past. At the same time it has a voracious appetite for new ideas, activities, and artifacts and can import them from other communities. Even if a few old traits are also discarded or relegated to the limbo of museums, still culture grows.

Though no individual can participate in every part of a rich, elaborate culture, he enjoys a range of choice beyond anything known in a small-scale society. Few Americans can ride in atomic submarines or become corporation executives or leading ballerinas, but opportunities exist to go into business, the arts, or science, or even to combine such fields. In some countries, like Swat, opportunity to enjoy rich variety directly is more restricted by caste-like barriers. A farmer's daughter will hardly become a dancer; nor do farmers turn carpenters. Even though in a large-scale community not everyone participates directly in variety, everyone experiences it indirectly: atomic power serves or threatens us; we enjoy a dancer's performance; we live from a farmer's skill and profit through the corporation executive's efficient management.

Variety also brings distress when persons invest exclusive value in narrow ways of believing, worshiping, dressing, dancing, or teaching. They then find deviant ways repulsive, try by force to restrict variety, and press their own values on others. Opposed to them are people who equally value their own forms of behavior, opposition to which strengthens their determination to persist in them. Such conflicts in the large-scale society keep groups, from families to nations, in nearly incessant tension. In Swat I observed the bitterness that divided a traditionally minded father from his heterodox son, who held a post in the government college. The young man's outlook was western; he had read widely and enjoyed wearing western-style clothing. The father regarded the English books and clothing as proof that his son had abandoned his religion to become an infidel. On one occasion he even locked up the books and his son was forced to appeal to the ruler of Swat for help.

Somehow man has failed. His reflective consciousness has endowed him with huge cultural variety which he cannot live with. Our heterogeneous society stands urgently in need of means to understand and appreciate a larger segment of the other fellow's culture. Only if we succeed in doing that will we assume the stature of tolerance proper for human beings in a large-scale society.

A POINT OF VIEW

Our venture in cross-cultural comparison has shown the advantage of asking how social systems cope with the world. The point of view can be applied to all types of social systems. The total culture of a U.S. Air Force bomber squadron is bent to the way that group copes with its intricate flying machines and flying conditions. Life in a leather factory revolves around the skins which workers tan. A tribe of pastoral herders shapes its culture to suit its dominant interests.

Narobachin Mongols of Outer Mongolia, who raise sheep, goats, horned cattle, yaks, horses, and camels, exemplify such a pastoral social system.[9] Sheep are their most important possession for they provide milk, butter, cheese, and meat to eat; wool to felt into mats for covering the Mongol tent; dung for fuel; and skins to tailor into coats and trousers. Herders face one primary problem: to provide grass, water, and winter shelter for their stock. To obtain these resources they must move frequently. The Narobachin exchange summer pastures for more sheltered winter grazing grounds and then in each locality shift from one place to another once the grass is cropped. Their narrow specialization as animal herders forces them to be large in scale and they depend on their society for tea, noodles, wheat flour, sugar, wine, dried fruit, cloth, needles, cordage, dishware, metalware, saddles, tobacco, and other things.

The way people secure food and cope with other problems of their physical

[9] Herbert Harold Vreeland, *Mongol Community and Kinship Structure* (New Haven, Conn., 1953); Lawrence Krader, "Culture and Environment in Interior Asia," in *Studies in Human Ecology*, Pan American Union Social Science Monographs, no. 3, 1957.

Mobility is indispensable for pastoralists. These Afghan transhumants are migrating in search of snow-free pasture. (*Pakistan Embassy.*)

world does make a difference in other elements of their way of life. If we apply this basic principle, we will enhance our understanding of culture.

FURTHER READING

My concept of scale parallels many attempts that have been made to distinguish between folk and civilized societies. For further discussion see Robert Redfield, *The Little Community* (Chicago, 1955). Godfrey Wilson and Monica Wilson use the notion of scale in *The Analysis of Social Change* (Cambridge, Eng., 1945), chap. 2. In *The World of Man* (New York, 1959), chap. 10, I compare scale to similar concepts. The definition of social system which I follow has much in common with one A. R. Radcliffe-Brown employs in *Structure and Function in Primitive Society* (London, 1952) and in *A Natural Science of Society* (Glencoe, Ill., 1957).

A British economist, William Arthur Lewis, explains technical development in *The Theory of Economic Growth* (London, 1955); see also John J. Honigmann, *The World of Man* (New York, 1959), chap. 18. A useful paper, "What Is Economic Development," appeared in *The United Nations Review*, 5 (1959), no. 8, 11-17; no. 9, 19-27; no. 10, 21-27; no. 11, 11-21; no. 12, 27-35.

Correlates of different subsistence systems are tested in L. T. Hobhouse, G. C. Wheeler, and M. Ginsberg, *The Material Culture and Social Institutions of the Simpler Peoples* (London, 1915). In "The Simplest Peoples, I, A Comparative Study," *British Journal of Sociology*, 7, (1956), 77-119, Hobhouse examines only the small-scale hunters and collectors, especially their means of maintaining peace and order. Melville Jacobs and B. J. Stern in *Outline of Anthropology* (New York, 1947) summarize correlates of the food quest. For a similar approach see J. H. G. Lebon, *An Introduction to Human Geography* (London, 1952), chap. 4; John J. Honigmann, *The World of Man*, chaps. 20-22; and Carleton S. Coon, *A Reader in General Anthropology* (New York, 1948). Subsistence is a source of energy. Fred Cottrell discusss the social significance of energy in *Energy and Society* (New York, 1955). A similar study is A. R. Ubbelohde, *Man and Energy* (New York, 1955). See also Leslie White, "The Energy Theory of Cultural Development," in K. M. Kapadia, ed., *Professor Ghurye Felicitation Volume* (Bombay, 1954) and his book, *The Science of Culture* (New York, 1949), chap. 13. Maximilien Sorre reviews many techniques of energy production in *Les Fondements de la géographie humaine, tome II, Les Fondements techniques* (Paris, 1948), pp. 209-391.

Oscar Lewis has written "Plow Culture and Hoe Culture—A Study in Contrasts," *Rural Sociology*, 14 (1949), 116-127. *Plough and Pasture* by E. Cecil Curwen and Gudmund Hatt (New York, 1953) is both a history of farming and a summary of operations involved in that occupation. What happens to culture in a setting that includes costly and extensive irrigation works is the subject of Karl A. Wittfogel's *Oriental Despotism: A Comparative Study of Total Power* (New Haven, Conn., 1957). For a shorter version of Wittfogel's thesis see "The Hydraulic Civilizations," in W. L. Thomas, Jr., ed., *Man's Role in Changing the Face of the Earth* (Chicago, 1956). Robert Redfield gives the defining characteristics of peasant cultures in *The Primitive World and Its Transformations* (Ithaca, N. Y., 1953), chap. 2, as well as in *Peasant Society and Culture* (Chicago, 1956). For an analysis of western industrial civilization consult Oscar Waldemar Junek, "What Is the Total Pattern of Our Western Civilization? Some Preliminary Observations," *American Anthropologist*, 48 (1946), 397-406. Types of pastoralism are described in Maximilien Sorre, *Les Fondements techniques*, pp. 633-660. For two important papers on large-scale pastoralism see John L. Myres, "Nomadism," *Journal of the Royal Anthropological Institute*, 71 (1941), 19-42, which is mainly historical, and Ralphael Patai's comparative study, "Nomadism: Middle Eastern and Central Asian," *Southwestern Journal of Anthropology*, 7 (1951), 401-414.

3

Another Side to Coping

We hang in perpetual suspence between life and death, health and sickness, plenty and want; which are distributed amongst the human species by secret and unknown causes, whose operation is oft unexpected, and always unaccountable. These *unknown causes*, then, become the constant object of our hope and fear; and while the passions are kept in perpetual alarm by an anxious expectation of the events, the imagination is equally employed in forming ideas of those powers, on which we have so entire a dependance.

David Hume (1757)[1]

INEVITABILITY OF STRESS

I admit that in the last chapter I gave a one-sided picture of man's ability to deal with problems of existence. In extracting food from his milieu to support life and culture he often falls short of being fully in command. Accidents, bad weather, and errors in their knowledge of animal habits hampered Kaska Indian hunters. Hopi farmers, despite their skill in farming a semidesert environment, confess lack of direct control over rainfall. This is also true in Swat; soon after the winter snow on Hindu Kush peaks has melted, the smaller streams in the side valleys run dry and leave the irrigation canals caked solid and useless. Even a technically competent civilization like ours is inadequate to deal with many aspects of the physical world. Inadequacy in any culture, including our own, is most evident when it comes to managing social relationships. As a matter of fact, by accentuating social problems our extraordinary technical proficiency has glaringly exposed our social ineffectualness. Industrial manufacturing has made us extremely interdependent both at home and abroad and thereby leaves us vulnerable to all kinds of

[1] *The Natural History of Religion*, ed. H. E. Root (London, 1956), pp. 28-29.

breakdowns in social relations: strikes, poor morale, international misunderstanding and tensions, as well as war. Who would say that our culture
possesses adequate skills to avoid or manage such disruptions? The fact that,
like Bronze Age man, most twentieth-century Americans still regard militarism as the best defence against threat of war proves how impoverished our
social skills really are. In 5000 years mankind has not succeeded in getting
rid of war. Instead, he has consistently intensified his ability to be destructive,
applying to war his brilliant scientific and technological achievements.

Well-intentioned people periodically revive the only popular alternative to
militarism we know, total disarmament. Political leaders urging disarmament
are like the animals who Salvador de Madariaga said once gathered together
for a security pact.[2] The lion looked at the tiger and said, "We must abolish
talons." The tiger looked at the elephant and said, "We must abolish tusks."
The elephant looked back at the lion and said, "We must abolish claws and
jaws." Each animal first proposed disarming some other, not himself. Finally
the bear stood up. "Comrades," he said with what he hoped would be convincing simplicity, "let us abolish everything—everything but the great universal embrace." Perhaps the animals were right. Given our lack of social skills
and the climate of international suspicion that stems from lack of world-wide
community feeling, how can any nation trust itself to disarm totally?

In lieu of more adept, positive skills we also rely heavily on legal codes and
penal institutions to manage social relations. But in the long run they also
fail. Legal norms depend heavily on penal institutions to make them binding.
Long ago the world learned that flogging, branding, mutilation, and torture
were ineffective to deter crime. American prisons have evolved into human
storehouses where guards herd thousands of men and women for a prescribed
period and then automatically release them. They have served their time;
little more is expected. A large proportion are bound to return to serve more
time before five years have passed. We are as helpless as the New York City
magistrate who, when confronted by a teen-age killer, exclaimed, "If only
their parents had made the boys repeat the Ten Commandments . . . particularly the Commandment, 'Thou shalt not kill,' we would not have these kill-
ings."[3] His premise is dubious but his frustration real. The incident demonstrates a point with which this chapter is mainly concerned.

Cultural inadequacy of whatever kind brings stress for some members of
the social system. To put it another way, every way of life fails to protect
people completely against stress. Physical dangers, we know, cannot be entirely controlled. In the realm of medicine, no culture is likely to forestall
death forever or even to avoid all costly, painful incapacitation from illness.
When a man competes against his fellows in examinations, applies for a job,

[2] *The New York Times,* September 19, 1959.
[3] *The New York Times,* September 23, 1959.

or solicits a grant to do research the outcome is as uncertain as when a Kaska hunter leaves to seek game, his wife sets a fish net, or a Hopi farmer plants his maize. Stress emanates from the very legal norms that keep a social system organized and guarantee members a certain measure of satisfaction. The norms press on people to pay taxes, to go through the long-drawn out procedure to win redress from injury, or to spend a term in military service. I am not asking the unanswerable, whether such rules are ultimately good or bad. I say they frustrate individuals who have other inclinations or none at all.

IN PROPORTION AS LIFE IS GOVERNED BY ACCIDENT

Cultural inadequacies whet the appetite for cultural change. We apply our intelligence to originate new devices, new rules to control interpersonal relations, and new remedies. All too well we know that necessity doesn't automatically conceive inventions. Unfulfilled wants have endured for centuries without solution.

Mainly, I want to talk about another response occurring when a partially inadequate culture leaves individuals exposed to physical danger, risk, uncertainty, and anxiety. "In proportion as any man's course of life is governed by accident," the philosopher Hume wrote in 1757, "we always find, that he encreases in superstition; as may particularly be observed of gamesters and sailors. . . ."[4] I prefer to avoid the word "superstition" in this context because too often it betrays a smug lack of respect and sympathy for other folks' beliefs and practices. One man's superstition is the reverent practice of another.

Hume is referring to purposeful behavior like petitionary prayer, to avoidances (taboos) such as fasting; and to manipulations (magic) undertaken to cope with problems. He notes that readiness to use such auxiliary coping procedures varies from one culture to another, a point fully substantiated by contemporary anthropology.

Cromwell's death in 1658 released confusion and anarchy in England that helped, in 1660, bring Charles II back to his throne. Five years after the Restoration, plague broke out. Daniel Defoe in his *Journal of the Plague Year* (first published in 1722) tells how at first he thought of fleeing from plague-ridden London to the country but finally decided to stay, "casting myself entirely upon the goodness and protection of the Almighty."[5] The *Journal* is an engrossing work of imagination, for Defoe was only 5 or 6 years old when plague struck. As a fictional account it vividly portrays panic-stricken Londoners responding to a threat against which they knew their cultural resources to be all too limited.

[4] Hume, *op. cit.*, p. 30.
[5] Daniel Defoe, *A Journal of the Plague Year,* Shakespeare Head Press edition (Oxford, 1928), especially pp. 15-46.

Apprehension mounted as the fatal illness relentlessly spread. Dire predictions by prophets, astrologers, and dream interpreters unnerved everybody. Anxiety made people see sights "that never appeared" and hear voices "that never spake." "Pretenders to Magic" found their trade booming and took full advantage of the people's hungry quest for control over their own fate and the fate of those they loved. The government appointed days of public prayer, fasting, humiliation, and public confession. People implored God to show mercy and "avert the dreadful Judgment" which hung over everyone's head. Worshipers thronged the churches for daily prayer and many families privately petitioned God in word and through fasting. Defoe describes citizens "led by their fright to extremes of folly. . . . running after quacks and mountebanks, and every practising old woman, for medicines and remedies; storing themselves with such multitudes of pills, potions, and preservatives, as they were called, that they not only spent their money, but even poisoned themselves beforehand, for fear of the poison of the Infection, and prepared their bodies for the Plague, instead of preserving them against it." Charms, philters, exorcisms, amulets, "and I know not what preparations were used to fortify the body." Defoe wrote during the Age of Reason in which philosophers held that nothing should be believed without good evidence that it is so. Hence the skepticism he reserves for the behavior of terror-struck Londoners.

China has also entered a new age. West Town in Yunnan province is no longer as it was in May, 1942, during a cholera epidemic that many people interpreted as a supernatural retribution for sin.[6] The same forces that sent the dire illness, people thought, could also revoke it and so they held prayer meetings at which they read scriptures, recited incantations, appealed to deities through incense, and burned papers bearing petitions addressed to gods. In written prayers and spoken incantations they admitted that they had sinned but implored the gods to withdraw their drastic punishment. Public authorities acted in the same spirit when they put up posters that exhorted moral behavior. People also avoided certain kinds of food, ceased to wash clothes and foodstuffs in public streams (in order, note, that the water should be left clean for the gods when they came), and wore amulets to frighten away evil spirits, invite good spirits, or arrest unwholesome activities by supernatural agents. From temples, sacred spots, and dispensaries families solicited "fairy water," efficacious, they thought, to prevent and cure cholera. On the fourth night of intense, prayerful activity an image of the ferocious God of Epidemics was carried in procession with clearly visualized strategy. The deity would assemble around his image all evil spirits responsible for illness. Then when the image was burned, they too would be consumed.

Even in 1942 China had at least one foot beyond the threshold of the

[6] Francis L. K. Hsu, *Religion, Science and Human Crises* (London, 1952). See also Charles J. Erasmus, *Man Takes Control* (Minneapolis, Minn., 1961), chap. 3.

supernaturalistic world view represented in this coping behavior. West Towners not only prayed and manipulated symbols. They also got themselves injected with cholera vaccine, boiled water, and took other sanitary precautions
recommended by public health workers. In other words, two coping traditions worked in harness. Many individuals accepted modern medicine without abandoning traditional methods. Even persons who had lost faith in the
incantations and in other old-time procedures continued to practice them.
They felt comforted in the face of threat doing as their neighbors did.

WHAT IT ALL MEANS

In examining coping through petitionary prayers and related techniques I
have leaned toward an existential perspective, that is, I have described what
many Londoners and West Towners themselves expected would come of
these activities. From an outsider's point of view, it is clear that both cultures
lacked substantial, effective control over threat of illness. (I do not deny that
there was a measure of control.) People felt their vulnerability. The plague,
says Defoe, so far defied all medicines that the very physicians were seized by
it. Yet, despite manifest vulnerability, Londoners and West Towners felt they
could cope by referring themselves to powerful protectors. Hence they fasted
to invoke divine mercy, symbolically lured the disease (or gullible agents
responsible for it) from the city, and wore amulets to ward off illness or fortify
the body. A varied assortment of procedures indeed, but from the standpoint
of the actors each procedure had a single purpose, to win protection. They all
add up to provide courage, a sense of greater security, and increased
confidence.

From an objective point of view, that is from the standpoint of outsiders
like us, these varied responses also have something else in common. They all
rise from a world view in which the universe with all its phenomena, including sickness, war, and the growth of crops, is controlled by personal
agents. Or the universe is viewed as capable of responding to commands much
the same way as living people respond when addressed. According to this
world view, symbolizing the death of an enemy is as useful as firing a shot
through his heart (and a good deal safer). The world view maintains that
simply planting and fencing a patch of yams won't suffice; incantations must
also be spoken to provoke the stubborn yams to grow and to keep away wild
pigs. According to this view certain things, like amulets, possess automatic
properties: they can protect a person, render him invincible, or make him
irresistible.

What general term can we use to refer to such behavior as petitionary
prayer, fasting, wearing amulets, and sticking pins into an enemy's image?
Magic at once comes to mind though usually the word doesn't connote prayer.

Religion is also too restrictive a term because in popular speech it implies the existence of deities, and deities aren't indispensable for coping in the manner I have just described. I will simply call these procedures petitionary prayer and magic. Remember, to be petitionary, prayer must be motivated by the intention of soliciting something in a fairly direct way. When we ask God's favor merely as a way of expressing our belief in God's power and our dependence on it, our prayer isn't petitionary. We will go wrong too if we impute coping *motives* solely on superficial evidence. In the Roman Catholic church medals are not supposed to be worn as amulets. They commemorate Christ, St. Christopher, one's first Communion, and other figures or events. No doubt some Catholics wear medals with the intention of winning protection but to establish this indubitably in any instance we must know the person's motives.

PETITIONARY PRAYER AND MAGIC

Next to some rare sexual customs, coping carried on confidently by means of petitionary prayer and magic is one of the most difficult things for cultural outsiders to understand. How can clouds, rivers, or illness obey verbal commands? How can anyone believe like the Hopi that masked dancers shaking rattles can bring rain? How can otherwise intelligent people stick pins into an image to shorten an enemy's life. We are powerfully tempted to regard such acts as laughable and misguided. Yet, once we cease to judge them in terms of our own assumptions and instead probe for their own underlying rationale we find that they make good sense. Petitionary prayer becomes quite logical when we bear in mind that people in this way address invisible, controlling deities or appeal to the whole universe that they believe is somehow in tune with man and can understand when he talks to it. What looks like an impersonal world of trees, game animals, clouds, and rain really pulses with hidden aliveness. Sentience pervades everything. Hence a woodcutter can appeal to a tree, for example. Then when he cuts it down it won't crush him.

What about acts not so clearly petitionary? For example, a Kaska Indian hunter formerly kept away from sexual intercourse the night before he went hunting; otherwise, he knew, he could hardly expect that any animal would allow him to slay it. This is what I call magic. A person expects that something, some prior procedure or avoidance, governs the outcome of an undertaking. He addresses no humble petition to game or to spirits that control animals. What beliefs can satisfactorily account for such conduct? People who behave this way act as though they conceive the universe to be made up of interrelated but not necessarily sentient parts, each one of which influences the others. A connection exists between sexual intercourse and animals hunted for food. Sexual relations and anything connected with woman's sexual physi-

TO SECURE LIFE AND FOOD — A POLAR ESKIMO'S CREDO

"We do not believe in any God, as you do. . . . We do not all understand the hidden things, but we believe the people who say they do. We believe our *Angáhut*, our magicians, and we believe them because we wish to live long, and because we do not want to expose ourselves to the danger of famine and starvation. We believe, in order to make our lives and our food secure. If we did not believe the magicians, the animals we hunt would make themselves invisible to us; if we did not follow their advice, we should fall ill and die."

Knud Rasmussen, *The People of the Polar North*, trans. G. Herring (London, 1908), p. 123.

ology, including birth and menstruation, repel animals. Sex and game are antithetical phenomena. Contrariwise proper amulets possess automatic power to attract animals within range of the hunters' weapons.

I fail to see anything immature in such coping maneuvers though Freud believed otherwise.[7] It is true that our children also endow trees with sentience or think a bit magically. We disabuse them of such notions knowing that they are incompatible with modern knowledge and belief. But this parallel does not mean that intelligent adults' behavior in an exotic culture is wholly equivalent to what our children do. Magical coping is grounded in thoughtful assumptions about nature and can be defended reasonably. Explicit rules govern such procedures and the whole community invests them with value. They are not only intended to protect entire social systems from threat but provide a common way of behavior that helps hold the group together. We blind ourselves if we dismiss such behavior as childish or as incompetent superstitions.

When we thoroughly know a culture, the view we obtain of coping behavior meshing with belief system is far richer and more convincing than anything a child might construct. Hopi Indians are quite explicit in their conception of the universe.[8] They believe that an active spirit world coexists with the sensory physical world. The spirit world encompasses, besides gods, all human beings, animals lesser than man, plants, and some natural phenomena, like the sun and clouds. All possess a spiritual component. Human prayer reaches, as it were, behind the obvious face of nature and makes contact with its spiritual component. Hopi don't exactly pray to the sun but to the sun's spiritual essence. All things by virtue of being linked with humans through a

[7] Sigmund Freud, *The Future of an Illusion*, trans. W. D. Robson-Scott (New York, 1953), chap. 4.
[8] Elsie Clews Parsons, *Pueblo Indian Religion*, 2 vols. (Chicago, 1939).

common spirit world can become aware of man's intentions. Existence of this continuous, systematic spiritual realm is taken for granted. It constitutes a basic assumption that needs no proof, just as for many Americans the efficacy of democracy and the jury system requires no demonstration.

Now let us see how the Hopi employ this belief in coping with the world. Hopi prayer doesn't resemble Christian prayer. Instead of voicing a request it expresses the wish or desire that certain things should come about. A prayer is a string of compulsive words. By virtue of this resolute element inhering in it, prayer operates on the spiritual counterparts of those objects (clouds, plants, animals) to which it is directed. The essential part of Hopi ceremonies is prayer. A ceremony itself is a mass prayer in which the village wills something: fertility, long life, or health. Many people praying simultaneously enhances the power of the wish. Yet, prayer becomes effective only if made with an untroubled conscience and a good mind free of hostile thoughts.

A Hopi prays with things and acts as well as words. Men undertake arduous eagle-capturing expeditions to secure downy breast feathers that possess potent, prayerful effectiveness. The feathers go on prayer offerings which are then deposited in a suitable place whence they reach the spirit world. Activities like dancing and running also constitute praying. The runner, whom the village chief appoints, garbs himself as Masau'u, god of death, owner of the earth, and controller of fertility. On successive nights he runs one counterclockwise circuit that each time becomes smaller. Nearer and nearer he draws the rain clouds and stimulates the corn to grow.

THE SYMBOLISM OF MAGIC

Like poetry in which allusions are indirect and thought is garbed in expressive similes and metaphors, so the magical wish often assumes a subtle symbolic guise. At times the symbolism is readily obvious. Even an outsider readily understands why the image of an enemy is being roasted; the underlying purpose is actually to torment him. A Kaska Indian mother whose child had just lost a milk tooth uses it to describe a circle over the child's head while she repeats, "Rabbit tooth! Rabbit tooth!" Let the tooth grow back, this symbolism says, as fast as rabbits multiply. When the symbolism is less obvious a suggestion or two from the people easily elucidates it. A Kaska hunter formerly ripped open his coat sleeve to celebrate the first game that his younger brother had killed. So, the Indians explained to me, would future game fall freely to the hunter. In New Guinea the hibiscus flower properly used promotes successful killing of wild pigs. When people explain that the flower is red just like blood flowing from a freshly killed pig, the symbolism becomes obvious. Its color makes it almost natural to use the hibiscus for this purpose. Of course, identification of blood with the flower occurs purely through convention, just as all meaning is conventionally assigned to symbols.

Understanding symbolism becomes more difficult when objects are employed in coping behavior without any apparent reference to color or any other physical property. Take corn meal, a product widely used among the Hopi. Ceremonialists pray or breathe on the meal. They sprinkle it on masks worn by impersonators of deities and on many other ritual objects as well as on rabbits taken in the ritual rabbit hunt. Before handling sacred things, priests wash their hands in corn meal. When naming a child, corn flour is rubbed on its face and chest as people pray: "With the meal they give you new life, you start afresh." These examples indicate that the Hopi endow corn meal with many useful properties. It helps to bring rain or general good fortune, blesses a child, and makes a person pure enough to handle sacred objects. But nothing obvious suggests why corn meal should be used in these contexts. We are reduced to a purely technical interpretation, namely that the use of corn as a staple food is the main feature which, like the hibiscus flower's color, recommends it for magical use. The lightness of the substance or its powdery nature seems to be another favorable property.

PRAYER AND "HAMMERING"

Apart from comprehending the symbols, to understand petitionary prayer and magic we ought to know more about the actor's state of mind. We know he is motivated to accomplish something. His behavior is instrumental, as instrumental as a woodcutter's chopping or a cook cleaning fish. Although prayer is sometimes reverent in the way it appeals to beloved ancestors or other hidden agents, magic can be as matter-of-fact as the cook's labors. Does a person who copes magically not distinguish between the efficacy of what he does and some other, more direct procedure which he might also employ? A farmer who painstakingly plants his yams and then sings for them to grow, does he equate one activity with the other? Puerto Ricans have a saying that applies to this question, "Pray to God but still keep hammering." Very likely the magician recognizes that the two procedures are different. But both are necessary.

What if there isn't also a more direct procedure? After all, the Hopi can't do anything more direct to bring rain than to utter their compulsive words and perform their complex ceremonies. Therefore they can't very well recognize that this mode of coping differs from another, more direct procedure. Apart from magic what "hammering" can a Hopi husband do to control in some measure the outcome of his wife's pregnancy? He takes care to injure no animal, for that would damage the unborn child's body; he is cruel to no beast, lest he endanger the foetus' life, and he feeds his wife weasel flesh and rubs her body with a weasel skin so that the baby will come out as swiftly as that sly, little animal slips through a hole. Magic constitutes his only defence against utter helplessness and anxiety. Then, too, we know that no empirical coping procedure is able to counteract situations only putatively dangerous, like the Hopi salt-gathering expedition or menstruation among the Kaska. The menace that Hopi or Kaska Indians feel from these latter two events is not objectively verifiable like the danger of miscarriage, for example, but arises from the way they define those activities. Naturally, that makes them no less real to the actors. However, the Kaska can have no way of "hammering" except to counteract such danger by prayerful petition, symbolic avoidance, or some other magical procedure.

Just because people deal with some of their problems in terms of petitionary prayer and magic is no sign that they regard all such procedures to be infallible or that they never admit change and experimentation into this area. The conviction with which prayers for help are said or magic is performed ranges from the highest degree of tentativeness to hardest certainty. Magicians may know several techniques for getting equivalent results and when one fails try another. They are quite capable of learning new routines, perhaps literally dreaming them up or borrowing promising methods from neighboring cultures. Clients who use professional magicians shop around if opportunity permits; they consult another practitioner if the first is unable to relieve an illness. Public opinion ranks curers who rely on petitionary prayer and magic. The community's most reputable specialists may quite rationally shy from tough cases lest they destroy his reputation.

THE SENSE OF COMMAND

Magic as well as petitions offered in the mold of prayer allow man a feeling of being in command of those very situations over which cultural inadequacy permits him least control. These coping devices reduce his sense of uncertainty and induce a more predictable view of life. As instrumental prayer and magical coping contribute to man's adjustment they simultaneously stimulate his morale and confidence to a point where they directly aid survival. Once he believes that deities have been marshaled to his assistance or that preliminary magic paves his way to success, man starts out with higher hopes, works harder, fights more forcefully, and tires less easily. Illness recedes and health returns under the patient's conviction that powerful forces have been enlisted in his behalf.

Shall we brand as illusory the beliefs that underlie indirect forms of coping? Illusions in the thought of Freud, Marx, and Lenin are ignoble compensations for human weakness.[9] To understand the strength of these indirect forms of coping we are obliged to take a considerably more positive stand and recognize the many useful functions that stem from them.

[9] Freud, *op. cit.;* Vladimer I. Lenin, *Religion* (New York, 1933).

A people's conviction that they possess successful coping techniques, their faith in ancestors or deities, and their confidence in magicians or priests represent a special class of sentiments. Powerful emotion envelopes these sentiments and enables them to hold together organized social systems. The sentiments provide a basis for social solidarity. Naturally magic and petitionary prayer also generate stress. They provide grounds for anxiety lest the prayer be said improperly or the magic performed by someone in an impure state. Conceivably coping through these channels in some circumstances even slows down acceptance of empirically surer modes of coping and thereby preserves a large measure of cultural inadequacy. But the fact that magic and solicitory prayer persist leaves no doubt whatsoever that by and large they contribute positively to human coping.

DO THEY WORK?

How do indirect forms of coping manage to persist? Our very different world view leaves us genuinely puzzled. Why have not petitionary prayer and magic long ago been dropped from culture? They don't work, do they?

Let's go slowly in offering a verdict of total ineffectualness. When inspired by faith and conjoined with more direct forms of coping—like fighting the enemy with weapons, keeping the patient warm and at rest, or planting seeds in the soil—it becomes nearly impossible without constructing a controlled experiment to tell what is working, the direct act or the accompanying spells, prayers, and magical manipulations. Furthermore, the latter actually do work, for example, when magic infuses confidence and this emotion then increases the farmer's care and effort. If magic convinces the fighter of his power it can insure a more successful outcome than would otherwise be the case.

In situations where the technique is employed to influence people's health or social effectiveness, to win their love, or to torment them with sickness and death, suggestions instilled through instrumental prayer and magic may bring about precisely the intended outcome. To be sure, success like this can only occur when belief is strong and full publicity is given to what has been done in the patient's behalf, for the victim's hurt, or to win the sweetheart's favors. Thanatomania, as death from sorcery is called, has been assiduously documented. An Australian tribesman "contracted a slight cold, but the local men told him that the members of a group about twelve miles away to the east had taken his heart out, and believing this to be so he simply laid himself down and wasted away."[10] Love magic is attested for the same part of Australia. A man "called some of his friends together [thereby insuring publicity] and performed the ceremony [of striking the grass] and in a very short time the de-

[10] Baldwin Spencer and F. J. Gillen, *The Native Tribes of Central Australia*, reprint ed., (London, 1938), p. 537.

sired woman, who was on this occasion a widow, came in from . . . about fifty miles to the west . . . and the two are now man and wife."[11]

Apart from the effectualness people feel in, or actually experience through, magic and solicitory prayer, other factors preserve their faith in these ubiquitous forms of coping. Authority of parents, headmen, and priests lends support to them to a point where it takes a resolute iconoclast to doubt their use. Should there be such a one in the community, he can expect to encounter the very firm hand of social pressure; others will laugh at his naïveté, shun him for his grossness, and determinedly reason him out of his obstinacy. Only in exceptional circumstances can a solitary man's opinions withstand so strong a barrage of criticism. Such exceptional circumstances are increasing even in small-scale, exotic corners of the modern world due to the impact of western cultures with new theories of nature and well-nigh miraculous machines and medicines. Culture contact shatters the consensus and consistency of hitherto largely isolated beliefs. Now traditional forms of magic thin out, perhaps to be replaced by magical use of Christian objects or reliance on petitionary prayer addressed to a new god.

Even people aware that their fervent use of petitionary prayer and magic is inconsistent with what they can realistically expect from those procedures do not invariably reject them.[12] When dissonance of this sort exists we can expect people to feel stress. Because of the uncomfortable nature of stress people will very likely do something to alleviate it. They will try to make their behavior more consistent, matching their use of magic with their knowledge that magic also fails. Oddly enough, one way of reducing dissonance is to step up the intensity with which the original belief is held or the fervor with which an act is carried out—the very act that accumulated experience has begun to contradict. Thus, up to a certain point, as magic and petitionary prayer encounter contradiction, people may increase their conviction toward these procedures and so reduce both dissonance and stress.

Magic and closely associated prayerful means of coping benefit from the very irregularity with which apparent rewards accrue, so that the behavior is never consistently invalidated.[13] Further support comes from the practice of haloing petitionary prayer, magic, and divining, remembering the occasions when, possibly through chance alone, they met intended results. In this way only the hits are counted and the misses easily overlooked. Daniel Defoe tells the story of a young girl with two sweethearts who went to the "cunning man to know which of those two shall have her." He tells the miss to lay two sticks crosswise under her pillow. This magical device will arrange things so that the

[11] *Ibid.*, p. 542.
[12] Theodore Rosenthal and Bernard J. Siegel, "Magic and Witchcraft: An Interpretation from Dissonance Theory," *Southwestern Journal of Anthropology*, 15 (1959), 143-167.
[13] Erasmus, *op. cit.*, chap. 3.

first man she dreams of will be her man. With the girl's mind full of her problem, of course she dreams of one of them "and it may be the right, as well as the wrong, so that it is an even lay," says Defoe. She marries that man and if all turns out well the cunning man can expect to draw all the young people of the country as his customers. If it turns out poorly, "that's forgotten, and does him no harm." [14] Specialists who depend on facilitating clients' adjustment through petitionary prayer and magic have special interest in doing all they can via haloing and otherwise to perpetuate what they and others agree is a socially most useful profession.

THE GLOW OF CERTAINTY

Plague-ridden Londoners in Defoe's imaginative account made much use of astrologers and other experts reputedly able to predict the future. Just as under conditions of uncertainty and danger magic enables man to feel that he can cope with threat, so divination, the clairvoyant view of the future, allays uncertainty. Even a bad prognosis gives some structure to an otherwise totally unknown end. Large-scale western culture in Europe and America has gone far in applying statistics to actuarial prediction. This is the best that we can do and it doesn't go far toward answering what will happen to me specifically. The client of the fortuneteller finds out what will happen to him, not to 300 motorists on a summer holiday weekend. Parents of a young couple in India consult an astrologer to learn whether the match they have arranged is suitable for two specific young people. They aren't concerned with the proportion of marriages likely to fail.

Man has discovered thousands of different means for learning the future. Scapulimancy, in which a hunter consults cracks that appeared in a roasting animal's scapula, ranges far in both the Old and New Worlds. The direction in which a crack runs indicates where the hunter will find game. Hopi and other Pueblo Indians have a variant of crystal gazing in which a crystal-like stone works about as well as better polished crystals of professional western fortunetellers. The diagnostician peers into the stone to find lost objects, discover causes of disease, and detect witches. The crystal also forecasts weather. Dreams, too, are loaded with meaning for the future and their interpretation seriously affects a Hopi's mood and outlook. In Swat many innocent events constitute omens. For example, a meteor flashing across the sky promises that sickness will strike. In mock autobiographical fashion Defoe tells of being undecided about whether or not to quit plague-filled London. To find an answer he opened his Bible at random and the first words he saw, "there shall no evil befall thee," induced him to stay. The seance, which arranges com-

[14] Daniel Defoe, *The Novels and Miscellaneous Works of Daniel De Foe. XII, A System of Magic* (Oxford, 1840), p. 353.

munication between a medium and his or her hidden sources of information, represents another far-flung means of divination. The infinite variety of omens and forms of divination is itself a most significant fact for understanding this form of behavior. Apparently almost anything that is not invariant can be made an index of something else.

Divination functions beyond providing a glow of certainty. Nothing about a scapula determines which way the cracks will run when the bone is heated; they can run any way. The hunter obeys the oracle whichever way it turns out. As a result he may head in a direction that he never would have chosen

The shaman on the platform is possessed by a deity. The advice he gives his client, therefore, is divinely inspired. (*Edward B. Harper.*)

if left to himself and thereby he reaches a relatively unfrequented area with game.[15] The oracle by randomizing behavior forestalls the likelihood of a hunter always being guided by past successes in choosing where to go. It prevents a curer from too readily applying the same and, possibly, no longer inspiring mode of therapy. Randomization increases chances of success.

It is sometimes hard to know when divination leaves off and empirical prediction begins, that is, to know whether the phenomenon which is taken as an index is independent or actually integrally related to the event to which it is supposed to give a clue. Many weather signs may be parts of a complex weather system and that accounts both for the success with which they predict

[15] Omar Khayyam Moore, "Divination—A New Perspective," *American Anthropologist*, 59 (1957), 69-74.

and their recurrence from one culture to another. Something similar is probably the case with prayersticks that Hopi men plant near a certain spring in a wish for rain. If on their return to the place they find the sticks and ground around them to be damp, then they know it will rain and crops will be good. Isn't it likely that prayersticks will most likely be found damp in a year of good rainfall when the spring is full and the surrounding earth moist?

The glow of assurance compensating man for his inadequate ability to cope straightforwardly can be provided in ways that have little to do with magic, petitionary prayer, or divination. In time of trouble and anxiety, people feel better after they have committed themselves to God or read a portion of scripture pregnant with promise and comfort. The Ninety-third Psalm cited by Defoe nicely illustrates the pattern. Talking about one's uncertainties also brings relief. Modern western culture includes ministers who act as pastoral psychiatrists for troubled minds. There are also laymen, listeners, who for a fee will sympathetically hear out a client's hopes and troubles. Later in this book I will examine one or two belief systems the purpose of which is to maintain or restore one's sense of personal adjustment.

FURTHER READING

Bronislaw Malinowski in "Magic, Science and Religion" explores the idea that magic is grounded in uncertainty and danger. The article appears in the book *Magic, Science and Religion and Other Essays* (Glencoe, Ill., 1948). Among the most important sources on magic are F. E. Williams, *Orokaiva Magic* (London, 1928); E. E. Evans-Pritchard, *Witchcraft, Oracles and Magic Among the Azande* (Oxford, 1937); and Hutton Webster, *Magic, A Sociological Study* (Stanford, Calif., 1948). Jean Cazeneuve, *Les Rites et la condition humaine* (Paris, 1958), believes that rites addressed to deities are more in accord with human nature than magic. "Confessions by Africans," by M. D. W. Jeffreys, *Eastern Anthropologist*, 6 (1952), 42-67, describes how that form of coping works. J. Franklin Ewing, S.J., a Catholic anthropologist, distinguishes between medals and amulets in the appendix, "The Religious Medals," in Ross Gordon Montgomery, Watson Smith, and John Otis Brew, *Franciscan Awatovi: The Excavation and Conjectural Reconstruction of a 17th-Century Spanish Mission Establishment at a Hopi Indian Town in Northeastern Arizona*, Papers of the Peabody Museum of American Archaeology and Ethnology, Harvard University, vol. 36, 1949, pp. 100-103.

A classic study deserving to be brought up to date is *The Medicine Man* by John Lee Maddox (New York, 1923). Ida Lublinski examines "Der Medizinmann bei den Naturvoelkern Suedamerikas," *Zeitschrift fuer Ethnologie*, 52/53 (1920-1921), 234-263. Part of her article tries to estimate how much of the shaman's therapy is "practical" and how much "symbolic." Her conclusion is that the latter predominates. G. Morris Carstairs, "Medicine and Faith in Rural Rajasthan," in Benjamin D. Paul, ed., *Health, Culture and Community* (New York, 1955) describes the experiences of a western-trained physician in India. Leland C. Wyman's paper on "Navaho Diagnosticians," *American Anthropologist*, 38 (1936), 236-246, should be read with William Morgan, "Navaho Treatment of Sickness: Diagnosticians," *American Anthropologist,* 33 (1931), 390-402.

Good accounts of divination include Evans-Pritchard, *Witchcraft, Oracles and Magic Among the Azande;* E. Z. Vogt, "Water Witching," *Scientific American,* 75 (1952), 175-186, which describes customs practiced in rural America; and S. F. Nadel's account of prediction among the Nupe and its integration with the rest of culture in *Nupe Religion* (London, 1954), chap. 2. *Gregorio, The Hand-Trembler* by Alexander H. Leighton and Dorothea C. Leighton, Papers of the Peabody Museum of America Archaeology and Ethnology, Harvard University, vol. 40, no. 1, 1949, is a careful examination of a Navaho Indian diviner's life.

4

Who Interacts with Whom?

PEOPLE ARE ORGANIZED

Social systems consist of more than just people. They arise when people become engaged with one another: employees work together in an office, comrades drink together in a tavern, children attend school, or a congregation worships in a common faith. Together all these groups interact when they affirm allegiance to a nation. In its turn a nation engages itself with other nations through trade, diplomacy, or war, so that, to a degree, even society is organized.

Obviously people hardly ever engage themselves completely at random; who interacts with whom is organized. Kaska Indian men, not women, join forces to hunt. A close core of female relatives, a woman and her daughters, remains together to form a Hopi household. In India a large household comprises a core of closely related men. To maintain standards a university restricts registration to well-qualified applicants of either sex. It is terribly disturbing when an emergency disrupts our organized modes of interaction and strangers bluntly force themselves upon us.

Understanding culture requires some acquaintance with the way social relationships are organized. To summarize, society dynamically viewed consists of interaction between people. Prescribing who engages himself with whom is a question which any social system must consider.

[1] *Ancient Law,* Everyman's Library edition (London, 1917), p. 179.

A core of female relatives, a mother and her daughters, remains together to form a Hopi household. (*Smithsonian Institution, Bureau of American Ethnology. Photograph by A. C. Vroman.*)

In large part social organization occurs through people being assigned to, or induced to join, groups. Much that an individual does in society satisfies the expectations of the many groups to which he feels bound.

Let us be clear about this thing, a group. To constitute a group, members need not be directly engaged with one another, like the women in a Hopi household cooperatively baking bread. Persons who sincerely acknowledge a sense of belonging together form a group though they never come into each other's physical presence. Thanks to writing and radio, even widely dispersed members can constantly strive to fulfill their group's purposes. Without necessarily meeting each other face-to-face, brethren in the Brotherhood of Railroad Trainmen support organizational goals and are aware of being united. Participation influences every member's self-image.

Organization, then, comes through the groups into which every social system and society itself are parceled. All groups are arbitrary, being created through men's decisions. No group is biological in the sense that people are

A BREAKDOWN IN SOCIAL ORGANIZATION AND SOCIAL DISLOCATION

Invasion and revolt against the Egyptian pharaoh around 2500 B.C. snapped the reins that held together the Nile kingdom. The ruler, source of order, truth, and prosperity, lost control. Social organization on a large scale evaporated.

Mournful texts that have come down from this time express the social dislocation people felt. "The country turns round like a potter's wheel," one text says. "Great and small say: 'I wish I were dead,' " another gloomily reports. "The land is in confusion. . . . The land is a misery."

Henri Frankfort, *Ancient Egyptian Religion* (New York, 1948), pp. 86-87.

---

instinctively driven into that form of organization. If groups were biological then they would hardly vary from one part of the world to another. Even the family is mutable. Contrary to what our experience seems to say, political organization is not inevitable. Gustav Landauer called the state a condition of human beings that we can destroy by contracting other relationships.

To work up a group you must in effect demarcate some people, few or many, from others who will be excluded. How is this accomplished? Groups are organized because everyone is not equivalent in all respects to everybody else. Individuals differ in age, kinship, experience, temperament, strength, and even in the distance they live from one another. Some differences, like inherent superiority or inferiority, are imputed. On the basis of meanings we assign to such individual differences we construct groups. For example, to attain protection geographical propinquity leads me to organize all adult men in my neighborhood for defensive action. Kinship, the fact that marriage or birth relates people, becomes the trustworthy basis of other groups, like the family. Previous experience becomes the criterion of membership when men who are divinely empowered through similar visions or who served honorably in war or who graduated Yale in 1945 enter a group. The selective factor may be far more practical. An entrepreneur who wants to set up a business to make and sell books needs authors with promising manuscripts, editors capable of checking on the authors' fallibility, competent typesetters, keen-eyed proofreaders, energetic salesmen, and sundry other specialists. Individuals with proper qualifications must be sought and hired before the group, a publishing house, can undertake its mission. Groups, then, originate when we apply one or more criteria in order to select those with whom we wish to associate for some purpose.

Not all groups are formed so rationally. Some, arbitrarily designed to include given persons and not others, cease to choose on the basis of individual characteristics. Hence the distinction between voluntary groups and those, like the family, into which we involuntarily fall by birth and from which we subsequently have trouble escaping.

Criteria that define membership provide only one basis of organization. A name, emblem, or motto for the group, some secret but expressive ritual, and a more or less creditable myth of heroic ancestry or fabulous destiny all contribute to the process whereby groups are formed. They also insure the continuity of groups in time. They bestow on the body a sense of distinctiveness or purpose that differentiates it and keeps it focused on its goals. Four walls help, too, whenever they effectively confine members' interaction to one another. The flimsy partition that separates shipping from assembly room and the hut into which the magicians periodically file strengthen each group's sense of membership. Annoying consequences follow when such devices by stressing propinquity create groups where none was intended. For example, men doing the same job may develop group norms that remain impervious to management's inducements to produce more. In addition, social control operates vigilantly to maintain an even tenor in group life. It prevents disagreements from reaching a pitch where members would find it impossible to attain the satisfactions for which they are organized.

THE "GROUP" THAT ISN'T A GROUP

We frequently use the term group imprecisely to cover mere assemblages. We label as a group all Africans, all Caucasoids, all college students, all the unemployed, applying the term to aggregates that never interact as a body. There exists no likelihood that all college students will ever band together. The word "group" is misapplied to such aggregates. It is better to refer to people as a category when they are identified solely because they possess one or more characteristics in common. An ethnic "group," like Italians in New Haven or Pathans in Pakistan, and a minority "group," like American Indians, lack special organization. The individuals in each of these cases form a category either because they speak a common language, trace common ancestry, possess similar legal rights, or have other attributes in common. Sometimes we can't easily decide whether a social aggregate is indeed a group or simply an unorganized category on the verge of banding together. There is no explicit, over-all organization for all the Hopi Indians. Yet they feel themselves to be a unity. In this case I am inclined to include them under the rubric of group.

WHO ONE IS

Grouping organizes society. Factories, families, churches, tribes, nations, and multinational organizations are among the groups that structure our society. Simultaneously social interaction is organized by allocating individuals to specific positions in groups and in society at large. We act and are responded to in given situations in terms of the position, or status, we occupy. Who one is depends partly on his status as he and others perceive it. The flashing bars on the captain's uniform identify his hierarchical position even when he is away from his base. Father, however, the position that a man occupies in his family, can less readily be recognized away from home. Consequently, dad, a hero to his small son, at the plant ranks only as an ambitious shipping clerk.

Everyone occupies a number of positions in society. Each provides him with a role to play in certain situations. The executive's role calls on him to make decisions for his company; the academic man reflectively chews his pipe stem and judges the chances of the student passing; a snowshoed Kaska Indian trapper sets traps for fur, and his wife plays her domestic role well enough but often finds it uncongenial for her temperament. Responsibilities, rewards, and stresses accrue from roles. An actor who seriously misplays his social role finds other members of the social system stepping in to bring his performance back into line, for there are norms attached to nearly every status. Naturally, an individual injects some of his own personal qualities into every role he plays. That's why one shipping clerk can be discharged and another, with more promising personal traits, hired to occupy the same position.

Society is made up of people engaging themselves with one another as representatives of the status that each happens to occupy at the moment. Statuses are ranked. Some carry more prestige, higher emoluments, and greater power than others. Hence a good deal of social interaction consists of striving by fair and foul means to change from a lower-ranking or frustrating status to a more rewarding one or to bring up the tone of a low-ranking status in which one is fixed. Other considerations also govern the energy people spend in circulating from one status to another or quitting one group and joining another. They are trying to maximize satisfactions or endeavoring to fit their personalities into more congenial roles. Some social circulation is involuntary; a child is born, a man fired, a patient discharged. Death, too, instigates social movement; it strips the group of members who may have to be replaced.

The number of statuses recognized in a social system varies directly with its size and scale. Kaska Indians, aboriginally as well as today, recognize relatively few positions carrying specific rights and duties. Kinship relations are especially important in standardizing behavior. Marriage and birth endow every Kaska with a number of kinship statuses. In Swat kinship status also regulates interpersonal relations, but in addition this larger social system possesses a greater number of diversified nonkin statuses. Men behave and are responded to according to whether they are nobles (khans), hereditary saints, religious scholars (mullahs), policemen, government officials (who come in many grades), tailors, barbers, shoemakers, farmers, or Gujar pastoralists precariously subsisting on cattle and a little piece of unirrigated ground. With greater differentiation of positions goes a marked diversification in types of groups. The schools, college, hospitals, government bureaus, political parties, courts, militia, and bus companies of Swat have no counterpart among Kaska Indians.

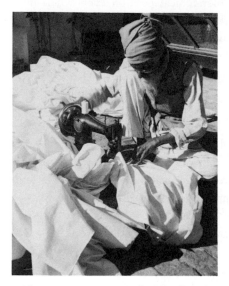

Extensive occupational specialization in West Pakistan demands many statuses.

A status implies goals for persons who occupy it. Occupants exert themselves to achieve maximum rewards or to defend their reputations. A dedicated executive pushes hard to bring his business out on top. A warrior wins decorations for loyalty, killing, and taking risks. Men, simply because they are men and not women, in many social systems must be untiringly assertive, dominant, and courageous. Some persons, neurotically unsure of themselves, become compulsive about nearly everything they do and in striving for perfection overplay their roles. Immigrants, because they are unfamiliar with their newly adopted culture don't quite know where the demands of a status end. Most of the time people respond judiciously to many kinds of cues that tell them how to rein their role playing. Here, instead of going into all aspects of social control, I will call attention only to cues that check a given line of behavior by extolling some counterpoised ideal quality: charity as well as competition; pity despite violence; reasonableness with impetuosity; relaxation along with industry.

In a large-scale social system special statuses guard counterpoised values. Every Sunday in America religious specialists routinely extol neighborliness, charity, and love to counterbalance self-seeking, competition, and morbid hate for rival social systems that endanger us. In Swat one set of leaders consists of landowning Pathans, khans, who have their wealth, power, and reputation to defend.[2] Khans who wish to be supreme recognize no superior chief. They collect followers from among their tenants and dependents with whose aid they zealously advance their own inexhaustible interests. They push against other khans who similarly raise followers to promote their own gains. Another set of leaders are called saints. Each saintly leader, too, has followers but rather than pursuing wealth and using his power to subordinate others, he

[2] Fredrik Barth, *Political Leadership Among Swat Pathans,* London School of Economics, Monographs on Social Anthropology, no. 19, 1959, chap. 11.

PEOPLE PASS IN AND OUT OF GROUPS AND STATUSES

The 21-year-old youth ran his fingers through his pompadour before answering.

"I quit because I got interested in other things. . . . Girls. That's one of the main reasons guys quit. . . . Sometimes the other gang won't let you quit—because maybe they're waiting to get revenge on your gang, and they want to get you too.

"I'm hoping to be an executive some day." The speaker, who had given up all the grim power and jungle prestige that being chief of an East Harlem gang had earned him, reflectively added, "I'd like to be the boss of a lot of people."

Gay Talese, "Gang Chief Who Quit Tells Why," *The New York Times*, October 2, 1959.

acts mildly as befits a student of religion. Khans should be proud, rivalrous, virile. Saintly leaders should be moderate, reasonable, and meek. The two opposite statuses complement and balance one another. When rivalry between chiefs builds up tension so intense that it could explode into open violence, a nearby saint hurries in to mediate. In any region followers of a khan simultaneously adhere to a saint. Hence they respect the authority of the saint when he intervenes. Especially in former times saintly intervention in the disputes of jealous khans prevented the social system of Swat from thoroughly collapsing into anarchy.

POWER AND AUTHORITY

In every group a few outstanding statuses carry relatively prodigious authority and power. The plant manager controls a multimillion dollar business; a minister has power to resolve intricate moral questions; a classroom teacher can promote or hold back her pupils; the ruler of Swat sentences men to death. Below these outstanding ranks, individuals in other positions aren't wholly powerless but command considerably less social strength.

The distinction between authority and power should be closely examined. Power means an ability, one often sought after, to be obeyed in a limited number of life's contexts. A man armed with a gun has power to rob; the victim obeys him through fear. Authority, however, denotes that a person is deemed worthy of being obeyed. He has the right to be heeded when he speaks, whether it be in church, doctor's office, classroom, through the pages of a professional journal, or from the polished height of a judicial bench.

Authority stems from varied sources. Sometimes it comes through birth. Don Talayesva, a Hopi Indian, acquired some of his authority because, he says, "I was a special baby—twins twisted into one. There was no doubt about this, for they could see the two whorls of hair on the back of my head, and those present at my birth told others how large and double-sexed I looked when fresh from the womb. . . . It was anticipated, therefore, that I would have a special power to protect myself, do many strange things before the people, and be able to heal certain diseases, even as a boy." [3] It turned out as you might expect. He did indeed reveal extraordinary abilities, no doubt because the authority legitimately bestowed on him by birth impressed people. Training and experience lend authority, usually in combination with age or seniority. Kaska Indians listened when a skillful hunter suggested where to look for game and even when, in quite a different vein, he encouraged them to behave morally. The physician wins authority in the same way he gains his license to practice—by many years of study and clinical experience. Ordination or a vision confers religious authority; people listen to a shaman because his vision brought him into direct contact with divinity. Formal rites of installation solidify a ruler's claims to power. In Hopiland members of a special sodality, the Kwan, legitimately install a village chief in his office. The Queen's far more resplendent coronation rite conferred no higher degree of authority. Authority also flows from personal charisma, that is, from the special quality that a rare person embodies in his personality. Charisma fires others to respect his counsel. Also, we cannot overlook possession of symbolic artifacts, like staffs of office, badges, uniforms, scepters, and other symbolic appurtenances that confer a convincing right to be obeyed. Finally, in some cultures wealth conveys authority. Among the Pathans of Swat, land or, better, wealth derived from land plus an unsullied honor support a khan's authority. [4] Any assault on a khan's honor damages his authority over his followers unless he retaliates appropriately. His retaliation need not be proportionate to the offense either, so that a mere insult to a khan may lead to murder. With foresight a khan will choose a style of revenge to enhance his reputation among potential followers. One thing a khan must never do—stoop to accepting money to repair an insult to his honor. Payment in Swat expresses the payer's superiority over the receiver and debases the latter's esteem. Whereas the Kaska Indians are little concerned with who has authority and how well he defends it, the khans of Swat, like some Americans, find this topic to be of engrossing interest.

In numerous social situations authority readily compels obedience. But in other areas men cannot successfully control human relationships simply through their strength of authority. Freud speaks bluntly, but he is basically accurate when he says, "It is . . . impossible to do without government of the masses by a minority . . . for the masses are lazy and unintelligent, they have

[3] Leo W. Simmons, ed., *Sun Chief, the Autobiography of a Hopi Indian* (New Haven, Conn., 1942), p. 33.

[4] Barth, *op. cit.*, chap. 7.

no love for instinctual renunciation, they are not to be convinced. . . ." [5] Therefore, the greater proportion of social systems invests chiefs or ruling bodies not only with authority but with physical force as well through which they can coerce others into obedience.

Authority and power make a difference in the way they coordinate activities in and between groups making up a social system. Power and authority confine behavior within tolerable limits, that is, they restrain diversity lest it go too far. The hopes with which people enter social interaction become more attainable thanks to the control exerted by people with power. On the other hand, any power can be abused unless balancing forces check it. The power which American editors and publishers have to influence public opinion checks political officeholders. Courts in turn check freedom of the press. Some social systems are poor in resources to manage vast concentrated power. Swat, for example, has no newspapers and few other channels that effectively bring public opinion to bear on the ruler. In fact, he threatens gossipers who talk unfavorably about him. Not that he claims to be perfect. But he fears that derogatory gossip will reduce his authority and so weaken his ability to rule.

WHO GETS WHAT?

Nearly every social system finds it convenient to use property as a means of organizing social interaction. Property can be used in this way not solely because it is always scarce or vital to survival. Such reasoning can't explain why a song, dance step, extra telephone, or deep-pile carpet becomes the keynote of a social status. The organizational virtue of property resides in the fact that possessions are tangible, visible or auditory, and readily transferable. By virtue of these qualities property can symbolize who a person is and helps focus his power over others. Individuals or groups, including nations, that claim rights to possessions, like land, a certain office, or a uniform, consequently set themselves off from other social entities. My relationship to my father or his lineage is expressed in my right to receive property in that line. Gifts that flow between kinsmen strengthen those relationships and keep alive the meaning of kinship ties. International trade to some degree cements our divisive, fragmented world society.

Property standardizes social relations by making manifest how important someone is. Possessions, whether they be gongs, pigs, slaves, mansions, or automobiles, are all capable of symbolizing prestige and authority. In the Hopi village of Oraibi the Bear "clan" claims to own all land by divine right; hence village chieftainship properly belongs to someone in this important kinship group.

[5] Sigmund Freud, *The Future of an Illusion,* trans. W. D. Robson-Scott (New York, 1953), p. 12.

BONDS OF KINSHIP

Without question, in relatively small-scale societies kinship exceeds any other factor governing social interaction. In much of the world unrelated strangers, regardless of their intentions, encounter reserve, suspicion, and even hostility. Any anthropologist who has lived in small-scale communities appreciates the vitality of kinship bonds. His work goes exceptionally slowly until a "father" or "brother" adopts him. Through his adopter he then acquires other relatives—brothers, sisters, aunts, and uncles who are willing to teach him their culture. Of course, kinsmen also fall out with each other. But when they do, efforts as strenuous as our own attempt to mediate a costly strike may be made to restore the disrupted relationship.

Why should kinship be stressed so much? Chiefly because it forms so obvious a tie. Biological facts of reproduction—sexual intercourse between a man and woman, conception, and birth—define everyone's relationship to two highly significant people, his parents. Usually they have other children, his siblings, with whom he grows up. His parents themselves have parents as well as siblings. And so a pool of genealogical kinsmen inevitably comes into existence that, despite loss and replacements, continues from one generation to the next.

Biological nature makes kinship inevitable but not the extent to which people acknowledge obligations to kinsmen. Nothing forces us to limit our dealings mainly to relatives. As social systems expand their scale and highly diversified responsibilities are flung farther afield, dealings necessarily cease to be confined to kinfolk. Other statuses involving relative strangers—employer, ruler, merchant, and teacher—become vital for sustaining life and well-being.

All integral social systems recognize kinship but differ in how many kinship statuses they distinguish. We have a separate term for mother and another for mother's sister (namely, "aunt") but Hopi and Kaska Indians merge both relatives in one term, "mother." They make do with one kinship status where we have two.

Why are there kin terms at all? Why does every social system distinguish father from mother, brothers from sisters, and parents from grandparents? And what is at work when people do not isolate one relative from another verbally, say, "mother" from "mother's sister"?

To understand how distinctions of kinship status are made let's take an imaginary human community, the Mafa. In this small social system living nobody knows where, people until now have been calling all kinsmen either em, if male, or am, if female. In other words, they recognize only what amounts to the primary criterion used in assigning kinship status, sex. Relatives are either male or female. (Sometimes even this primary factor is overlooked—we call all cousins "cousin" regardless of sex.) An exceptionally thoughtful Mafa elder became troubled by the generality of the em-am distinction. His mother was an am; so were his sister, wife, and niece. When he said "am" half-a-dozen heads looked up. He complained of his am's nasty temper and his friends couldn't always tell from context if he was talking about his wife, mother, or mother-in-law. This elder noticed that individuals differed in generation as well as in sex. He and his wife belonged to different generation from their son and son's wife. The youth and his wife stood one step lower, generationally speaking. His son's children in turn stood on a level two steps down. At the same time our Mafa noticed a correlated phenomenon. By virtue of inescapable inequalities in growth and experience each of these three generations behaved somewhat differently. He assumed rights and responsibilities denied to his son; both he and his son faced duties quite beyond the power of youngsters in the second descending generation. Hence, the elder thought, generational differences, which everybody manifestly recognizes would provide an excellent criterion for further reducing the number of ems and ams. Why not call men and women in my generation by terms different from those used for them in my son's and grandson's generations? By the same principle, why not have separate terms for male and female kinsmen in my parents' and parents' parents' generations?

Like sex, generation is universally recognized through the kin terms by which people make status distinctions in their pool of relatives. Our own terms, "mother," "son," and "grandson"—despite whatever else they do—recognize the basis of generation. However, when we lump cousins and children of cousins under one label, "cousin," we turn our backs on a potential refinement in our kinship nomenclature. We choose to override generational differences just as in our term "cousin" we override sex distinction.

The Mafa can now recognize 10 different relatives:

Male Relatives	Female Relatives
Two generations up	Two generations up
One generation up	One generation up
One's own generation	One's own generation
One generation down	One generation down
Two generations down	Two generations down

But, no known culture is content with such a simple kinship system.

The observant Mafa elder noticed another factor, one considerably more subtle than sex or generation, and incorporated it in his thinking to make yet further status distinctions in his pool of relatives. He observed that he is related to his son by an actual biological tie. Knowing nothing about sperm, ova, and genes, he is nevertheless aware that he begot his son while another man begot his son's wife. Generalizing a bit and somewhat more abstractly speaking, a genealogical tie ("blood tie" we sometimes call it) links him to his son. The same kind of a tie links his son and his son's son; indeed, he himself is con-

AMERICANS MINIMIZE KINSHIP

No integral social system ever completely ignores kinship as an element governing behavior. *Potentially* every living person has hundreds of relatives (aunts, uncles, brothers, sisters, nephews, nieces, and in-laws). Therefore, it is reasonable to assume that people will *actually* know a large number of their kinsmen in a community where kinship is important. Where kinship is a relatively minor element organizing behavior, they will know only a small number of relatives.

Two hundred U.S. college students, most of them unmarried daughters of middle-class business and professional families, knew only about 30 relatives each:

In their own generation they knew an average of 10.9 relatives each;
In the generation of their parents an average of 11.1 relatives each;
In the generation of their grandparents an average of 7.5 relatives each;
In the generation of great-grandparents an average of 1.7 relatives each;
And in the generation of nephews and nieces an average of 1.6 relatives each.

Helen Codere, "A Genealogical Study of Kinship in the United States," *Psychiatry*, 18 (1955), 65-79.

nected to his son's son by a genealogical link. These links are definitely different from the marriage tie joining him to his wife and to his son's wife. Apparently, this Mafa student of human relations reasons, people are related in two ways. Some are affiliated with one another through actual, genealogical connection and others as a result of marriage only, that is, by affinity. His relationships to his wife, wife's brother, and son's wife are in the second category. Why not recognize this distinction between genealogical and affinal connection in assigning status terms to people who comprise his pool of relatives? Once the Mafa add this criterion to their other criteria for making kin distinctions they can identify 20 relatives:

	Male Relatives		Female Relatives	
Second generation up:	Genealogical	Affinal	Genealogical	Affinal
First generation up:	Genealogical	Affinal	Genealogical	Affinal
Own generation:	Genealogical	Affinal	Genealogical	Affinal
First generation down:	Genealogical	Affinal	Genealogical	Affinal
Second generation down:	Genealogical	Affinal	Genealogical	Affinal

Thoughtfully our Mafa originator next speculated on the closeness in genealogical ties that bind him to his own father and to his father's brother. Biology connects him to both these relatives but he is closer to his father than to his father's brother. A straight line as it were links him to his father; the other man with his own descendants is off on a branch. The elder has recognized a distinction between kinsmen of different degrees or between lineality versus collaterality. Were this criterion adopted with the other bases for making kin-term distinctions the Mafa could recognize 30 distinct relatives:

	Male Relatives			Female Relatives		
	Genealogical			Genealogical		
Second generation up:	Lineal	Collateral	Affinal	Lineal	Collateral	Affinal
First generation up:	Lineal	Collateral	Affinal	Lineal	Collateral	Affinal
Own generation:	Lineal	Collateral	Affinal	Lineal	Collateral	Affinal
First generation down:	Lineal	Collateral	Affinal	Lineal	Collateral	Affinal
Second generation down:	Lineal	Collateral	Affinal	Lineal	Collateral	Affinal

In English we recognize the close connection between ouselves and our siblings and the collateral link that connects us to cousins. Often, though, social systems overlook collaterality at this point and refer to cousins as though they were actually brothers and sisters, lineal relatives. What is more appropriate than for children of two Kaska Indian sisters to ignore collaterality and call each other by sibling terms. Don't these children also call both women "mother"? Aren't children who have the same mother siblings? Such is the logic inherent in kin term systems!

I won't carry this fiction further. Let me summarize. I have described how relatives are distinguished from one another to create kinship statuses. Such distinctions recognize that the pool of relatives is marked by sex differences, generational differences, genealogical as well as affinal connection, close as well as more remote bonds. Frequently a distinction on one or more of these grounds is overlooked in the case of a particular kinship tie. Thereby a potential status is ignored. We overlook sex and generational differences in cousins. Hopi and Kaska Indians ignore collaterality when they classify mother and mother's sister in a single category. Ignoring certain criteria of differentiation keeps kinship statuses at a relatively small number.

Kin terms embody more than these four bases of differentiation. They often employ age to distinguish between certain relatives. Pathans of Swat regard the difference between an older and younger brother as very significant. Seniority carries more serious responsibilities and greater privileges. Hence they assign distinct terms to each brother.

Bifurcation may figure in a kin-term system. If so, then a relationship is singled out for attention on the basis of whether it is traced to the speaker (Ego) through a male or female connecting relative. The Hopi Indians categorize father's brother separately from mother's brother. The former is the brother of a male parent, while in the other case the connecting relative, mother, is a female. English speakers, however, disregard sex in intervening relatives. They indiscriminately speak of uncle or aunt regardless of the link connecting them to Ego. A surprising number of social systems make it their business to distinguish between cousins by whether the connecting relative,

KASKA CHILD AND HIS "MOTHERS"

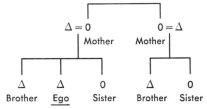

Kaska Indian sisters live together after marriage and cooperate in many tasks. Here they scrape flesh from a good-sized bear hide. Sisters also care for one another's children. In the kin-term system both women occupy a single status and are called "mother."

Put yourself in the place of Ego in the diagram. Do you see why it is quite logical in such a kin-term system to call your cousins by sibling terms?

the parent's sibling, has or has not the same sex as the parent. The Kaska regard children of two brothers or two sisters as siblings not cousins. But when the intervening relative is of the sex opposite to the parent, then they use cousin terms. In their professional discourse anthropologists who have to deal with cousins of these two types speak of two kinds of cousins:

Parallel cousins: the cousins are children of siblings of the same sex; my father's brother's children and mother's sister's children are my parallel cousins.

Cross cousins: the cousins are children of siblings of opposite sex; my father's sister's children and mother's brother's children are my cross cousins.

Decedence, too, may call for a distinct kinship status. In rare cases where it does, it is not the sex of a connecting relative that counts but whether he is dead.

Kinship terms, I repeat, stand for statuses. As such they order behavior, especially in a small-scale social system. Even large-scale social systems assign important roles to people who occupy certain kinship statuses, for example, parents.

Roles played by persons classed together, like mother and mother's sister among Hopi and Kaska Indians or cousins among ourselves, share similar features. For example, sisters called "mother" nurture and help rear each other's children. They also possess similar rights. Children will behave to their "mothers" in similar (but not identical) fashion, treating both with marked respect.

Role behavior, however, can change before kin terms change. Anthropologists predict that when divergence in role behavior goes far enough, kin terms will also alter so that distinct social statuses will become fully apparent.

SOCIAL SOLIDARITY

Social relationships, groups, and social systems of all kinds possess varying degrees of solidarity. When solidarity is strong, people want to remain together at work or play, in trade, or under the same flag and government.

Social solidarity differs in kind. The solidarity of lineally related kinsmen is automatic, mechanical, unplanned. People who feel they owe each other loyalty because the same tribal "blood" flows in their veins (obviously, my language is popular rather than biologically accurate) also reveal what Émile Durkheim, the French sociologist, called mechanical solidarity. Another kind of solidarity, organic, welds social relations increasingly as scale grows. It joins persons who depend on each other's services. Organic solidarity links baker to wheat farmer; it binds the housewife to the baker, butcher, schoolteacher, and other occupational specialists. Any disruption of organic links, for instance through a strike, profoundly upsets the social system and great effort goes to heal the costly breach. Along with the automatic feeling of oneness an element of organic solidarity fuses a family. Husband and wife depend on one another for sexual satisfaction and wife and children live on the husband's income. In many social systems children themselves play valuable economic roles that help organically to maintain the group.

Internationally the modern world contains less solidarity than it might. Regional blocs exist, it is true, and international specialization creates some quite firm organic bonds. On the other hand, we insist on national borders, separate flags, intensive patriotism, passports, and visas, that, even more than our mutually unintelligible languages, reduce over-all international solidarity. Paradoxically, modern technology in the form of fast ships and planes, radio, and intercontinental weapons has obliterated the weakening factor of distance. Much of our current trouble springs from the discrepancy between close interdependence of all living people brought about by modern technology and the isolationism each country persistently maintains. The way the world is organized internationally was suitable years ago when travel was difficult and nations self-sufficiently met most of their own needs. Still, current isolationism has its reasons. The very prosperity rich nations enjoy frightens them from risking closer ties with poorer nations whose teeming millions might swamp and undermine their abundance. The cultural antithesis between capitalism and communism also forestalls effective cooperation between west and east. Each side is eager to promote somewhat stronger international organization, provided it be on its own terms.

If we wait until the world has only one way of thinking, feeling, and doing before risking tighter international cooperation than we will wait forever. The tough problem lies in learning to live with cultural differences.

FURTHER READING

Social organization in one of the most heavily worked areas of English-speaking anthropology. The literature is vast and any selection must necessarily eliminate much that is both pertinent and good.

Status and role are treated in Ralph Linton, *The Study of Man* (New York, 1936), chap. 8. See also the chapter on "Social Relations" in J. S. Slotkin, *Social Anthropology* (New York, 1950), chap. 13, and Siegfried F. Nadel's discussion of "Groupings" in *The Foundations of Social Anthropology* (London, 1951), chap. 7. Prestige, power, status, and role are discussed in John W. Bennett and Melvin M. Tumin, *Social Life* (New York, 1948), pp. 106-110. Chapters 6-8 in J. A. Pitt-Rivers' ethnography on *The People of the Sierra* (London, 1954) are devoted to an examination of male and female statuses in a modern Spanish town. Gladys Reichard's chapter "Social Life," in Franz Boas, ed., *General Anthropology* (New York, 1938) discusses prestige with the aid of many ethnographic examples. Carl J. Friedrich has edited a symposium on *Authority* (Cambridge, Mass., 1958).

Many mechanisms related to the longevity of groups are cited by Stuart C. Dodd in *Systematic Social Science* (Beirut, 1947), p. 107. "How Groups Originate and Become Organized" is treated by Pitirim A. Sorokin in *Society, Culture, and Personality* (New York, 1947), chap. 21. Karl Loewenstein's paper, "The Influence of Symbols of Politics," in R. V. Peel and J. S. Roucek, eds., *Introduction to Politics* (New York, 1946) examines group emblemization. My idea of counterpoised values helping to regulate behavior extends Gregory Bateson's concept of complementary schismogenesis. See his paper, "Some Systematic Approaches to the Study of Culture and Personality," *Character and Personality*, 11 (1942), 76-82, as well as his book *Naven*, 2nd ed., (Stanford, Calif., 1958).

Kin terms and how they arise are discussed systematically and concisely in George P. Murdock, *Social Structure* (New York, 1949), chaps. 6–7. See also

A. L. Kroeber, "Classificatory Systems of Relationship," *Journal of the Royal Anthropological Institute*, 39 (1909), 77-84. Max Gluckman examines "The Origins of Social Organization," *Human Problems in British Central Africa*, 12 (1951), 1-11. More facets of group structure are examined in John J. Honigmann, *The World of Man* (New York, 1959), chap. 23, and kin terms on pp. 406-412. A. R. Radcliffe-Brown's "Introduction" in A. R. Radcliffe-Brown and Daryll Forde, eds., *African Systems of Kinship and Marriage* (London, 1950) overlaps with this and the next chapter of this book. It is a comprehensive, if somewhat technical, statement of an analytical point of view for understanding culture which enjoys considerable popularity in contemporary anthropology. This viewpoint, structuralism, is more provocatively examined and debated in Rodney Needham, *Structure and Sentiment, A Test Case in Social Anthropology* (Chicago, 1962) and F. L. K. Hsu, "Structure, Function, Content, and Process," *American Anthropologist*, 61 (1959), 790-805.

5

The Groups That Kin Form

"Women have to be provided for . . . and it is we who have to do the providing. They cling to us because we give them food and clothing. See! when I was well and strong, and caught seals in abundance, I had a wife who was very fond of me. And then the Evil Fate laid its grip upon me, and my body died. Then I had to be content to eat what others caught, and see! my wife ran away, and let herself be taken by one who could feed her better—ha! that is what they are like,—but if we are to be the providers, then we must be masters too. And if the woman gets fancies into her head, then she must be beaten; that will bring her to her senses again."

Knud Rasmussen[1]

VARIETY IN KIN GROUPS

Of all the groups men form, those organized by kinsmen invariably turn up in every integral social system. Relatives united genealogically or through marriage do no less than maintain life itself and provide a number of other, less basic gratifications. The only "school" where a child learns to live as a human being in many communities is the kin group in which he is reared, his family. Although ties of kinship thin out under highly industrialized conditions, even then most people grow up in a family. And once grown, they marry to enjoy the emotional gratification that their own family will bring. Yet, we shall see that the family has begun to weaken. It remains as a group, but other organizations are trusted to perform some of its former tasks. One anthropologist in effect asks, without noticeable alarm, whether the family is even necessary.[2]

There is danger in becoming infatuated with simply the peculiar forms which kin groups take in one culture or another. If a group of kinsmen is

[1] *The People of the Polar North*, trans. G. Herring (London, 1908), p. 60.
[2] Melford E. Spiro, "Is the Family Universal?" *American Anthropologist*, 56 (1954), 839-846.

worth noting at all, it is because organization confers something on its members. It gives them rights to property, interests in rearing children, land and ancestral shrines, or specific duties to perform. A kin group significant in its members' lives involves them in economic or religious undertakings, makes them dependent on one another for affection and emotional security, or compels them to provide each other with legal help when needed. Kinship groups engage people around tasks and interests. As soon as kinship ceases to regulate these topics in a culture the importance of kin groups gradually lapses and nonkin organizations grow prominent.

It is too neat to speak only of kin and nonkin groups for, like all dichotomies, this one oversimplifies. Kin and nonkin groups overlap. A family may adopt nonkinsmen and bestow on them the status of a brother, daughter, or other close relative. The head of the Kaska Indian camp where I wintered in 1945 adopted my wife as a daughter. The young women, his daughters, always called her "sister" and I became their brother-in-law. Many other anthropologists have been adopted by their hosts simply because small-scale people unaccustomed to strangers feel comfortable only when they deal with kin. For that reason American colonists found marriage with Indian women of leading families useful in dealing with the Indians.[3] Not only do kin groups contain relatives who are kinsmen in name only, but in some kin groups relatives find it impossible to trace their kin ties. In addition we have groups like college fraternities which frankly recognize that their members are unrelated; yet members fictionally refer to themselves as "brothers."

Kin groups are clearly not all the same. Some, like the family, gather all members in one place. In others the members are widely dispersed so that they rarely or never assemble in a single locality.

THE HINDU JOINT FAMILY

When we think of a family we visualize father, mother, and two or three children living independently, solitary in the privacy of their own house or apartment. This tiny, isolated nucleus is remote in type from the family that serves people in many exotic social systems.

By way of contrast let me first describe the classic family in Hindu India.[4] Mainly wealthy, rural people in India who belong to high-ranking castes and are orthodox Hindus live in this type of family. In fact, the family itself is religiously justified; certain of the Hindu scriptures prescribe it. The group consists of a number of related men (brothers, their sons, son's sons) the

[3] William T. Hagan, *American Indians* (Chicago, 1961), p. 12.
[4] David G. Mandelbaum, "The Family in India," *Southwestern Journal of Anthropology*, 4 (1948), 123-139; Pandhari-Nath Prabhu, *Hindu Social Organization*, new rev. ed. (Bombay, 1954), chap. 6.

wives of all these men, and their unmarried daughters. Ideally, the home also includes members who are dead and members yet to come into being. Living members in some places occupy premises enclosed by high compound walls in which nobody has much privacy or feels the same need for it that we do. Marriage creates a bond so firm between a woman and her husband's family that she remains within these walls all her life, even when she is widowed, for ideally a widow should not remarry. Girls born to the intact core of men will someday be lost to the family for they will marry into another household.

Women and children belonging to a Hindu extended family pose for an anthropologist in their household courtyard. (*Stanley A. and Ruth Freed.*)

The Hindu joint family, as this group is known, resembles a corporation that owns property and creates goods in common. The much respected senior man manages family lands and organizes joint agricultural production. He controls the single purse. Ceremonies celebrated in the group periodically reinforce members' loyalties to their "great family." A particularly strong, affectional link binds a mother to her sons, though a woman scarcely stints her daughters of love. The father remains more remote; children find it difficult to establish companionable ties with his authoritarian figure. Older siblings, especially boys, hold authority over younger ones, and another senior member, a husband's mother, has authority over brides. Wives literally worship their husbands. The power of parents, uncles, and elder brothers is used to arrange a younger relative's marriage. Often a boy never sees his bride prior to the ceremony. But slowly the couple develops mutual, warm, affectionate ties.

THE COMMUNAL FAMILY

Compared to the three generations that live together cooperatively in a Hindu joint family, the communally oriented family in Israel is small indeed.[5] Only husband and wife share a combination bed-sitting room; they eat in a communal dining hall and work in whatever shop they are detailed. Children, instead of sharing a home with parents, sleep in a dormitory from which they go to school and, when the day's work is done or they are on holidays, visit with parents. According to kibbutz philosophy, after age 2 the sole responsibility of a parent is to love his child. Verbal and physical affection are generously, even intensely, given, the intensity perhaps compensating for the physical separation of mother and child. But parents also transmit values to children by praising their school work, rewarding obedience, or commiserating unsuccessful competition. Play and reading aloud are other activities that fill the evening's Children's Hour.

This type of family no more prevails all over Israel than the classic Hindu family exists all over India. Marxist-oriented kibbutzim (collective farms) endorse this type of family. A kibbutz is a communistic organization in which members own and produce wealth in common. It attempts to realize a vision of a planned new world that goes back to the first half of the nineteenth century. Bolsheviks successfully incorporated the ideal in the Soviet Union and certain Jewish farmers applied it to Palestine to bring that land of the Jews back into flower. Justification of the communally oriented family is philosophical rather than scriptural. It is designed to avoid the authoritarian, patriarchal climate of European peasant communities which planners of the kibbutzim believed overwhelmed and crushed personal spontaneity in both women and children. Wives' economic dependence on men under capitalism fosters extreme masculine dominance. The kibbutz is designed to free women from depending on the father as sole provider. Women have social and economic equality with men and child care does not tie them down, preventing them from contributing labor and ability to society. Financial, physical, and economic responsibility for children belongs to the community as a whole, not to either parent. The kibbutz family, like the kibbutz itself, belongs to the future.

Unlike the classic family in India, in which members jointly produce goods, the kibbutz family itself creates no wealth. In it are centered intimacy, affection, psychological security, and sexual satisfaction (though an unmarried kibbutz couple is also permitted to secure sexual gratification). Psycho-

[5] Melford E. Spiro, *Kibbutz. Venture in Utopia* (Cambridge, Mass., 1956).

COMMUNAL CHILD CARE AND DINING FACILITIES IN AN ISRAELI KIBBUTZ

(Israel Office of Information)

Care and training of kibbutz children represents a social revolution. At the age of 4 or 5 days an infant joins the kibbutz's child-care system. First he joins a nursery. Then he moves to a toddler's house, where he is gradually toilet trained, taught to feed himself, and learns to interact with other children. Kindergarten comes when he is 4 or 5 years old and a year or so later he starts school.

In the first picture kindergarten children are painting. The group partially shown will remain together through high school. Except for toys, kept in the parents' rooms, kibbutz children know that they possess no private property. Actually, even their desire for personal possessions is weak.

The second photo shows adults of another kibbutz in a communal dining hall. Diners and staff all work for their collective agricultural settlement.

Melford E. Spiro, *Children of the Kibbutz* (Cambridge, Mass., 1958).

logical identification, love, and security are important rewards which a child receives from nobody else in the kibbutz except his parents. So, although the kibbutz family has shed child rearing—a task that families execute in most other parts of the world—it still fulfills affectional and other psychological functions for which, so far, no adequate substitute has been found.

The fate of the communally oriented Israeli family will be worth watching. Will this experiment in a new form of living succeed? The ideal of equality between men and women has proven difficult to achieve. Women work, but 88 percent of their jobs are service jobs, like laundering, cooking and cleaning, which no man wants to do and in which women can't utilize all their talents. Women also begrudge having their children sleep under a separate roof. Also, the kibbutz has not eradicated all desire for private property. Some members have become disillusioned with the very collective ideal that brought the kibbutz and the kibbutz family into being.

THE INDIVIDUALISTIC FAMILY

Now consider the family in which many Americans already grow up and in which all someday may live. I call this the individualistic family of Crestwood Heights, adopting a pseudonym for an upper-middle class Canadian suburb where a team of researchers closely studied domestic life.[6] This small group, consisting of two parents and about two children, is justified, people believe, because it allows every member, especially children, a chance for maximum satisfactions. It is supposed to be well suited to maintain good mental and physical health. It guarantees respect for everyone's individuality. Through it an independent adult develops, a person capable of choosing for himself—choosing a spouse, a career, or a political party.

The individualistic family exists to consume, not to produce. Father works for a salary. The woman presides over her mechanized home and carries on liaison with relatives. Her efforts keep the home an attractive place where the family can display its wealth to validate its middle-class status. The neighborhood school assumes a large share of the work of rearing children. Nothing, however, supplants this intimate, little group as a center wherein each member finds affection and other psychological gratifications. Husband and wife divide authority, neither dominating the other, though in emergency the man is expected to take over leadership. In contrast to India, seniority brings no pronounced respect. In fact, adults at times act as if they wanted to deny an actual gap in age and rank between themselves and their children. Obviously, then, discipline remains inconspicuous. Only if everyone treats everyone else considerately will each member's sacred individuality be protected. How different from India, or Bali where a woman speaking of her husband said, "Even for my pleasures I must follow his wishes. Foreign women do what they themselves please, is there any joy in that?"[7]

THE ESSENTIAL FAMILY

Kibbutz and individualistic Crestwood Heights families omit many tasks which the Indian joint family still handles by itself. In the process of becoming simpler they have also grown more highly specialized for psychological gratification. The lower-class British Guiana Negro family omits the father as the figure of authority and main source of support.[8]

Ancestors of the Negroes came to British Guiana in 1616 as slaves. Emancipated in 1838, the former slaves built villages on small plots of purchased land and raised crops mainly for home consumption. Today their overriding

[6] John R. Seeley, R. Alexander Sim, and E. W. Loosley, *Crestwood Heights, A Study of the Culture of Suburban Life* (New York, 1956), chaps. 3-5, 7.

[7] Santha Rama Rau, *East of Home* (New York, 1950), p. 232.

[8] Raymond T. Smith, *The Negro Family in British Guiana* (London, 1956).

problem is how to acquire sufficient cash income to buy goods and services which their households cannot provide.

The core of what I call the matricentric Negro family, namely, a woman and her unmarried children, is embedded in a larger household including a number of additional children, including those of her unwed daughters. Eventually all these children will marry and move away, whereupon the family will disappear. Without ceremonial to-do, a man founds such a household once he sees his way clear to assume financial responsibility for a spouse and for children whom he has probably already fathered. He has delayed this move, partly because it takes time to accumulate enough money to provide a house and partly because he is far from eager to assume a duty that, among other things, will no longer allow him to provide for his dependent mother. Into conjugal life the couple also brings children they have had by other liaisons; all these children are treated precisely like their own offspring. Illegitimacy in this social system carries no stigma and involves no social disabilities.

Early in the household's life cycle wife and children depend economically mainly on the husband and father. Youngsters tie a woman to her home, which slowly begins to accrete additional members, like a juvenile brother of the husband or children of his dead sister. A wife remains sexually faithful to her husband but he is often unfaithful and may father a series of children with other women. His authority at home is mostly nominal, as are his rights and responsibilities. He interferes very little in the group which he helped to establish. Working away from home on a plantation or in a mine he contentedly leaves control to his wife, whom he continues to support. Children derive practically nothing else of importance from their father, whom they see very little. In this social system it is not even crucial to have a father. As time passes and children grow older, the woman becomes an ever stronger focus for holding the group together. Adult children who start working give her money. In middle age she herself embarks on minor economic enterprises, selling a little farm produce or prepared food. A woman who is widowed or, as frequently happens, separated from her husband, remains economically quite secure, supported by her unmarried sons.

To upper-ranking people with quite different values, such a woman-headed family appears loose, disorganized, and overly tolerant of immorality. The critics fail to understand that it, too, is governed by unmistakable standards which demand conformity.

Attempts to explain matricentric, lower-class Negro families, both in the West Indies where they are common and in the United States, have stirred up controversy. Melville J. Herskovits gives most weight to historical factors.[9]

[9] Melville J. Herskovits, The Myth of the Negro Past (New York, 1941), chap. 6; "The Ahistorical Approach to Afroamerican Studies: A Critique," American Anthropologist, 62 (1960), 559-568.

He sees the group as a New World persistence of traditional African family organization. A rival, but still historical, theory regards the U.S. matricentric family as the product of social disruption grounded in slavery.[10] Under the slave system a man could easily be torn away from his family; hence, if necessary, a woman and her children had to be able to survive alone. Dissatisfied with both these historical explanations, Raymond T. Smith argues that matricentric households are a "natural" solution that arises in any social system—be it made up of lower-class West Indian Negroes or depressed Scottish coal miners—when people occupy a very low ranking, economically hazardous position that they can't do anything to raise.[11]

WHY MEN FORM FAMILIES

From one culture to another the family recurs in some form. What does man find in this ubiquitous social arrangement?

Husband and wife find the family a convenient arrangement whereby each spouse can readily secure sexual gratification with the other. To enumerate, we can call this the first task which the family successfully meets. So powerful is sex that every social system finds it must somehow be regulated. To allow completely free play to erotic impulses would quickly lead to havoc. Confining sex to the family gives approximately every male at least one sex partner and so forestalls strong, aggressive men from each monopolizing many women, thereby denying ready sexual gratification to weaker men. Families, then, prevent sex from unduly complicating the business of survival and personal adjustment. Nevertheless, other social arrangements also exist to provide erotic gratification. Like the Israeli kibbutz, a number of social systems allow as yet unmarried young people to have sex relations. Prostitution, found mainly in large-scale social systems along with other kinds of trade and specialization, is another means whereby married or unmarried men can experience sexual pleasure. In other words, sexual gratification can also be found through other, far less permanent, social relationships than the family, so this factor cannot by itself explain how families regularly come into being.

Economic cooperation in the family in many communities guarantees both individual survival and personal adjustment. Usually it unites a woman, who bears and nourishes helpless children, with a man, who most conveniently is never encumbered by pregnancy and nursing and is therefore ideally suited to uninterruptedly supplying mother and child with food, protection, and shelter. By maintaining their well-being he also insures ultimate survival of the social system. Economic cooperation is the second task of the family, one in which even children may play major roles as in British Guiana. By per-

---

[10] Edward Franklin Frazier, *The Negro Family in the United States* (Chicago, 1939).

[11] Smith, *op. cit.*, chap. 9.

forming small tasks requiring little skill, like fetching water or setting snares for rabbits, young Kaska Indian children augment the family's well-being. In the Hindu joint family a larger group works together to provide food and cash crops. Part of the wealth which the group produces it consumes; the rest it trades for other goods. In contrast, the small kibbutz, Crestwood Heights, and Guiana Negro families are economically quite unproductive. The family can dispense with cooperative economic production and still survive as a group.

Children are reared and culture transferred from one generation to the next in the family. We can group these activities together as the family's third task. Helpless at birth, a human baby is also unendowed with instincts which, given appropriate circumstances, might enable the unaided and untaught individual to create his own survival. Education, or cultural transmission, provides human beings with skills to pursue survival and adjustment. The family thus maintains not only continuity of the social system but continuity of culture as well. But here again the family can be replaced by other groups. In an Israeli kibbutz a nursery rears children practically from birth until school takes over. Yet the kibbutz family survives, though it dispenses with economic production, child rearing, education, and exclusive sexual gratification. What other need does the family meet that holds the group together?

For the answer let's look into the fourth major task of families. The family is a social center which liberally dispenses emotional security, reassurance, and affection. It is a bank from which each member regularly, as well as at time of crisis, draws emotional fortification. The family stabilizes its members' personalities through companionship, affection, and relatively unconditional acceptance. The West Indian Negro family concentrates these tasks in a matricentric household that largely dispenses with a husband and father; the Indian joint family entrusts them to a group of brothers, their sons, their wives, and children. In Crestwood Heights and the Israeli kibbutz the group is smaller, the time it spends together face-to-face briefer, but the task is still met. Although individuals can find jobs, amusement, sexual gratification, and satisfy many other needs in other groups, in all social systems people find some emotional satisfactions in the family not served elsewhere. In fact, in an industrialized community as the family sheds other tasks, it, like other groups, becomes highly specialized and concentrates on the task of providing emotional gratification.

In performing any or all of these tasks family life generates social solidarity, a desire of the group to remain together, that counterbalances disruptive forces. There is reason to believe that as families shed tasks they become less stable, less able to withstand disruptive stress. This partially explains our high divorce rate. Yet the family continues to be popular with each new generation.

FAMILIES STILL HOLD ATTRACTION

"In view of the major changes and loss of functions, does the family still serve purposes of sufficient importance to assure its survival? The available data, fragmentary as they are, leave no doubt as to the affirmative answer. Marriage is more popular in the United States than ever: People now marry at a considerably younger age than, for example, in 1890; a much larger proportion of men and women are married today than two generations ago, and, though divorce rates are high, the remarriage rate is also high."

Halbert L. Dunn and Mort Gilbert, "Public Health Begins in the Family," *Public Health Reports*, 71 (1956), 1003.

ONE SPOUSE OR MORE?

In the world as a whole, most families are monogamous. Here in the U.S., despite our vaunted respect for religious freedom, the Supreme Court decided in the case of the Mormons that to advocate plural wives as a tenet of faith "offended the common sense of mankind." Monogamy here is legally enjoined. Among aboriginal Kaska Indians and many other people monogamy prevails simply because, for one reason or another, men don't choose to marry a second or third time. Monogamy also prevails in Swat, but Muslim religion allows up to four wives and some wealthy men avail themselves of this permission. Despite the prevalence of monogamy, out of a world-wide selection of 554 social systems, in 419 a man is permitted to live with more than one wife or a woman with more than a single husband.[12]

I will quickly pass over cases in which men, usually brothers, become the plural spouses of one woman, a custom called polyandry. This is really an uncommon way of forming a family. In the 554 sampled communities only 4 practice polyandry. But its very occurrence indicates that the combination is by no means unnatural.

Polygyny, the common form of polygamy, turns up in 415 of the 554 cases we are using. However, as I have already pointed out, circumstances render it quite impractical for every man in a community that allows polygyny to win more than one wife. More active, wealthier, or elder men (as they mature they inherit widows of deceased brothers) become polygynists. When the wives are sisters, their accustomed relationship to each other removes several dangers that polygynists must otherwise cope with, such as wives' jealous unwillingness to cooperate and their perpetual bickering that threatens

[12] George P. Murdock, "World Ethnographic Sample," *American Anthropologist*, 59 (1957), 664-687.

ly unity. Separate houses for each woman and her children is a device
.at sometimes helps to maintain tranquility. But to keep harmony between
two or more unrelated wives requires a polygynist to exercise constant, administrative finesse. Plural wives increase the family labor force. By cooperat-
ing together they contribute substantially to the whole group's well-being and
raise the prestige of its polygynous head whose reflected glory they too enjoy.

A man who keeps a concubine or mistress in town while he supports a
wife in the suburbs is still monogamous. The mistress is outside the cooperative family group in which children are reared and receive emotional gratification. Wife lending is something else again. Eskimo in Canada's central
Arctic who exchange wives or bestow a wife's sexual favors on a friend intensify bonds of solidarity. Let an Eskimo woman tell how easily she accepts
the custom: ". . . it is quite a common thing among us to change wives. A
man does not love his wife any the less because she lies with someone else
now and again. And it is the same with the woman. They like to know about
it, that is all; there must be no secrets in such matters."[13]

WHO SHALL REMAIN?—RULES OF RESIDENCE

By grafting on new members the classic Hindu family continues in existence from one generation to the next. But the small family in Crestwood
Heights and the mother-centered family among Guiana Negroes disappear
once the children have married and gone off and parents die. Families that
persist from one generation to another are suitably called extended families.
They form when children stay at home after marriage. The son or daughter
brings in a spouse with whom he has children thus establishing a new nuclear
family that overlaps the nuclear family headed by his parents. This, in turn,
overlaps the nuclear family containing his grandparents, provided they still
live. Sometimes, however, married siblings stay home only until their parents
die. Then they divide the inheritance between themselves and each moves
into an independent household. This custom doesn't set up continuing extended families. In Murdock's study of social systems, 245 maintained independent families containing one or more spouses and 303 had some type of
continuing extended family.[14]

Practically all social systems enforce a rule of incest that absolutely prohibits sexual relations or marriage between parents and children and between
brothers and sisters. Therefore, once maturity prepares children for marriage
they, or whoever arranges the marriage, must seek a spouse beyond the

[13] Knud Rasmussen, *Intellectual Culture of the Iglulik Eskimos*, trans. W. E. Calvert,
Report of the Fifth Thule Expedition 1921-1924, vol. 7, no. 1, 1929, p. 25.
[14] Murdock, *op. cit.*

POLYGYNY REQUIRES ITS OWN TYPE OF HOUSING

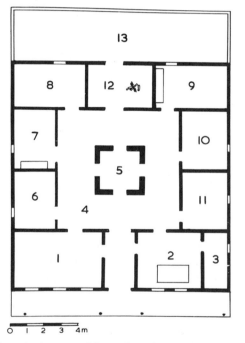

These drawings show the house and floor plan of a Yoruba (Nigeria) polygynist who is married to four wives. On the floor plan room 1 serves as a parlor; 2, the husband's bedroom, contains a large comfortable bed; in 3, the wardroom, the husband keeps his clothing; 4, is a central hall where the family does most of its living and work; 5, the impluvium, catches rainfall; rooms 6 to 9 are the wives' private bedrooms; 10 and 11 are storerooms; 12, a kitchen, and 13 the yard.

C. G. Feilberg, "Remarks on Some Nigerian House Types," *Folk*, 1(1959), 15-26.

THE EXTENT OF POLYGYNY

A census of some Likouala villages, Congo Republic, reveals first, the proportion of men married to more than one wife and, second, the tendency of more extreme degrees of polygyny to increase with a man's maturity.

The Marital Status of 257 Men in an African Tribe

Average Age	Number of Men			Number of Wives								
	Unmarried	Widowed or Divorced	Married	1	2	3	4	5	6	7	8	9
75		1										
70			1		1							
65			5		1	1	1	1				1
60		1	6			3	1	2				
55		1	5	1	2		1					1
50	3	3	13	4	4	3		2				
45	2	1	18	9	4	2	3					
40	2	3	39	23	13	2	1					
35	4	2	21	17	3	1						
30	11	1	16	13	3							
25	6	1	9	6	3							
20	37		7	7								
15	38											
Totals	103	14	140	80	34	12	7	5				2

Jean Crocquevieille, "Étude démographique de quelques villages Likouala (Moyen-Congo)," *Population*, 8 (1953), 491-510.

nuclear family.[15] So much is generally true everywhere. What follows once a spouse is found varies according to culture. Among Guiana Negroes and in Crestwood Heights marriage ideally begins a new independent nuclear family which locates itself apart from both parental households. Neolocal residence occurs giving rise to independent families. The Kaska and Hopi Indians expect only sons to move upon marriage. Daughters stay home, a girl's husband joining her in her parents' home. This custom is called matrilocal (or uxorilocal) residence. In the ideal Hindu family of India as well as in Swat where sons remain with their parents and brides move in, patrilocal (or virilocal) residence is practiced. In ambilocal residence (also called bilocal) either a son or a daughter moves, depending on particulars in each case. Ideally, in half the marriages brides join a husband's family and in half grooms join a wife's family. Avunculocal residence, in which a boy brings his

[15] George P. Murdock, *Social Structure* (New York, 1949), pp. 12-13.

FAMILIES THAT PERSIST

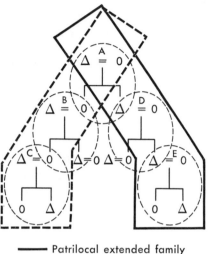

——— Patrilocal extended family
with four generations

– – – Matrilocal extended family
with four generations

The overlapping circles indicate how in an extended family several nuclear families (A, B, C, D, E) overlap. The diagram by showing only one daughter or son remaining at home each generation simplifies what may occur. Large extended families have two or more siblings or cousins in adjacent generations.

spouse to the home of his mother's brother where he himself has been living for some years is the rarest of all these forms.

THE RELATIVE IMPORTANCE OF MEN VERSUS WOMEN

Residence certainly is fundamental to extended families but it doesn't automatically produce them. Residence may endure only for a year or two, as most often happens in Swat, after which the young couple set up an independent household. Extended families arise only if married children remain continuously in their parental home.

Whether son or daughter stays home is far from a matter of chance.[16] Other

[16] *Ibid.*, pp. 201-208.

cultural facts make a difference in whatever rule of residence a community follows. In general, who stays home and who moves are questions decided by the relative social and economic importance of men versus women. Such importance, in turn, hinges on the tasks allocated to men and women as well as on the wealth and other prerogatives which each sex controls.

Where activities magnify the importance of men, sons stay home so that patrilocal extended families are likely to appear. Large herds of cattle, agriculture by plow rather than hoe, and frequent warfare encourage patrilocal residence. So does a complex political system in which men hold authority and wield power. A religion, like Islam, emphasizes masculine authority. Turning to the opposite sex, if women contribute substantially to subsistence, as they do when they cultivate the crops, men merely clearing the ground before the planting season, then women achieve enhanced importance which favors matrilocal residence. Of course, countervailing factors, like warfare, may always swing the balance. Female control of property and relatively simple government also encourage the custom of girls staying home after marriage. The latter two conditions hold true among Hopi Indians, where, however, men take charge of cultivation. Except simple government, none of these rules helps explain matrilocal residence among Kaska Indians. We would expect the Kaska to be like most other hunting people, either bilocal or patrilocal. Yet they are matrilocal, a fact not easily explained functionally. A plausible historical explanation exists. Ancestors of the Kaska and related people in northwestern North America may have crossed Bering Strait with a constellation of traits including matrilocal residence.[17] No pressures in the New World forced them to give up that trait and so it has been retained. I offer this not in lieu of a functional explanation but merely as an interim answer.

So far I have described factors elevating the social and economic importance of men or women and thereby favoring either sons or daughters to remain home after marriage. With ambilocal residence, now men bring spouses home and now women do so. Obviously, if my basic assumption is true, variable factors favorable to both sexes must underlie ambilocal arrangements. To take one example, when women are free to inherit property or titles equally with men and the privilege sometimes goes to sons and sometimes to daughters, ambilocal residence is favored.

Matripatrilocal marital residence remains to be explained, the custom by which a man first joins his wife's parents and then, perhaps a couple of years later, brings his wife to his parents' home to live. Before saying more about this it will be helpful to say something about marriage. Many means are employed to establish a valid marriage. Usually, however, some kind of

[17] George P. Murdock, "North American Social Organization," *Davidson Journal of Anthropology*, 1 (1955), 86.

get-together occurs, attended by relatives and other community members. This assembly publicizes the fact of marriage. Frequently, too, a prestation solemnizes marriage. In Swat three prestations, or payments, are necessary for a valid marriage. In accordance with Islamic custom, the husband's family settles an endowment of jewelry, called *mahr,* on the bride which she may later contribute to finance a family undertaking. In addition, the bride's family furnishes an elaborate dowry of beds, bedding, kitchen equipment, and clothing—possessions to equip the couple's new home. Finally, there is bridewealth, a custom usually found whenever patrilocal residence severs a bride from her family. Bridewealth means that the husband's kin purveys cattle, hoes, salt, money, or other wealth to the bride's kinsmen. In Swat, where a monetary prestation is the rule, amounts range from $60 to $1500, depending on economic status. Bridewealth varies in meaning from one social system to another. Generally it denotes appreciation of the girl, of the rearing she received, and of her reproductive powers. Now to return to matripatrilocal residence. In place of a prestation, bride service may validate marriage. A new husband for some years serves his father-in-law's family, where he also lives. After his term expires he takes his bride, abandons matrilocal residence, and rejoins his paternal home.

Avunculocal residence is conveniently understood in primarily historical terms as having replaced earlier matrilocal residence. Why was matrilocal residence abandoned? Culture changed in a way that weakened feminine and strengthened masculine importance. Since patrilocal and avunculocal residence both act in a similar way, assembling genealogically related males in a group, it is easy to see how the latter can serve in lieu of the former.

It may happen that a spouse after shifting from his natal group becomes so thoroughly assimilated to the group he joins (whether a family or one of the linearly organized descent groups which we are about to describe) that he sheds all rights and duties with respect to his own kinsmen. In Swat, for example, marriage transfers full authority over a woman from her father to her husband, with the result that she retains no further rights in her father's or brother's home, not even if she becomes widowed. Not so among Hopi Indians. Here the man who leaves his natal group to join the household containing, perhaps, his wife, her mother, and her sisters retains many rights and responsibilities in his own kin group. He continues actively to exercise authority over his sisters' household, just as his wife's brother does over his. No wonder that his authority as a husband should be so attenuated! He just barely belongs to his wife's extended family. Should she die, he returns home, leaving his children with their maternal kinsmen.

WHO FOLLOWS WHOM?—DESCENT GROUPS

At one extreme we have social systems which support life through hunting, collecting, and fishing. Habitations are temporary; settlements unstable; the number of people in interaction paltry. Scale is minimal. At the other extreme stand large, world-dominating cities, tremendous in scale, richly endowed with productive capital and labor. Between these extremes are the middle-range, village-dwelling farmers and migratory herders. Kin groups of the kind we shall next examine flourish in this middle range. Once middle-range social systems become thoroughly implicated in an urban-dominated society, whether capitalist or 'collectivist, these kin groups break down. They cease to function as bulwarks for the individual, promoting social services and regulating inheritance of wealth and office. Status then comes to depend heavily on achievement and practically ceases to be ascribed through birth and descent.

In a kin group of the kind I have in mind relationship ties connect only persons who succeed in tracing their descent in it from the same real or hypothetical ancestor. Hence these groups are collectively called descent groups. Anthropologists have used a variety of names for such units: clan, gens, sib, lineage, and sept.

Let's use sib to cover a large, dispersed body of kinsmen who trace their descent unilinearly, that is, through only one parental line—mother or father —and who cannot specify an actual apical ancestor from whom the group descends.[18] A patrisib traces descent from a hypothetical founder only through men; from a child of either sex to its father, father's father, and so on. Membership in a matrisib descends through women, from mother's mother, to mother, to her son and daughter. Mishongnovi, a Hopi Indian village, around the turn of the century contained 14 matrisibs each totemically named after an object, animal, or supernatural person. The totem, the sib's spiritual partner, gives the group its special quality.[19] A fetish, preserved and ritually fed by the sib's leading family, symbolizes the group's partner. Each sib member feels intimately related to his sib's totem. "One night in a dream," Talayesva, a Hopi Indian belonging to Sun sib in Oraibi village, relates, "I saw a strange being coming to me in the form of a middle-aged man and as white as snow. He kept his face hidden but said with a friendly voice that he was the Sun god himself and that he saw and heard everything I did."[20]

Although all the members of a sib cannot really trace their actual genealogical relationship to one another, they nevertheless affirm common descent

[18] Murdock, *Social Structure, op. cit.,* chap. 3.

[19] Fred Eggan, *Social Organization of the Western Pueblos* (Chicago, 1950), chap. 2. He follows traditional usage and calls these groups "clans."

[20] Leo W. Simmons, ed., *Sun Chief, the Autobiography of a Hopi Indian* (New Haven, Conn., 1942), p. 87.

and so, quite logically, act as if their mutual kinship could be traced. A Hopi Indian who belongs to a sib bearing the same name as sibs located in other Hopi and even other Pueblo villages also counts members of those groups as kinsmen. Each sib in a village forms a little corporation that controls land, owns certain ceremonies, and in other ways regulates its members' lives. Hopi sibs are exogamous, which means that a person dare not marry anyone in his own sib. To do so would be equivalent to incest. Therefore, husband and

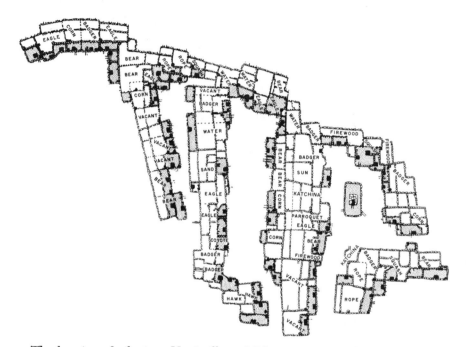

The location of sibs in a Hopi village, Mishongnovi, around 1883. (*Adapted from Cosmos Mindeleff, Localization of Tusayan Clans, Annual Report of the Bureau of American Ethnology, no. 19, 1900.*)

wife come from different unilinear descent groups. A child belongs to his mother's sib though he learns that all members of his father's descent group are also his relatives. In this way a middle-range social system surrounds individuals with a web of kinship.

Sibs sometimes contain segments of more modest genealogical depth called lineages. Each segment contains only members who can explicitly trace their descent in it unilinearly from a known ancestor. A maximal lineage has the same dimensions as a sib, except that its ancestor at least could have been real. A minimal lineage is the core of an extended family; it contains all members except in-marrying spouses. Hopi Indians have matrilineages. The landowning Pathans of Swat trace their membership in patrilineages through their fathers, father's father, and back through males to founding ancestors

UNILINEAR DESCENT GROUPS ARE SELECTIVE

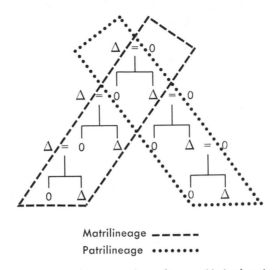

Matrilineage ━ ━ ━ ━
Patrilineage •••••••

This diagram contrasts a patrilineage and matrilineage. Notice how in-marrying spouses are only peripheral to the descent group.

who, around A.D. 1500, invaded the country and divided its land among them.[21] Actually all Pathans in Swat are related inasmuch as they all claim descent from a more remote common ancestor, Yusuf. But only landowning families keep genealogies by means of which they can, more or less accurately, show ancestry going back to one of Yusuf's descendants. Upon arriving in Swat these descendants are assumed to have founded lineages which in time segmented into smaller and smaller units each explicitly connected with the others. Lineage membership confers rights to land. In Swat, however, no lineage ever acts as a unit. Rivalry between brothers and sons of brothers (cousins) keeps relationships too strained for that. Contrary to the preference of Muslims in the Middle East, Pathans in Swat see little merit in marrying parallel cousins, that is, children of two brothers, though occasionally lineage endogamy of this kind does occur.

Both matrilineal and patrilineal unilinear descent groups flourish under fairly definite social and cultural conditions. Generally speaking, they fail to appear in social systems based on food gathering in which only a sparse population lives together. Middle-range social systems provide the requisite number

[21] Fredrik Barth, *Political Leadership Among Swat Pathans*, London School of Economics, Monographs on Social Anthropology, no. 19, 1959.

A CLOSE LOOK AT SOME SEGMENTS OF A LINEAGE

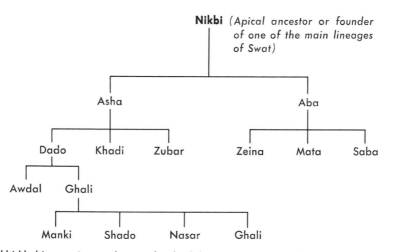

Nikbi khel is a region on the west bank of the Swat River. It takes its name from Nikbi, descendant of Yusuf, the more remote ancestor of one far-flung branch of Pathans. Nikbi khel contains about 2000 men. It has given its name to a region which, including landless persons without lineage affiliation, contains 40,000 people. Ghali khel, a segment of Nikbi khel, contains about 200 men. They inhabit 5 or 6 villages with a total of 1000 men. Each of the minor khels (Manki, Shado, Nasar, and Ghali) contains 20 to 50 men. Remember, a diagram ten times as large would be required to show in as much detail as this the segmentation of all the main lineages of Swat.

Members of Nikbi khel own land by virtue of belonging to their patrilineal descent group. In fact, should they lose their land they would cease to have any valid standing in the lineage. This diagram mentions no women for two reasons. First, the privacy surrounding women makes it difficult to learn their names. Second, when women marry into another lineage they tend, in the thinking of Pathans, to be lost to the lineage of their birth. Thus Pathans see a lineage as primarily aggregating agnates.

Fredrik Barth, *Political Leadership Among Swat Pathans*, London School of Economics, Monographs on Social Anthropology, no. 19, 1959, pp. 26-28.

of people for such organizations without the extreme degree of individualization brought about by industrialism.

It is easy to overestimate the importance of unilinear descent groups and contemporary social anthropology has been accused of doing so. An observer who concentrates too heavily on a community's unilinear ideal will miss noticing the many meaningful roles played by kinsmen not unilinearly affiliated to an individual. Overemphasis is easy because even anthropologists are impressed by the strong sentiments and marked religious activity that often envelope unilinear kin groups. They become like monuments and public buildings lit up by flood lights that leave other important parts of the city in darkness. It is wise to start with tasks that people do and interests that concern them and then to examine organizations that control those interests.

Whether descent in kin groups is patrilineal or matrilineal depends on the relative importance a community attaches to men or women, on the rule of marital residence it observes, and on the kind of extended family that the rule of residence creates. These three factors work together. When for any reason male social importance is enhanced, then patrilocal extended families are likely to aggregate unilinearly related males in a particular locality. The men's sisters upon marriage move away to join their husbands' families. A social situation is created that favors affiliating a child predominantly with the father's kin, who are so visibly aggregated on the scene. Thus a patrilineal descent group originates. In the same manner a matrilocal extended family aggregates unilinearly related women in a locality, providing the stimulus to create matrilineages and matrisibs. Bilocal and neolocal residence, which fail to aggregate exclusively kinsmen from either the paternal or maternal side of the family, don't encourage the creation of unilinear descent groups. Some social systems trace descent doubly; for example, both patrisibs and matrisibs are present and an individual belongs to both.

DESCENT MORE VARIABLE

Unilinear kin groups bestow membership automatically, depending on whatever descent rule—for example, patrilineal or matrilineal—the culture espouses. Usually no choice exists regarding the kin group which a person will join. Double descent adds nothing new; instead of one, he acquires two memberships, one in his father's kin group and the other in his mother's.

In another kind of descent group, status comes more variably. I am speaking now of a nonunilinear descent group, a subtype of descent group of which anthropologists have recently become increasingly aware.[22] It contains some members who are in because their mother belonged and others who join following a brother, mother's father, or some other relative. Hence, descent in these groups follows multilinearly; it runs through both sexes rather than unilinearly along one line. Like unilinear descent groups, nonunilinear descent organizations also have ancestors. The latter may be fictive or, in the case of a lineage segment, a clearly known, real forbear.

A Samoan village contains from 10 to 30 named, exogamous nonunilinear

[22] William Davenport, "Nonunilinear Descent and Descent Groups," *American Anthropologist*, 61 (1959), 557-572; George P. Murdock, "Cognatic Forms of Social Organization," in George P. Murdock, ed., *Social Structure in Southeast Asia*, Viking Fund Publications in Anthropology, no. 29, 1960; and Ward H. Goodenough's extensive review of the latter paper, published in the *American Anthropologist*, 63 (1961), 1341-1347.

kin units, membership in which extends beyond the village boundaries. A given individual belongs to as many as 7 or 8 such groups. Should he, however, fail to participate in group events, for example, neglecting to send food to a kinsman's wedding or funeral, then his membership lapses. This is much the way failure to pay dues quickly dislodges us from a club or professional association.

HOLDING COMPANIES—PHRATRY AND MOIETY

Unilinear and nonunilinear descent groups are sometimes grouped in larger divisions. Hopi sibs, for instance, are grouped into 12 larger, unilinear kin groups, some of which combine into still larger aggregates. Each such "holding company" constitutes a phratry. To some extent a Hopi phratry, in a logical way, groups together species and objects to which component sib names refer. The Snake-Lizard-Sand phratry is founded on the logical relationship that exists between sand (earth) which feeds people, benevolent snakes who serve as messengers for the life-giving rain and guard the springs, and rain-bringing lizards. Hopi mythology substantiates such ideas.

When two holding companies suffice to contain all descent groups in a social system, or when the social system makes do with only two linearly organized descent groups, then each division constitutes a moiety.

EGO-ORIENTED KIN GROUP

One more kin group must be described, this one very different from the linearly organized, ancestor-based kin groups of which I have been speaking in the preceding pages. It is the ego-oriented, or personal, kin group and is laterally rather than linearly organized. No ancestor, real or imaginary, holds its members together. You are familiar with such a kin group. It contains those relatives, on both your mother's or father's sides of the family, whom you invite to weddings, funerals, or family reunions, and to whom you send Christmas cards. It is organized on the principle of close collateral relationship, that is, beyond a certain degree of relationship a person is not included. However, unlike our kindred, all ego-based kin groups don't select members bilaterally, that is, from both father's and mother's sides. Such a group may, for example, be restricted only to certain members belonging to one's own unilinear descent group.

We know that each person's personal kindred is variable. To understand why this is so, note how membership in such a group is established. My kindred includes relatives of my father and mother approximately as far removed as second cousins and grandparents. My mother's kindred, however,

---

KINSMEN ORGANIZE THEMSELVES LINEARLY AND LATERALLY

Ancestor-based kin groups are linearly organized. Members trace descent from a real or imaginary ancestor who remains a fixed point of reference which all hold in common. In time, as new segments bud from the descent group, they trace descent to an ancestor genealogically later than the apical one, whom they often continue to recognize.

Ego-oriented, or personal, kin groups are laterally organized. Members lack any ancestral point of reference, though they do have a common relative. Principles by which membership is assigned vary; for example, the group may, like our personal kindred, only be open to close kinsmen or it may be restricted to kinsmen who live in the same village.

---

ranges to her grandparents and outwards to cousins too distant for me to know.

Unlike a descent group, the personal kindred doesn't count for much. Appropriately, kindreds predominate in large-scale, industrial social systems. Here, as we well know, mobility quickly weakens contact with relatives. Individualistic self-sufficiency joined with neolocal residence makes each independent nuclear family independent of any larger set of kinsmen. Bilocal residence leading to extended families also favors emergence of personal kindreds. Unlike descent groups which continue for generation after generation, a personal kindred lasts only briefly. It disappears once the individual who holds it together dies. But one arrangement allows a kindred to acquire almost the same continuity as a descent group. This requires a single individual in each generation who inherits rights and property and then exercises his heritage for his own personal kindred. Or else he redistributes property to these kinsmen. When he dies he bequeaths his rights and wealth to only one of his descendants who again utilizes them within his personal kindred. Such a continuous kin group is called a stem kindred.

OTHER POSSIBILITIES

There are people in the world who consider the whole tribe, band, village, or other local group to constitute a kin group. In India and Pakistan local castes think of themselves as comprising kinsmen. Such local kin groups may be linearly organized—tracing descent from a common ancestor—or laterally. They may expect either endogamous or exogamous marriage.

LOCUS OF POWER

Matriarchy, rule by women, is a figment. The fact is that whether descent goes through men or women, it is mostly men who possess formal authority in domestic as well as in public affairs. Partly, no doubt, masculine dominance hinges on the physical power which men can exert to subdue women. But men nowhere regularly defend their authority through physical combat with wives and sisters! Their authority is maintained through other ways. For it is they who execute the most important responsibilities in defense and government and who have dealings with deities. Such tasks, possibly in an unfair way, confer more glory and repute on those who execute them than bearing children and maintaining a home confer on women.

Even matrilocal extended families assign leadership to men. The brother who moves out to join his wife's household continues to exercise authority over his sister's children. Conversely, fathers in a matrilocal household exercise limited authority over their own youngsters. A matrisib charges brothers of the women through whom descent is traced to make decisions for the whole corporate descent group. The role of women, who sometimes perform ceremonial tasks in the sib and even induct a masculine officeholder into power, must be understood correctly. Their impressive ritual acting should not be confused with real power. The true state of affairs resembles a constitutional government that is sworn into office by a venerable, black-gowned justice. Who would identify real power with him?

Social systems like the Israeli kibbutz and Crestwood Heights with their independent families that attempt to equalize power between husband and wife nevertheless still allocate more prestigeful public roles to men. And in Crestwood Heights, remember, "togetherness" in decision-making ceases once a crisis arises. Then responsibility in large measure falls on the husband. Even the matricentric British Guiana Negro family ideally ascribes family authority to the husband as long as he supports it. On the other hand, nowhere are women stripped bare of all authority and power. Only naïve travelers return from exotic places and improbably report women to be completely browbeaten and insignificant. Often the female voice prevails when the door to the street is shut.

What about seniority? Do old men rule more than their sons and nephews? Gerontocracy and seniority should not be confused. Patriarchs are biblical figures. In actual kin groups men don't possess power simply by virtue of extreme age. Rather they usually lose or surrender power once advanced age forces them to retire from the active side of life. People stress not age but seniority. Older males often enjoy marked respect and their prestige strengthens their opinions, which juniors carefully refrain from contradicting. Seniority comes in grades. Father's elder brother is more senior than father and an elder brother outranks his juniors. All these men are paid deference and all enjoy some power in circumstances for which they are qualified. The custom that allows alternate generations (grandparents and grandchildren) to joke informally with one another restricts the likelihood of the senior generation exercising power exceeding that of the intervening parents. Socially expected familiarity easily draws together grandparent and grand-child. In contrast the relationships of the middle generation to its parents and to its children are much more difficult because they are ambivalently compounded of love, discipline, and fear.

FURTHER READING

Introductory works on marriage, the family, and other kin groups are abundant and this can be only a selected list. I recommend John Layard, "The Family and Kinship," in *The Institutions of Primitive Society* (Oxford, 1954); Raymond Firth, *Human Types,* rev. ed. (New York, 1958), chap. 4; Robert H. Lowie, *Social Organization* (New York, 1948), chaps. 5, 10, 11; Ralph Linton, *The Study of Man* (New York, 1936), chaps. 10-12; Gladys A. Reichard, "Social Life," in Franz Boas, ed., *General Anthropology* (New York, 1938); and E. C. Parsons, *The Family* (New York, 1906). Parsons' book is quite thorough although much more understanding has come from work done during the last half century. Weston La Barre, in *The Human Animal* (Chicago, 1954), chaps. 6-7, approaches the family from a unique perspective which employs psychoanalytic theory in a broad evolutionary framework. The theoretical significance of woman-headed house-holds is examined by Richard N. Adams, "An Inquiry into the Nature of the Family," in Gertrude E. Dole and Robert L. Carneiro, eds., *Essays in the Science of Culture in Honor of Leslie A. White* (New York, 1960). Jacquetta Hawkes speculates on how the earliest human families emerged in "Society in Palaeolithic Cultures," *Cahiers d'histoire mondiale,* 4 (1957), 481-496. An interesting paper on Soviet life by Kent Geiger examines "The Family and Social Change," in Cyril E. Black, ed., *The Transformation of Russian Society* (Cambridge, Mass., 1960).

Incest has interested many writers. Cases of communities permitting occasional marriage between siblings are reviewed in Edward A. Westermarck, *The History of Human Marriage,* 3 vols., 5th ed. (London, 1921), vol. II, chaps. 19-20. A general survey of "Incest Prohibitions in Primitive Culture" by John M. Cooper appears in *Primitive Man,* 5 (1932), 1-20. Two penetrating studies of the functions of the incest rule in the nuclear family are L. A. White, "The Definition and Prohibition of Incest," *American Anthropologist,* 50 (1948), 416-435, and Talcott Parsons, "The Incest Taboo in Relation to Social Structure and the Socialization of the Child," *British Journal of Sociology,* 5 (1954), 101-117. Samuel Kirson Wein-berg's *Incest Behavior* (New York, 1955) is encyclopedic in its range.

The advantages of polygyny in the life of a West African community are dis-cussed in David W. Ames, "The Economic Base of Wolof Polygyny," *South-western Journal of Anthropology,* 11 (1955), 391-403. Samuel W. Taylor describes a Mormon family in *I Have Six Wives* (New York, 1956). Some indication of the functions of cousin marriage is given by Camilla H. Wedgwood in "Cousin Marriage," *The Encyclopaedia Britannica*, 14th ed. (Chicago, 1929). An elaborate structural theory of cross-cousin marriage, which is certainly not recommended for the beginner, is Claude Lévi-Strauss, *Les structures élémentaires de la parenté* (Paris, 1949). For a synopsis see J. P. B. de Josselin de Jong, *Lévi-Strauss's Theory on Kinship and Marriage*, Mededelingen van het Rijksmuseum voor Volkenkunde, Leiden, no. 10, 1952.

The significance of unilinear kin groups is well described by Meyer Fortes in "The Structure of Unilineal Descent Groups," *American Anthropologist*, 55 (1953), 17-41. The sib and phratry of ancient Rome and the way kinship there fused with religion are described in Numa Denis Fustel de Coulanges, *The Ancient City*, 3rd ed., trans. Willard Small (Boston, 1877), especially Books 1 and 2. A. R. Radcliffe-Brown's "Introduction" in A. R. Radcliffe-Brown and D. Forde, eds., *African Systems of Kinship and Marriage* (London, 1950) has more theoretical than ethnographic significance. Another regional study, *West Indian Family Structure*, by M. G. Smith (Seattle, 1962) also discusses matricentric families in the Caribbean.

6

Other Possibilities of Organization

> People living together at a given time and in a given space are only to a certain
> degree capable, of their own free will, of living together rightly.
>
> Martin Buber[1]

ORGANIZATIONAL COMPLEXITY

People organize on bases other than kinship alone. Some groups are literally grounded in a territory, wide or restricted, which they occupy or control. Tribes and nations that possess guarded boundaries, kings, and other officials illustrate territorial organization. For clarity I will try consistently to make at least a nominal distinction between relatively large territorial groups and more restricted local groups. Units ranging from cities down to open country neighborhoods are local groups. Other groups exist to do a quite specific task, like producing automobiles or books. And within such instrumental groups even more narrowly specialized subunits carry out more particularized tasks, like binding the books or keeping records of the number of items sold. Finally, we have rather loosely organized groups or associations. People form them because of congeniality, common background, or to pursue a variety of general interests. For example, the tall, bony Manhattan youth with scarred face and alert eyes who joined a juvenile gang said he had done so for "Fun, excitement, to be constantly doing something. . . . I wanted to get a rep. . . . I was stabbed eight times. That's how I got the scars on my chin and

[1] *Paths in Utopia,* trans. R. F. C. Hull (London, 1949), p. 47.

head."[2] I don't propose to become overdefinitive, trying rigidly to separate territorial, local, narrowly task-oriented, and interest-centered groups from one another. Experience tells me it can't be done. Furthermore, in practice two or more types of groups overlap; the instrumental factory capitalized to manufacture books is also localized and satisfies more goals in workers' lives than turning out the daily quota.

To obtain a realistic understanding of some of these possibilities of organization I propose to examine them mainly as they are known from three contrasting social systems: the food-gathering, aboriginal Kaska Indians, the village-dwelling Hopi Indians, and Swat. This comparative view will demonstrate that particularly the number of such groups together with the intricacy of their internal organization differs substantially from one culture to another. To put it another way, organizational complexity varies between social systems. The reasons for such differences we will try to understand.

LOW POINT OF COMPLEXITY

Food gatherers, like the Central Arctic Eskimo or Kaska Indians, reveal a low point of organizational complexity.[3] All the people who today acknowledge they are Kaska Indians aboriginally possessed no sense of identity and, therefore, little or no organization. Each of the major river basins flowing through Kaska country, however, supported a collectivity of people which did feel a minimum sense of identification. They didn't designate themselves with a tribal name, but their neighbors called them after some characteristic feature of the country they occupied. Here, then, was a territorial group, a tribe, but one with an utter minimum of effective organization. The tribespeople possessed no officers and did not assemble regularly as a whole. Hunting and trapping kept their small bands dispersed during much of the year. In the cold, winter months a number of families clustered around a dependable fish lake and then something like a village briefly emerged. A tribe never asserted its unity by claiming to own the land which its members exploited. Territorial proximity of individuals, endogamous marriage, and kinship links alone gave some degree of structure to such a territorial group. Task-oriented organization appeared for brief intervals in war parties and caribou drives, groups with short lives and bare internal organization. Potlatch feasts, in which the members of one moiety bestowed gifts and food on the other, can be looked upon as short-term interest-centered associations. Such occasions helped to settle disputes between members of the loosely organized tribe and probably gave feuds a chance to rest or even heal.

[2] Gay Talese, "Gang Chief Who Quit Tells Why," *The New York Times*, October 2, 1959.

[3] John J. Honigmann, *The Kaska Indians: an Ethnographic Reconstruction*, Yale University Publications in Anthropology, no. 51, 1954, pp. 84-87.

More than the tribe the small band of people who traveled together constituted an effective social unit. It, rather than the larger territorial group, represented the maximum unit of effective social organization among the aboriginal Kaska Indians. The mobile band represented a local group, comparable to larger, sedentary local groups like open-country neighborhoods, villages, and cities. Men and women in the band, most of them kinsmen, cooperated in hunting, trapping, and setting fishnets and also enjoyed sociability. In a large-scale modern nation activities like these fall to specialized instrumental and interest groups but the Kaska did nearly everything in a single, small group broken down only into families. Here we have minimal organizational complexity. Although the band marked the largest enduring unit possessing effective social organization, this idea must be understood in the context of aboriginal Kaska life. In the first place, the band was small, consisting of two or three extended families and, perhaps, some unrelated hangers-on; it contained not more than 50 people at most. One man was leader. His principal distinguishing characteristic, the basis of his effective authority, was his outstanding ability as a hunter. Contact with supernaturals probably also augmented his impressive personality, giving him charisma that impressed his followers. But he advised and counseled rather than commanded. He suggested where to hunt in a given season or when to move. If he ruled on moral questions he did so quite without being able to force anybody to follow his decisions. People who strenuously disagreed with him could pack up and quit the band. As a result bands were fluid.

Man has lived in social systems with even less organization than the Kaska. The Great Basin Shoshoni Indians of eastern Idaho, Nevada, and northeastern Utah, for example, who survived primarily by gathering wild vegetable foods rather than by fishing and hunting, lived most of the year in individual families.[4] Family and local group were one. In winter, however, a number of families camped together and drew on the food resources that they had stored.

The low point of organizational complexity occurs when production of food or other commodities is insufficient to support a large aggregate of individuals. Population density remains small. People live spread over a large territory on which they fish, pursue game, trap furs, or collect roots and nuts. They find it impossible to command or buy supplementary food from the wider society, which would allow population to increase. They lack vehicles and energy for trade or war as well as an economic surplus to offer in exchange for imports. Basically minimal organizational complexity reflects absence of people to organize. Simple social organization still holds among the Kaska and other northern forest people today, particularly in winter when families move onto

[4] Julian H. Steward, *Basin-Plateau Sociopolitical Groups,* Bulletin of the Bureau of American Ethnology, no. 120, 1938.

trap lines for fur. What new permanent groups exist in Kaska country, like a trading post and airport, have been introduced by white Americans.

INDEPENDENT VILLAGES

The Hopi Indians, divided into some 13 independent pueblos or villages, bring us to a higher level of organizational complexity.[5] Although they possess a common name that gives them a sense of social distinctiveness, the Hopi disdain any tighter basis of territorial organization. Each of the relatively autonomous villages resembles a tiny city-state. Its relations to others are reaved by jealousy and suspicion strong enough to block any but rare cooperation. In 1936 the U.S. Government persuaded all the Hopi to adopt a Tribal Constitution but no real, all-tribal political unity has developed. There is a Hopi reservation but white officials rather than Indians directly sustain it as a territorial group. No chief or formal council firmly regulates affairs within any of these Hopi principalities. In fact, each matrisib in a village remains politically independent. Yet anarchy is avoided because the independent matrilineal kin groups cooperate freely, willingly, and intensively for the benefit of the entire village in one respect—religious activity.

Each independent Hopi pueblo—Old Oraibi is a good example—contains more task-oriented groups than ever existed in a Kaska tribe. Compared to the instrumental groups of Detroit and New York which give employment to millions, these Hopi task groups are quite remarkable. Each focuses its energies on religion and exists primarily to put on certain ceremonies. We will see the vital importance of these ceremonies in a moment.

One sib in Old Oraibi, that of the Bear, stands first among its peers, its claim backed by myth. According to this myth, after the Hopi Indians left the Underworld and came on earth, Masau'u, God of Death, gave Matcito, mythical ancestor of Bear sib, all the land of Oraibi and appointed him chief. The village chief still comes from the Bear sib, though his office carries very little power outside of his own kin group. Myth says that Bear chief Matcito gave all other sibs their land. As long as Bear sib doesn't try to upset present landholdings nobody cares to dispute seriously this harmless assertion. For its integration and survival Old Oraibi does not depend on action organized by the village chief.

What over-all action villages undertake is confined almost exclusively to ceremonies, a number of which the people feel are vital. Firmly convinced of the importance of these rituals, the village no more leaves their performance

[5] Mischa Titiev, *Old Oraibi*, Papers of the Peabody Museum of American Archaeology and Ethnology, Harvard University, vol. 22, no. 1, 1944, chap. 5; Fred Eggan, *Social Organization of the Western Pueblos* (Chicago, 1950), chap. 2; Laura Thompson, *Personality and Government* (Mexico, D.F., 1951), chap. 6.

to chance than Jews and Christians leave ceremonies to chance but instead train rabbis and priests to carry them out correctly. Old Oraibi, like other Hopi villages, doesn't support full-time, wholly specialized priests. Instead each adult villager belongs to one or more secret groups whose traditional task it is to perform ceremonies. Some of the groups allow only men to join and a few only women. A ceremonial group overlaps with several unilinear kin groups—lineages and sibs—of the village. One matrisib provides the chief priest of each ceremonial sodality and also controls that group's ceremonies. More important than this element of control, however, is the fact that members from several sibs belong to every ceremonial body. The group, therefore, acts as a social device which engages separate sibs in cooperation that ultimately benefits the whole village. The most important task carried out by men's ceremonial groups is the annual cycle of major ceremonies which bring ancestors, Katchinas, back in the form of clouds and rain and thereby sustain life in the desert. The secret portion of these ceremonies, generally lasting seven days, takes place in rectangular, underground ritual chambers called kivas. Here, through ritual smoking, praying to the accompaniment of shell and gourd rattles, and sand painting, men institute the ceremony. They also build an altar, prepare potent liquids ("medicine water"), and occasionally leave the kiva to make prayerful offerings at shrines located around the village. On the eighth day private and public rituals are combined. Then on the ninth day the main public dance occurs to which other villagers are drawn as spectators.

It might seem out of place to discuss these ritual acts in a chapter that deals with social organization. But they are quite pertinent because they bind together the independent sibs and give them common tasks to do in behalf of the total village. The ceremonies organize a village and hence are equivalent to the thousands of detailed acts that make up a large factory's instrumental task and insure that organization's organic continuity. Did the Hopi invent complicated ceremonials in order to have a basis for village integration? Not likely. The Hopi system of organizing a village through ceremonial sodalities and the rituals assigned to these groups probably materialized unselfconsciously. We nevertheless admire the result. In these pueblos where women form the solid core of the unilinear kin groups and men upon marriage are compelled to join the households of strangers, men are firmly reorganized by being made responsible for the year's paramount events, those ceremonies which, as Don Talayesva of Old Oraibi says, were "handed down by our fathers" and "mean life and security, both now and hereafter."[6] It is quite fitting that the nearest thing to an all-village council in Old Oraibi should occupy itself primarily with religious matters. Annually the chief priests of

[6] Leo W. Simmons, ed., *Sun Chief, The Autobiography of a Hopi Indian* (New Haven, Conn., 1942), p. 178.

the main secret ceremonial groups, who actually represent the village sibs they head, meet and lay plans for the coming ceremonial season. Religion for the Hopi is truly the basis of social life. Instrumental groups concerned with manufacturing, trade, and defense, have no place in organizing them. Interest groups that unite men or women simply on the basis of congeniality are subordinated to the business of religion. One of the leading students of Hopi culture seems too short-sighted when he claims that "Whatever other talents they possess, the Hopi do not have the gift of statecraft." He is right, of course, if he merely compares the Hopi to social systems with kings and other familiar routines of government. But he ignores the skill with which the Hopi, preferring to avoid the constraint of political centralization, have worked out a more congenial basis of integration.

Culture change in some Hopi villages has begun to break down the traditional religious basis of local integration. Emigration from Old Oraibi, for example, severely depleted membership of the groups responsible for ceremonies. Men remaining in the pueblo have thereby lost a former outlet for creativity and village solidarity has been further weakened. Deprived of the opportunity for self-expression formerly provided by their ceremonial roles some Oraibi men listen sympathetically to Mennonite preachers and drift ever further away from traditional Hopi ways.

Out of 562 social systems distributed around the world for which we have requisite data, political integration in 225 goes beyond the family but does not exceed the boundaries of an autonomous local group, like a wandering Kaska band or Hopi village.[7] Greek cities, like Athens and Sparta, clung to this organizational groundplan from the sixth to the second pre-Christian centuries. Local autonomy also centered in Italian cities, like Venice, Genoa, and Florence, between the eighth and fifteenth centuries A.D. and in German trading cities on the Baltic coast until in the thirteenth century they merged into the powerful Hanseatic League. However, in contrast to an acephalous Hopi village that lacks even a political council, these cities possessed far more clear-cut, responsible internal organization.

WHEN TERRITORY AND KIN GROUP COINCIDE

Anthropologists in recent years have studied closely social systems which, even more clearly than the Hopi, consist of independent unilinear kinship segments, that is, politically autonomous lineages or sibs. This form of organization is called acephalous segmentary social organization, the word acephalous denoting absence of any head, like a chief, with power to coordinate the autonomous segments by force if need be. In some acephalous segmentary

[7] George P. Murdock, "World Ethnographic Sample," *American Anthropologist,* 59 (1957), 664-687.

social systems territorial and kinship groups coincide. These middle-range communities, in keeping with the great emphasis they put on kinship, avoid any political control except that of a lineage elder, that is, a kinsman.

Inasmuch as no superior power exists to prevent a stronger kin group from encroaching on another's rights, one lineage's "foreign relations" with another may approach a permanent state of war. Grim as it may seem, competition and feuding between equal segments of kin are fundamental to each main-taining its equivalent status and dominance. Often, though, ways exist to remind lineage segments of a general good for which they should cooperate,

In villages like this, surrounded by terraced fields and barren hills, the political leaders of Swat sought to extend their advantages and increase their power. (*Government of Pakistan.*)

as Hopi sibs do through ceremonies. Simultaneously, however, each kin group remains vigilant to protect its own rights and identity, even though belief in one apical ancestor, the parent of the tribe from whom all lineages descend, promotes a sense of wider identification as also do personal kinship ties created by interlineage marriage. Where strict lineage endogamy is the rule, as among Arabs who favor marriage between brothers' children, even this personal link between lineages vanishes; hence a basis of common action is hard to secure in the Arab world.

ANARCHY IN SWAT

Swat a hundred years ago exemplified a social system with acephalous social organization.[8] Land, the basic economic resource, belonged to patrilineages

[8] Fredrik Barth, *Political Leadership Among Swat Pathans,* London School of Economics, Monographs on Social Anthropology, no. 19, 1959.

descended from the conquerors who several hundred years previously had invaded the country. Where one of these ancestors received his real estate holding, there his male descendants still lived and farmed. Although everybody depended on land, only a relatively small fraction of persons belonged to lineages controlling land. Membership in such a group gave a man prestige and authority. A lineage member owned not a definite piece of ground but, rather, rights to definite amounts of land. Periodically the time came around to reallot lineage land and then a landowner had to move, taking up his rights in a new place on the lineage territory. The narrow main valley of Swat, with its barren, unirrigable hills on either side, held all too little arable land. Many more people wished to own land than in fact did and many landowners sought to expand their prestige by acquiring more land. But anyone with land was reluctant to sell. To sell was tantamount to renouncing membership in a lineage together with all one's prestige and authority. Hence an ambitious man had to employ other ways to gain control of property. A strong landlord tried to encroach on his weaker neighbors' possession. In the absence of written records he put forward a fraudulent claim to land which the actual owner found difficult to disprove. A strong man also employed cold war tactics to terrorize others into selling or abandoning their claims to land.

Lineage membership governed inheritance of land, a father transmitting his rights to his sons. Inheritance, therefore, served as a mechanism to continue the lineage. A man defended his right to own land in terms of being a patrilineal descendant of a previous landowner and could even trace his ancestry all the way back to one of the sixteenth century invaders who settled down in Swat. Landowners in a given territory recognized their descent from a common conquering ancestor but also emphasized their membership in smaller segments within the maximal lineage. As is customary in acephalous segmentary social systems lacking any organized central control or police, close lineage relatives cooperated to defend a fellow member's interests. Close patrilineal kinsmen, like a man's brothers, shared his insults and therefore jointly avenged such affronts. They took revenge against the actual offender or against his close patrikin. If necessary, sons who inherited a man's land also avenged his murder. Sometimes lineage segments combined for a common purpose but the minimal unit, a man and his sons, also stood alone against brothers and cousins. Segmentary lineages without over-all unity provoked a Pathan poet, Khushhal Khan Khattak, himself the member of a minor lineage of repute, to say:

> Would the tribes but be of one mind amongst themselves,
> Emperors would prefer to bow down before them. . . .

By "tribes" he meant his people's many sovereign lineage segments which were having trouble defending themselves against the organized might of Mughal conquest.

Swat landholders pursuing mainly personal goals left their lineage weak. With only small lineage segments occasionally available to act in his behalf, a man had to look elsewhere to defend his interests. We have here a social problem that favors the emergence of one strong lineage whose head acquires sufficient adherents to keep other kin groups and individuals in check. Something like this came about only recently in Swat. Prior to the appearance of centralized government powerful men depended on private, armed bands to protect their interests, which the lineage was too weak to defend. Such a task force consisted of whatever followers a leader could induce to join him, but mainly tenant farmers made up its ranks. For more ambitious forays or stronger defense two leaders allied themselves, each partner remaining the other's equal. Serious wars were carried out through still larger forces built up with smaller alliances.

Alliances between men aspiring to power compensated for the weak, disrupted lineages. At the same time they sapped more strength from the kin groups. A landlord who commanded followers with whose power he could aggrandize himself at the expense of his neighbor was bound to be in a state of war with other members of his own maximal and minor lineages. Remember, lineages were localized descent groups; hence a man's landowning neighbors (but not landless tenant farmers) belonged to his lineage. Alliances also fell apart readily due to envious intrigue and internal factionalism. From such instability and virtual anarchy there emerged the modern nation of Swat.

POWER AND THE CITIZEN

Each of our three levels of organizational complexity contains a social system in which political integration does not exceed the local group (Kaska band, Hopi village) or in which territorial group coincides with lineage. However, a large number of the world's people (237 out of a sample of 562[9]) have willingly or unwillingly moved under a central political authority. To this type of territorial group, varying in size from over a thousand to millions of people, I will now turn.

Because of its relatively small size Swat can be regarded as a model of these organizationally complex, national groups dividing the modern world. The legal status citizens enjoy in such leviathans assures them of many tax-supported services to increase their satisfactions and provide protection. In return a citizen owes obligations to his nation; if need be, he must die for it. Rarely can he conscientiously resist committing acts in its name whose brutality or immorality would repel him in more intimate social relationships. The gas chambers of Dachau and Auschwitz and the atomic flash released on Hiro-

[9] Murdock, *op. cit.*

shima are only two examples. Citizens have reason to be wary of the mighty, efficiently organized power centers in the national groups.

Many factors combine to bring nations into being. Modern Swat owes its foundation to the efforts of Akhund Sahib, a mystic and saint, who in the nineteenth century sought to quell the land's near anarchy by supporting a strong leader. But even a holy man's authority was not enough and furthermore the leader mismanaged things so that the first attempt at nation-building ended

Roads and bridges, like this one crossing Swat River, knit together the modern nation of Swat. (*Government of Pakistan.*)

in failure. Around the turn of the century the Akhund's eldest son, whose inherited sanctity people respected, himself sought assume temporal power but the alliance he controlled failed. Next the Badshah, son of Akhund's junior son, commenced the struggle. Nation-building can be cruel and in Swat it was. Under the Badshah's direction kinsmen fought and killed one another and the Badshah banished some of his own close relatives. Kinship, predominant value of middle-range social systems, had to be replaced by other ideals. Clever manipulation of alliances helped by external danger raised by a neighboring ruler, intrigue, and military power enabled the Badshah gradually to consolidate his control. He established forts to dominate the unruly land and pushed roads, bridges, and telephone lines into the remote valleys. He strengthened his prestige by marrying the daughter of a powerful ruler in a nearby mountain state. It must have been a heartening token of success when in 1926 Swat won recognition from the British Government in India. Twenty-three years later the Badshah abdicated in favor of his son, the land's present ruler.

In this tomb the Akhund of Swat lies buried. (*Government of Pakistan.*)

For all their might and importance, nations themselves can't be seen. There-fore, attempts are made to reveal them symbolically. In Swat the national emblem is a flag bearing a turreted fort that recalls the forts from which the Badshah established control over rebellious chiefs. A distinctive license tag for automobiles also proclaims Swat's independent social existence. In the capital, surrounded by an impressive mosque, stands the Akhund's marble tomb, symbol of both the ruling family and its saintly ancestor who encouraged the first attempt to centralize political power. In effect it symbolizes the nation itself. The tomb's reputation for miracles draws many pilgrims who travel to the capital to appeal to the dead saint. Nearby in 1958 the Badshah from his hillside palace could watch his own tomb rise, a new national symbol in the making.

Territorial groups are complex organizations. They are subdivided into smaller, task-centered groups that are then coordinated with one another in bureaucratic fashion. The government of Swat depends on courts, ordinance shop, police, public works staff, telephone personnel, chief-medical officer, and hospital staffs. Each of these bureaus performs certain duties for the country. Swat contains 35 administrative districts each managed by a central government official. Groups of districts are coordinated under a governor. The 7 governors come under 3 regional officers who are in frequent and direct contact with the ruler. Between this hierarchy and the people a more traditional system of organization interposes itself. Leaders of the localized landlord lineages serve the government as local leaders. In somewhat similar fashion British colonial governments in Africa utilized native leaders for indirect rule. Advantages accrue from relying on grass-roots leadership; the knowledgeable local authorities accurately reflect public opinion. Like modern nations everywhere, the central government of Swat watches carefully lest power drain off from the center and concentrate too heavily in some subordinate group. The ruler relies on intelligence to inform him of disloyalty. He shifts district administrators frequently so that they cannot build up personal followings. And he watches lest any alliance of chiefs grow too great, in which case he throws his personal support to a rival bloc.

Swat is small enough to allow the ruler to take personal, even paternalistic, interest in his realm. The personal bodyguard that cordons the ruler's office can be penetrated by any citizen who wishes to see the ruler and who isn't content to relay his message through the Private Secretary or Chief Secretary. In distinction to Swat, in large nations that include millions, people act as if shell-shocked when they have to deal with government.[10] Rulers hide themselves under a shroud of mystery and take on the appearance of supermen.

As territorial and local groups become organizationally complex, replete with subgroups that specialize in government, education, trade, treating the sick, and managing transportation, high value is placed on technical proficiency. Membership in task-centered groups cannot be left simply to birth and tradition or purely to individual choice. Only a man or woman who can prove he possesses requisite experience, training, and other qualifications is eligible to become a clerk, machinist, policeman, telephone serviceman, bus mechanic, merchant, teacher, doctor, or nurse. And only a trained person can succeed in those undertakings. Membership qualifications are rationally fixed with a view

[10] Leopold Kohr, *The Breakdown of Nations* (New York, 1957), pp. 74, 98-99.

toward meeting the goal for which the group is organized. Individuals are cautiously selected to receive necessary training for which in Swat and other underdeveloped countries they sometimes have to go far from home. I have been to Swat and cannot deny that traditionalism still persists there. Nevertheless, with rationalism emphasized in at least a section of group life, Swat today is a truly modern social system.

GOVERNMENT SHOWS ITS HAND

Government as we are familiar with it—bureaucratically organized, responsible to a people's legislature, and topped by an executive who is flanked be secretaries or ministers—belongs to Europe and America. Recently these lands exported it to new nations in Africa and Asia. By the hand of government I mean its process, a process of administration. Government is basically administration: making plans for a group, guiding a group out of certain kinds of dilemmas, following through on plans in executive fashion, and, at last, receiving information on the outcome of the plans in order to have a basis for future action.

Possibly all human activity carries a trace of administration, even if only an individual by himself plans and does a job and afterwards appraises his degree of success. Certainly every group that does things together, whether an independent nuclear family in Crestwood Heights or a mammoth Detroit factory, requires administration. In a family the process is carried out by parents, casually and loosely, from day to day. In task-oriented groups, long-range planning centers in one or several highly qualified persons who chart procedures, coordinate activities, impose sanctions, and study reports on results. One man can scarcely administer a mammoth corporation by himself; that task alone occupies hundreds. Overseeing the vast administrative staff itself keeps several full-time specialists busy. The general manager oversees all but delegates much to his subchiefs who are lined up on the organizational chart in a bureaucratically fixed hierarchy of command.

But administration of a family, Hopi ceremonial group, Indian war party, or university is not government as I mean it. Government means administration undertaken over a territorial or local group: a tribe, nation, segmentary lineage tract, band, village, or city. The hand of government may have a span smaller than a single social system. Formerly no government administered all the Kaska, Hopi, or Pathans of Swat valley. These social systems were organized into a number of smaller groups, each of which possessed some, no matter how rudimentary, degree of administration. Government, then, turns out to be a matter of degree. Rather than say that people have the kind of government they deserve we will understand government better by observing that people live or smart under the degree and form of government that suits their total way of life. To this I shall return when, after surveying the hand of government, I turn to some of its faces.

POWER TO GOVERN

No matter how complicated a modern government's communications, how powerfully equipped with hidden stores of nuclear weapons its army, air force, and navy, or how well endowed it may be with ponderous mechanical brains to help it arrive at decisions, from a human point of view government (and administration) rests on our capacity to influence one another's actions. Government means certain persons are influencing others through appeals, threats, promises, and more subtle, wordless signs that arouse loyalty and obedience. All too often these sources of influence fail, particularly if we want others to do something that is untraditional or that conflicts with other loyalties. At that point government as we know it is apt to fall back on a capacity we humans share with a number of other animals. Influence is exerted in what euphemistically we call "a more direct way," namely, through physical force.

The important point, however, is that governments rely mainly on other than purely physical power. A ruler may be obeyed because he has power to withhold rain. Disobedience or disloyalty may carry automatic retribution that will affect the whole realm. Perhaps it is the chief's curse that dooms a resister to illness or death. Such powers imputed to government heads are existentially as real as the physical force exerted by a police riot squad. A political authority, like a Kaska Indian headman, relies on moral persuasion and even more on the common sense and traditionality of his advice, qualities which undoubtedly make him effective most of the time.

Governmental power is effected through the prestige of those men—elders, saints, or good hunters—who wield it. However, power by itself brings respect; holders of power accumulate prestige for the very fact that they occupy an august position.

Power, whether persuasive or coercive, always tries to become legitimate. Or so it seems, because even a tyrant who seizes office attempts to legitimize his position as quickly as possible. He tries to acquire authority to back his rule. Authority confers the right to make administrative decisions, to follow them up, and to receive feedback. Government uses many means to acquire legitimacy. The belief that an officeholder had divine ancestors, was himself personally chosen for his role by a divinity, or enjoys an unusual degree of divine protection can confer authority even on a fool. Being born in a recognized ruling group—to be of "royal blood"—confers authority. Several of these criteria operate in the chief of Hopi Oraibi. He belongs to Bear sib, whose mythical ancestor, Matcito, won a special favor from the God of Death by virtue of which Bear sib alone may provide the village chief. Modern, large-scale social systems pay much less heed to hereditary succession and its accompanying myths. Many end up choosing occupants for top offices through what amount to big popularity contests. It is hard to see any alternative. The technically specialized, complex roles which the successful candidates will have to play, combined with the public's ignorance or disinterest concerning such technicalities, prohibit elections from being based on a careful evaluation of rival candidates' qualifications. Hence the candidates' popular appeal carries. Here we border on another source of authority, personal charisma; the right to administer falls to a man not by virtue of tradition or his technical qualifications but by virtue of the force of his personality which commands others to follow him.

Whatever the basis of authority, inheritance, election, or charisma, all but the smallest scale social systems buttress it with symbols and ceremony. The Oraibi headman owns a chief's staff and a special stone, red splotched, incised, and carved with human figures, which Bear sib long ago brought up from the underworld and still treasures. It is some 16 inches long, 8 inches wide, and 1½ inches thick and signifies Bear sib's authority to preempt the village chief's office. Ceremonial investiture frequently symbolizes assumption of authority. The reigning British Queen was crowned; the President took his oath from the Chief Justice on a Bible. In Oraibi the chief priest of the Agave ceremonial group inducts a new village chief saying: "Now I make you chief. . . . Now you are our father." The accompanying ceremony brings the chief into close touch with the rain-giving ancestors on whose aid he will count. Following inauguration authority continues to be symbolized throughout a government official's life. Rulers receive deference that is exaggerated when compared to normal respect. Heads of state are entitled to especially noisy salutes. Communal work that benefits the whole village expresses respect for the Hopi village chief. Illnesses of rulers and their infirmities are minimized and some middle-range communities hold that such august personages are incapable of dying a natural death. Royal and presidential funerals in Europe and America rather belatedly symbolize authority. They grow ever more impressive and in these days of mass media vicariously involve international participation by millions.

People in small-scale and middle-range social systems understand that the occupants of governing positions will do little which departs widely from tradition. Steady consultation links a village headman and his followers. In large-scale systems the governed stand in vigilant, fearful suspicion lest those who govern become too powerful or act against public interests. Remember, the community is divided into producers, merchants, and consumers, labor and capital, rich and poor, rural farmers and urban folk engaged in manufacturing or service roles, and into numerous religious denominations. Action taken by government in favor of one of these interests jeopardizes the welfare of others.

THE GOLDEN STOOL

(*Information Services Department, Government of Ghana*)

"In the interior of Gold Coast Colony [Ghana], West Africa, lies the land of Ashanti, known to our fathers as the seat of a fierce barbarism that had its centre in the capital— Kumasi. . . .

"Early in the eighteenth century there came to the court of Osai Tutu, the fourth King of Ashanti, a celebrated magician named Anotchi, who announced that he was commissioned by Onyame, the god of the sky, to make Ashanti a great and powerful nation. In the presence of the King and a great multitude he drew down from heaven a black cloud from which issued the rumblings of thunder and a wooden stool. The stool sank slowly through the air till it rested upon the King's knees without touching the earth. Except for the gold which partially covered it, the stool was such as Africans commonly use. Anotchi proclaimed that it contained the *sunsum* (the soul) of the Ashanti people, that with it was bound up their power, their honour, their welfare, and that if ever it were captured or destroyed the nation would perish.

"Thereafter the Stool was cherished as the most sacred possession of the tribe. . . . Not even the King ever sat upon it. Whenever on great occasions its power was evoked the King would pretend three times to sit upon it and would then seat himself upon his own stool and rest his arm upon the Golden Stool. Once a year it was carried in solemn procession, under its own umbrella and accompanied by its own attendants who in pomp and number exceeded the attendants of the king who walked behind it."

Edwin W. Smith, *The Golden Stool, Some Aspects of the Conflict of Cultures in Modern Africa* (London, 1927), pp. 1-2.

SYMBOLS UPON SYMBOLS

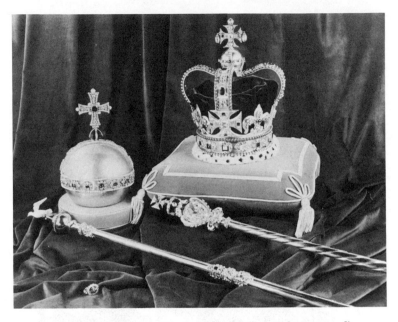

(British Information Services, Crown Copyright Reserved)

The intrinsic value of the British Crown Jewels is great. Equally potent is their symbolic value. Putting on the enormously heavy Crown of St. Edward forms the grand climax of the coronation service. At this point Westminster Abbey rings with acclamations, guns boom, trumpeters blow fanfares, and Abbey bells peel. The Orb symbolizes independent sovereignty under the Cross. Both sceptres are symbols of regality and each carries a symbol of Christianity. The ring also symbolizes royal dignity and is placed on the former marrying finger, the third on the right hand.

Jocelyn Perkins, *The Crowning of the Sovereign of Great Britain and the Dominions Overseas,* 2nd ed. (London, 1953).

Out of fear lest undue advantages be given to a rival interest group or lest government become too strong, social inventions which attempt to limit governmental power develop. Democracy is one such social innovation. Because democracy has many meanings and often denotes an ideal state of affairs which nowhere exists, we might more neutrally call the process polyarchy. The German scholar Max Weber lists some specific devices to establish polyarchy: limited term of office, possibility of recall or impeachment of officials, rotation of office, constitution-like mandate that limits leaders' powers, regular reports due from officials, and powers divided between offices so that one office can check another's power.[11] At times all these devices have been circumvented by governments acting basely or with the highest motives. Only eternal vigilance can restrict the progressive erosion of liberty.

Let us be wise enough to recognize that everything which pretends to rule over a territorial group is not government. Some governments exist in name only. The administrators avoid as much as possible testing their power with the result that their territory seethes with factions each trying to control others, almost like Swat before it achieved centralization of power. In a prolonged interregnum, such as intrudes between the death of one authority and the selection of his proper successor, not even a fictive administration is perceptible.

Officeholders don't wield power alone. Behind the front of elected officials in the United States are self-selected, powerful men.[12] The top positions that they occupy in business, religious organizations, armed services, and labor unions earn them their places in state and national power elites. It is they who approve the more important plans which elected leaders officially formulate and execute. Although these top-flight power wielders avoid publicity, they are not conspirators. Do they have authority? With some citizens they do, but not with all. In fact, they feel a little guilty about their role. It is the passivity shown by the majority of citizens that keeps the elite in power. They accept what most of us disdain, that ideal of polyarchy, a large measure of government "by the people."

SIZE AND TOTALITY OF GOVERNMENT

The size of a government, that is, the number of people more or less busy with administration, depends partly on the number of persons organized in a territorial group and partly on the volume and complexity of tasks that territorial administration encompasses. The all-Kaska chief today elected at the behest of Canadian authorities has little to do, largely because the Canadian authorities won't entrust him with responsibilities but also because Kaska life demands little coordination. This is what I mean by saying that people live under government that suits their way of life.

Hopi village government, too, is modest. The village chief sets himself up as a shining example of good living. His prayers are vital for good crops. In more secular fashion he gives permission to use free land, settles land disputes, and assesses damages when livestock destroy crops. It sounds odd that Hopi even consider it improper to worry a chief with petty grievances and thereby

[11] Max Weber, *The Theory of Social and Economic Organization,* trans. A. M. Henderson and T. Parsons, ed. T. Parsons (New York, 1947).

[12] Floyd Hunter, *Community Power Structure* (Chapel Hill, N.C., 1953); Floyd Hunter, *Top Leadership U.S.A.* (Chapel Hill, N.C., 1959).

destroy his tranquility or "good heart." But on the chief's equanimity as on everyone's, village health, prosperity, and welfare depend. Swat, where a central government seized power to pacify the unruly land, is numerically far larger than a Hopi village and the tasks of administration are also more numerous. The ruler has too much work for one man to deal with. Hence the capital and realm are organized into government bureaus and districts, several tiers of courts, and police and militia.

Governments grow in scope when social systems become organizationally complex. Many task-centered groups arise to produce, move, or trade goods; each depends on others to accomplish its mission successfully. Groups and categories of people in the community begin to pursue conflicting interests which are hard to reconcile. These developments are predictable in a society with increasing population and technical development. The Industrial Revolution, for example, encouraged them mightily. Government does not expand arbitrarily and never automatically. Administrators may even seek to avoid having more work to do. But as soon as groups begin to agitate for aid, protection, or arbitration of their differences they compel government to perform new tasks: protect commerce, manage communications, finance industry through loans, boost farm prices, support the unemployed, regulate air traffic, provide old-age assistance, contribute to education and research. Individually each step in expanding administration may be resisted by some part of the population but rarely does anybody object consistently to all.

Increasing the scope of government spells totalitarianism. Like most useful concepts, totalitarianism viewed nonpejoratively is a matter of degree. Its early stages coincide with the normal span of government in any fairly large-scale social system. It reaches full-blown maturity when government adjudicates in a wide range of activities, fixes production and regulates consumption, attempts even to set tastes and personal values, and officially records and licenses practically each step an individual takes from birth to death.

In another form of governmental expansion one territorial group's administration imposes its power over another. Perhaps unstable conditions on the border invite this effort to maintain stability. Perhaps lust for tribute, raw materials, or markets spurs conquest. During the colonial era in Asia, Africa, the Pacific, and the Americas several of these motives operated simultaneously. The colonial powers further ethnocentrically defended their imperialism in nobler terms, claiming they had shouldered the "white man's burden."

The next step in territorial organization has already appeared. I mean the painful process by which national units become organized as segments of larger, supranational organization. Dogged resistance limits the growth of effective supranational units. Even nations eager to joint international bodies like the United Nations jealously guard their political autonomy in the same way that Hopi villages cherish their sovereignty and some chiefs in Swat still resent the ruler's monopoly of military force. Will supranational political organization on a world-wide scale someday be successfully achieved?

ONLY LIMITED STABILITY

Man's nature leads him to organize into groups for survival, collective action, aggression, production, worship, play, and many other purposes. The sheer number of groups in a society and their types keep pace with population, scale, and technical productivity. Every group to which he belongs calls for a share of a person's loyalty. As a result people run into difficulty. The goals a man pursues in one group conflict with goals he pursues in another. He is torn between conflicting loyalties to different associations. If he reserves his basic loyalty for his family and refuses, as he sees it, to jeopardize their welfare for the sake of national goals, then he is punished. Yet he looks to his nation for aid and protection. American corporations and state governments resist the central government's encroachment on their autonomy but at the same time claim federal assistance. Political life is replete with clashes between groups as well as between nation states.

Man's nature leads him into groups but his group life knows only limited stability. Even Hopi Indians have not been able to prevent intravillage struggles over power. Absolutist kingdoms could not maintain stability even though they claimed that God backed their rule. Modern day, affluent democracies cannot forestall divided loyalties and resultant conflicts. Nor can monolithic states like the U.S.S.R. or Communist China do so. Every group uses means to strengthen loyalty to it and to forestall internal disputes. Ritually we pronounce or enact obedience to parents or lineage heads, reiterate our duties of citizenship, and affirm national patriotism. Difficulty arises, however, because in competing groups members are simultaneously affirming loyalty with equal intensity.

Must we not conclude that man has much to learn about living effectively in a large-scale society segmented into diverse, overlapping, and rival groups, organized to achieve special and, at times, incompatible satisfactions? Granting that we still have much to learn, how can we hope that stable, supranational political organization can soon be successfully achieved?

FURTHER READING

Varied approaches to associations and political institutions will be found in Julius E. Lips, "Government," in Franz Boas, ed., *General Anthropology* (New York, 1938); Robert H. Lowie, *Social Organization* (New York, 1948), chaps. 13, 14 (incidentally, Lowie shows social organization in action by means of four case studies ranging from the Crow Indians to imperial Austria); John Gillin,

The Ways of Men (New York, 1948), chap. 19; E. Adamson Hoebel, *Man in the Primitive World,* 2nd ed. (New York, 1958), chaps. 23, 28; and Ralph Pidding-ton, *An Introduction to Social Anthropology,* 2 vols., (Edinburgh, 1950, 1957), vol. I, chap. 5.

Essays on political organization written from a theoretically more specialized point of view are Max Gluckman, "Political Institutions," *The Institutions of Primitive Society* (Oxford, 1954), and his volume of broadcast lectures, *Custom and Conflict in Africa* (Oxford, 1955). S. N. Eisenstadt, "Primitive Political Systems: A Preliminary Comparative Analysis," *American Anthropologist,* 61 (1959), 200-220, provides a very broad, over-all view.

Evolutionary anthropologists have been much concerned with organizational complexity. Julian H. Steward discusses this phenomenon as he reviews levels of growing sociocultural integration in *Theory of Culture Change* (Urbana, Ill., 1955), chaps. 3, 6–9, 11. See also Walter Goldschmidt, *Man's Way* (New York, 1959), especially chaps. 3-5. These provide a macroscopic point of view. For a microscopic anaylsis there is Laura Thompson's *Culture in Crisis* (New York, 1950), an analysis of changes in Oraibi ceremonial organization which accompanied other cultural changes. Her analysis, however, does not make use of evolutionary theory. Célestin Charles A. Bouglé, *The Evolution of Values,* trans. Helen Stalker Sellars (New York, 1926), chap. 4, describes how value differentiation keeps pace with social differentiation.

Acephalous lineage organization has received its due share of attention. A number of types are contrasted in John Middleton and David Tait, eds., *Tribes Without Rulers, Studies in African Segmentary Systems* (London, 1958). Meyer Fortes, "The Structure of Unilineal Descent Groups," *American Anthropologist,* 55 (1953), 17-41, offers a more general view. Edward P. Dozier observes a shift from lineage to village organization in certain southwestern U.S. Pueblos and traces the shift to the influence of irrigation. See his paper, "The Pueblos of the South-Western United States," *The Journal of the Royal Anthropological Institute,* 60 (1960), 146-160.

My definition of administration is adapted from Edward H. Litchfield, "Notes on a General Theory of Administration," *Administrative Science Quarterly,* 1 (1956), 3-29.

This chapter has touched on questions that perplex political scientists, namely, what is political life and how shall it be studied. For a professional view of the topic see Charles S. Hyneman, *The Study of Politics* (Urbana, Ill., 1959), chaps. 8, 9. Studies of comparative government by anthropologists include the book by Max Gluckman mentioned above; M. Fortes and E. E. Evans-Pritchard, *African Political Systems* (London, 1940); M. Gluckman, J. C. Mitchell, and J. A. Barnes, "The Village Headman in British Central Africa," *Africa,* 19 (1949), 89-106; and I. Schapera, *Governments and Politics in Tribal Societies* (London, 1956). As these titles indicate, anthropologists have been very active studying African forms of government. *The Journal of African Administration* devotes many pages to the emergence of new administrative forms in the developing territories of that continent. I hope nobody reading the preceding pages has tried the practically hopeless task of distinguishing sharply between a tribe and nation. In *From Empire to Nation* (Cambridge, Mass., 1960), chap. 5, Rupert Emerson points out difficulties with the nation concept. Concerning the suitability of government and culture, Robert W. King, "Technology and Social Progress," *Political Science Quarterly,* 76 (1961), 3-10, points out how useful Communism is in a country whose elite want to surmount the twin hurdles of little free capital and trained labor. Theodore R. Anderson and Seymour Warkov discuss the relationship between the size of an administrative group and its task in "Organizational Size and Functional Complexity: A Study of Administration in Hospitals," *American Sociological Review*, 26 (1961), 23-28. I find useful the concept of polyarchy advanced in R. A. Dahl and C. E. Lindblom, *Politics, Economics, and Welfare* (New York, 1953), chap. 10. My concept of totalitarianism derives from Carl J. Friedrich, *Totalitarianism* (Cambridge, Mass., 1954) and Carl J. Friedrich and Z. K. Brzezinski, *Totalitarian Dictatorship and Autocracy* (Cambridge, Mass., 1956).

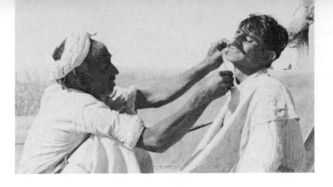

7

Maintaining Social Distance

We hold these truths to be self-evident, that all men . . . are endowed by their Creator with certain unalienable Rights, that among these are Life, Liberty and the pursuit of Happiness.

Declaration of Independence

The enumeration in the Constitution of certain rights shall not be construed to deny or disparage others retained by the people.

Article IX, Constitution of the United States

SHARED EXPERIENCE AND COMMON INTERESTS

The very nature of society impels men to differentiate themselves into units. Assemble enough people who are unequal in age, sex, experience, authority, wealth, or power and regularly they will segregate themselves according to one or more of these attributes. Some will keep their distance from those who are younger, possess less authority, exert weaker power, own less wealth, or have had different experiences. In practice several such attributes always work conjointly. For example, shared experience and the common interests that experience creates draw together persons of the same sex or similar age.

To see why this is so consider, first, that universally men and women carry out different tasks and responsibilities. Inevitably, therefore, one sex shares experiences about which the other couldn't care less. We see the result at a party where, to the hostess' intense annoyance, men draw off into one animated corner while their wives, high and dry across the room, talk about children and food prices. Many women resent their segregation, yet women in many small-scale and middle-range social systems insist on publicly staying apart from men. In church the aisle divides one sex from the other. When my wife and I attended summer dances among the Kaska Indians, we separated once we entered the dance house. My wife edged in with girls on their bench and I huddled around the door with young men. As soon as a dance number ended, girls and boys flew apart, each sex hurrying back to its own side. In such communities it would be immodest for an unrelated man and woman to appear together brashly in public. Their companionship could mean only one thing—sex.

Age like sex brings with it differences in experiences but here another factor intrudes to promote social distance. Young people and, at the farther end of the continuum, the aged both possess limited capacities that restrict their behavior. Seniors find it useless to talk at length about sacred subjects to impatient juniors who can't comprehend theological subtleties. The wisdom of age lies partly in being wise enough to retire from active involvement in many concerns of life. Let these be the province of the responsible middle generation.

The gap, compounded of experience, maturity, and capacity, that divides men and women or young and old readily becomes institutionalized. Clubs take in only members of similar age or only those of the same sex, or only men who fought together in the same war, or only shamans who acquired their power from a similar inspiring vision. Small-scale cultures, however, usually limit associational life to men, or at least men find more opportunity than women to band together. For one thing, men have so many more varied experiences that can become bases for solidarity and social distance. Also, women's routine duties, especially caring for children, tie them down and leave no time for exclusive club life. Some male sodalities initiate youths under circumstances whose dramatic intensity testifies to the momentousness of this step in their lives. The initiation drama shocks boys loose from their hitherto close identification with women who raised them and pushes them to join the ranks of men. The purely masculine problem of overcoming childhood identification with the opposite sex also explains why some men's associations feature clear-cut opposition to women. Secrets must be religiously concealed from women and masked men, representing spirits, periodically ceremonially terrify both women and as-yet uninitiated boys. Masculine associations, remarkably similar in traits like these, are known from cultures located as far apart as the southwest Pacific islands, the remote tip of South America, and West Africa.

Associational life furnishes men with abundant opportunities to share common interests and at the same time fortifies still more their fund of common experience. Thereby a high degree of solidarity results precisely where it counts most, among men, the sex that assumes the heaviest social responsibility. Club life offsets the disunity that jealousy, rivalry, and competition constantly aggravate among men. These tensions, should they run unchecked, would sporadically flash into violence and produce social anarchy in which the social system would dissolve.

Youth dormitories, found among India's aboriginal inhabitants and in Melanesia, bring together unmarried boys and girls of both sexes. At adolescence each discovers in the other its most engrossing interest, so it should hardly surprise anyone that dormitory customs openly recognize youth's intense erotic drive. African age classes belong to a different order of age groups. Each such class really forms a grade in a men's association, a group that can be compared to a school. Members, children and young men, win promotion to successive higher grades in the association as their training and maturity ripen them to master advanced communal responsibilities.

Segregation nurtured by differential age, experience, and interests varies a great deal from culture to culture. So do its functions. Generally, whenever segregation occurs it can be counted on to reinforce bonds of solidarity between those persons who confine a significant portion of their interaction to one another. Strong segregation by age is impossible. The young need care and training; therefore adults dare not leave them too much alone. Rigorous segregation by sex can continue lifelong and strengthens the conviction that men are utterly different from women. On the other hand, minimal sexual segregation, like we have in cities, conveys a contrary but just as extreme notion, namely, that men and women are largely equivalent. According to Ernest Crawley, the male, the sex that conclusively controls what a community believes, in all communities perceives a mystical, contagious danger exuding from women.[1] Despite their periodic need for sexual satisfaction, men strive to forestall this mystical danger by keeping women at a safe distance. Some social systems, including the Kaska Indians, do indeed fear that women (particularly during menstruation and childbirth) contaminate men's hunting ability and scare off game, and this belief supports sexual segregation. But one can also usefully turn Crawley's theory around and say that fear is bred and danger suspected whenever people—whether men and women or two ethnic groups—draw themselves apart too widely.

ALL MEN ARE NOT EQUAL

All don't share equally among Kaska and Hopi Indians. Some Kaska families trap more fur which brings them a higher income from the trader. Personal ambition motivates some Hopi men to become prosperous. Yet, prosperous and less prosperous Kaska and Hopi families live together in the same neighborhood. They associate easily, without constraint or discomfort. Marriage joining families with unequal means is quite natural and promotes no difficulties

[1] Ernest Crawley, *The Mystic Rose* (London, 1902).

PREMARITAL SEX RELATIONS IN MURIA GOND YOUTH DORMITORIES

" . . . everything is arranged to prevent long-drawn intense attachments, to eliminate jealousy and possessiveness, to deepen the sense of communal property and action. . . . A chelik [boy member of a youth dormitory] and motiari [girl member] may sleep together for three nights; after that they are warned; if they persist they are punished. If a boy shows any signs of possessiveness for a particular girl, if his face falls when he sees her making love to someone else, if he gets annoyed at her sleeping with another chelik, . . . he is forcibly reminded by his fellows that she is not his wife. . . .

" . . . I heard the phrase 'so that they will not be ruined by love.' This is certainly a genuine consideration. . . . A strong and lasting attachment to a girl in the pre-nuptial period may lead to an elopement and an irregular marriage. Such a marriage disturbs the serenity of the home—which ultimately depends on the parents; it destroys the old alliances of families and prevents the repayment of ancient debts; it often turns out unsuccessful.

" . . . the Muria temperament . . . is fundamentally hostile to individualism, to exclusiveness, and to any kind of 'possessiveness.' The Muria believe that if everyone belongs to everyone else in the ghotul there will be no room for jealousy. . . .

"The result of this arrangement is—according to Muria theory—that everybody in the ghotul is in love with everybody else."

Verrier Elwin, *The Muria and Their Ghotul* (London, 1947), pp. 343-345. By permission of Oxford University Press. The Muria Gond live in Central India.

---

of adjustment in married life. In other words, among these Indians differences in prosperity that arise from inequalities of skill and motivation do not create social chasms.

Compare this sociable picture with a modern U.S. town in which families of about the same means and background tend to cluster together and possess a common rank. "There's just no one in this town for a person like me to marry," a 28-year-old Smith College graduate complains, obliquely appraising the social distance dividing her from others. Even those outside the upper class ungraciously admit that there are superior grades when they sneeringly refer to a "fancy crowd." A person is recognized not only as an American citizen, female, age 28. Everyone is graded by his class rank in relation to other people. Visiting, club activities, and marriage are confined to families and friends of the same class and of approximately equal social worth.

Our class-stratified social systems are tiered like a layer cake, one social stratum hierarchically superimposed on the other, and each set back from the one below because the number of people shrinks toward the top. How many social classes comprise a U.S. community? Some authors have been content with three; others describe five or six. More than six classes become too cumbersome to handle and distinctions between strata then grow too fine to be easily handled. I would look for at least three social levels: an upper, middle, and lower. Then I would expect to find people themselves distinguishing further in the middle social class, say between a bustling upper-middle level (who stand directly below the very highest ranking families) and a lower-middle level of "good, solid, ordinary people." In the lower social class, judging from work that has been done by W. Lloyd Warner and others, my attention would probably be called to "poor but honest, hard-working, and respectable" upper-lowers and "dirty, immoral, chronic reliefers" lower-lowers, who, still quoting others in the community, "live like animals." But the boundaries between strata would not be easy to fix. In actuality gradations between families and individuals flow continuously. Particular cases might be hard to classify. Conceivably parents might rank high in social estimation while their son, due to his "wrong" friends, stands far below them. Equally tragically, a son and daughter might move up and leave their parents lower on the social-class ladder.

Each social class in an American town possesses a distinct culture, though, of course, it also shares many of its customs and artifacts with other social levels. Toothbrushes, monotheism, monogamy, English, handshakes, shaving, and cooking are a few of the many traits most Americans hold in common. Important, too, are beliefs that the whole town shares: the government has a right to tax (but shouldn't do so excessively), science and progress are good things, religion is vital, and democracy is a fine form of government. In other things—recreation, drinking habits, diet, dress, house furnishings, reading matter, topic of conversation, taste in music, painting, and other pure arts, the style in which English is spoken, and ways of handling emotion—social classes diverge.

TO REACH THE TOP

Like a ladder that attracts children to climb, our social classes invite upward mobility. Due to cultural differences between strata and for other reasons that I shall take up immediately, it is hard to climb in the social-class system. A person born in the lower-lower class has only a remote chance of acquiring the motivation, education, occupation, income, and other props that will make him accepted and allow him to move confidently in upper-class circles. Nothing prevents him from trying to climb, and in that sense we do have an open-class system. Plays, soap operas, and magazine fiction offer the fantasy of marriage as a means of social climbing. Cultural differences, however, severely limit the possibility of romance skipping across social-class boundaries. A suitor of lower standing finds an upper-class girl's manner stiff and affected.

CULTURE VARIES WITH SOCIAL CLASS IN METROPOLITAN SAN FRANCISCO

Upper class   These people are not compulsive about attending church every Sunday; they take religion casually. They keep aloof from neighbors' opinions and avoid becoming involved in neighborhood affairs. They enjoy a before-dinner cocktail and have one at least twice a week. They heavily stress manners and decorum in rearing children and frequently use physical punishment.

Upper-middle class   Husbands in this social class like to "do-it-themselves"; they build furniture, paint and plaster their homes. On this level people are generally trusting and nondogmatic in their attitude toward others and in their relationship to children, whom, however, they spank frequently. They put much stress on moving up in the social-class hierarchy and perceive that occupation and education strongly influence success. They go in for sports, both as participants and spectators, and believe that boys should play rugged games.

Lower-middle class   These are people much concerned about men and boys acting masculinely and women femininely. They are easily shocked by taking the Lord's name in vain. They prefer to stay home rather than go out, especially on weekends. "Togetherness" is practiced when the whole family engages in the same activities. Husbands like to garden. Men are also fond of recalling their experiences while they served in the armed forces. Being puritanical, especially with respect to drinking and sex, it is not surprising that these people also attend church regularly and spend considerable time in church groups.

Upper-lower class*   The husband dominates the family, as indeed people in this social class believe he should. Children should be neat, obedient, orderly, and subservient to parents. Men prefer a tough, outdoor, masculine role. Yet husbands help their wives in many tasks, like dishwashing and shopping. One has to get ahead, these people believe. When men drink they prefer beer and drink it in a neighborhood tavern.

Lower-lower class*   On this level people express the greatest amount of authoritarianism. They are harshly intolerant of children who flaunt parents' orders or who are messy. They don't like to hear off-color stories told in mixed company.

* Both upper-lower and the lower-lower folk tend to be other-directed. They are people afraid of losing popularity. Hence they try to conform and teach children not to be characters. They are ambitious for their children, expecting that youngsters can and will reach a higher social position than they did. Yet, they don't evaluate formal schooling very highly. They often complain of sleeplessness, ulcers, migraine headaches, nightmares, and inability to relax. Economic security concerns them very much. They tend to feel that the lot of the average man is getting worse, not better.

Harold M. Hodges, Jr., "Social Stratification in a Pacific Coast Metropolitan Area: An Exploratory Analysis," unpublished, c. 1960.

Her behavior inhibits him and dampens his ardor. His actions and speech strike her as graceless and uncouth.

Upward mobility is severely impeded because it costs money. To move in upper-ranking circles requires living in the right neighborhood. A large, attractive house set in a landscaped plot brings higher rank than a dilapidated two-room cottage of nondescript design huddled in a row of monotonously similar dwellings. The right possessions displayed inside the house are equally essential for high social rank. They are the props which, when viewed by visitors, validate social worth. All these credentials cost money, which means that income is fundamental to social-class position. How income is earned itself counts for a great deal. Professional men, proprietors, and managers of big businesses rank above clerks, who in the hierarchy of occupations stand above semiskilled and unskilled workers. A large-scale social system contains a heterogeneous assortment of jobs that pay a wide range of wages and salaries. Jobs that require considerable training not only carry highest prestige but pay top salaries. Therefore, families of men who hold top positions can afford to—in fact, for the sake of the husband's career they must—live as befits people who are up near the social pinnacle. More routine jobs pay less. Therefore, middle-income families build or buy smaller, less elaborate houses and furnish them more modestly. They also move in middle social circles. Ranked near the bottom are no less vital but far more poorly paid jobs that unskilled workers fill. The community assigns these people to the lowest social ranks. For lower-class men to win more prestigeful jobs that pay more money, with which in turn they can "buy" higher social esteem, they must have burning ambition. They must be able to afford long years of schooling and then restlessly strive after promotion. The road to the top is longest for lower-class folk. As a class they show the smallest inclination to fight their way up.

Promotion up the social-class ladder is one of the choice rewards we offer people who are both willing and able to acquire the special skills that our industrial social system requires. Higher standing in America means greater opportunities for the best medical and psychiatric care, though it no longer carries longer life expectancy since advances made in medicine are available to all social classes. People of high prestige receive more consideration from their peers and even from public servants who rank below them. They have more power in economic and political affairs. They have greater access to those things which they believe bring happiness: bigger houses, cleaner heat, choicer food, opportunity to travel. Even in public schools their children receive a better education and more readily win admission to whatever college they prefer to enter. True, not everybody at the top is making a very important contribution to society; the class system works far too imperfectly for that. Also, everybody isn't supposed to strive to reach the top. If upward mobility were completely free, what would we do with millions of managers, doctors, and other professionals? Who would wash dishes, sweep the floor, load trucks, and keep records? These low-ranking jobs are also important but don't require special skills. Hence persons who fill them can't acquire as much of what our culture defines as happiness as highly trained people.

Now we understand why Kaska and Hopi Indians are spared from both the incentives and stresses found in a social-class system. Among them all men do practically the same kind of work; a professional-managerial class and an unskilled labor component are not present. Income differences actually are small. Small-scale or middle-range social systems with their slight division of labor lack the degree of social differentiation and cultural elaboration neces-sary to institute systems of social inequality. Even though their life expectancy is lower and they have a smaller range of goods to choose from, compared to an American town all Kaska or Hopi Indians are much more nearly equal in their opportunities for life, liberty, and the pursuit of happiness.

Despite social class inequalities, ours has been a stable country. Revolution-ary dissatisfaction has at times almost reached explosive thresholds but on the whole it has been kept in check. One reason the system has worked so well, that is, with so little friction and resentment offered by our lower-ranking mil-lions, is our growing national prosperity. We have always managed to produce enough wealth to permit low-ranking families to add constantly to their mate-rial comforts. Dissatisfaction remained mild; its expression in apathy and delinquency never became grounds for questioning the class system. Social leg-islation, too, although it has not gone as far as in poorer European countries, has helped stabilize our social system. Particularly during the Great Depression it drew heavily from the wealthy to finance government-supported social secu-rity for the needy. The wealthy grumbled darkly about socialism and high taxes but they paid up and so bought stability for the pyramid on which they sit.

INFLEXIBLE SOCIAL DISTINCTIONS—QUOM AND CASTE

Compared to us, Swat makes far more inflexible social distinctions,[2] for in Swat a son inherits his father's position and expects to retain it throughout his life. Main Swat valley contains more than two dozen quoms. (I will not translate the word quom yet because I cannot do so without contaminating its existential meaning. Later, when I have made you perceive the concept as it is understood in Swat, I will introduce a rough, English equivalent.) The first two quoms are nearly tied for top rank: Saints, who claim a special relationship to Heaven or descent from the Prophet Muhammad, and Pakhtuns, landowning descendants of the valley's conquerors. Below them

[2] Fredrik Barth, "The System of Social Stratification in Swat, North Pakistan," in E. R. Leach, ed., *Aspects of Caste in South-India, Ceylon and North-West Pakistan,* Cambridge Papers in Social Anthropology, no. 2, 1960.

come the quom of Mullah, several craftsmen quoms (like carpenter and black-smith, who claim descent from biblical King David), the quoms of agricultural tenants and laborers, of herders, and, finally, very, very low-ranking quoms like those of washerman, barber, rope and thong maker, and dancer. A Swati will tell you that each quom is rigidly endogamous, marriage occurring only between members of the same social level. Endogamy actually does occur but marriage is also readily hypergamous, a wife rising from a quom lower in rank than her husband's. Hypergamy saves a groom's family considerable bridewealth.

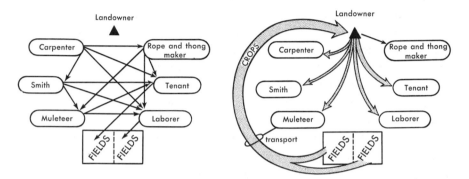

The caste system in Swat and other parts of Pakistan and India provides specialized services to support agriculture. How various castes cooperate to farm a landlord's fields is diagramed in the drawing on the left. After the muleteer has brought in the crop the landlord (in North India he is called the jajman) remunerates the specialists (the village kamins) with traditionally fixed amounts of grain and straw. (*Fredrik Barth, "The System of Social Stratification in Swat, North Pakistan," in E. R. Leach, ed.,* Aspects of Caste in South India, Ceylon and North-West Pakistan, *Cambridge Papers in Social Anthropology, no. 2, 1960; courtesy of Cambridge University Press.*)

Although all quoms are not found in every village, when they do exist together each contributes a distinctive service or plays a specific, useful role in social organization. To see the quoms collaborate let us look at a village. In any Swat village land is owned either by militant Pakhtuns or by holy Saints who have received it as gifts from landholders. Whatever his quom the owner supplies the main capital, land. He makes contracts with members of the tenant and farm-laborer quoms to work the land with plows and other equipment that members of the carpenter and blacksmith quoms will provide and maintain. The rope and thong maker supplies cordage, bridles, sieves, and brooms for the tenants as well as for the transport worker, who under contract moves produce off the fields. The landlord enjoys top rank and is the pivot around whom these specialized relationships revolve. Once the harvest is cut he divides part of its yield among the members of the other quoms who worked for him. No money changes hands. To each specialist goes a traditionally fixed

amount of produce, regardless of market value, as remuneration for his productive role. The lion's share belongs to the capitalist. Services performed by
still other village specialists belonging to other quoms, like the barber and
potter, also earn a reward in kind rather than cash. The term jajamani system
is convenient to designate South Asian systems of this type in which several
specialists cooperate in return for fixed rewards.

Nobody in Swat can rank precisely all quoms of the valley in terms of relative power and esteem. No more could anybody rank the thousands of castes
of India in a continuous series, from highest to lowest. Only quoms found
together in a given locality are significant in a person's life. Therefore, within
a given village relative power and rank are clear. Major power, as I have said,
lies with the landowners, Pakhtuns or Saints. Wealth enhances a landlord's
social esteem. Additional power comes to Pakhtun chiefs who, formerly more
than today, organize followers in defensive and offensive military blocs. Be-

Barbers are the professional message carriers of rural
Pakistan and India. Of course, they also cut men's hair,
shave beards, shave them under the arm and cut their
fingernails and toe nails. A barber helps to dress and
anoint a bridegroom and in many places his wife acts
as a village beautician. For large wedding parties in
some villages barbers cook huge quantities of rice and
meat. The recompense which rural barbers receive for
these duties under the jajmani system by no means
leaves them poor, yet their caste ranks relatively low.

low the landowners, quoms are ranked by the degree of respectability conventionally attached to their nominal calling. Families in the tenant-farmer quom outrank those in the goldsmith, carpenter, and blacksmith quoms, though all these quoms pass as somewhat respectable. Lower down in the hierarchy, but still respectable, come cotton-carder, oil presser, and leatherworker quoms. Why they are below the carpenter or goldsmith quoms no Swati can explain and no anthropologist can determine. Then we cross the line to utterly unrespectable quoms, some of whose members may be fairly well off financially: barber, dancer (the women appear unveiled before strangers and, even more disgracefully, prostitute their bodies), washerman, and rope and thong maker. A quom's rank is symbolized in behavior and with the aid of artifacts. For example, landlords dress in white, carry pistols or rifles, and wear bandoliers. Others accord them deference, rising when they enter a room. A laborer acknowledges his low rank by accepting payment from a person above him or by entering into a contractual relationship with a landlord. In feasts Pakhtuns and Saints symbolize their high prestige by forming an inner circle while persons of lower standing make up the two outer circles which eat later.

As I said, a man inherits his quom from his father, but nothing compels him to follow the occupation called for by his quom name. It does not follow, however, that a Mullah (the word means religious scholar) who acts as a carpenter loses membership in his quom and becomes a carpenter. As long as he and his descendants associate mainly with kinsmen known as Mullahs they will remain Mullah. If the larger community forgets the original quom of his descendants then they will become known as carpenter. In similar fashion new quoms appear as a hitherto unknown occupation grows up. Only specialists from traditional quoms are available to perform the new roles and in time some of these specialists become known by the tasks they do. A Pakhtun loses his quom and his rank if he sells his land, the principal foundation on which his status depends.

Quoms in Swat jar incongruously with Islamic religious values which assert that all men are equal. How, then, can such a hard and obvious system of inequality be maintained? The answer to this question enables us to understand all the caste systems found in other parts of Muslim Pakistan, through much of Hindu India, and in Buddhist Ceylon. People in South Asia assume, largely implicitly, that individuals born in different ethnic groups, castes, or quoms differ inherently from one another. People who stem from different social backgrounds automatically possess unequal social worth and diverse backgrounds can never blend. This underlying belief, which is almost nonexistent in the west, is stronger than Islam and perpetuates the quoms of Swat. Whenever someone measures the amount of respect he should accord to another, depending on the latter's quom, he perpetuates the caste system. Whenever a man is ashamed lest he or his family do something that is appropriate only to a lower or higher standing quom, his shame keeps the lines demarcating one quom from another firmly defined.

Explicit and rigid borders are essential to caste. They distinguish castes from nameless social classes across whose vague boundaries mobility and marriage take place with ideal impunity. The weight of Hindu scriptural authority in India heavily justifies India's caste system; it makes caste sacred for the Hindus, though not for Indian Muslims who follow the same form of social exclusiveness. In order to maintain the world, Hindus believe, God created four main orders of man. The first sprang from his mouth. They are the Brahmans to whom he assigned by right the tasks of teaching, study, charity, and performance of sacrificial rites. The second order of men sprang from his arms. To these Kshatriya he assigned the hereditary duty of protecting people as well as of charity, sacrifice, and study. Vaisya, who sprang from his thighs, have cattle tending, commerce, and agriculture as their ascribed occupations but they, too, may study, give charity, and perform sacrificial rites. To serve these three ranks is a Sudra's inherited duty. These are the four varnas of Hinduism and the yardstick that ranks some of India's thousands of castes or jatis. All jatis belonging to the Brahman varna possess the greatest in-dwelling purity. Just as everything below the navel is impure compared to anything above, so pollution rather than purity is the inherent quality of the Sudra, who sprang from God's feet. Sudras are not even privileged to overhear the sacred scriptures being recited. Even more polluted are millions of people who belong to lower-ranking jatis, the Outcastes. With great sympathy and imagination Mahatma Gandhi renamed these Untouchable millions Harijans, meaning Children of God. He, like other reformers, dedicated much of his life to enhancing these spiritually polluted people's prestige and privileges.

The scripturally founded belief that impure castes can pollute the pure ones enforces social distance between them. Precise rules sometimes govern the proper distance that must be maintained. For example, a member of a higher jati may refuse to take food or drink from a caste inferior to his own. Marriage, of course, is prohibited (except for hypergamy). Formerly even sitting or traveling with a low-caste person was forbidden but the advent of buses and railroad trains helped to eradicate that avoidance.

European scholars have offered several explanations to account for the Indian caste system. A favorite theory carries the foundations of caste back to that dim period when speakers of an Indo-European (or Aryan) language first entered North India, probably around 1500 B.C. These so-called Aryans are supposed to have conquered autochthonous Dravidians (the overwhelming portion of Dravidian-speaking people today live in South India) and devised caste rules in order to keep their descent uncontaminated by inferior, subject people. Regardless of how the custom began, Hinduism gives sharp reasons why everyone should accept his caste station, no matter how low and un-

COMPLEX TRADITIONAL RULES GOVERN CASTE RIGHTS AND SERVICES

Naggal village (Punjab, India) has castes of Hindu cultivators and castes of Hindu and Muslim artisans and menials. The artisans and menials, as the following examples illustrate, have rights to perform definite remunerative duties.

The Hindu watercarrier supplies water to such families of cultivators as can afford to make use of his services. There are three men who do this work and each has a certain number of client families allotted to him. He receives 27 pounds of grain every harvest for each pipkin of water which he filled during the previous 6 months and claims 2 garments each year. Besides regular payments he also gets certain dues at marriages and on other special occasions. One watercarrier family also farms.

The ten Muslim barbers in addition to their professional duties join the minstrel in taking news of marriage and other important events to other villages. For this each receives small cash payments from each person to whom he is sent as well as from whoever employs him. For barbering he receives at each harvest 9 pounds of grain plus one extra bundle of crop consisting of about 4 pounds of grain and 8 pounds of straw for every plow owned by his clients. All barbers also cultivate land and formerly this caste performed considerable petty surgery.

Fourteen families of Hindu leatherworkers live in Naggal but most of the men work for wages as whole-time field laborers. Two families do cobbler's work for which they receive cash payments. Ten families serve cultivators by repairing their clients' shoes or the harness of clients' yoke animals and doing other necessary leather work. Dues at each harvest are 9 pounds of grain for each plow owned by clients. At marriage and on festive occasions the leatherworker also helps his client and for this he is paid in food and cash. Skins of dead animals, except young stock, by right belong to the leatherworker.

The five Hindu scavenger families help out farmers with field labor for which they are

---

privileged. A person is born many times and dies many deaths. In each of his incarnations he incurs a certain karma, which stems from the good and evil that he is capable of performing. Good deeds earn good karma and allow a person to be reborn into a higher caste station than someone who incurred bad karma in his former incarnation. As one sows, so one reaps; only reaping, in Hindu belief, doesn't come until rebirth. Once he is reborn in a given caste, a man's future karma depends on dutifully carrying out the obligations that belong to his position. His duties, or his dharma, he owes both to himself (so that by performing them he may earn good karma) and to his social system, which can thrive only through every caste's God-given contribution. Confusion would reign if hewers of wood, that is, members of the Sudra varna, chose to live like Brahmans. Everyone's "salvation," then, depends on properly fulfilling the roles of the station where, in accordance with his former conduct, he rightly belongs. Unquestionably, it is preferable that a man perform his God-given duty imperfectly rather than execute the tasks properly belonging paid wages. In addition women of this caste clean the cultivators' houses and cattle sheds. Each receives 46 pounds of grain at every harvest and 1 garment each July from every client family plus some bread daily. A scavenger himself, for removing dead animals, gets 9 pounds of grain every harvest and a handful of grain every third day for every plow owned by his clients. Unlike elsewhere, scavengers in Naggal need not remove human excrement from houses because people use the village fields as latrines. In case of illness women of the family perform sanitation duties.

There is only one family of Muslim minstrels. The man's chief role is to deliver messages. For this he is paid cash. His womenfolk beat a small drum and sing at marriages. For these services at each harvest they receive 9 pounds of grain and a bundle of unthreshed crop from each family of cultivators or from each group of three farmers who cultivate jointly. At marriages the minstrel by right gets food for his whole family plus cash.

The village lacks resident carpenters and blacksmiths, these Muslim specialists coming to Naggal from a neighboring village. They repair all wooden and iron implements used by cultivators and also make such implements as are simple to construct. The customer always supplies wood, iron, and coal. Every harvest these men each receive 36 pounds of grain for each plow they service and a bundle of straw (weighing about 80 pounds) for each unit of three or more farmers cultivating jointly.

Before the British came to India the Muslim drum beater caste possessed quite an important role. Whenever two villages fought, drum beaters led the men by the beat of drum to the place of battle. Today their main task is to call back by drumming parties that have gone out to search for lost animals. Each man gets 9 pounds of grain from each family of cultivators or from each unit of three farmers who cultivate jointly. At a marriage he claims food and cash and he also begs for extra grain at harvest time. Five of the six village drum beater families also farm.

Sher Singh, *An Economic Survey of Naggal, a Village in the Ambala District of the Punjab,* Punjab Village Surveys, no. 5, 1933.

to another caste well. This is Hinduism's philosophical justification of caste. However, remember that caste is also justified in terms of a popular, implicit belief that people born from diverse backgrounds are inherently different and basically unequal.

Ethnocentric prejudice makes it hard for many westerners to appreciate how logically caste and religion integrate in Indian culture. Nearly two hundred years of democratic revolutions have made us blind to the genius by which caste justifiably allocates people to unequally privileged statuses and can count on each status performing duties that will maintain a full life. Priests, warriors, rulers, farmers, merchants, shoemakers, and scavengers—all contribute. A constant supply of specialists is guaranteed by the rule that a son must follow his father's caste and occupation. As in Swat, at least in villages, the caste system requires little money. Each farmer is a pivot who rewards his carpenter, blacksmith, barber, watercarrier, and other specialists with grain and extra gifts on stated occasions. The specialist in turn exchanges some of his grain for other necessities. The system has always been flexible enough to permit new jobs to be filled when they arose. Even upward mobility is allowed, though scarcely for an individual. Rather, an entire local section of a caste can rigorously discipline itself and change its style of life in order to rise in purity. Say the group gives up meat, foregoes alcohol, and refuses any longer to accept food and water from a caste that formerly it recognized to be superior. In effect the mobile group subordinates this other caste as it pushes upward, narrowing social distance between itself and the top flight Brahmans.

I have emphasized the way Hinduism justifies caste and expects the system to work. As in many well-designed social systems, people in India haven't always adhered to the ideal. Many low castes have found Hinduism's justifications very poor solace for the deprivation and frustrations they had to endure. There have always been critics who condemned one or another feature of caste: Gautama the Buddha, who lived 500 years before Christ, was one such critic; Nanak, the fifteenth-century Sikh prophet, was another. Caste survived both. In the British period reformers like Keshub, Vivekananda, and Gandhi arose and sought to reconcile traditional Hinduism to more egalitarian western dogmas. The Constitution of republican India today forbids caste discrimination. In effect it also prohibits enforcement of scriptural caste privileges. Any practice smacking of untouchability has been made a punishable offense. Time-tried flexibility still stands caste in good stead. Unwillingly the system yields to these new demands based on western values. Yet it persists, for example, by becoming an active force in democratic political life.

PREJUDICE AND FEAR

Man has found other means in addition to class and caste to maintain social distance in his social relationships. They need not all be reviewed in detail. One principle shows up, for instance, in segregation based primarily on any known degree of Negro ancestry, a form of social segregation which in the United States is currently being driven from its legally entrenched position in the South. As in India with respect to caste, constitutional rights have been invoked to protect Negroes from discrimination that violated their rights as Americans. By declaring school, bus, train, and restaurant segregation illegal in the South the courts succeeded in reducing social distance between persons of known Negro and non-Negro ancestry, at least in public places. A vast gap, of course, remains including a ban on intermarriage. In the northern states, too, Negroes and non-Negroes each enforce strong prejudice against intermarriage and informally whites are able to prevent Negroes from moving into non-Negro residential areas and enjoying many facilities.

Nationalism supports another kind of chafing social distance. About a hundred sovereign nations comprising the international society stand divided by customs barriers, immigration policies, mutual mistrust, and language. Advances in transportation have made it easy and cheap to visit almost any of these countries and education fans the urge to see new places. Yet, foreign travel depends on whether the citizen's own country considers him qualified for a passport, that "vicious instrument," as Myrdal calls it, of state control. Then a would-be visitor must usually induce the prospective host country to visa his passport, thereby granting him permission to enter. In some respects affluence in the world's richest countries militates most strongly against our society's achieving closer international integration. Particularly in economic matters, centripetal national integration is actually increasing, with exceptions like the Common Market, and economic integration between nations growing weaker. What rich nations fear, of course, is that cheap goods and labor from abroad will flood them and grievously upset their high standard of living. Skilled labor and professional persons are allowed some freedom in international mobility, but unskilled labor is rigidly excluded. Most of us agree that this is only reasonable. What other course do we know and dare follow? Myrdal says, now that the welfare state has brought almost everything that dreamers, planners, and fighters of an earlier generation sought in the way of a "better life," it is time that "there should again be dreamers, planners, and fighters, in the midst of our nations, who would take upon themselves the important social function . . . of raising our sights—so far ahead that their proponents again form a definite minority in their nations. This is only possible if they enlarge the scope of their interests to encompass the world scene. They must again become internationalists. . . ."[3]

FURTHER READING

Robert H. Lowie introduces the topic of social stratification in *Social Organization* (New York, 1948), chap. 12, as do Charles P. Loomis and J. Allan Beegle in *Rural Social Systems* (New York, 1950), chaps. 10–11; Arnold M. Rose, *Sociology* (New York, 1956), chap. 8; and John J. Honigmann, *The World of Man* (New York, 1959), chap. 27. Oliver C. Cox, *Caste, Class, and Race* (Garden City, N. Y., 1948) offers more substantial coverage and so do the many papers that make up Reinhard Bendix and Seymour Martin Lipset, eds., *Class, Status and Power* (New York, 1953). Kurt B. Mayer, *Class and Society* (Garden City, N.Y., 1955) is a succinct summary. A number of these books also consider estates and race as isolative devices used in social systems. A classic source on age and men's associations is Heinrich Schurtz, *Altersklassen und Maennerbuende* (Berlin, 1902). S. N. Eisenstadt, *From Generation to Generation* (London, 1956) provides a systematic understanding of age groupings and their relationship to other features of culture.

J. H. Hutton reviews *Caste in India: Its Nature, Function and Origins,* 2nd ed.

[3] Gunnar Myrdal, *An International Economy* (New York, 1956).

(Oxford, 1951). McKim Marriott surveys complexity of *Caste Ranking and Community Structure in Five Regions of India and Pakistan,* Deccan College Monograph Series, no. 23, 1960. See also R. P. Masani, "Caste and the Structure of Society," in G. T. Garratt, ed., *The Legacy of India* (Oxford, 1937). A Hindu philosopher's idealized view of caste and its scriptural sanctions will be found in Pandhari-Nath Prabhu, *Hindu Social Organization,* new rev. ed. (Bombay, 1954), chap. 8. William H. Wiser examines *The Hindu Jajmani System* (Lucknow, 1936), as do Oscar Lewis and Victor Barnouw in their paper "Caste and the Jajmani System in a North Indian Village," *The Scientific Monthly,* 83 (1956), 66-81. All of these accounts also examine recent changes in intercaste relations. L. S. S. O'Malley describes earlier aspects of such change in "The Hindu Social System" in a book he edits, *Modern India and the West* (London, 1941). *Untouchable,* a novel by Mulk Raj Anand (London, 1947), grippingly follows a Harijan's life. To finish it requires a strong stomach. Similar in subject matter is Hazari's autobiography, *An Indian Outcaste* (London, 1951). Bryce F. Ryan's monograph, *Caste in Modern Ceylon* (New Brunswick, N.J., 1953) helps to understand caste as it is practiced anywhere in South Asia.

Closer to home, anthropologists and sociologists have written several accounts of the class system in specific American communities. Three recent books deal with the South, Morton Rubin, *Plantation County* (Chapel Hill, N. C., 1951); Hylan Lewis, *Blackways of Kent* (Chapel Hill, N. C., 1955); and John Kenneth Morland, *Millways of Kent* (Chapel Hill, N.C., 1958). Lewis is concerned primarily with the Negroes and Morland with white mill workers of the same South Carolina town. Written earlier but still enlightening are John Dollard, *Caste and Class in a Southern Town,* 3rd ed. (New York, 1957); Hortense Powdermaker, *After Freedom* (New York, 1939), both of which deal with the same Deep South community; and Allison Davis, Burleigh B. Gardner, and Mary R. Gardner, *Deep South* (Chicago, 1941). A. B. Hollingshead describes the impact of social class on school-going adolescents in *Elmtown's Youth* (New York, 1949). The same midwest community is described in W. Lloyd Warner and Associates, *Democracy in Jonesville* (New York, 1949). See also "A Sociologist Looks at an American Community; He Finds that Rockford, Ill., like the Rest of the U.S. Has Six Social Classes," *Life,* 27, no. 11 (September 12, 1949), 103-119. The classic anthropological study of social class and the first in a multivolume New England community study is *The Social Life of a Modern Community,* by W. Lloyd Warner and Paul S. Lunt (New Haven, 1941). Roy Lewis and Angus Maude examine *The English Middle Classes* (New York, 1950) and C. Wright Mills the American middle class in *White Collar* (New York, 1951).

8

Agreeing to Communicate

Our reverence for the nobility of manhood will not be lessened by the knowledge that Man is, in substance and in structure, one with the brutes; for, he alone possesses the marvelous endowment of intelligible and rational speech, whereby, in the secular period of his existence, he has slowly accumulated and organised the experience which is almost wholly lost with the cessation of every individual life in other animals; so that, now he stands raised upon it as on a mountain top, far above the level of his humble fellows. . . .

Thomas H. Huxley[1]

THE SIGN THAT ISN'T A SIGN

How thin human relations would be without the traffic of communication. Lacking means to exchange messages, no individual could share a fraction of his experience or, what is even more important, explain to others any discovery he makes that leads to coping more effectively with his world. How, then, without communication could there be much culture? Groups, principles of descent, political organization, authority—all would be virtually non-existent in the absence of humans' ability to transmit ideas. Communication also reinforces group morale and social solidarity, thereby strengthening organizations so they continue to yield the satisfactions we expect from them.

We communicate whenever we design something—a window display, book, commencement address, high-fi record, alarm bell, musical composition, mask of a god, or travel poster—that succeeds in calling attention to its inbuilt message. But suppose I construct a simple, attractive sign in which an olive green circle of paint on a pure white background stands for the message, "Stop, danger ahead!" Why when I try it out doesn't it register as I intend? How does it happen that others do not see the message which I thought I

[1] *Man's Place in Nature*, authorized ed. (New York, 1902), pp. 155-156.

had built into the sign? People admire my sign, commend it for its use of form and color, and admire its simplicity, but they don't stop or even experience any feeling of caution. What I neglected is only the most important element in communication; I failed to get anybody to agree beforehand that a green splotch on a white background means "Stop, danger ahead!" Successful communication depends on prior agreement concerning the meaning of any message-bearing elements.

Eyes, ears, speech organs, prehensile hands that can gesture and paint signs, man's extensive power to reflect on experience and to symbolize experience in signs are the biological bases of communication. But they won't suffice for communication without social conventions that establish common meanings concerning what the signs mean. Once agreement over meanings is reached, then it makes sense to use a red signal to stop a train, or for a hard-working laborer to accept a piece of paper in payment of his week's work, or to put sheets of engraved paper away in safe-deposit boxes, or to use any of the countless other signs with which our culture is filled. Signal lights, money, and bonds are more than they seem to be, just as a uniform and its insignia are more than cloth and metal. But whatever significance they have, they assume only through convention. Agreements make them so and if agreements are changed or lost, then their significance will also alter or will vanish completely, the way Egyptian hieroglyphs lost their meaning not to regain it until Champollion found their key.

LANGUAGE IS ARBITRARY

Communication in all its aspects, from sign language to mass communications, is too vast a subject for this chapter. I shall narrow the topic down to language, a system of agreed-upon vocal sounds with agreed-upon rules for combining them in messages. More creatures than man use vocal sounds to bear messages which ear picks up and brain decodes. Animals signal one another with mating calls and birds utter shrill cries of assembly and alarm. Birds that have grown up in distant areas cannot always "understand" one another's cries, so apparently even among birds growing up together brings about a measure of conventional agreement.[2] But a big gap separates animal calls from every known human language.

We haven't much choice when it comes to choosing between contradictory accounts of how language is supposed to have originated. One theory is no better than the next. According to Genesis man simply began to name the separate parts of God's creation. How this extraordinary ability arose the Bible doesn't specify. Later theorists made good this Biblical deficiency.

[2] Hubert Frings and Mable Frings, "The Language of Crows," *Scientific American*, 201, no. 5 (1959), 119-131.

Language is God's direct gift to man. This idea nicely supplements the Bible but for most people it fails to explain anything.

The onomatopoeic (better known as the bow-wow) theory of language maintains that speech arose through imitating natural sounds. Now, a few words in many languages, like the name for the cuckoo and the peewit and apt terms like "slosh" in English, perhaps are onomatopoeic, but what about the bulk of our vocabulary? The theory can't explain most of language. Another version of this fancy supposes that a natural tendency exists for words to take on sounds to suit their meaning. A moment's thought exposes the weakness of that idea. Is it "eat," "essen," or "manger" that more perfectly suits the act of biting into a roast-beef sandwich with mustard? Personally I might find the Cree Indian verb "miitchiisiw" to be the perfect combination of sounds to represent this particular gustatory experience but how can I convince you in the event that you see gemlike perfection in the Urdu verb "khana?" Words are arbitrary. Save for a few onomatopoeic exceptions, words have no intrinsic connection with the task, object, or relationship that they are by convention supposed to designate.

The interjection (pooh-pooh) theory claims that speech originated in cries resembling animal cries. But it fails to explain how interjections of dismay, pain, joy, determination, and fear ever came to be converted into words. And how shall grammatical rules that govern the meaningful arrangement of words be accounted for? Nor is the harmony (ding-dong) theory a bit more useful. In fact, it complicates things because it supposes that every experience calls up a specific set of sounds which harmonize with it. Sighting a dog moving rapidly strikes the observer as akin to the sound of a bell and so he exclaims bell-like, "dog runs." We are back in the deathless fallacy that words bear an intrinsic relationship with what they refer to, a notion that any comparative study of language easily demolishes. According to gesture theory, language arose from nudges, imitative acts, pleading looks, and similar expressive bodily movements like those we still use to amplify our spoken remarks.

Composite theories of no greater helpfulness combine several of these pat little formulas. For example, one recent essay says that speech began with consonant-plus-vowel combinations like maa or baa. Such sound units, the writer argues, are easiest to produce; don't children delight in these very syllables, speaking them early in life? Early men uttered such syllables involuntarily in the course of putting out maximum effort to accomplish some heavy task. Gradually the words came to stand for commands to join in and help. Language, the writer concludes began with verbs for commanding attention and help. In time the proportion of verbs in spoken utterances declined while that of nouns and adjectives increased.

One reason why it is impossible to choose between any of these theories is that none has any more support than the other. Lacking direct historical

Radio Corporation of America

Gebildete Dame, 65/I,65, mit guter Figur, o. Anhang, mit 3
Raum - Neubau - Wohng. u. Ba
(I. Etg.), wünscht sich z
2. Ehe, feinen, gebildete
Herrn in guter Position. Nich
raucher! Zuschr. u. A 117
an die Geschäftsstelle der NR

You will not understand the meanings of one or more of these symbols. You have not been in situations where, by word of mouth or through their acts, people apprised you of their meanings and you agreed to accept them, that is, you agreed to respond to the sign as they intended you should. A child growing up, a college student enrolled in German, a motorist who studies a foreign road map, and an anthropologist attentively observing greetings in an exotic community are all learning to share conventions governing the meaning of symbols.

evidence, they simply speculate about what happened. One thing is certain. Men didn't originally agree to communicate vocally through self-consciously discussing the possibilities of doing so! With that warning, I propose to observe the rise of language among a hitherto languageless people, the imaginary Mafa. My object is simply to demonstrate a few simple facts about how every language is constructed and works. Not only are the Mafa imaginary; I will describe them acquiring language through an impossible process. My fable further credits the unsophisticated Mafa with far too much comprehension of language principles. Only someone who has studied linguistics, the subject-matter of this chapter, would possess an equivalent knowledge of how language operates. Most people in the world, including Americans, even if they give occasional thought to grammatical rules, have never learned to be as self-conscious about their verbal habits as the Mafa will turn out to be.

AN IMPOSSIBLE FABLE

Long ago the forest-dwelling Mafa somehow managed to live without language. Then a wise elder observed a simple but highly significant fact about the structure of his own and other human bodies. Every person, using his nose and mouth, constantly inspired and expired relatively long streams of air into and out of his lungs. With some amusement, the elder discovered that he could employ various parts of his mouth and throat to disturb the air column as it moved into or out of his lungs. For example, he could stop it by pressing his tongue up against the gum-ridge just behind his upper teeth or by clamping his lips shut. By not vibrating and then vibrating his vocal cords (muscles in his throat), he could make the escaping column of air alternately soundless and audible. He found this discovery fun but as with many idle discoveries that occur to intelligent men this one led the Mafa to think. (Whether or not he could think much without help from language has nothing to do with the point of this fable and the question would distract us unnecessarily if we pursued it.) Before following his thoughts, however, let me explain why the Mafa's discovery is highly significant for understanding language. Language relies on speech and speech is communication achieved mainly through disturbing in an agreed-upon series of ways a column of air passing from and into the lungs. Few languages interrupt inspired air and use it in communication; generally exhaled air is stopped, constricted, deflected, or rolled around in the mouth to make the basic sounds by which speakers transmit messages.

The clever Mafa elder thought about these possibilities and worked out a system of about a dozen specific ways of disturbing the air column during its passage from the lungs. That is, he devised a number of minimal unit sounds which could serve as basic elements in a communications code. Since language is meaningful only because at each point it has been made a matter of convention, we cannot suppose that the Mafa elder devised his code alone. Others must have accepted these elements as the basic sound units on which Mafa language would depend.

One sound our elder formed by stopping the column of air simply by momentarily pressing his tongue tip against the ridge just behind his upper teeth, at the same time not vibrating his vocal cords. We write this sound t. Then repeating the position of his tongue, he allowed his vocal cords to vibrate. We write that sound d. Now he had a pair of closely related yet contrasting sound units, t and d, one unvoiced and the other voiced. Such minimal sound units (not necessarily t and d, but these and similar units) form the basis of every language, though in themselves they have no meaning. Phonemes, as such agreed-upon, minimal units of linguistic significance are called, constitute the basic bricks with which every language is built. In some languages closely related sounds like t and d constitute a single phoneme; it is insignificant whether one is substituted for the other. Mafa is like English in that it makes a difference whether a speaker substitutes unvoiced t for voiced d. Try it; substitute t for d in "din" or d for t in "ten." Notice how the meaning of your utterance changes?

One cannot build a house with two bricks or communicate with two phonemes. The Mafa elder and his group continued to add to their collection of agreed upon phonemes. Our innovator next constricted the air as it passed between his lips and teeth; once he left his vocal cords loose and then he did it again with vocal cords vibrating. Thereby he added the contrasting units f and v to the Mafa stock of phonemes. Now they had four phonemes, still a far smaller number than any known language gets along with. He devised a third contrasting pair of sound units. He would stop the air column as it arose to the top of his throat by blocking it with his velum or soft palate. Thus he obtained voiceless k and its voiced companion g. At this point one of the group who had been following these oral maneuvers attentively and agreeing that each contrasting pair of phonemes which the elder produced would possess significance himself suggested some sound units. By performance he indicated that it might be a good idea to make a further distinction. In addition to the pair k and g, why not modify each by a little puff of breath placed after the sound itself? From two phonemes would come four, k, g, kh, gh.

There are languages, it is worth interrupting, that distinguish between aspirated and unaspirated consonants as zealously as English speakers distinguish between voicing and unvoicing. For example, in Urdu, the national language of Pakistan, it makes a difference whether one says taap or thap. The first means warmth, the second a slap or tap. It is not the vowel length (aa vs. a) alone that helps convey different meanings but aspiration of the voiceless stop, t, as well. The Mafa elder, however, would not accept the breath of air as a significant discriminating feature. He showed his dissent vigorously in gesture and so, failing agreement, the Mafa forewent the opportunity of making this kind of distinction between phonemes. English doesn't regard aspiration as significant either and, thanks to the Mafa elder's veto of the aspirate, we find it a bit easier to pronounce Mafa words correctly than we find it to pronounce correctly Urdu words in which aspiration is significant. The Mafa conclave considered and rejected other potential modifications of consonants, too, like palatalization, so common in Russian, in which the tongue acts as though it were going to pronounce a y during or directly after certain sounds. They rejected glottalization in which the vocal cords are firmly closed, compressing the air stream just before or during pronounciation of a sound. However, the Mafa did accept the voiceless glottal stop itself as a significant sound unit. I shall write it in these pages with a little hooked sign (').

As he continued developing a stock of workable phonemes, the elder produced a sound by completely shutting up air in his mouth. Instead of releasing it via the lips he passed it through his nose, the soft palate being conveniently lowered away in order to allow him to perform the deed. With his voice box vibrating during the operation he produced what English speakers recognize as a familiar voiced nasal sound, m. But the Mafa also made a contrasting voiceless sound for which English has no use. I invite you to agree that this latter phoneme of Mafa shall be written m̄. A voiceless nasal is not difficult to make; just keep your lips shut and sniff down your nose, as in the deprecatory hm, or, rather hm̄. You see, we do employ this sound, though not as part of language.

Much later when the Mafa learned to write they did what anthropologists who want to classify systematically the phonemes of a new language always do. They arranged their phonemes by the vocal organs and vocal techniques that go into producing them. Anthropologists make a chart. The kind of disturbance made in the air stream they list vertically along the left-hand margin. Horizontally across the top they note the organs mainly responsible for each phoneme, designating these organs by their adjectivial forms. In each contrasting pair of phonemes they wrote the voiceless variant first and then the voiced:

	Bilabial	Labiodental	Dental-alveolar	Velar	Glottal
Stops			t d	k g	ʼ
Spirants		f v			
Nasals	m̄ m				

No language contents itself solely with consonants. The Mafa elder further devised a small series of vowels which gave the consonants some substance. In forming this class of sounds he contorted his mouth into different shapes, each shape altering the sound of the escaping air stream. The conclave of Mafa agreed upon three vowels, one made high in front of the mouth (i, the vowel of English eat), one resonated low in the middle of the oral cavity (a, the vowel of English cot), and another high in back of the mouth (u, almost as in English loot but more like German gut). The group surrounding the elder allowed two significant (that is, phonemic) modifications of vowels; they accepted as a separate phoneme nasalization of i, made by sending part of the air stream up through the nose (pronounce the vowel of "eat" through your nose), and rounding of u, made by pronouncing u with the lips nicely pursed. Rounding produces the effect Germans call an umlaut.

So the Mafa ended up with 14 phonemes, a relatively small stock of building blocks with which to construct a language. Most languages fall within the range of from 12 to 60 phonemes. Languages situated at the lower end suffer no inability to communicate. At this point I must confess to having committed another oversimplification. Linguistic messages rely not only on significant consonants and vowels, that is, on so-called segmental phonemes, but also on the degree of stress words carry. Note what happens when you shift major stress from the first to the second syllable in the four-syllable utterance "lighthousekeeper." The way a speaker intones an utterance is further significant. In English, for example, it makes a difference in meaning whether or not I send my voice up at the end of a sentence. If I do, I ask a question; if I don't, and the sentence contains no clue in words like "when" or "why," then I am stating a fact. Stress and intonation are two examples of prosodic phonemes. The Mafa with 14 minimal, significant segments of sound and a small number of significant differences in stress and intonation, were quite well equipped to begin adding other elements that make a language.

Let us be clear about what the Mafa had. They possessed 14 distinctive segmental phonemes, each of which, they agreed, would make a difference in verbal communication. Now by combining these consonants and vowels with appropriate stress and intonation in a previously agreed-upon manner, they would be able to utter the most commonplace remarks, basest calumnies, most abstract ideas, and noblest sentiments of which they were capable. They would not always be quite able to say what they really meant, but can any speaker of Latin, Russian, English, or German claim more for his language? All of which indicates that there is no such thing as a language so primitive that it is barely able to communicate. But Mafa really couldn't yet communicate because they had not yet decided how the bricks should be laid, how phonemes should be used to express units of meaning. Only when a single phoneme, or more likely a combination of phonemes, is assigned a definite meaning, creating a morpheme, can proper linguistic communication begin. What the Mafa needed was a vocabulary.

Need I repeat that it is utterly fantastic to imagine that any language could have begun in this rational, deliberate fashion? Whatever the origin of language actually was, it is certain that languageless men didn't—couldn't—first decide on a stock of phonemes and then employ them to build words. Language evolved through use, not through deliberation. So please don't mistake my fable for speculative history.

HOW THE MAFA ACQUIRED A VOCABULARY

To design a vocabulary is to associate a particular meaning with a particular unit or units of vocal sound. We see the result when a Mafa today tells us that ma means forest, fa designates people or human beings, and the compound noun mafa is their name. The process of constructing a vocabulary occurs with rare self-consciousness whenever a scientist or manufacturer searches to find an expressive and hitherto unused name for a newly discovered phenomenon or marketable product. Words are much more frequently created spontaneously through use. What happened among the Mafa is what usually happens and it went something like this.

A Mafa found it useful to call others' attention to the forest. Each time he did so he regularly, for an unknown reason, employed the sound combination ma and no other. I want to stress that he originally employed this particle not because it already possessed any agreed upon meaning or because something about it harmonized with the bank of towering green trees and made ma peculiarly suitable to designate that kind of experience. Whatever social or linguistic meaning the particle ma eventually acquired, it acquired only through being used regularly to designate the same sector of experience. Other Mafa thus learned to look expectantly into the forest whenever they heard ma. More and more Mafa confidently said ma whenever they wished to direct attention to the forest. And so ma gradually acquired its meaning of forest. Unself-conscious convention had succeeded in taking a meaningless flow of disturbed air and had endowed it with specific meaning, a feat of no small magnitude. The particle ma became a morpheme, a minimal unit of sound with meaning. It would continue to bear that meaning until usage, again acting arbitrarily, associated it with some new bit of experience, with something other than the forest. Of course, the Mafa, like other people, were alert lest this happen too readily. A child who used ma for grass instead of for the woods was either ignored or reminded that a word regularly used for forest logically means forest and nothing else. Still, occasionally meanings do shift or else several meanings accrete to the same word. Changes in environment and culture help bring about altered meanings. Transporting the Mafa to a treeless desert before they could invent a word for desert might encourage them to rely on ma to designate the sandy waste. Centuries of agriculture might denude their home landscape in which case ma might either fall into obsolescence or be reassigned to designate something else.

Now I will describe how the morphemes t and ut originated in Mafa. The Mafa regularly suffixed t to the name of anything when they wished to designate two objects of that kind. They regularly attached the combination ut to the end of names when they wished to designate three or more objects of a kind. Thus t and ut came to "mean" dual and plural number respectively. But t and ut, like English s, en, es, are morphemes of a different type than Mafa ma and fa or English hat, ox. and box. It makes good sense if I simply utter the word hat, but it makes no sense (outside of certain restricted contexts) if I speak the morpheme s by itself. It has power of meaning, no question about that; but its meaning is less readily apparent than the meaning of free forms, like hat, ox, and box. We call morphemes bound when they are spoken only in conjunction with a free morpheme.

In time the Mafa through use invented several thousand morphemes, each of them appropriate to a certain sector of experience, that is, each with a particular meaning. With a few onomatopoeic exceptions, none of these morphemes corresponds "naturally" with whatever phenomenon it designates. They have all been assigned meaning quite conventionally. Primarily, of course, the Mafa vocabulary refers to things especially significant in Mafa life. For example, their vocabulary contains a rich assortment of terms to designate forest phenomena, just as the Eskimo language is well stocked with words to describe caribou and snow, items of experience highly significant to many Eskimo. But even a vocabulary of several thousand words would enable the Mafa to transmit only the most rudimentary ideas. They could utter words, like boy, mother, big, hard, strike, and struck; indicate the duals and plurals of objects; and specify the time when an act was or would be performed. But they couldn't yet indicate who was striking whom, or what word in the sentence possessed the quality to which a speaker referred. They needed another series of grammatical agreements to specify how morphemes were to be arranged to produce longer meaningful utterances. Again through use rather than deliberatively the Mafa developed rules of syntax. Mafa associated the form "big boy strikes mother hard" with the actual dastardly act which it designates for us and not with what we feel is a more customary act of mothers, that is, the mother striking the boy. Word order, they agreed, would make a difference in their linguistic messages. Adjectives, for example, would customarily precede nouns; predicates and objects would follow subjects. In time the Mafa wrote down their grammar and then, like all written grammars, it became quite confining. True, in vigorous argument people occasionally ignored grammatical custom, but when they wrote so that others could carefully follow the structure of their utterances, they were forced to be careful. Grammar had become more than customary usage; it had become normative and difficult to alter.

MIRACLE OF LANGUAGE

Miracle forms the key word in the title of a book, The Miracle of Language, whose author wants his readers to appreciate fully the achievement that language represents. With less than 50 discrete segments of sound plus a few stresses and intonations, social systems like ours are able to preserve their vast cultural heritage from one generation to the next; teach children and young adults life-saving, anxiety-reducing, and face-saving coping techniques; describe their gods and appeal to them for help; marshal armies and construction gangs; compose enobling myths that extoll their history; revile and curse their enemies; and make the sick well. And what a few, simple principles underlie use of language! Basically there must be a code, consisting of a few significant sound units which have been arbitrarily selected from the wide range that man can produce with little trouble using his throat, mouth, and nose. Meanings are conventionally assigned to combinations of phonemes (occasionally to single phonemes), converting them into enriched and more serviceable morphemes. Agreed-upon ways are found for stringing morphemes together to form larger, relatively unambiguous units of meaning. By the time a normal child is 6 years old he has mastered these principles in every culture. So apparently there can't be much in the way of fundamental differences between one language and another. One language can't be much more difficult than another. On the other hand, even well-motivated pupils commonly find trouble learning a second language, especially if it deviates markedly from habits involved in speaking the first. But such difficulty probably arises from the force of cultural momentum and not from any inherent difficulty in the second language.

Each of the world's languages pretty well performs the task to which its speakers regularly put it. At the same time, every language strains and stumbles and proves ineffective when it must suddenly undertake new tasks for which the necessary vocabulary or other resources first have to be found. And, as I have already said, in every language words sometimes can't be found to capture the full flavor of what someone wants to express.

Despite the equal efficiency of languages to cement social interaction, produce cooperation, and relieve feelings, people often assert the inherent superiority of one language over others. In India and Pakistan members of some speech communities have resorted to violence to resist attempts by government to substitute a single, national language. The newly independent governments have found it hard to conduct national business in three, four, or half-a-dozen languages or in a foreign language, English. But those speakers whose language did not receive the honor of becoming the lingua franca cared relatively little about achieving national unity. They were more afraid that ultimately their beautiful language, which they spoke as children, would disappear. Nobody can prove that one language is superior to another. There are no tests objectively verifying the superiority of a language. But linguistic ethnocentrism is not less powerful for being based purely on feeling. Emotional attachment to a language may stem from the literature written in that language. Poetry, myths, or God-given scriptures are dear and their value transfers to the language itself. Should a language with a literature of great books be overwhelmed by another language, then much of the literature and the truths the great books enshrine might become restricted to a small coterie of bilingual scholars. Translation gifted enough might or might not be forthcoming to render the spirit of the original.

LANGUAGE AND CULTURE

Language interweaves with practically everything in culture. Kinship, so important in most of the world, pivots around statuses, and each status is known by a linguistic term. Variations in speech index a person's rank, education, or foreign background. Ritual depends heavily on words. Almost every profession and branch of work—from medicine to carpentry—constructs its own argot or idiom by which phenomena important to specialists can be identified expeditiously and unambiguously. Learning the argot forms a major obligation in professionalization. With language so basic an underpinning of social life, Edward Sapir surmised that language might have been the part of culture that man developed earliest.

Claims have been made for language that go much further. Ethnolinguists like Benjamin Lee Whorf claim that language is not just a vehicle of communication. It also confines the way persons think of and perceive their world. Since action often follows from the way men think and perceive, language thus shapes a large part of human culture.[3] To demonstrate this assertion Whorf picks two languages, English and Hopi, and first proceeds to show a few ways in which they differ. English allows us to pluralize not only phenomena we can objectively see and feel, like men, masks, and houses, but also phenomena we experience only subjectively, like days. Blithely we apply cardinal numbers to both and say "two pencils" as easily as we speak of "ten days," as though days could be gathered up like pencils. English grammar leaves us no choice but to treat both kinds of experience as though each was objectively real. Hopi, however, never equates subjective experience, like the passage of time, with objective entities, such as men or houses. A Hopi speaker doesn't group days like corn kernels by saying, "he stayed 10 days." Instead he indicates time as a flow saying, "he stayed until the eleventh day" or "he left after the tenth day."

Both languages deal very differently with periods of time, like summer, winter, morning, or noon. English classifies them simply as nouns. Furthermore, we talk of arriving "in the morning" as though morning were a place one could physically enter. This is another example of how English encourages us to objectify time and obscures its purely subjective nature. Summer, morning, and noon are not nouns in Hopi. They are in a class by themselves, a class called temporals. Where in English we say "in the morning," a Hopi Indian says "when it is morning." Thereby he conveys the notion of duration, progressive movement, or becoming.

The three tenses of English—past, present, and future—help objectify time. Through them we are led to picture time as if it were lined up physically, the past stretching into the future. Actually past and future exist only here and now in my consciousness. Hopi verbs, which lack tense, go far toward recognizing this fact. Instead of putting an act into a tense category, Hopi language insists that a speaker pay attention to his assertion's validity. If a Hopi refers to an act of running that he sees occurring before him, he indicates this indubitably clear, present fact by using a special form of the verb

[3] Benjamin Lee Whorf, "The Relation of Habitual Thought and Behavior to Language," in Leslie Spier, A. I. Hallowell, and S. S. Newman, eds., Language, Culture, and Personality, Essays in Memory of Edward Sapir (Menasha, 1941). Also Benjamin Lee Whorf, "Time, Space and Language," in Laura Thompson, Culture in Crisis (New York, 1950), chap. 8.

"run." When he is less positive he uses a form of "run" that indicates he speaks from memory. In such cases English speakers would use the past tense, putting an act "in" the past. The Indian also has a verb that allows him to say he only expects somebody to run; here we would put the act "in" the future.

Another way English objectifies is by applying to an abstraction, like duration, words also employed for objects—words like long or short that also designate the size of physical things. Hopi avoids such metaphorical use of words. Action is designated by aspect to express duration. (If you have ever studied Russian you will be familiar with this grammatical device.) Where we would say long or short, in Hopi a special class of words known as tensors call attention to duration. Tensors allow speakers to express duration and other qualities subjectively without recourse to metaphors.

The point of these contrasts is to show how each language confines its speakers to different ways of speaking about time. Whorf claims that each language also affects how its speakers think about time. Ultimately language further determines the way we act with regard to time. "People act about situations in ways which are like the ways they talk about them"—so runs the principle of ethnolinguistics.

Let me illustrate with the example of thought. No more than they talk metaphorically of time do Hopi Indians talk about thinking metaphorically, as though it, too, were like an object. They describe thought qualitatively, as a process, and this grammatical habit, Whorf maintains, readily allows them to conceive of thinking as a force. The Hopi conceive that thought is capable of being directed for the benefit of crops. It can produce illness, bring rain, and become purified. Perhaps Hopi grammar does help the Indian to visualize man influencing his universe through directed thoughts. But, as Lévy-Bruhl documents exhaustively, many other small-scale, exotic people live by a similar world view. Must they too have Hopi-like languages that avoid objectifying a subjective experience like thought? English does objectify thought, but that doesn't debar English speakers from grasping the notion of mind influencing matter. I would argue that how we speak and how we think and act are more independent of each other than confirmed ethnolinguists assert.

But these questions can't be settled by arguing back and forth. We must find out if people with different languages really do think, perceive, and act differently, that is, in accordance with the way they talk.

HOW FAR DOES LANGUAGE GOVERN BEHAVIOR?[4]

Vocabulary in every language reflects interests that its speakers hold. A vocabulary is attuned to environmental and other distinctions useful to

[4] Joshua A. Fishman, "A Systematization of the Whorfian Hypothesis," *Behavioral Science*, 5 (1960), 323-339.

people. It makes sense that Eskimo should be linguistically armed with several words for snow when they find it vital for survival to distinguish different kinds of snow. Because vocabulary resources between languages are unequal, speakers of one language may find it easier to express some ideas than persons who converse and write in another. Hebrew in Israel and Urdu in Pakistan must refurbish their vocabularies in order that universities in those countries can teach the concepts of modern physical and social science.

There is a second way vocabulary interweaves with what people do. An extensive series of terms for colors, parts of a seal, or parts of culture is helpful when it comes to recognizing very fine color differences, to carving up and sharing a seal meticulously, and to understanding culture anthropologically. In the absence of the words, these tasks would probably be hard to carry out. So, for example, Kaska Indians with only one word to cover both blue and green encountered a bit of difficulty when a troublesome anthropologist demanded that they discriminate between those two colors.

So much for vocabulary and the way it mirrors and facilitates behavior. Whorf goes further and claims that grammar shapes a community's ideas and in doing so encourages people to act the way they speak. The way Hopi Indians talk about thinking first influences their conception of thought. They then use thought as a force, directing it into the environment. Let us take another example. Commonly when we speak or write English we place the adjective before the noun it modifies. In French, however, adjectives follow nouns. English usage, someone has suggested, encourages particularistic thinking. It is well suited to induction, drawing broad generalizations from discrete experiences. French usage, on the other hand, favors an opposite approach to experience. It encourages thinking deductively, moving from broader generalizations down to particular instances. Inevitably we ask whether English speakers are in fact more inductive than French speakers? This is far from easy to answer. We find it hard to resist selecting elements of behavior that will demonstrate what we expect to find. We too easily ignore contradictory facts. Precisely because proof or disproof is so difficult to secure, ethnolinguistics still remains largely unverified.

If ethnolinguists are correct in their assumption that language governs behavior, then every people is hopelessly trapped by whatever language it happens to speak. At best we can escape the confining world view of English only by exchanging English for another equally confining language. The true state of affairs can't possibly be so bad. We do experience phenomena apart from language and such experience, too, shapes our ideas. As we all know, thought at times outruns the confines of linguistic usage. Surely, then, our thinking is not wholly at the mercy of the way we speak.

ANOTHER MAFA BREAKTHROUGH

Every language has limitations, an important one being that it only works at relatively close range. A messenger entrusted with an oral message may forget what he has to say or inadvertently twist the information so as to distort its meaning. Message sticks and other mnemonic aids don't incorporate language; they merely jog memory. The Mafa, as their social system grew in scale, recognized this limitation in linguistic communication. Their first attempt to overcome it followed precisely what happened in early human history; they tried to invent a communications code fully independent of spoken sounds.

A Mafa innovator suggested sending forth a courier with pictograms. Simply sketch the outlines of a scene corresponding to the message. A recipient of the picture will read the drawing and reconstruct the message from purely visual cues. Furthermore he will be able to read the picture even if he speaks a language other than Mafa! What a convenience in a growing society! It took no time at all to demonstrate that pictographic writing was not a perfect solution to long-distance communication. It turned out to possess insurmountable limitations. Some ideas just couldn't be drawn. The Mafa could draw a weapon reasonably well but how should they represent the fear-inspiring idea that many more weapons were on hand and would be used mercilessly if the other party didn't promptly desist in the trouble he was creating? Recipients can't read everything that an artist intends to say in his picture; prior agreements are lacking. Hence pictures are notoriously ambiguous. Stone-age cave paintings discovered in southwestern Europe have provoked interminable discussion about their true meaning. Nobody is yet sure that he understands what the paleolithic food-gatherers intended to set down with their colorful representations.

Mulling over the limits of Pictographic writing a sagacious Mafa saw three solutions. One way continued to desert language. It required coining a distinct sign for every word that was to be communicated graphically. Not only names of objects would have their logographic representation but signs would be provided for such abstract words as mind, power, and royalty. China adopted this mode of writing but the Mafa did not because they realized the tremendous burden it would put on scribes. A proficient secretary would have to learn thousands of logograms and anybody wishing to read would need equally lengthy and patient training to stuff his mind with the meanings of thousands of arbitrarily created signs. The cost of reaching agreement concerning the meaning of signs promised to outweigh the value of this form of writing. Ever since China's seventeenth-century contact with the west, reformers there have contemplated altering the cumbersome Chinese logo-

PICTOGRAPHIC WRITING HAS ITS PROBLEMS

Some knowledge of Plains Indian culture might help you to gauge the general interests of the Blackfoot Indian who painted these figures on his tipi cover. But your understanding would hardly go far enough to enable you to tell that the top center painting narrates how a man captured a Gros Ventre Indian woman and boy. In the second the artist boasts of how he and a companion killed two Crow Indians. In the third he tells of a Cree Indian killed while running off with Blackfoot horses.

Robert H. Lowie, *Indians of the Plains* (New York, 1954), p. 110.

graphic script and today the Communists propose to substitute a mere 30 phonetic signs for the thousands of traditional logograms in which China's literature is written.

A second suggestion occurring to the Mafa was also rejected as overly cumbersome. This involved not a sign to stand for each word, regardless of how the word is pronounced, but a phonetic logogram (or phonogram) that would be read as the word is pronounced. For example, it is as though we agreed that the image of a date would be read aloud and thereby signify either the fruit, the calendrical day, the first part of the word "dative" or "data," and so on. Other signs would stand for the other parts of the latter two words or we might trust a bit perilously that context would fill in the reader. Not a very happy solution!

The third solution which the Mafa innovator earnestly recommended to his community, and which others adopted enthusiastically, consisted of a relatively small stock of signs each standing for a rather discrete sound. The Mafa suggested signs to stand for consonant-vowel combinations: ti, tu, ki, ka, and so on. A few signs to represent single consonants and vowels also promised to be useful; they could signify morphemes consisting of only a single consonant or vowel. By adopting this system of syllabic writing the Mafa

Writing helps to organize work teams. Members of an Israeli kibbutz check the work-assignment board to find out where they have been detailed. (*Israel Office of Information.*)

with only a relatively small stock of syllabic graphemes were able to express any idea they uttered in speech. They had fused language and writing. From now on what a man said could be held against him as long as the records were preserved free from tampering. The past could be securely preserved into the future; history became possible.

Mafa historical records tell present-day scholars that the Mafa did not stop with syllabic writing. They went further. For unknown reasons the Mafa dropped syllabic writing and adopted an even more expeditious way of representing language graphically, namely by reserving one sign for every phoneme in the language. They adopted the principle of the alphabet in place of the syllabary. Chances are overwhelming that the Mafa did not discover this alphabetic principle independently. The principle of the alphabet was discovered only once 3000 years ago in Southwest Asia. From there it diffused, like ripples in a pond, to other parts of the world. Adopting this principle the Mafa were stimulated to devise a mere 14 signs each representing one segmental phoneme. Oh yes, they invented an additional sign to represent the intonation at the end of an utterance that indicates a direct interrogation. Otherwise, though, they didn't try to mark significant prosodic features of their language, leaving that chore to highly precise linguistic scholars. Their alphabet, with one grapheme standing for each discrete, significant unit of

MAN, A TIME-BINDING ANIMAL

(*Eastman-Kodak*)

Linguistic and nonlinguistic forms of communication don't merely facilitate social interaction. They bind time by helping us to hold fast to the otherwise swiftly vanishing past. They make the past available in the present. Language initially made man a time-binding animal. Other innovations—writing, phonograph records, films, and magnetic tapes—intensified this human talent.

sound, was even more perfect than ours, which occasionally makes a single sign do for more than one phoneme (a, for example, in words like hat and father).

The Mafa now possessed both linguistic and extralinguistic means of communication. Their minimally significant speech sounds had become the base for a nonvocal system of coding. Our Morse code is another example of extralinguistic communication and so, in a very different way, is the radio in which spoken language is first converted into radio waves that are then reconverted to sound.

Naturally the Mafa also occasionally used their hands and grimaced to communicate more effectively. These gestures have no connection with the elements of language. They, like the boar's head outside of an English tavern, a barber pole outside of a hair-cutting shop, and the mortar and pestle hanging in front of a druggist's, constitute instances of nonlinguistic communication. But these signs, too, as I stated at the outset of this chapter, communicate only because we have agreed beforehand that they will stand for such enterprises.

Even writing has its limitations, as the Mafa discovered before long. It takes time to write a letter that is destined for one man and takes longer to copy the same message for ten men. As a social system grows in scale, communicating with many persons extralinguistically becomes arduous and expensive. Printing solved this difficulty. The time required to cut graphic signs into blocks of wood (type) and arrange the type in a machine for reproduction was infinitesimal compared to hand-copying a large number of messages. But printing, too, has its limitations. Even by hiring a gifted stylist it is hard to get the speaker's insistent tone or a sense of intimacy into a mass-circulated printed message. Radio and, better yet, television, when they appeared some half a millennium after the invention of printing overcame that obstacle. Now a personal appeal, closely resembling what takes place in face-to-face communication, can, for good or evil, be directed simultaneously at millions of people in an attempt to sway their thoughts, feelings, and actions.

FURTHER READING

A number of introductions to linguistics expand on many points I have taken up. These include: Stuart Chase, *Power of Words* (New York, 1954); H. A. Gleason, *An Introduction to Descriptive Linguistics* (New York, 1955), for which a workbook also is available; Robert A. Hall, Jr., *Leave Your Language Alone!* (Ithaca, N.Y., 1950), chaps. 5-10; Charlton Laird, *The Miracle of Language* (Cleveland, 1953); Eugene A. Nida, *Learning a Foreign Language* (New York, 1950), the title reflects only one of the author's aims; Edward Sapir, *Language* (New York, 1921); also an article by Sapir with the same title in *Encyclopaedia of the Social Sciences* (New York, 1934); Margaret Schlauch, *The Gift of Tongues* (New York, 1942); and George L. Trager, "Language," *Encyclopaedia Britannica* (Chicago, 1959). J. R. Firth, "Personality and Language in Society," *Sociological Review*, 42 (1950), 37-52, and Leslie White, "The Symbol: The Origin and Basis of Human Behavior," *Philosophy of Science*, 7 (1940), 451-463, are comprehensive introductory papers.

Alf Sommerfelt sums up much thinking that has been done about "The Origin of Language: Theories and Hypotheses," *Cahiers d'histoire mondiale*, 1 (1954), 885-902, while Weston La Barre reviews language with reference to primate behavior in *The Human Animal* (Chicago, 1954), chap. 10. The concept of linguistic change is well treated in *Three Keys to Language* by Robert M. Estrich and Hans Sperber (New York, 1952), chaps. 5-12. Language as related to class consciousness forms the substance of Chapters 4 and 5 in Mario Pei, *The Story of English* (Philadelphia, 1953).

An excellent study of the history and functions of writing has been written by Alfred C. Moorhouse in *The Triumph of the Alphabet* (New York, 1953). See also I. J. Gelb, *A Study of Writing* (Chicago, 1952). Joseph Needham's *Science and Civilization in China, 1, Introductory Orientations* (Cambridge, Eng., 1954), pp. 27-41, discusses Chinese writing. In "The Japanese Language," *Life*, 13, no. 10, (September 7, 1942), 58, 61-64, 67, Francis Sill Wickware offers a picture essay on Japanese writing. For gesture and sign language see Macdonald Critchley,

The Language of Gesture (London, 1939); D. Efron, *Gesture and Environment* (New York, 1941); and William Tomkins, *Universal Indian Sign Language of the Plains Indians of North America,* 3rd ed. (San Diego, Calif., 1929).

Edward Sapir has written on "Communication" in its cultural setting in the *Encyclopaedia of the Social Sciences* (New York, 1934). Stanley Rundle's book, *Language as a Social and Political Factor in Europe* (London, 1946), not only reviews the continent's language map but discusses the social implications of linguistic diversity. See also Harold Goad, *Language in History* (Harmondsworth, 1958), and the review of language problems in the modern world in *Unesco Courier,* 7, no. 1 (1954). The Communist Chinese writing reform is described in Nigel Cameron, *The Chinese Smile* (London, 1958), chap. 5. *Language in the Modern World* by Simeon Potter (Harmondsworth, 1960) is a fairly comprehensive introduction to linguistics, including the historical branch of that discipline with which I have not dealt in this chapter.

Religion:
The Rite That Binds

Ceremonies are the bond that holds the multitudes together, and if the bond be removed, these multitudes fall into confusion.

Book of Rites (1st Century B.C.)[1]

COMMON UNDERSTANDINGS EXPRESSED THROUGH RITUAL

Religion is a most general and notoriously unprecise word. It has been used to cover many things: magic, Christianity, Hindu philosophy, atheistic Buddhism, and the emotional appeal of Communism. I will apply it to a very specific kind of behavior, one often stringently standardized in society, ritual. The title of this chapter hints at only one of many differences ritual makes; I shall deal with others too. Please note that coping with life's difficulties through petitionary prayer and magic, a subject sometimes shunted under that obliging label, religion, has been treated earlier and will be introduced again only as it, too, exhibits qualities of ritual.

From one situation to another in every social system persons openly express understandings or sentiments they share. Such understandings sometimes resist being captured in words but can be acted out genuinely and unselfconsciously. Dinner table etiquette, for example, ritually brings out into the open common understandings that are impossible to describe. But as everyone knows, failure to exhibit proper mealtime ritual brings painful consequences. However, in a greeting or condolence, words quite explicitly say the sentiments people feel or are supposed to feel.

[1] Cited in A. R. Radcliffe-Brown, *Structure and Function in Primitive Society* (London, 1952), p. 159.

Dinner manners, a greeting, and offering condolence are simple rituals. They contribute to a way of life a measure of its distinctive quality. The disparity between mealtime rituals in two cultures is apt to be substantial. Ignorance of the correct behavior can be most discomforting and lead to gross misunderstanding. Cultures also differ in that they go to unequal lengths in elaborating such social rituals. Kaska Indians live a life stripped down in ritual expression. Yet they too share mutual understandings and in their own way express them. For example, when a winter camp runs short of meat, a man obliquely reminds his son-in-law that the ptarmigan, an easy-to-kill bird, is likely to be found nearby. And in discussing people who fail to live up to social expectations, the Kaska Indian shrugs his shoulders and says resignedly, "It's up to him." Both behaviors express a common sentiment which I shall try to put into words: by exercising deference in interpersonal behavior we respect one another's autonomy; a human being can't be bossed like a dog.

For other examples of everyday ritual, let's look at Hopi culture. A woman from one village who visits a woman in another avoids coming empty-handed. She always brings a small gift of food. Similarly, the hostess bids her friend farewell with a countergift. Many social systems rely on gifts to convey openly sentiments never precisely expressed in words. When we observe how Hopi Indians express grief at death we learn about a new side of ritual. Only people actually in the house weep on this occasion. They weep in a restrained way. No protracted mourning conveys the idea of relatives utterly crushed or deeply agonized by tragedy. There are communities that indulge in wildly dramatic expressions of grief but that would shock the Hopi. As it is, bereaved Hopi feel vulnerable enough to attack by malevolent witches. They must get over their grief quickly and restore their serene, confident outlook so as to become reasonably safe again. By warning members of the dreadful consequences that will follow if ritual is not carried out in prescribed fashion, social systems insure that the proper ritual will always be forthcoming. Like many American Indians, Hopi extend ritual respect beyond the circle of human beings. They also show respect to animals. A hunter never kills wantonly out of excitement or sheer love of killing. And animals must be placated lest they become angry when one of their number is killed.

In self-conscious fashion a sect seeking to dissociate itself from the majority may, like the Puritans, imbue nearly everything in life with special significance, making it the channel of ritual. Nearly every act expresses the understandings that bind members into a distinctive group. Over 90 percent of sixteenth- and seventeenth-century Puritan culture resembled that of other Englishmen, but the Puritans by their scrupulous values introduced a new spirit into that culture.[2] Puritans regarded themselves as chosen people pre-

[2] Ralph Barton Perry, *Puritanism and Democracy* (New York, 1944); Perry Miller, *Orthodoxy in Massachusetts, 1630-1650* (Cambridge, Mass., 1933).

destined by God to salvation. In their eyes the Reformation had fallen far short of thoroughly purifying religious life, so they sought to carry reform further. Success failed them in England and they migrated to New England Colony where they established a theocracy. For our purposes, what is important is their attempt to ritualize nearly everything they did. I do not claim that Puritanism consisted solely of a revolution in ritual, though I will stress this aspect more than the philosophical and theological issues which Puritans as part of the broader Calvinist movement raised.

What was the principal common understanding they sought to express ritually in word and deed? Puritans believed that God shed his grace on some people more than on others and that they had been vouchsafed his great gift. They were predestined to salvation. They expressed their common feeling of electedness by exemplary moral behavior, Sabbath observance, thrift, wise use of time, hard work, and even worldly success. The Puritan did not work, speculate for profit, conquer the New England frontier, and fight Indians only pragmatically. Ideally "his heart [was] not set upon these things," as John Cotton said in 1651. His worldly success proved that God's grace operated in his life. Puritan culture, therefore, made even ordinary behavior pregnant with religious significance. But why should these particular symbols, replete with worldly success, have been chosen to express the Puritans' understandings? Economic opportunities prevailing in England and New England during the 200 years from 1500 to 1700 undoubtedly helped the middle-class bourgeoisie, the class to which most of the Puritans belonged, to choose these particular vehicles of ritual expression. Avoidances, whose roots lay in the Protestant Reformation, also assumed expressive meanings. Puritans rejected liturgical art, sculpture, and other sensuous accouterments of worship because these worldly things distracted man in venerating God.

Some rituals consist of simple everyday observances which direct sentiments to other people or animals. Other rites focus on supernatural beings. Muslims in Swat, for example, worship God through the rituals that are obligatory for 450 million other Muslims. The meaning of Muslim rites is far more explicit than the significance attached to the deference one Kaska Indian pays another or the sentiment that lies behind the Hopi visitor's gift. This meaning is learned quite formally. From the Atlantic coast of West Africa to the islands of Indonesia specialists keep these meanings alive and preserve them relatively unchanged.

At least once in his lifetime every Muslim must ritually recite the confession: "There is no God but God and Muhammad is His Prophet."[3] Five times daily he should worship in prescribed fashion. Annually he is commanded to fast during Ramadan—a rite that commemorates God's gift of the Quran, which occurred in that month. Every Muslim is enjoined to give

[3] Carleton S. Coon, *Caravan* (New York, 1951), chap. 7.

alms, and at least once in his lifetime, if he can afford it, he should go as a pilgrim to visit the sacred places of Mecca in Saudi Arabia. However, few of the world's Muslims can afford to become pilgrims to express their faith. The trip would cost a person from Swat at least $75 minimum fare, a sum greater than most people there see in a year. Through all five Islamic rituals a Muslim expresses his submission to God's will and acknowledges the greatness of Muhammad, who was the final prophet. God will never honor another with His revelations.

Let us look closely at one of the five Pillars of Islam, the prayer a Muslim says as each day starts, to note how it fulfills the primary task of ritual expression. The ritual begins even before the actual prayer, for a Muslim

Not only words but prescribed body postures express the understandings that unify Muslims everywhere in the world. (*Edward W. Lane, The Manners and Customs of the Modern Egyptians*, Everyman's Library Edition, London, n.d., p. 78.)

always symbolically first purifies himself so he will be fit to approach God. With running water he rinses his mouth, rubs his teeth, snuffs water into his nostrils, splashes his face, hair, and beard, and washes his ears' orifices, hands, forearms, and feet. Now he may address God. He turns toward the Prophet's city, Mecca (in Swat he faces westward), and lays his hands on his hips as he formally declares, silently or aloud, his intention to worship God with a sincere heart. Then he places both thumbs to his earlobes, opens the hands on either side of his face, and praises God: "God is great." Next he places right hand over left and holds both at navel height while reciting the ringing Fatihah, the Quran's opening verse: "In the name of Allah, the Compassionate, the Merciful, Praise be to Allah, Lord of Creation. . . . You alone we worship, and to You alone we pray for help. Guide us to the straight path, the path of those whom You have favoured, not of those who have incurred Your wrath, nor of those who have gone astray."[4]

The prayer is not yet finished. Peasant, bureaucrat, and ruler (on Fridays all worship together in the same mosque) now bow and then fall to their knees. Each man presses his face to the ground and extols his Lord.

Do people actually experience all the sentiments they express so dramatically in ritual? Sometimes they do, as when zealous Hungarian patriots hire Madison Square Garden to demonstrate rousingly their faith in a non-Communist Hungary. The grief of a mother for her dead child, no matter how closely its expression conforms to pattern, is undeniably and tragically real. Sometimes, however, mourners pretend sorrow; friends who care little act out gladness when they meet; and worshipers in a congregation bow, ostensibly in humble submission, when they feel no emotion at all.

At still other times the true state of affairs lies in between. Then as we murmur the joyous greeting due at Christmas, bow our heads in prayer, or join in a pledge of allegiance, we feel the ceremony catch us up. Everyone's cheerfulness infects us; the solemnity grips us too, or the emblem, replete with a symbolism to which in early life we learned to respond, works on us again. If we give in, even a little, the sentiments that the pageantry expresses roll over us. Even Scrooge mellowed at Christmas and ended by saying what he actually felt!

THE DIFFERENCE IT MAKES

Sentiments held in common which regularly find their way into the open through ceremony make individuals conscious of themselves as a group and cut them asunder from other human aggregates. This is the general function of ritual. Social classes diverge from one another in formidable etiquette. By insistent avoidance rites, or taboos, castes rigidly exclude each other. In the southern United States whites separate themselves from Negroes whenever they ritually refuse to sit down and eat with Negroes (who, however, may prepare and serve the food). Churches are organized around dogmas and rites that give dogmas their expression. And there are ceremonies that express national understandings as they regularly honor national heroes or celebrate historic events. They keep the nation conscious of itself as a distinct social entity.

Let's not forget the small, everyday gestures of friendship and respect that we exchange with friends, customers, and acquaintances. These rites also bind. A smile, gift, cigarette, or cup of tea not only breaks the ice. It offers warm assurance that common understandings exist between giver and receiver, that the visitor is welcome, or that circumstances are favorable for discussing

[4] *The Koran,* trans. N. J. Dawood (Harmondsworth, 1956).

a business contract. Persons who ritually display such sentiments find it easy to remain in each other's company and to transact business comfortably.

Ritual, then, creates social solidarity in small or large areas of society and helps to perpetuate social ties through time. But keep in mind that while firmly preserving some ties, ritual in any group neglects strengthening bonds with other persons in society. Ritual, in fact, may consist of deliberately avoiding close contacts, so that instead of expressing the sentiment of incorporation it betrays feelings of extreme difference, superiority, and uncompromising exclusiveness.

INSTRUMENTAL AND CONSUMMATORY ENDS

Looking for the difference ritual makes is, of course, distinct from assessing a rite's meaning and purpose. The meaning of an elaborate rite, like a nine-day Hopi ceremony such as will be examined, is enormously complex. For an outsider fully to unravel this meaning requires analysis, in contrast to the forceful, immediate impact which the ceremony makes on participants who have been familiar with it since childhood. Many ideas are interwoven in such a ritual and each possesses its own emotional significance. All the objects and costumes which are a part of it carry intricate symbolism that contributes to the over-all meaning.

On the other hand, we can usually discover quite easily when a ritual is carried out instrumentally, that is, with a magical purpose. People then regard it as a means to an end. It promises fertility, health, or safety from accidents, witches, or demons. Other rituals have a consummatory, purely expressive meaning. The ceremony is an end in itself. When we stop to honor God or a bygone national hero we have no other purpose. Complications arise in a large-scale social system where theologians condemn worship if it is carried out magically instead of purely reverently. Islamic scholars in Swat point out that the Fatihah offered at the tomb of a saint is not efficacious in curing barrenness. Still women who don't conceive persist in magical prayer. The great tradition practiced by scholars is imperfectly geared with the unlettered folk's little tradition.[5]

Between instrumental and consummatory ritual is a third class, consisting of well-designed consummatory rituals rationally performed with a calculated view of achieving something through them. The boss is dined to put him in the proper frame of mind to grant a raise. Honors are showered on a foreign head of state from the moment he deplanes in Washington as part of a deliberately contrived attempt to promote U.S. foreign policy. For certain distinguished vistors the welcome is purposefully lukewarm and reveals only

[5] Robert Redfield, *Peasant Society and Culture* (Chicago, 1956), chap. 3.

AN ANTHROPOLOGIST ADOPTS THE FATHER-IN-LAW TABOO

"Since I was with Sitting-Standing's family every day, I eventually made arrangements to move out from the nearby town, where I had been staying, and live at the farmhouse. Gradually, I came to have a place in the family organization, and it was made official when Elizabeth's grandmother adopted me as her granddaughter. At first I thought of this only as an interesting and flattering formality, but soon I perceived that it was considerably more than that. Instead of being simply a welcome visitor, I was now actually a member of the family. My duties, responsibilities, and privileges were no less than Elizabeth's own.

"As Elizabeth's sister, I was, by [Kiowa] tribal custom, a potential wife of her husband, and so, by extension, I was also a potential daughter-in-law of Sitting-Standing [Elizabeth's husband's father], and the taboo applied to me. No longer could I say good morning to him if we met at breakfast. My back must be turned to him; if that was impossible, my eyes must be averted. I had to be careful to wear long sleeves and high necks in his presence, in spite of the midsummer heat. And the old man was equally careful. If departure was feasible, he left any room when I entered it; otherwise, he turned his back and ignored me with the most profound politeness and respect."

Alice Marriott, "Father-in-law Taboo," *The New Yorker*, 28 (September 13, 1952), 94-101.

polite respect, acknowledging the visitor's august rank, combined with disapproval for his regime.[6]

RITES OF DEFERENCE

Simple rites of deference illustrate easily and clearly how ceremonious behavior acts to bind social relationships. The cheerful greeting to a friend or office-mate goes far to perpetuate a warm relationship. Try deliberately to omit a response when the boss says good morning and see what happens! The warm embrace between kinsmen who have not seen each other for many months expresses emotion of a more overwhelming kind but it also gives assurance that binding affection still exists. The full prostration or deep courtesy acknowledges the paramountcy of a ruler and his subject's subordination. A salute between officer and enlisted man symbolizes the distinction between two ranks. Such ritual recognition of authority affirms the validity of the social system in which those persons have unequal rights and duties. By

[6] James Reston, "Washington Sets Tone. Reserved Reception for Khrushchev Unusual for Demonstrative Capital," *The New York Times*, September 16, 1959.

acknowledging the social order's validity we accept it with all its inequalities. On occasions of state, magnificent glamour surrounds the staging of rites of deference. A slight mishap, for instance turning one's back a few steps sooner than it is polite to, threatens disastrous international complications.

HALLOWED REFERENCES AND SOLEMN PROMISES—
RITES OF INTENSIFICATION

Another type of ceremony occurs more or less regularly. Among us these recurrent ceremonies occur at intervals which our calendar conveniently notes as red-letter days. Changing seasons or the movement of stars are calendars by which certain small-scale social systems recognize that the time has again come around to celebrate these rites. Such rituals involve a congregation, a whole village, or an entire large social system. The group gathers or, nowadays, tunes in to hear appropriate sentiments expressed under stirring circumstances that conveniently also renew and fortify the strength of those sentiments. Unlike rites of passage, which I will take up presently, recurrent rites of intensification are general in nature. In them a *group* celebrates its anniversary or recalls its historic triumph over forces of evil. In a Sunday rite of intensification a church congregation reaffirms and acts out its sacred understandings; a factory pursues good fellowship through a picnic; and a club gathers many more members for an annual banquet than normally attend less enlivened business meetings.

We are all intimately familiar with rites of intensification because from childhood we have participated in them at Thanksgiving, Christmas, and Easter, on Memorial Day, and the Fourth of July. Part of the ceremony takes place in the home and is for the family; we embody the season's significance in special family greetings, a symbolic Christmas tree, and festive meals. The church, cemetery, or town square may be a more inclusive rallying point. And nowadays we almost unwittingly join in such rites when we encounter them in the pervasive mass media that carry expressive seasonal music, advertisers' timely greetings, and chosen words solemnly pronounced by prominent men in public life. Such days bring time off from work, invite recreation, and stimulate business.

The excitement they kindle makes persons in a social system (or other group) intensely aware of themselves as a group. This heightened sense of membership intensifies the group's solidarity and helps insure its continuity. Striking emblems, like a flag, remind people of their allegiance to a nation. Emotion-filled references to sacred ideas on which the group depends or from which it stems—ideas of God, the Resurrection, justice, freedom, and the October Revolution—undoubtedly quicken self-awareness. Hallowed references to the group itself almost unfailingly arouse a warm sense of identifica-

CHURCH RITUALS IN YANKEE CITY GIVE EACH YEAR AN EMOTIONAL RHYTHM

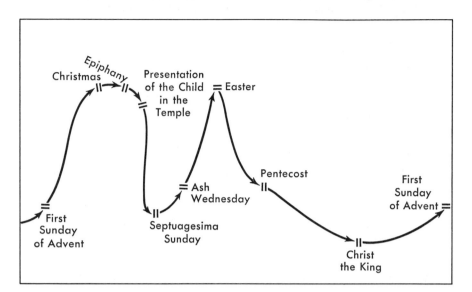

In this New England town, like elsewhere in the United States, Christmas and Easter represent joyous rites of intensification. The chart shows how they bring with them the emotional peaks of the year's ritual cycle. Of course, the chart would look different if in addition to church rituals it included secular holidays, like the Fourth of July and Labor Day. These would add two relatively low crests of emotional intensity in summer and fall, seasons when this community celebrates no important church rituals.

W. Lloyd Warner, *The Living and the Dead* (New Haven, 1959), p. 406.

tion. We solemnly reiterate the promise that this group will continue, grow in size and strength, and always be vigilant to repel its enemies. These sentiments are calculated to marshal idealism latent in nearly everyone. We feel proud, carried away by the group's nobility and what it stands for. Our emotional commitment leaves us unwilling to look too frankly at the group's shortcomings. To do so might shake our faith, prove our emotion to be wrongly invested. Hopefully the sense of commitment will stay high until the next occasion of intensification, unweakened by the call for taxes or the notice that club dues are due.

Occasions for intensification are frequent in a large-scale social system where a constant battle of rival ideologies persistently nags at all allegiances. Each person who stays away from a rally or shuts his ears to sentiments ritually expressed in a rite of intensification reveals his disenchantment with the group, its purposes, and its carefully cultivated memories. He also deprives himself of the emotional nourishment that rites give and so quickens the pace at which his disaffection proceeds. He speeds up dissolution, a process running counter to social solidarity and social continuity. In relatively small-scale social systems such rituals are seldom purely consummatory. For that reason they are not readily ignored. Instrumentally conceived, they guarantee fertility, well-being, and life itself. The very organization of the universe compels their regular performance in order that man may live safely and comfortably. Their instrumental purpose further enhances the ceremonies' capacity to stimulate group awareness and protect social continuity.

The Hopi leave ritual performances up to secret ceremonial groups each of which includes members of several sibs, though one kin group controls it. Each ceremonial group in a village exemplifies a centripetal process working to overcome the centrifugal forces that beset the acephalous, segmented village. Let us see the rituals these groups perform to benefit their pueblo.[7]

Rituals must be held someplace. Hopi secret ceremonial sodalities carry out most of their activities in rectangular, underground chambers called kivas, each about 12 feet wide, 25 feet long, and 10 feet high. One enters a kiva by climbing down a stout ladder perched in a hatchway cut in the roof. In an acephalous Hopi village a kiva gets built through the efforts of one enterprising sib, which then collectively owns the building. This kiva becomes headquarters for the secret association headed by that sib. An emblem flying over a kiva where a ritual is in progress gives notice that none but authorized personnel may enter. At other times the kiva serves men as a clubhouse. During the ceremony's duration and for four days afterwards the kiva ceremonialists must not eat salt or fat, they renounce sexual pleasure, and, above all, they keep steadfastly tranquil, that is, aloof from angry or depressing thoughts. Compulsory avoidances like these remind the participants of their solemn duty.

Usually seven or eight days are devoted to secret kiva ritual in which the sodality members sing and pray, that is, exercise their wills. Hopi rituals are intended to promote a favorable relationship between the village and the universe, not to request it. Further techniques by which the ceremonialists work to maintain a harmonious balance between human life and the rest of nature consist of sand painting, symbolic smoking, and offerings (mainly feathered prayersticks deposited at shrines and before the kiva altar). Although these services bar outsiders, during the nineteenth and early twentieth centuries visitors did manage to penetrate the kivas. Men like J. Walter Fewkes, G. A. Dorsey, and Henry R. Voth painstakingly recorded the details and published

[7] Mischa Titiev, *Old Oraibi, A Study of the Hopi Indians of Third Mesa*, Papers of the Peabody Museum of American Archaeology and Ethnology, Harvard University, vol. 22, no. 1, 1944, chap. 8-14; Laura Thompson and Alice Joseph, *The Hopi Way* (Chicago, 1944), chap. 4.

comprehensive accounts of Hopi ceremonials. Modern scholars find these accounts invaluable and irreplaceable but their step-by-step descriptions are dry and tedious to read through. Naturally the Hopi were shocked when these volumes appeared but they have certified their contents to be on the whole accurate.

Usually on the ninth day members of the ceremonial group, brilliantly costumed and masked as deities, Katchinas, present a dance in public. These colorful exhibitions have brought renown to Hopi and other Pueblo Indians. Dancers don't merely impersonate spiritual beings. Actually their masks trans-

As soon as he dons his mask, symbol of a particular Katchina, the Hopi ceremonialist becomes that Katchina, a supernatural visitor to the pueblo. The other paraphernalia he carries help to identify the particular Katchina he represents. (*Smithsonian Institution, Bureau of American Ethnology. Photographs by J. W. Fewkes about 1891.*)

form them into Katchinas! Little children, obeying adults' Santa Claus-like hoaxes, go even further and believe that the masked men from whom they anticipate rewards or dread punishment are incarnated deities, not simply masked villagers. Spectators on crowded rooftops watch participants below in the dusty village plaza. The dances with their meticulously practiced songs are the high points in the big rites of intensification making up the Hopi religious calendar. They fortify religious convictions as they bring safety and fertility and provide the whole community with release and recreation. Clowns furnish comic relief, often satirizing whites and engaging in scatological or pornographic humor. Their antics are tremendously relished. Furthermore, clowning prevents sadness and worry from spoiling people's thoughts and so undermining the rituals' magical power.

The main ceremonial season coincides roughly with that part of the year when Katchinas cease to be confined to their underworld homes and become free to travel. This season begins about the time of the winter solstice (December 22) and lasts till just after the summer solstice (June 22). Conflict be-

A rite of passage, like this Muslim Punjabi wedding in West Pakistan, involves considerable preparation and a wealth of complex detail. (Top right) Female relatives assemble for several nights before the ceremony to express in singing the occasion's joyful significance. (Top left) Adorned in a headdress that veils his face, the groom goes to visit the mosque where he pays his respects to God. Then, seated on a white mare, he starts for his bride's home. Here bride and groom separately consent to be married. (Bottom left) The groom is garlanded in his bride's home. Money is pinned to his garland but it offers small compensation for the relentless teasing his own and his bride's female kin inflict on him. (Bottom right) Only after the bride has given her consent does she adorn herself in wedding finery. In a palanquin she is carried to her husband's home where she will live at least for a while. When they arrive there the couple, whose marriage parents and other relatives arranged, are for the first time allowed to see one another face to face.

tween religion and subsistence activities is obviated in this period when the Indians are conveniently free of heavy farm work. The season opens with the Soyal ceremony which directs the sun, a major deity, northward and commemorates the Hopi emergence from the underworld. In July the closing Homegoing Dance occurs. It bids the Katchinas farewell and thanks them for past favors. Minor ceremonies take place during the rest of the year. These include Katchina dances to promote cures, to celebrate recovery from illness, or to mark a birthday. On such festive occasions the whole village cements its unity anew through pleasurable relaxation and affirming belief in common symbols.

RITES OF TRANSITION

Social systems in which the effectively organized groups are not much larger than extended families rarely have separate rites of intensification. But no culture omits opportunities for ritual expression at times when individuals pass from one status or condition of life into another.[8] Rites of passage are often occasions for spectacular ceremonies that, like rites of intensification, intensify the sentiments of a whole band, village, or tribe. But they are primarily relevant to an individual or a group of individuals who together are undergoing a similar status transition. Birth or the assumption of parenthood, betrothal, marriage, death, initiation into new responsibilities, and inauguration into leadership are the major circumstances celebrated in rites of passage. The birth of a child confers additional responsibilities on parents to which they are ritually alerted. Betrothal and marriage usher a couple into social positions where they acquire new responsibilities and are no longer free to act or to be treated as before. Death ceremonies help convey the deceased to his afterworld but also repair the emotionally disrupted lives of surviving kinsmen. Mourning rites enable the bereaved to recoup morale with which to continue caring for their own needs and the needs of others dependent upon them. Initiation stresses that the time is at hand when a youngster must discard relative dependence and irresponsibility and pay serious heed to the moral and practical order by which adult life is organized. Inauguration reminds leader and followers that authority has been transferred to a new officeholder.

Such transformation rites make a difference. They help persons to accept roles attendant upon a new status or to bear up under loss. By their intensity or the prestige they confer upon participants they emphasize the importance of a social change. Their dramatic intensity forestalls backsliding to an outgrown status. Their attendant publicity reminds kinsmen and others to treat the individual as befits his new position. In a more far-reaching way rites of passage help guarantee that duties attached to important social positions will be performed adequately. Thereby they help maintain the social system. Occupants enter and may leave those positions but the meanings, purposes, and functions attached to the positions themselves continue.

Best known of all passage rituals found in small-scale cultures are those which promote children nearer the rank of adult. Frequently three steps can

[8] Arnold van Gennep, *The Rites of Passage,* trans. M. B. Vizedom and G. L. Caffee (Chicago, 1960).

be detected in such initiation rites (as well as in some other rites of passage). First comes seclusion. The initiate withdraws from his customary social activities, that is, from the life in which he played minor roles compared to those which he will soon assume. Isolation focuses the youth's attention and that of his community on the momentous social change underway. Secondly comes a transition. Gradually the initiate moves into his new role. In the seclusion of the bush, where with other initiates he spent months learning and undergoing tests of endurance, he is visited by his parents. The transformed youth (some cultures describe him as "reborn") returns home parading through the village. In the final stage of reintegration he picks up his new life in earnest.

A first initiation ritually introduces Hopi children of both sexes to their deified ancestors, the Katchinas, to whom henceforth they will own ritual obligations and in return receive blessed rain and fertility. A later rite makes boys into full-fledged Hopi adults. Certain features of this latter ceremony resemble other making-him-man ceremonies found in distant parts of the world.

Two adults (godparents) sponsor a child in his first initiation. In return the initiate joins their sib (as though he had been born in it) and, in due course, becomes a member of the secret ceremonial groups to which they also belong. Choosing sponsors, therefore, deserves careful thought. Furthermore, in Oraibi village the ceremonial godfather's affiliation determines whether a child will be initiated into the weightier Powamu ceremonial sodality or the less restricted Katchina group. Most children between the ages of 6 and 10 go through the dramatic passage ritual which affiliates them with the Katchina group. In this rite they hear a Katchina describe at length the Katchinas, their underworld homes, and their shrines. Then three additional Katchinas, armed with long yucca whips, rush down into the kiva. One after the other each initiate is whipped on naked flesh, boys more severely than girls. Don Talayesva explains that "If a ceremonial father wishes to do so, he may let the boy get two stripes, then pull him out of reach . . . and receive the other blows on his own bare thighs. My ceremonial father failed to do this, letting me take the four blows full force. I stood them fairly well, without crying, and thought my suffering was past." But then another Katchina struck Don repeatedly "and cut me to pieces. I struggled, yelled, and urinated. . . . Blood was running down over my body."[9] The people in the kiva shouted angrily for the Katchina to cease. It turned out that Don's father had requested an especially severe whipping in order to discipline his mischievous son.

A startling revelation follows the whipping. For the first time children learn that the Katchinas, from whom they have received gifts and punishment, are not gods incarnate but human beings. "I recognized nearly every one of them,"

[9] Leo W. Simmons, ed., *Sun Chief, the Autobiography of a Hopi Indian* (New Haven, Conn., 1942), p. 83.

Don says, "and felt very unhappy, because I had been told all my life that the Katcinas were gods. I was especially shocked and angry when I saw all my uncles, father, and clan brothers dancing as Katcinas. I felt the worst when I saw my own father—and whenever he glanced at me I turned my face away." The rite concludes by warning the initiates never to reveal the Katchinas' identity to uninitiated children.

The Hopi Katchina initiation combines fear, pain, and a startling revelation in its attempts to promote discipline and responsibility in youngsters. The rite symbolically expresses the power Katchinas wield over men, the power men control through rituals. A new name conferred in the ceremony denotes a step in growing up. From now on, each time a child joins a secret sodality he undergoes another, milder initiation, or symbolic rebirth, and receives a fresh name. At each such step his ritual responsibilities increase.

Soon after adolescence nearly every Hopi boy joins in a second rite, the Wuwutchim ceremony, by whose efficacy he is reborn into adult status.[10] Four secret ceremonial sodalities cooperatively execute the complex Wuwutchim rite at the end of which each "little chicken hawk," as the initiate is called, becomes a member of one. During the nine days of ritual, novices wear chicken hawk feathers. They flap their arms like wings as their sponsors feed them. Each initiate sleeps with his sponsor under the same blanket. So in childhood he slept with his mother who reared him as his sponsor rears him now. The fourth night is filled with mystery and terror. The dead throng into the pueblo where only ceremonialists dare venture outdoors. For one night dead are reunited with those still living. The novices join the dead; symbolically they die as children to be reborn as men. The terror possesses specific functions. We know that terror can cause a conversion in the way people think and feel; hence the prominent use revolutions make of it. It vivifies the Wuwutchim transformation rite, not only for the initiates but for all their kinsmen and village-mates. In other cultures, too, initiation rituals, by including a night of fear and mystery, dramatically achieve the same function.

On the fifth day, Wuwutchim ceremonialists exaggerate their masculinity by painting phallic designs on their partially naked bodies. Then they climb out of the kiva and in a bawdy way revile village women who are watching them from rooftops. With well-simulated anger the women respond and douse their detractors with pots of cold water, foul-smelling urine, and garbage. Women again taunt and defile male dancers later that day when the men—some disguised as women—dance backwards while carrying very realistic images of a vulva. Dammed up tension is discharged through this ritual license but here I want to call attention to another aspect of the day's symbolism, the pseudo bitterness and aggression exchanged between men and women. In many other

[10] Titiev, op. cit., chap. 10; Simmons, op. cit., chap. 8; J. Walter Fewkes and A. M. Stephen, "The Ná-ac-nai-ya: A Tusayan Initiation Ceremony," Journal of American Folk-Lore, 5 (1892), 189-217.

cultures male initiation rituals also call for simulated opposition between men and women. In that way the rites effectively dramatize the boys' severance from the women who reared them and to whom they are still deeply attached. Even though the novices, isolated in a kiva, remain out of the altercation, the fifth day's ritual stresses the solidarity of men, the sex category with which the boys are being merged. On the ninth day each novice reintegrates himself in everyday family life. The sponsor leads him to his mother's house along a path strewn with sacred corn meal. At the door the sponsor addresses the boy's mother: "I have brought our son home. Now he is a man and is called——." He informs her of her son's new name.

AN OUTSIDER INTERPRETS

Long, complex ceremonies, like the Hopi Wuwutchim or Roman Catholic Mass, comprise many symbols. Some are verbal symbols—words; others consist of meaningful acts, artifacts, or designs blazoned on artifacts. No doubt a number of these symbols have reached the culture from other cultures, the whole ceremony slowly accreting over many centuries. Alone or in combination with one another these symbols trigger emotional responses which range from veneration or dependence to objectless feelings of awe, excitement, and delight. Even an outsider in time learns to feel as people feel who regularly participate in such rituals.

To understand the many symbols which constitute a ritual we sometimes go further than learning, for example, that an image stands for a female deity who arouses respect and affection in her worshipers. The fact that the deity is female and other clues tempt us to go further and identify her with fertility, though until they themselves are told this, members of a community may remain oblivious to such significance. I interpreted the acts in the Wuwutchim, which realistically simulated sexual opposition, as dramatizing how the ceremony draws boys away from women. This enhanced my understanding of the rite. The Hopi, as far as I know, offer no such interpretation. Yet an outsider, armed with a plausible theory, can legitimately support reading that meaning into the sexual opposition. Seeing the opposition as an enacting of a breaking point in boys' development is not an existential interpretation but a technical assessment. Such an assessment of meaning is akin to the interpretation a psychoanalyst offers when he elucidates his patient's dreams.

COLLECTIVE REPRESENTATIONS

Following trends in modern anthropology I have emphasized the array of outward activities and rituals that comprise what is loosely called religion. I spent much less time delineating vigorously held motivating beliefs that often underlie expressive ritual acts. Yet, such beliefs, too, must be understood. They are the dynamic source from which much ritual springs.

Participants in many (though far from all) rituals dedicate their ceremonial acts to collectively endorsed ideas like God, saints, ancestors, spirits that control illness, weather, or fertility, or to the alert, animate universe itself with which they wish to establish personal contact. Ritualists treat collective representations as though the deities, ancestors, or spirits actually existed and could hear the paeans of praise and appeals for assistance addressed to them. Rituals directed toward supernatural beings are sometimes called sacred rituals. Cultures that regularly refer even humdrum activities to God (in Pakistan our Muslim cook murmured "In the name of God" even when he began to prepare a meal) are called sacred cultures.

Much ingenious speculation has been devoted to answering the still unsolved question: How did beliefs in supernatural beings originate? In 1757 David Hume, writing in the spirit of the Enlightenment, reasoned that deities stand rooted in human fear, uncertainty, and hope. "Agitated by hopes and fears . . . men scrutinize, with a trembling curiosity, the course of future causes, and examine the various and contrary events of human life. And in this disordered scene, with eyes still more disordered and astonished, they see the first obscure traces of divinity."[11] They garb their intimations of deities in the guise of beings like themselves, only more powerful or immortal. Hume's explanation comes very close to what Freud said 170 years later when he branded religious beliefs as illusory. He called them illusory because he believed that they are grounded only in human hopes and wishes. Longing to be spared the dangers with which nature threatens him, yet helpless, man personifies nature or else peoples it with beings like himself. When we have done this "we can breathe freely, we can feel at home in face of the supernatural, and we can deal psychically with our frantic anxiety."[12]

Hume and Freud looked into human nature to find ever-present springs of religious belief. Other scholars took the word "origin" literally. They tried to account for supernatural beings with the aid of very bad history—bad because they lacked evidence with which to document the occurrences they described. For example, Edward B. Tylor in 1871 published a book in which he surmises that early man hit upon the notion of a soul as a device to account for the difference between a live and dead body and to explain dreams.[13] Death comes when a soul permanently quits its body. Should a soul merely travel a bit during sleep, then a person dreams about whatever the errant wanderer

[11] David Hume, *The Natural History of Religion*, ed. H. E. Root (London, 1956), p. 28.
[12] Sigmund Freud, *The Future of an Illusion*, trans. W. D. Robson-Scott (New York, 1949), p. 29.
[13] Edward Burnett Tylor, *Primitive Culture*, 2 vols., 3rd rev. ed. (London, 1891), I, chap. 11.

experiences. Now, some contemporary communities did indeed hold beliefs like these. But that fact alone hardly allowed Tylor to claim that he had uncovered man's original beliefs. Tylor went on to describe prehistoric men modeling spiritual beings according to the way they conceived of the soul and endowing those beings with superhuman power to control all nature. Tylor's theory, proved unsatisfactory even in his day and scholars hastened to improve on it, unfortunately without any more evidence than he had. Today all these theories have become curiosities, survivals from anthropology's early history.

Émile Durkheim was another searcher eager to understand the origin of religious beliefs. He floundered between a dynamic explanation like Hume's and a fake historical reconstruction like Tylor's.[14] Promising to deal with ever-present sources of belief he rummaged for these in books describing the Australian aborigines. In their culture Durkheim thought he had discovered the most primitive and simple religion in existence. Here he made Tylor's error, hoping to discover sound evidence of history in documents dated at least half a million years too late. Durkheim believed that totems were the prototype of many supernatural beings. Originally totemic birds or other animals merely symbolized a group. But the constant association of a totem with the constraint, elation, and other feelings that group life arouses in people led early men to ascribe these emotions to the totem. They could not account for them naturalistically, as the social scientist does when he attributes them to social life itself. Through this error of early man totems came to be conceived as sacred sources of self-confidence, strength, and vitality, feelings that grip people in groups. The totems became gods.

SENTIENCE AND POWER

Some ideas honored in ritual (Durkheim called them collectively held representations) possess both sentience, so that they know the wishes of people, and power, with which they are able to meet their worshipers' needs. Hopi Indian Katchinas fall into this category. I do not mean the masked dancers who file from a kiva on the ninth day of big ceremonies and dance in the crowded, dusty village plaza, but those 200 or more beneficent and evil supernatural beings, some of whom the dancers represent and embody. They are also modeled in dolls (though not in the spurious "Katchina dolls" tourists buy). Ordinarily Katchinas are supposed to live in the snow-covered San Francisco mountains near Flagstaff, Arizona. To these supernatural targets—gods, messengers of gods, and ancestors—the Hopi, in behalf of health and prosperity, direct their ceremonies. In addition

[14] Emile Durkheim, *The Elementary Forms of the Religious Life*, trans. Joseph Ward Swain (London, 1915).

Hopi Katchina dolls. (*Harold S. Colton*, Hopi Kachina Dolls, *Albuquerque, 1949, by permisison of the University of New Mexico Press.*)

to Katchinas the Hopi recognize some 32 additional major sentient deities, a few of whom they also impersonate and model in figurines. They also believe in souls of Hopi who live on without becoming Katchinas. These, however, largely lack any power over the affairs of the living.

In addition to heeding a profusion of minor supernaturals, many social systems also acknowledge a high god who carries over-all authority, power, or omniscience. Outside of large-scale communities, however, his worship tends to be neglected. Rituals pay greater attention to more specific, less august power entities with attributes closer to those of the ordinary man. Even under large-scale conditions communicants often attempt to reach the high god through appeals made directly to lower ranking saints or minor deities. Thus, Muslims in Swat seek relief from many ailments and success in passing an examination by praying to dead saints who lie housed under imposing tombs located in cool, verdant groves. Yet these Muslims admit that only God's will counts for He alone is supreme.

Duties assigned to sentient, powerful collective representations always reflect a social system's problems, its state of technical development, and its range of knowledge. Hence any important change in those aspects of culture swiftly ushers into the culture new conceptions of the deities, particularly new expectations of what can be awaited from them. In this way cultural change has weakened religious faith in Europe and America. The revolution in technical development—the Industrial Revolution—greatly

SHAMANS ACQUIRE POWER THROUGH DREAMS AND VISIONS OF COLLECTIVE REPRESENTATIONS

Many communities depend on shamans, men and women who won their supernatural power through dreams or visions and use it to help their fellows. American Indian youths spent several days fasting in lonely places waiting for the supernatural to vouchsafe itself in helpful visions.

These two drawings were made by Anarqaq, an Iglulik Eskimo shaman, who saw spirits while awake and asleep. To the left is the Spirit of the Musk-Ox. Eyeless, it senses everything through its ears, which resemble horns. Anarqaq met it one day while he was hunting. It explained that it had been looking for a shaman to serve and henceforth would always follow him. But he must never turn around expecting to find it, for then it would disappear at once. Musk-Ox spirit enabled Anarqaq to heal many ailments. To the right is the same shaman's drawing of Water-Man, a spirit that alternates between dog and man. Always it lacks a belly. Among Eskimo, where illness frequently results because supernaturals have stolen souls, Water-Man proved to be of great assistance, for his special talent is finding stolen souls. He exercised this talent in Anarqaq's behalf.

Knud Rasmussen, *Intellectual Culture of the Iglulik Eskimos,* Report of the Fifth Thule Expedition, 1921-1924, vol. 7, no. 1, 1929, pp. 160, 208.

---

shortened the span of control that people left in God's hands. Men began to rely on expert knowledge, drugs, surgery, and science more than on submission to God's omnipotence and mercy. Naturally churchgoing fell off. With things as they are today, it is unlikely that the third of the U.S. population currently without church affiliation[15] will ever join a congregation. Members of the clergy need not expect soon to regain their practically extinct public authority.

In small-scale social systems transformation of the gods proceeds quite easily for it encounters resistance from no vested interests. Should the community encounter an appealing new deity it either makes place in the pantheon for the stranger or else fuses him with a compatible existing deity. Let the his-

[15] According to the Board of American Missions of the United Lutheran Church, reported in *The New York Times,* April 30, 1960.

torians later delightedly peel off each added layer of meaning imposed on the protean concept. In a large-scale community change in religious conceptions comes more slowly. Theologians strive mightily to keep collective representations immutable and bitterly contest as heresy even small changes.

CONSECRATED HISTORY

Man fashions some collective representations with the aid of his memory. He recalls revered historic personages, their legendary brave deeds, or the mighty trials which they successfully overcame. We consecrate these ideas just as we consecrate ideas about supernatural beings, that is, we invest them with ultra significance. Once consecration is done, who cares if the idea can be accurately documented or not? In forward-looking fashion even the millennium becomes a collective representation, and who can document that? Ceremonialists don't, of course, address these nonsentient collective representations in man-to-man fashion. That would be absurd. But they take pains to honor the idealized hero as he deserves, to commemorate the notable event, or to hail the group's steady progress toward the perfect millennium. In this religious spirit Americans celebrate Memorial Day, Lincoln's birthday, and the Fourth of July.

Nonsentient collective representations are quite important in large-scale social systems. Along with related concepts, like capitalism, communism, and freedom, they absorb some of the emotional fervor which in sacred cultures goes to powerful, feared, or loved supernatural beings. A cultural outsider can see similarity in both kinds of collective representations. Don't they both invite people to express their sentiments toward symbols ritually? Both possess extremely complex meanings. In God as well as in George Washington is bound up our certitude that goodness is worthwhile and inevitably more powerful than evil. Both embody conceptions of history and endorse the rightness of our laws and our social order. Attributes invested in God, Jesus, Lincoln, and Muhammad specify very precisely the virtues they symbolize, yet they don't do this too specifically, for then the heroic figures would cease to be models that could continue to be emulated for centuries despite vast cultural changes. Generality of meaning insures their viability.

The most sacred collective representations, as Durkheim pointed out, symbolize the social system itself. People who celebrate what happened in their national past in a sense worship themselves. In a community segmented into classes, castes, sects, and rival power blocs powerful symbols like God and George Washington call for a unity that transcends segmental loyalty. Hence care must be taken lest the symbols be "stolen" and identified too narrowly with either capital or labor, rich or poor. If that happens they lose their function of helping to bind together the whole.

FLAGS, FOODS, PHARMACEUTICALS

In addition to collective representations ritual comprises techniques by which the celebrants manipulate objects or their own bodies in an effort to express understandings bound up with the ceremonial occasion. Techniques, too, serve splendidly as symbols: bride and groom eat together, thereby symbolizing their newly established unity; worshipers bow in prayer and thereby express respect; ceremonialists bathe, wash, and vomit to establish their outer and inner purity; occasionally sexual intercourse serves ritualists as a technique with which to manifest their hope for a fertile harvest. Some ritual techniques lend extra excitement. They stress the occasion's importance. Chastising the initiate in becoming-a-man ceremonies impresses everyone with the momentous transition that is underway. Bodily mutilation, like circumcision, inflicted on a boy or girl in such ceremonies leaves a permanent badge of earned status. Generally, a social system favors a relatively small repertory of basic ritual techniques that recur from one ceremony to another. They constitute the culture's ritual idiom. For example, Hopi Indians wash their hair in yucca suds, induce vomiting, and sprinkle corn meal as frequent gestures of purification.

Techniques by themselves won't suffice; they must be carried out by someone of proper status and must be accompanied by the right objects or substances. Things people use to express themselves ritually—flags, foods, ointments, pollen, vestments, dolls, staves, and esoteric objects reverently wrapped in bundles—are loaded with symbolism and are powerful stimulants of emotion. A complex ritual may revolve around only a small ritual specific pregnant with meaning, for example, a cross, image, or pharmaceutical. Many U.S. Indian tribes practice Peyote Religion, a system of worship which spread from Mexico into the Great Plains late in the nineteenth century. Compared to the formalism characteristic of many established American churches, Peyote Religion (chartered as the Native American Church) lacks any codified doctrine to bind the tribal groups which practice it. The central collective representation is Power, something God bestows on man to keep him successful and healthy. Peyote, the flat top of a low-growing desert cactus, is the chief ritual specific. It incarnates Power. To eat peyote means to absorb directly God-given Power. The pharmaceutical's remarkable physiological and psychological effects when eaten easily support this belief. However, plain water drunk during the ritual also contains Power. Peyote Religion embodies the Peyote Road, a loose ethical code that enjoins brotherly love, care of one's family, self-reliance, and abstinence from alcohol. Peyotists celebrate their ritual at regular intervals in a tipi resembling the old-time Plains Indian dwelling. Peyote, being a chemical "mind changer," induces visions, heightens participants' ability to introspect, and sensitizes their consciences. Thus aided worshipers silently confess their sins, resolve on a better life, and experience a self-transcending state of blessedness. Let a Menomini Indian describe his feelings: "suddenly I hear something. . . . a sound . . . kind of a ring, like if when those telephone wires get hit by something. It got louder and louder. I was just sitting there, then a light from far off, way up, like a star . . . like as if I was outdoors like now, come towards me. It come fast, coming right towards me. Then it come real close, right up in front of me, and busted. . . . just like one of them fireworks. . . . I could see everything clear. That was good. It meant everything was going alright. It was a message from heaven. It showed me I was doing good, doing the right thing, that I should keep on."[16]

Although peyotists call themselves Christians, missionaries and others have repeatedly but so far unsuccessfully tried to suppress Peyote Religion on grounds that it is harmful. They often call peyote a drug to brand it unfavorably and outlaw its use. The ritual successfully functions to maintain a degree of tribal cohesion. It creates a sense of pan-Indian solidarity and contributes to personal adjustment. Its rapid spread in the nineteenth century can be attributed to the way it helped depressed Indian tribes adjust to the grim conditions that followed white encroachment on their lands. It has provided the Indian with an opportunity to blend meaningful traits of Christianity with cherished elements of his traditional religion, like visions.

The variety of techniques and objects potentially suitable to promote ritual expression is nearly unlimited. It ranges from human sacrifice to polygyny to intoxication. No social system is strong enough to tolerate complete religious freedom. At some point ritual expression is guaranteed to clash with other norms. Sects that spring up believing they are executing divine will won't allow their rituals to be tampered with. Their rituals protect their identity as groups and they will fight to maintain their integrity. Only armed might can suppress some obstinate ritual practices. The U.S. Government needed armed force to crush the Plains Indian Sun Dance and then made laws by which it became a criminal offense to perform this and other "pagan" ceremonies. By such steps we hoped to hasten the Indians progress toward standards unblushingly called "Christian civilization."

Not only what people do and use goes into constructing ritual but also what they avoid. Taboos, too, mean something and through their symbolism contribute to a ritual's expressiveness. For example, sexual abstinence enjoined on a Hopi ceremonialist makes him pure. From an outsider's point of view, refraining from sexual intercourse before a ritual points up the importance of the role about to be performed. The Catholic's abstinence from meat on Fridays acknowledges Christ's sacrifice. We refrain from light conversation and

---

[16] George D. Spindler, "Personal Documents in Menomini Peyotism," *Microcard Publications of Primary Records in Culture and Personality*, 2, no. 13 (n.d.), 22.

laughter during a funeral because they would clash with the gravity called for by that solemn occasion.

Not all rituals are equally rich in expressive symbolic components. But the grand ceremonies do make their impact from the way they organize dozens of elements, integrating them artistically in a well-knit assemblage that has clear-cut meaning for participants. Myths are repositories of this over-all meaning. They also perpetuate the significance attached to specific ritual components and may link each step in the rite with some momentous event of the past. But times do change and in an altered culture myths lose their force. Ceremonies too lose their validity for persons who identify whole-heartedly with a foreign way of life. A fictional Apache Indian world war veteran who sneers at the girls' puberty rite of his tribe sees no incarnation of White Painted Lady but a tired little bobby-soxer. " 'I'm supposed to think that kid in that tent who was down at the trading post yesterday in bobby socks listening to a Frank Sinatra record is a *goddess*. Look at those fools—holding their kids up to her so she can *bless* them!' " The young veteran's face grew tight. " 'It makes me sick,' he said. . . . 'This stuff belongs in some jungle somewhere, in Africa maybe. When are they going to grow up?' "[17]

FURTHER READING

Good introductory accounts to comparative religion viewed anthropologically are abundant and I shall select only a few. Eliot D. Chapple and Carleton S. Coon, *Principles of Anthropology* (New York, 1942), chaps. 21-23, is a book from which I have learned much; therefore I list it first. Parts of Chapple and Coon's theory are used by Charles P. Loomis and J. Allan Beegle in examining rural American religion in *Rural Social Systems* (New York, 1950), chaps. 12-13. Also see A. R. Radcliffe-Brown, *Structure and Function in Primitive Society* (London, 1952), chaps. 6-8. It consists of papers originally published much earlier. My own approach stems from these men and is developed more fully in John J. Honigmann, *The World of Man* (New York, 1959), chaps. 31, 38. Franz Boas, *The Mind of Primitive Man,* rev. ed. (New York, 1938), chap. 12, illustrates at length the conventional nature of etiquette.

Accounts in other textbooks are more traditional. See, for example, Ruth Benedict, "Religion," in Franz Boas, ed., *General Anthropology* (New York, 1938); Alexander Goldenweiser, *Anthropology* (New York, 1946), chaps. 14-18; Joseph Haekel, "Religion," in Leonhard Adam and Hermann Trimborn, eds., *Lehrbuch der Voelkerkunde* (Stuttgart, 1958); Robert H. Lowie, *Primitive Religion* (New York, 1925); and William Howells, *The Heathens* (Garden City, N.Y., 1948).

Edward Norbeck, *Religion in Primitive Society* (New York, 1961), one of the most recent textbooks in the anthropology of religion, stands apart from others because of the author's functional orientation. An interesting focus on interpersonal ritual is given in two papers by Erving Goffman, "On Face-Work: An

[17] Elliott Arnold, "Spirit of Cochise," *Collier's,* 135, no. 4 (February 18, 1955), 68, 70-75. Dialogue slightly rearranged.

Analysis of Ritual Elements in Social Interaction," *Psychiatry*, 18 (1955), 213-231, and "The Nature of Deference and Demeanor," *American Anthropologist*, 58 (1956), 473-502. Edward Sapir's article "Symbolism" in the *Encyclopaedia of the Social Sciences* (New York, 1934) serves nicely to explain the symbolism inherent in ritual and so does Bronislaw Malinowski's article "Marriage" in the *Encyclopaedia Britannica*, 14th ed. (Chicago, 1929).

An excellent review of theories coined to explain religious origins is given in Wilhelm Schmidt, *The Origin and Growth of Religion*, trans. H. J. Rose (London, 1931). Schmidt's own contribution is no better than those he demolishes. For a brief account of shamanism see Mircea Eliade, "Shamanism," in Vergilius Ferm, ed., *Forgotten Religions* (New York, 1950). Max Gluckman has a fine discussion of ritual license in *Custom and Conflict in Africa* (Oxford, 1955), chap. 5. Raymond Firth's "Religious Belief and Personal Adjustment," *The Journal of the Royal Anthropological Institute*, 78 (1948), 25-44, analyzes how European religious belief changed in step with other changes in culture. Another study in the reinterpretation of beliefs is Lawrence Wilson, "The Gods of New England," *Pacific Spectator*, 9 (1955), 141-153. Clyde Kluckhohn systematically relates "Myths and Rituals," *The Harvard Theological Review*, 35 (1942), 45-79.

Islamic ritual is reviewed in Carleton S. Coon, *Caravan* (New York, 1951), chap. 7, and the Five Pillars of Faith more fully in G.-H. Bousquet, *Les Grandes pratiques rituelles de l'Islam* (Paris, 1949). Among accounts of Hopi religion I can recommend Mischa Titiev, "The Religion of the Hopi Indians," in Vergilius Ferm, ed., *Forgotten Religions*. J. Walter Fewkes reproduces in color *Hopi Katcinas Drawn by Native Artists*, Annual Reports of the Bureau of American Ethnology, no. 21, 1903. A similar article for pueblos in general is Paul Coze, "Kachinas: Masked Dancers of the Southwest," *National Geographic Magazine*, 112 (1957), 219-236. The difference traditional ritual makes in Hopi village life can be seen from Laura Thompson's comparison of Hopi villages where it broke down and where it remains relatively intact in *Culture in Crisis* (New York, 1950).

John Collier describes the former significance and ultimate fate of the Plains Indian Sun Dance in *The Indians of the Americas* (New York, 1947), pp. 230-242. Much has been written on the Peyote Religion. Three important works are Weston La Barre, *The Peyote Cult*, Yale University Publications in Anthropology, no. 19, 1938; J. S. Slotkin, *The Peyote Religion: A Study in Indian-White Relations* (Glencoe, Ill., 1956); and Weston La Barre, "Twenty Years of Peyote Studies," *Current Anthropology*, 1 (1960), 45-60. On how U.S. courts have limited freedom of religion see R. F. Bellamy *et al.*, *A Preface to the Social Sciences* (New York, 1956), pp. 442-448.

Anthropologists have studied some exotic religions very throughly. To mention only a few recent book-length reports: E. E. Evans-Pritchard, *Nuer Religion* (Oxford, 1956); Clifford Geertz, *The Religion of Java* (Glencoe, 1960); Godfrey Lienhardt, *Divinity and Experience, The Religion of the Dinka* (Oxford, 1961); J. Middleton, *Lugbara Religion, Ritual and Authority among an East African People* (London, 1960); B. A. Pauw, *Religion in a Tswana Chiefdom* (London, 1960). Also, LeRoy Bowman looks at *The American Funeral* (Washington D. C., 1959) as a display of guilt, extravagance, and sublimity. Camara Laye's memories of a West African childhood, *The Dark Child*, trans. James Kirkup (London, 1955), provide a wonderful perspective for understanding childhood initiation rituals as practiced in the Republic of Guinea.

10

A Variety of World Views

. . . ideas . . . are not personal and are not restricted to me; I share them, to a large degree, with all the men who belong to the same social group that I do. Because they are held in common, concepts are the supreme instrument of all intellectual exchange. By means of them minds communicate.

Émile Durkheim[1]

ALL MEN POSSESS A WORLD VIEW

Every culture possesses a body of ideas and values which guide people's behavior. The fund of knowledge and belief may be so vast and detailed that it must be divided into many impregnable academic monopolies: history, philosophy, zoology, physics, psychology, religion, and others. Usually the stock of ideas is far more modest, homogeneous, and systematic; it is possessed by practically everyone in the social system, rather than being broken down among specialists.

"World view" is a good term to describe the aggregate of ideas and values that form the basis of a social system. Facts have fully quashed the supposition that there is any social system whose members are intellectually too feeble to reason coherently and build a logically defensible world view. Though, like us, man in a small-scale, exotic community may err, inherently he is nowhere predisposed to think in an inferior way or "prelogically." His thinking often looks erroneous to us but that is because *we* are ignorant of his assumptions about man and nature. All social systems, large and small, first reason from a few unproven, underlying assumptions, possibly self-evident axioms, which as long as they work remain unchallenged. The modern scientist's faith that

[1] "The Dualism of Human Nature and Its Social Conditions," trans. Charles Blend, in Kurt H. Wolff, ed., *Émile Durkheim, 1858-1917* (Columbus, Ohio, 1960), p. 327.

nature is orderly and, therefore, that he can know it through careful, objective procedures is an unproven but so far consistently useful assumption. Understanding culture depends much on grasping the often unspoken assumptions in which a group trusts.

That man holds assumptions and through reason builds world views reflects a peculiarity of human beings. All animals are physiologically equipped to experience the world through their senses. But evolution gave man more than it bestowed on other animals, namely, enhanced ability to reflect upon what he experiences. Since all men possess this power (except subnormal individuals, who don't concern us), by itself it fails to explain why world views vary between cultures. Ideas entertained in any social system depend on the total situation in which people find themselves, especially on the rest of their culture. As total situation alters, ideas also alter, though I don't mean that ideas alter *only* after something else has changed. They may well change initially, and other things will then follow from man's altered perceptions. What is relevant knowledge for a hunting band is irrelevant to farmers, just as termites in an organ loft enjoy no note of Bach but only the wood. A capitalist or communist country puts high value on thrift and extols its importance for creating wealth but people who subsist through food gathering can't save. Where costly machines depreciate whether they are used or stand idle, time literally equals money. In contrast, patient Hopi farmers evaluate time in a much more relaxed fashion. Through its specialized equipment a large-scale culture enables intensive probing of nature that augments the fund of knowledge. It allows professional scientists and philosophers time to search, doubt, test, and revise what they formerly believed. A small-scale community adds ideas less deliberately and so its knowledge changes slowly. A small-scale, nonliterate culture contains no specialized equipment for research or statuses devoted to learning and without writing people cannot conserve their reflections. These are some reasons why world views vary.

WHAT IS IMPORTANT?

A world view proclaims how man and nature are organized and also registers decisions about the value of such knowledge. World views consist of perceptions informed by values.[2]

Self, God, or group? Which comes first?
What group deserves loyalty? Family, tribe, neighborhood, nation, or an as yet hardly emerged international society?
Shall priority go to the poet, scientist, priest, warrior, administrator, or entrepreneur?

[2] Florence R. Kluckhohn, "Dominant and Substitute Profiles of Cultural Orientations; Their Significance for the Analysis of Social Stratification," *Social Forces*, 28 (1950), 376-393.

Is the most significant time dimension the past from whence we come, the future toward which we aspire, or simply the present?

Can man dominate nature, should he surrender to it, or should he contrive to live with it harmoniously?

How important are originality and variety and, therefore, tolerance? Should stress properly be on tradition and conformity?

Armed with values men decide how to act, sit in judgment on one another, and appraise other ways of life. Some psychologists once believed that they could condition human beings to accept anything—even something monstrous or absurd—as good, beautiful, or true. Our fear of propaganda, while justifiable, reflects this outmoded doctrine. Values are indeed learned but only if they accord with an individual's personal beliefs and his culture. Otherwise, how easy it would have been to convert the Plains Indians into farmers and make Soviet writers content with state control! If propaganda can sell anything, South Sea missionaries and technical assistance experts in underdeveloped countries might have successfully persuaded their pupils to renounce sex more stringently, work harder, and provide themselves with better sanitary facilities. Only when a propagandist knows what is likely to appeal and is able to cast his message masterfully in that mold, can he control other men's minds.

Some values, like health, in-group harmony, courage, and respect for elders, range freely across many cultural boundaries. So do negative values placed on murder, adultery, and theft. But even these, like all values, are situationally anchored. In war we are ready to undermine an enemy's health to destroy him. Most of the time we tell the truth, but not under certain conditions. Few people, reviewers excepted, would truthfully tell a proud author that his book is puerile. Nobody expects the President to compose "his own" speeches. Yet, without qualms we expel a university student who hands in a ghost-written thesis. And a congressman, wise in hindsight, is allowed to correct his remarks, so that what appears in the *Congressional Record* isn't what he said on the floor. In every loosely structured cultures, like that of Ceylon and others in Southeast Asia, people even more readily overlook paramount values should circumstances be inconvenient.[3]

SCIENCE AND TESTING KNOWLEDGE

Testing knowledge is at least as old as human life. Even animals act as if they form tentative conclusions on which they hopefully or apprehensively approach some mysterious object. In all social systems men inadvertently test some of their knowledge. A community with craft specialists who make goods

[3] John F. Embree, "Thailand—A Loosely Structured Social System," *American Anthropologist*, 52 (1950), 181-193; Bryce F. Ryan and Murray A. Straus, "The Integration of Sinhalese Society," *Research Studies of the State College of Washington*, 22 (1954), 179-227.

to be marketed gives added inducement to deliberate experimentation. The craftsmen try new ways which, if they succeed, rapidly change culture. Naturally people don't or can't test everything. That in-group murder is evil needs no experiment. That kind or angry supernatural beings send rain, illness, drought, and children is, in one sense, tested each time these things occur.

Deliberate procedures for testing vary between situations and also between cultures. To ascertain an accused criminal's guilt one doesn't apply criteria reserved for discovering whether a certain clay will make good pots. And we ascertain guilt differently from the East African Azande. Our intricate laws of courtroom evidence insist on fairly direct proof that the accused actually committed the offense with which he is charged. Hearsay evidence isn't allowed. The Azande recognize quite well the merit of direct evidence but nevertheless employ very indirect means to reach what usually turns out to be a satisfactory decision.[4] They administer poison to a fowl. If it survives the ordeal then the defendant is innocent. We look on most such criteria of truth as wholly unacceptable. And, indeed, we ought to. Ever since the Renaissance, Europeans dissatisfied with customary bases of certainty have sought more reliable techniques through which to substantiate knowledge. We have succeeded in finding some, though much more effectively for impersonal natural phenomena than for human behavior.

Simply to experiment doesn't equal science. Science is considerably more than saying in a common-sense fashion, "Let's try it and see." A Kaska Indian who tries to repair a broken snowshoe with a piece of wire, even if he succeeds, doesn't earn a place in the ranks of Marie Curie and Albert Einstein. Science is not skilled craftsmanship. A Hopi potter and Kaska fisherman are technologists. Fully capable of controlling their respective techniques, they lack the vision that accredits scientists.

Science consists of two accomplishments. It starts in, or leads up to, a theory—a vision—of order inhering in some phenomena. The vision may turn out to be false, but science means striving after systematic, general knowledge. Science aims at broader information than determining when fish bite in a particular lake. It wants to understand fish in general. Anthropology is more than ethnography of Kaska or Hopi Indians. Its goal is understanding culture in general. Sometimes a general theory of order guides the scientist from the moment he starts making observations. Or sheer curiosity may impel him to observe and only later does he construct a statement which in general terms accounts for what he observed.

As a second accomplishment, science critically tests its theories, using whatever means a scientist commands. The astronomer tests when he scans the

---

[4] E. E. Evans-Pritchard, *Witchcraft, Oracles and Magic Among the Azande* (Oxford, 1937), pp. 258-351.

skies, the chemist when he repeats another man's experiment, and a physicist when he offers data to a computer to mull over. Just as people's wants outrun their resources, so theories grow faster than means for testing them. Some theories are tested only logically. The author and his peers examine the work for fallacies and plausibility. They weigh it against rival theories which purport to cover the same subject.

There is not merely one scientific method. The world's scientists do not possess any unified orientation to research. Methods vary with subject matter and with culture. An abrupt break separates American and Soviet scientific traditions. American scientists believe they should pursue discovery without regard for religious or political convictions. Soviets believe that Marxism-Leninism gives added meaning to scientific theories which in turn invigorate and transform that philosophy. Hence scientists in the U.S.S.R. try as far as possible to interpret their theories in harmony with their guiding philosophy.

Like some other notable traits in world culture, science originated more than once. Long before the Renaissance it emerged in ancient India, Egypt, and Greece. Never, though, has the combination of systematic thought, empirical observation, and experimentation proven as fruitful as it did in western Europe following the sixteenth century. The eighteenth century then applied scientific knowledge to technology, a feat that revolutionized world culture.

IDEAS ABOUT TIME

To examine the diversity of world views more closely, consider time. At first it might seem that time is time. True, some people count it by clock or calendar. Others calculate by new moons and by the flow of seasons saying, "that child is four winters old" or "its father died two moons back." Still another form of time reckoning is social; instead of calculating how many years a man has lived, his friends consult his social responsibilities: he is an initiate, or well into his career period, or he is retired. Bygone time may be seen not as elapsed years but as a genealogy that culminates in a fabulous ancestor. But apart from diverse ways of tracing time, time means different things in various cultures. Time is valued in different ways or lacks value as an end in itself. People who don't own clocks can tell time to suit their purposes but, unlike us, they evade being pressured by time. For them time passes; it can't be wasted, and therefore doesn't have to be saved and rationed as though it were money. Such people—rural Greeks fit the type—hate to schedule their activities rigidly. Among them neither guests nor meals arrive by the clock. Nor does Mass begin on the hour. Such casual attitudes disconcert and shock Americans, who feel their time is too valuable to waste in waiting. Hence we stress promptness, make agendas, and terminate appointments with dispatch so that the next person will get in on time. Identical intervals of time have unequal significance between cultures. In Latin America to be kept waiting 30 or 40 minutes in an outer office is as insignificant as five minutes in New York City.

All social systems have a past which, if people choose, can become the dimension of time invested with maximum importance. A community can also emphasize the future or it can act as though only the present matters. Americans for the most part dismiss the past; we value practically nothing simply because it is old. (Antique hunters, bibliophiles, and archeologists obviously don't fit this generalization.) Ambitious immigrants coming to the New World from many parts of Europe shed their feeling for their several, unrelated pasts.[5] They focused attention on their children and on what a great thing the future would be for them. Spanish-Americans in the southwestern United States also fail to venerate the past. But for them the present is most important. The future, they feel, will be much like the present, so why plan ahead? Future-oriented folk find this attitude impossible to grasp sympathetically. Kazakh and Uzbek pastoralists in Soviet Central Asia are profoundly involved with the past.[6] Through their lineages they trace ancestry many generations back. All lineages are related to one another on a master genealogy by means of which the whole tribe affirms its unity. Strangers who meet search for kinship by counting back to when their lineages segmented from a common stem. Should two lineages become allies, they "register" their relationship, amending their genealogies if necessary to show that both descended from a common ancestor. They rewrite the past in order to validate the present. Central Asian pastoralists value a thing because it is old. Leading men are always seniors to whom juniors respectfully defer. Offices are inherited by primogeniture, which is another way of showing respect for age and for the past where age is anchored.

All over the world traditional orientations to time have been attacked, especially those that favor past and present. Urban Greek citizens urge rural Greeks not just to pass time but to budget it. People who live primarily for the present are told to give more thought to the future, so that it won't be like the present. In Soviet Central Asia, where a radical communist world view emphasizes youth and originality and culture is changing under forced draft, elders are no longer able to guide and their authority has been reduced.

Even we who invest great emotion in that which will be are retrospective enough to write histories and cultivate myths. History is the scholar's interpretation of the past based on documented facts. Myths affirm the value of past events, even those unsupported by sound documentary evidence. A social sys-

[5] Margaret Mead, *The American Troops and the British Community* (London, 1944), p. 6.

[6] American University, Bureau of Social Science Research, *Soviet Central Asia,* 3 vols., Subcontractor's Monograph, HRAF-49, American U.-1, 1956, vol. I, pp. 330-350.

A NEW ENGLAND TOWN REVIEWS ITS HISTORY

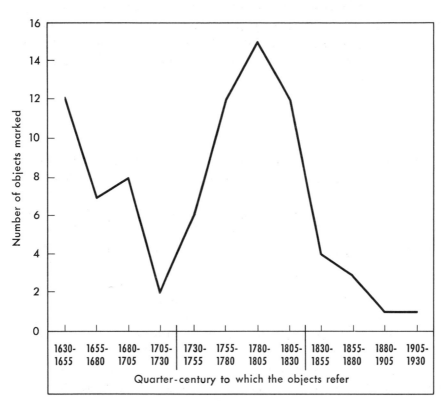

Yankee City held a historical procession to celebrate its 300th birthday and the anni-versary of Massachusetts Bay Colony. Attentive anthropologists counted the number of marked objects displayed in the procession and noted each 25-year period to which the objects symbolically referred. The table gives results of this analysis.

The peak period, 1755-1830, was Yankee City's golden age and holds the greatest significance for contemporary Yankee City. Over half of the 83 objects marked and car-ried in procession come from this time, a time when the town stood at the pinnacle of prestige and prosperity. And it includes the Revolutionary War, an episode for which Americans reserve profound reverence.

W. Lloyd Warner, The Living and the Dead (New Haven, 1959), p. 134.

tem's value-charged mythology is a distillation of the past prepared from selected facts and beliefs. Although people vouch for their myths' historical accuracy, anthropologists have learned to be wary about depending on such cherished accounts of "really old times." Even communities equipped with writing to conserve facts readily distort bygone phenomena. Consider, for example, Washington's unblemished reputation or how utterly gloriously we view the War of American Independence. Take away writing and the enticement to distort becomes irresistible.

Myths justify present behavior in terms of what is supposed to have gone before. Forms of government, land ownership, social obligations, ceremonies, or almost anything can be haloed through a mythologized antiquity. Or, as I have already said, people add to their myths in order to keep pace with changing times.

SPACE IN DEMAND

An American purchases land after he has appraised the plot in terms of his purposes. A shipyard needs access to water; a factory benefits from a nearby highway or railroad; a house is warmer if oriented southward. Other social systems go further in evaluating space. Chinese, who can afford to, traditionally site their homes and their revered ancestors' graves wherever the landscape's configuration promises to bestow good fortune and prosperity. In their world view a properly located grave does much to further prosperity in the living. Specialized geomancers with instruments pronounce on the suitability of a site. Descendants who prosper sometimes exhume their ancestors and belatedly inter the bones in more favorable places for continued good fortune. Families even compete for gravesites replete with good influence and sometimes poach by planting their dead too near the auspiciously situated graves of another family. Rural Japanese also invest space with special significance.[7] Fortunate things enter a house from the southeast, therefore a wise owner orients his house that way. The storeroom he puts in the extreme northwest corner of the compound where it will catch all possible income flowing from southeast to northwest. In both these Oriental countries western ideas have undermined faith in such traditional beliefs.

A professional geographer conceives of global space quite differently from a layman. We all know that the Sahara is in northern Africa but most of us are pretty vague about how much space it occupies or how long it takes to fly across its length. Thus, there are several kinds of maps, the professional employs one and laymen others. Small-scale social systems cannot imagine magnitudes of space that U.S. high school students take for granted. I tried to tell an Eskimo how many miles intervened between his country and mine. Soon I realized that even though he knew the concept of a mile, he didn't comprehend so vast a number of them. So I translated the information into the days it would take to cover the distance by plane and train. He had never traveled those ways and so knew nothing of their speed. Then I tried to explain in

[7] Richard K. Beardsley, J. W. Hall, and R. E. Ward, *Village Japan* (Chicago, 1959), pp. 77-81.

terms of dogteam days, figuring a dog team pulling a sled covered about 20 miles daily. But that proved equally incomprehensible to the Eskimo. Who would undertake a sled journey of 90 days? I gave up trying to describe how far away I lived.

The way urban and suburban Americans appraise space would mystify a Hopi farmer. City land is not valuable because it is fertile, provides rich pasture, or has a good spring but because it is scarce—more individuals wish to live and work on it than it can accommodate. Manhattan Island and other business districts are built up into the air to accommodate everybody who wishes to locate in that restricted space.

Lacking concepts like miles or kilometers into which to divide long distances, people calculate space in terms of time. We do this too. We estimate that we live an hour from the office or ten minutes from town (train or automobile understood). You recall that for us time equals money. Therefore space expressed as time can also be converted into money. Land costs more when it is close to the business district than when it is far out. Another way we appraise space is by the social worth of those persons who currently live in it. Property in an exclusive upper-class neighborhood commands exorbitant prices. With such property plus other qualifications an ambitious family might manage to reach the top of the social-class pyramid.

USES FOR THE SOUL

Universally man conceives himself as uniting a body with an intangible, hidden self or selves. He calls upon the covert side of his being to explain illness, death, good-fortune, courage, and similar phenomena. At the same time he is mindful of properly caring for his inner self and so ponders momentous questions like: "What is a man profited, if he shall gain the whole world, and lose his own soul?"[8]

Proof of the soul's existence is easy. Like many American Indians, the Kaska endow a man with plural souls. One of these, the taiyush, can safely leave its mortal shell temporarily but death follows should it stay away. Sometime after death the taiyush is reincarnated in a newborn baby. Déjà vu—the fairly common, vague feeling of having previously been in what obviously is a new place—constitutes proof for the Kaska that souls are reincarnated. Unlike his taiyush, a man's shadow after death lurks around his grave. It reveals itself in ghosts that make people uneasy. Dreams furnish Hopi Indians with proof of the soul. Dreams, they say, mirror whatever the errant soul experiences while it is free outside the body.

The atman, a Hindu believes, is man's true self because it incorporates

[8] Matthew 16:26.

Brahman in everyone.[9] Brahman can loosely be translated as world-soul, or God, but you must not then think of God as a Father possessing human attributes like wisdom and power. Brahman is neuter and it pervades the whole universe. Most people, busy making profit or achieving fame, completely overlook the atman within themselves. They have mislaid their souls under a thousand details.

> Smoke hides fire,
> Dust hides a mirror,
> The womb hides the embryo:
> By lust the Atman is hidden.

Hinduism expects a person to be wise enough to lock out the world and to look deeply into his self, there realizing his atman. In doing so he identifies himself with the all-pervasive Brahman. Mystically he fuses himself with the world-soul. Worldly sensations and desires cease to count for this individual. No wonder the experience is said to liberate a person. Hinduism makes belief in the atman the keystone of an elaborate doctrine to which I shall refer later.

WHY SOME MEN ARE SUCCESSFUL

Closely related to ideas about souls are concepts of integral abilities comprising part of a person. Biologists explain that aptitude, health, courage, and fortitude derive from joint action of an individual's hereditary endowment and his life experience. Other people, who also wonder why some men are strong and clever but others weak and foolish, offer other explanations. The Burmese, for example, point to the kan, that part of an individual which increases or declines but whose potency basically depends on whatever merit an individual accumulated during his previous existence.[10]

> . . . each man's life
> The outcome of his former living is,
> The bygone wrongs bring forth sorrows and woes,
> The bygone right breeds bliss.

No use counting on luck. Only a strong, potent kan keeps a man well and strong. If he is rich and powerful it is because he has inherited a vigorous kan and then further enhanced it through good deeds. Constant vigilance keeps his kan energetic. Only he can do so, without help of priests, magicians, or doctors. Carefully he must outweigh bad deeds that weaken his kan with good ones that earn him merit. Good deeds lie within everyone's power to

[9] Swami Prabhavananda and Christopher Isherwood, trans., *The Song of God: Bhagavad-Gita* (New York, 1951).

[10] Margaret Mead, ed., *Cultural Patterns and Technical Change* (Paris, 1953), pp. 43-66; Shway Yoe, *The Burman, His Life and Notions* (London, 1896).

perform. For example, one can give food daily to a mendicant Buddhist monk. Every man while growing up joins a monastery. Even living a few days as a monk boosts his kan. Some periods in life, like pregnancy, are dangerous because they reduce a woman's kan to a very low ebb. At such times hostile spirits can easily hurt her unless precautions are taken. Note how ideas of the kan function to induce Burmese to perform approved behavior. The kan provides these people with an explanatory concept as handy as the soul.

Nearly all American Indians formerly shared the Kaska concept of power. A person at birth lacked full ability to become a creditable man or woman. He acquired this extra power by "dreaming of animals in a lonely place," as one young Kaska put it to me.[11] Isolated in a lonely forest camp, a young man fasted and earnestly wished to be visited by a supernatural experience featuring some part of nature, a moose, deer, or tree, water, or thunder. When it came, the dream or apparition bequeathed him a song that in any emergency would augment his natural capacities. It gave him power to hunt well, cure illness, locate lost objects, kill enemies, and emerge from war unscathed. A successful man was one who during his lifetime managed to enlist support from several "helpers." Yet other searchers were inexplicably turned down. "Something, he don't want me," a Kaska youth sadly complained to me. Although girls could also win spiritual helpers, they sought them less assiduously than young men. Today in some American Indian tribes men regularly seek to replenish their individual spiritual power by ceremonially eating peyote, that mind-changing narcotic from a desert cactus.

One famous idea accounting for human abilities is mana.[12] The New Zealand Maori held mana to be an impersonal efficacy that resides in certain words, a name, land, the person of a chief, and a tribe. Because it is the basis of a person's power, mana induces others to obey his commands. I am aware that this definition, adapted from an expert's work on the Maori, leaves mana very unclear for a cultural outsider. Yet these Polynesians find mana no more mysterious than we do radio waves. In war Maori tribes used to force their mana across enemy lines to help weaken foes. Like a blessing the victors then absorbed into their own lives mana of the conquered. Like all beliefs of this genre, mana conveniently explains individual differences. Individuals unequally possessed this ineffable quality; poor people without social standing had very little. A person or thing possessing mana warranted special consideration; in other words, mana made individuals and objects tapu (taboo).

[11] John J. Honigmann, *Culture and Ethos of Kaska Society*, Yale University Publications in Anthropology, no. 40, 1949, pp. 218-219. Also see John J. Honigmann, *The Kaska Indians: An Ethnographic Reconstruction*, Yale University Publications in Anthropology, no. 51, 1954, pp. 104-108.

[12] J. Prytz Johansen, *The Maori and His Religion in Its Non-Ritualistic Aspects* (København, 1954), chap. 3.

KEEPING A GOOD MIND

A surprising number of cultures assume thought and action to be more or less equivalent. As a result, certain dangerous thoughts carry practically the same significance as parallel evil deeds. With beliefs like this, thought-control becomes a matter of practical importance.

Hopi Indians show clear faith in thought-control. Unhappy or hostile thoughts, they hold, affect one's total well-being because they corrupt body and mind. A person's thoughts also ruin others' welfare and spoil the efficacy of ceremonies for rain and prosperity. Dwelling on infirmities, Hopi believe, only makes them come more quickly. By urging one another to "keep a good heart" the Hopi encourage vigilant thought-control. The South African Lovedu reflect Freudian principles in their belief that even unconscious resentment between relatives leads to illness. Hence people in this African kingdom try mightily to reconcile kinsmen whom disputes have alienated. A number of juridical procedures in Lovedu culture show them bending their genius toward ending festering animosities.

Soviet communism conceives the link between thought and action in somewhat different terms.[13] One must have faith in the Truth as, at any given time, Communist party leaders know it. Any iota of doubt in the party line amounts to open treason. Doubt in the party's wisdom wrung the consciences of some Soviet officials so hard that they found relief in being accused of overt conspiracies they had never committed. We must see this behavior in terms of their own world view. They were patriotic enough to be frightened by their doubt, which they felt threatened their country as much as open sabotage or betrayal. Russians' tendency to equate thought and deed, though retained in Soviet culture, is older than communism. The idea appears in Dostoyevsky's work. Mitya in *The Brothers Karamazov,* for example, is overwhelmed with guilt for hating his father and wishing him dead, quite as if he had really committed patricide.

Some neurotic patients also suffer intense guilt simply because of forbidden thoughts. Normally, though, people don't become neurotically incapacitated, loaded down with burdensome guilt, because culturally they put thought and action on a par.

PROPERTY BECOMES SIGNIFICANT

Everything man does with property stems from a socially standardized conception of what is significant. And what is significant in turn reflects the

[13] Margaret Mead, *Soviet Attitudes Toward Authority* (New York, 1951), pp. 25-30; Nathan Leites and Elsa Bernaut, *Ritual of Liquidation* (Glencoe, Ill., 1954).

situation obtaining at a given time and place. Aboriginal Kaska Indians being food gatherers troubled themselves little about owning land. Unmarked boundaries separated band territories. Two bands simply couldn't afford to dispute the same ground for long and survive. Hunters avoided trespass not from a sense of mine and thine but because they knew that more people in a given area meant less food to go around. Individual hunters did own beaver creeks. Beaver are nonmigratory animals and Kaska Indians knew that private control allowed a man to kill these rodents selectively and thereby to maintain a permanent supply on which to draw for food and skins. Ideas toward land changed once fur-trapping came North. Now land guaranteed income and the Kaska established explicit boundaries between family trapping grounds. Trespass became a serious offense. But make no mistake, even previously the Kaska had recognized *some* private property. In fact, no social system fails to admit individual claims to certain tangible possessions or intangible rights, like the right to sing a given song or perform a dance. Even communistic Israeli kibbutzim are forced to admit private property, though wealth produced by the whole kibbutz is communally owned. Food gatherers, as though to balance the constant threat of starvation under which they live, often severely limit rights to private ownership. They insist on a kind of social insurance. A hunter is obliged to share any large animal he has killed with other families in his band. In turn, his family benefits when another man returns to camp loaded down after a successful hunt.

In middle-range social systems, like the Hopi or traditional African folk, harvested crops guarantee subsistence. Yet, even here, individuals seldom own agricultural land in the European sense. Generally, families merely have the right to use land. Primary control rests in the lineage or some other descent group. These circumstances forbid a man to sell ground he happens to cultivate, a point that European colonists too readily overlooked. Headmen and chiefs likewise have no greater power to alienate land. They are merely custodians, precisely as New York Tuscarora Indian chiefs argued before the Federal Power Commission in 1957 in protest against government's seizure of one-fifth of their tribe's land.

When subsistence farming breaks down and peasants begin to trade with townsfolk, land assumes cash value. Quickly individual land tenure replaces communal tenure with far-reaching changes in social relationships. In Swat, a peasant state, land can be bought, sold, rented, and pledged for credit. A man who succeeds in controlling more land than he can farm hires landless tenants to work it for him. In return he gives them an agreed-upon fraction of the wealth produced. Such economic relationships are unknown in smaller-scale agricultural communities. In their wake they bring disputes over boundaries and over agreements made with respect to land or its cultivation. Resolving such disputes enhances a government's power and rapidly stimulates bureaucratic growth in the form of new administrative organs, like courts and record offices.

In a number of communities persons use wealth to augment their personal esteem in the eyes of others. In some social systems a man establishes and maintains his renown through assiduously accumulating property in order to give mammoth feasts or bestow wealth on others. Social climbing feasts, or potlatches, come high when measured in terms of the energy they consume. They require sustained collaboration by a considerable number of people, usually a lineage. They take place in social systems which lack means to store food and have no trade outlets capable of siphoning off surplus goods into the larger society. Mammoth distributions that earn prestige for their entrepreneurs utilize food surpluses more wisely, perhaps, than if food were simply left to rot or went to support an army of rats. In Melanesia pigs provide the pièce de résistance of social climbing feasts. Without periodic feasts to keep down rapid increase in pigs they would soon overrun the island and depredate its gardens.[14]

Technical development enables a social system to produce durable consumer goods, like cars, furniture, and houses, in huge abundance. Money facilitates distribution of this great wealth. People who live in an affluent society substitute conspicuous consumption for ostentatious giving as an avenue to social prominence.[15] Each man holds on to what he earns, or rather displays it with varying degrees of taste, in an effort to validate his social rank. Everyone works hard to accumulate proper symbols with which to command respect. Signs indicate that today America has come over the crest of sheer pecuniary emulation such as Thorstein Veblen vividly describes in *The Theory of the Leisure Class*. Our current affluence permits nearly everybody to own mass-produced houses, furniture, and cars. Many possessions have lost their service as markers of social distance and so more subtle criteria must be found.

RIVAL WORLD VIEWS

Ideas, by explaining whence come illness, accidents, death, uncertainty, and threat, furnish a sufficiently convincing basis for people to safeguard themselves and their dependents. Danger stalks everywhere. Modern large-scale communities impersonally pin threats down to war, drought, invasion of tissues by disease agents, or complications of the physiological apparatus that cause coronary and other failures. Small-scale societies express their fears considerably more personally. At certain stages of life, say pregnancy, an indi-

---

[14] A. Vayda, A. Leeds, and D. B. Smith, "Pigs in Melanesia," unpublished paper presented to the VI⁰ Congrès Internationale des Sciences Anthropologiques et Ethnologiques, 1960.

[15] Charles J. Erasmus, *Man Takes Control* (Minneapolis, Minn., 1961).

vidual is vulnerable to attack by spirits or witches who are always alert to spread trouble. To understand concepts of this sort and the complicated maneuvers adopted to escape injury and win relief it helps to know how people regard their universe and man's role in it.

Speaking very generally, society is divided by two types of world view; one is impersonal, the other personal. People in large-scale modern nations espouse (but don't always follow) an impersonal world view. With many compromises it took form starting in the sixteenth century, accompanying the growth of western science. It teaches that experience yields truth and that any form of supernaturalism is suspect precisely because it does not conform to the public experience of each person. The world can be explained better without God and the Bible. No truth is ever final. New experience can some-day be expected to revise any judgment once reached. However extraordinary the human animal may be, the impersonal world view holds him to be still part of nature and subject to natural laws. The ideal, which nobody really achieves, is to repudiate any beliefs that can't be sensed or that experience proves to be false.

Predecessors of today's impersonal world view appeared long before the Renaissance. In India naturalistic ways of thought flourished between 600 B.C. and 400 B.C. that flatly contradicted traditional beliefs.[16] Knowledge, exponents of Indian materialism explained, comes solely through the five senses. Nothing exists except what can be perceived. They discarded belief in a deity, immortal soul, and sacred literature. Man, they affirmed, consists of the same elements as the rest of nature and no evidence indicates that he alone will enjoy a celestial future or endure a painful hell. Nothing is inherited from a previous existence and the mind in one body can't influence consciousness in another. These teachings have persisted in India but on the whole Indian philosophy has developed along a very different path, becoming increasingly idealistic.

During the sixth century B.C. there arose independently in Greece a remarkably similar tradition of original, creative thought.[17] In a setting of booming prosperity, philosophers like Thales pictured a world that required God neither to set it going nor to maintain it. Heraclitus, consulting his experience, denied permanence and stability and held them to be merely relative. Constant flux is the rule in everything, not because of constant battle between rival spiritual powers, but simply because change is inherent in the nature of things. Far from being absolute, justice is unsettled, for it consists in reconciling conflicting claims. One expects to hear Heraclitus go on to say

[16] William T. de Bary, Stephen Hay, Royal Weiler, and Andrew Yarrow, compilers, *Sources of Indian Tradition* (New York, 1958), pp. 43-44; Dale Riepe, *The Naturalistic Tradition in Indian Thought* (Seattle, 1961), chap. 4.

[17] Benjamin Farrington, *Greek Science*, 1 vol. ed., (Harmondsworth, 1953), chap. 2; Henry B. Parkes, *Gods and Men* (New York, 1959), pp. 184-190; Arthur Koestler, *The Sleepwalkers* (London, 1959), chap. 1.

that society itself exists only because conflicting social groups are balanced in a way that creates a dynamic equilibrium. Without teaching atheism, Heraclitus made God into a kind of ideal that couldn't possibly explain the workings of nature.

A completely impersonal world view is impossible for anyone as is its opposite, a fully personal world view typical of small-scale, exotic social systems. According to this way of thinking the world our senses "sees" is merely one face of existence. The other face pulses with animism, life, intellect, understanding, and feeling. Man can reach this hidden face, for example, through prayer and magic. Because of the way everything is organized it is quite possible for our wishes, wills, and feeling states (for instance, rankling animosity) to affect directly other people and parts of nature. The personal world view puts greater value on the more potent, hidden side of nature because it produces so much that happens to man, both good and ill. It is a homocentric world view, affirming that man enjoys a central place in nature. Practically everything—drought, rain, illness, successful crops—happens because the world is favorably or unfavorably disposed toward man. People who live by this world view seldom trouble themselves with how the animated or animistic hidden face of existence operates, what it is like, or how prayer and magic manage to influence it. They take for granted constant, voluntary and involuntary reciprocal interaction between man and the rest of nature. It never occurs to them to be systematically skeptical, to test their beliefs against experience, or to experiment with rival theories in order to see if perhaps they would work as well as traditional beliefs. In the precise terms I have just used, the personal world view does not exist. I have created a construct useful only because with it the thought of exotic people—the Hopi, for example —can readily be compared to other ways of thought. Although personal world views are widespread in small-scale, exotic social systems that have resisted western ideas, they are by no means limited to these. Overt acts by many Americans show that we too think animistically.

When challenged, each of these world views defends itself against the other with equal tenacity and conviction. Impersonal philosophers rigorously repudiate the possibility of divine intervention in nature. People who think personally find purely impersonal explanations absurd. They insist that some controlling mind (they would capitalize the M) guides the universe that scientists study. Proponents on each side most readily admit contrary evidence against that belief system for which they have least sympathy.

SOURCES OF THREAT

"If somebody looks at a handsome man enviously," a young man told me in Swat, "the person who is looked at will become sick. Or some kind of trouble will come to him." Belief in the evil eye—that looks can kill—recurs with minor variations from one culture to another. To people steeped in the personal world view it is a threat as real and lethal as atomic weapons. The belief is founded on the expressive power of the human glance[18] and on psychological insecurity. Man feels apprehensive even when he enjoys good fortune. He projects his apprehension on others expecting not only envy but malignancy powerful enough to destroy his well-being. Countervailing techniques normally exist for warding off evil eye. At curbside bus stations in Swat small boys push through the crowd carrying a brazier in which burn leaves and twigs of a plant resembling oleander. Sniffing the magical fumes prevents ill effects from an envious glance. Customers, who can hardly miss breathing the fumes, reward the urchins with a small coin. Broken pots and goat jaw-bones (symbols of poverty?) mounted on newly built homes in this Hindu Kush land also magically ward off baleful effects of evil eye.

Witchcraft is a closely related source of fear. A witch is a man or woman endowed with a special propensity for evil which he usually exercises involuntarily. (In this respect witchcraft differs from sorcery, ill deliberately promoted by magical manipulations.) Unconsciously a witch serves people as a scapegoat, someone to blame for inevitable stress and misfortune. Hopi Indians call witches "two-hearts" and resentfully point out that much crop destruction, illness, and death start from their persons.[19] Extraordinary capacities are ascribed to two-hearts. For example, they at will transform themselves into coyotes, cats, dogs, or crows. Witches force back the clouds almost at the instant when it is about to rain. But the really horrible thing they do is steal a relative's heart and implant their's in its place, thus prolonging their own wicked lives. Hopi Indians guard themselves against witchcraft. Also, they blame witches more often than they outrightly accuse anyone of this crime. If they detect a witch correctly and confront him openly, he would take powerful revenge, causing severe misfortune or death. In no culture are suspected witches chosen randomly. Suspicion assails mainly people who behave deviantly, irreligiously, or neglect other social obligations. Therefore, oddly, belief in witches helps maintain social control. People conform lest they be suspected of witchcraft. When culture change is swift, stress and deviance are encouraged. At such times (for example, today in Africa) complaints of witchcraft also mount. In much the same way when stress and uncertainty gripped the United States after the last war we hunted Communists and fellow-travelers hoping that exposing or punishing them would protect our culture from Soviet Communism.

That omitted rites and committed sins automatically unspring fearful retributive action is another idea that maintains conformity. Retribution

[18] Hutton Webster, *Magic, A Sociological Study* (Stanford, Calif., 1948), pp. 151-152.
[19] Mischa Titiev, "Notes on Hopi Witchcraft," *Papers of the Michigan Academy of Science, Arts and Letters,* 28 (1943), 549-557.

HOPI CONFRONT A SUSPECTED WITCH

Don Talayesva was plagued by misfortune and deaths. "I realized more than ever that the old people were right in their claims that the Two-Hearts cause most of the trouble in the world, and that every person has someone against him. It may be a next-door neighbor, a very close relative, or a kiva brother. I had been told these things from my childhood, but they meant more to me year by year; and I began to suspect some of my neighbors."

People blamed Don for the death of his own children, hinting that he himself was a witch. In desperation he confronted Nathaniel, a kinsman and one of his detractors. "I told him that he had no right to call me a Two-Heart, and that I had never attended a secret meeting of the underworld people, that I had not caused the death of my children, and that I had no power to defend myself. I reminded him that I had caught him crying in the field and that he had fled like a coward.* 'When was it?' he asked. I described the occasion about twenty years before and gave all the details. He could not deny this and was speechless for a moment. Then I out-talked him, reviewing his complete record for the people, how crazy he had acted, how his wife and children had died one after the other, and how he had even let the missionaries bury them without food and a grave ladder. . . . I almost struck the Two-Heart; but my Guardian Spirit checked my fist before it fell. . . . I had him cornered; the people cheered me, and a few spat at Nathaniel."

*At the time white people labeled Nathaniel insane but Don, puzzled by his unusual behavior, suspected he was a witch.

Leo W. Simmons, ed., Sun Chief, the Autobiography of a Hopi Indian (New Haven, Conn., 1942), pp. 257, 307-308.

takes many forms, including illness, death, and a hunter's persistent failure to kill game. Public confession, however, may halt the train of catastrophic consequences launched by an illicit deed. A surprising number of cultures into which Catholicism has never penetrated—including Eskimo—recognize efficacy in confession.

Automatic retribution overtakes not only the heedless sinner. Through no fault of his own a man who kills an enemy or a woman who becomes pregnant like a lightning rod attracts danger to himself and transmits it to others until prophylactic steps make him safe. This idea preoccupies the South African Lovedu who expect that a warrior runs the risk of becoming quarrelsome and even insane until he is rid of the monstrous shadow that his warrior role casts over him.[20] Shadows also fall over Lovedu girls at puberty, over anybody who attends a funeral or loses a close relative, over a woman who has miscarried, and over a married couple who have engaged in sexual intercourse. Shadows harmlessly carried by well people endanger others who are sick. Therefore, parents with a sick child protect him from complications by

[20] E. Jensen Krige and J. D. Krige, The Realm of a Rain-Queen (London, 1943), chap. 12.

abstaining from sexual relations. Lovedu also believe that at critical periods of life—death, initiation, childbirth, and others—a dangerous though nontransmissible force invades the body and must be neutralized. The force automatically besets domesticated animals if a woman enters a cattle kraal or if death occurs in a village. Going one step further, Lovedu say that human events make the world awry and it remains so until normal order is magically restored. Death of their queen causes the realm to become hot, whereas its normal state is coolness. Then rain ceases, vegetation burns up, and the dry earth becomes defiled. By extinguishing in a prescribed way all fires in the kingdom and undertaking other rites they cool the country in preparation for a new ruler. Cooling "medicines" are included among the powerful specifics that Lovedu use in rainmaking.

IN PURSUIT OF HEALTH

Concepts like evil eye, witchcraft, and involuntarily cathected danger, among other services they render, provide small-scale communities with meaningful explanations for illness. However, even small-scale cultures recognize that some ailments "just come," perhaps on the wind, through diet, or inexplicably. As one might expect, individuals feel more helpless toward such illnesses than toward those they ascribe to evil eye, wrathful ancestors, or confirmed witches. The personal world view offers them logical grounds for proceeding prayerfully or magically against diseases that stem from nature's hidden face, but what can they do to counter illness that "just comes"?

Large-scale social systems like Swat employ dual theories of illness. The folk fear illness sent by evil eye. But the hakims of Swat prefer to diagnose with an impersonal world view. They are physicians trained in the international tradition of Unani (Greek-Muslim) medicine, a system rooted in ancient Egyptian and Greek thought, particularly in the treatises of Galen (A.D. c. 129-200). Around the middle of the eighth century Arabs translated and enlarged his books and in this form they reached western Europe where Galen's ideas dominated medicine until the sixteenth century. Persians made further original contributions to Galen's theory before it reached Swat, in company with Islam, around A.D. 1000. Unani diagnosis needs no close knowledge of anatomy and physiology and its teachers ignore dissection. The hakim impersonally reasons that ill health stems from imbalance in the body's four primary elements (heat, cold, moisture, and dryness) or in its four humors (blood, phlegm, yellow bile, and black bile). Therapy combines diet, medication, repose, and applications, all having the aim of restoring a healthful equilibrium. Medicine that hakims prescribe is purchased in bazars from Unani pharmacists. Some hakims provide their own medication and rely heavily on penicillin to effect speedy recovery. Observe how impersonal Unani theory is. No place does diagnosis refer to animistic properties in nature. Therefore, the clinician, who very likely is a devout Muslim, can't logically employ strategies like prayer in curing nor does he concern himself with counteracting a witch's baleful influence.

Health is a cherished goal people pursue as ardently in Swat as elsewhere. To promote it Swat even supports a few physicians trained in the impersonal western theory of internal medicine who are skilled in X-ray and surgery. They operate in government hospitals and utilize their own pharmacists. Impersonal medicine competing with urchins who peddle safety from evil eye! The contrast strikingly discloses the transitional character of modern Swat. So does the steady trickle of ailing pilgrims who despair of help from either of the two impersonal medical traditions and bestow their faith on buried saints whose tombs adjoin modern, state-supported hospitals and dispensaries.

MYSTERIOUS, PERVASIVE POWER

A few small-scale communities possess concepts that explicitly explain the intimate link between man and other parts of nature. Perhaps if they had been able over the years to conserve these ideas in writing, they would today be less obscure, at least to outsiders. Still, we have fairly good information on two such similar philosophies.

Siouan-speaking Indians in North America, like the Dakota, erected their theory around Wakonda.[21] This power, which they called mysterious, permeated all nature—trees, animals, rivers, mountains, and people—and thereby bound man to every other component in his world. Wakonda ordered creation and directed man's fate, partly according to ethical considerations. Improper behavior invited automatic retribution through the agency of this power, perhaps in the guise of a fatal lightning bolt. But Sioux Indians didn't fatalistically accept whatever blows or blessings Wakonda sent. Prayer, ritual pipe smoking, and other rites reached the mysterious power and sought to bend it or make it serve human welfare.

Manitu, an omnipresent property with ethical implications recognized by Algonkian Indians in Northeastern North America, belongs to the same class.[22] It resided in many things but some situations, for example a sweat lodge, partook of it more intensely than others. Fox Indians while sweatbathing sometimes punctured their skin to allow Manitu, in the guise of dense, hot steam, unobstructed access into their bodies. A youth who successfully

[21] Alice C. Fletcher and Francis La Flesche, *The Omaha Tribe,* Annual Reports of the Bureau of American Ethnology, no. 27, 1911.

[22] William Jones, "The Algonkin Manitou," *Journal of American Folk-Lore,* 18 (1905), 183-190; Walter B. Miller, "Two Concepts of Authority," *American Anthropologist,* 57 (1955), 271-289.

appealed for supernatural assistance directly felt the immanence of Manitu when he saw a vision or heard voices. The all-encompassing presence of power, for which he couldn't find words, overwhelmed him. In a circumlocutory way the recipient of Manitu later explained that "the mountain beings have taken pity upon me." Indians could best grasp the abstract notion of an all pervasive Manitu by localizing the power in specific objects or by speaking of it in anthropomorphic language. After missionaries began to teach the Algonkians, Christian and pagan ideas fused. Kitchii Manitu, "Great Spirit," became the Indian name for God.

DOGMAS OF PERSONAL ADJUSTMENT

"Let thy fortune be what it will, 'tis the mind alone that makes thee poor or rich, miserable or happy." So said Robert Burton in 1621, succinctly explaining how beliefs make a difference in personal adjustment.[23] The formula works for both individuals and social systems whose philosophical and religious dogmas prescribe attitudes of personal equanimity. Best-sellers, like Vincent Peale's *The Power of Positive Thinking,* offer a very simple prescription indeed: Believe in yourself and in God. In the strangulating grip of worry repeat some comforting Biblical verse, pray, or just sit silently, deliberately flushing everything from your mind. But dogmas of personal adjustment don't all depend on inspirational slogans or congregational rituals. It is true that periodic gatherings of believers fortify everyone's faith in the comforting power of certain ideas. But fundamentally it is the idea in which the group believes that counts. Whether the idea gets ritual embodiment, takes form in a philosophical tome, or is the underlying theme in clinical psychotherapy is beside the point.

In India, both Hinduism and Buddhism have produced systems of thought designed to achieve personal serenity. I will describe only a few aspects of Hinduism and Buddhism, and will not discuss worship of deities, prayer, purification, and other popular elements. Nor are the ideas I will take up widely applied, for reasons you will understand in a few minutes.

Let me start with how Hinduism explains lack of peace of mind.[24] Life possesses two aspects. There is the world of appearance, of surface, which we sense whenever we experience color, smell, taste, power, pleasure, and pain. There is another dimension of life, one much more difficult to define, which can't be known through sense organs, but can be experienced vividly and immediately by anyone who really wishes to get to it. Sense objects hold most people thoroughly in thrall. Is such captivity good or bad? Consider the evi-

[23] Robert Burton, *The Anatomy of Melancholy,* eds. Floyd Dell and P. Jordan-Smith (New York, 1927), p. 528.

[24] Puragra Parampanthi, *The Cardinal Doctrines of Hinduism* (Dibrugarh, Assam, 1955), pp. 68-74 and chap. 8.

dence. Captivity by sense objects certainly gives pleasure. We enjoy food, sex, power, bask in our parents' love, enjoy realizing our skills, and triumph in our careers. The world constantly adds to the number of pleasurable sense objects, so obviously the realm of appearances must be good; otherwise why should people work so hard to expand it? But you haven't yet heard all the evidence. Not one of the satisfactions which we try so hard to achieve lasts, not taste of food, thrill of sex, or satisfaction in power. Those who love us and whom we love die or prove inconstant. Our senses bring pain as regularly as pleasure. We inevitably grow angry, frustrated, sad, annoyed, disillusioned, and disappointed, Now let's ask the question again: is captivity by the realm of appearances good or bad? A fair answer would be that it is never as good as we pretend it to be. Yet we stick to things of the senses, knowing perfectly well that sensory gratification can't last. As if hypnotized, most men and women, lured by hope, strive to be satisfied and never are. All they earn is more desire and restlessness. History undoubtedly reveals the futility of pursuing appearances for the sake of happiness. Yet few heed the lesson.

The Hindu-Buddhist dogma of personal adjustment explains how anyone can win release from being captive to the overrated world of appearances. Many teachers have dedicated their lives to this explanation. Basically release is conceptual, that is, it requires belief or certain ideas. One famous teacher, Siddhartha Gautama, better known as Buddha, around 500 B.C. gave a sermon at Benares (still famous as a North Indian religious center) in which he offered four keys to liberation.[25] First, the key to pain: pain is inevitable from birth to death; all life contains suffering. Second, the key to what causes pain: pain is caused by wanting. Wanting what? Paradoxically, pain is caused by wanting pleasure. Third, the key to stopping pain without any remainder: stop wanting. Free yourself from passionate striving. When it came to the fourth key, the key to how pain could be entirely banished, Gautama, who knew the answer very well, like so many Hindu and Buddhist teachers found himself unable to state in words the purely conceptual maneuvers involved. He could not be more explicit than he had already been in the third key which says, stop wanting. And so he simply added, the way to stop wanting lies in right living.

The Bhagavadgita, Song of the Lord, is a Hindu book that prescribes keys to liberation.[26] Composed between 100 B.C. and A.D. 100 it contains (in addition to other material) one of the most remarkable ideas ever discovered. It explains how one can live in the world of appearances while escaping sensory captivity and, therefore, maladjustment. One can be like a lotus leaf that floats on water but never becomes wet. The Song of the Lord consists of a dialogue between two men, King Arjuna, who is about to enter a crucial battle, and

[25] *The Teachings of the Compassionate Buddha*, ed. E. A. Burtt (New York, 1955), pp. 29-30; de Bary, Hay, Weiler, and Yarrow, *op. cit.*, pp. 101-102.
[26] Prabhavananda and Isherwood, *op. cit.*

Buddhist nuns have learned that the key to stopping pain
is to stop wanting. (*Consulate General of Japan,* N.Y.)

Krishna, a chariot driver who in the manner of some metropolitan taxi drivers
is free with advice. (Some Hindus worship Krishna as God incarnate; hence
his title, Lord, and the book's name.) The disturbing fact that the enemy include his own kinsmen gives Arjuna no taste for fighting. He asks Krishna,
"How can we hope to be happy slaying those people, even though they are
evil? Perhaps to let them kill me would be the wisest policy." Krishna's reply
is not only for Arjuna, but for all men who find wise action difficult to determine in this confusing world of appearances. He tells Arjuna to carry on with
the social obligations of kingship. Otherwise Arjuna would be disgraced. Then
he explains that Arjuna is asking trifling questions as though they were matters of importance. Whether to fight or not to fight is a superficial problem
belonging to the world of appearances. Such problems, like sensations of heat
and cold or pleasure and pain, come and go. They are inconsequential. There
is another, indestructible side of life—Brahman—that pervades the whole universe though it cannot be known through the senses. It is within everyone's
reach; in fact it is within everyone, waiting to be discovered. To discover and

merge with it is to transcend the world of appearances. People who have discovered Brahman and who understand it speak of it as wonderful beyond understanding.

Arjuna demands how to identify a man who has gone beyond the senses and his question enables Krishna to describe the bliss of one who has found liberation, the bliss at which Gautama also hinted:

> He knows bliss in the Atman [soul]
> And wants nothing else.
> Cravings torment the heart:
> He renounces cravings.
> I call him illumined.
> Not shaken by adversity,
> Not hankering after happiness:
> Free from fear, free from anger,
> Free from the things of desire.

The Bhagavadgita offers a simple key to such perfect adjustment. A man should perform his role without being ego-involved in results. The central message of the Gita (as the Bhagavadgita is often called) recommends nonattached action. In Krishna's words:

> The ignorant work
> For the fruit of their action:
> The wise must work also
> Without desire. . . .

Let Arjuna and anybody who wants peace liberate himself from sensory captivity by killing the evil tendency that obstructs discrimination and binds him to appearances. Without fleeing the world for a hermitage let him give up attachment to the fruits of action. The Gita adds that correct worship of a personal God can also help man free himself from undue attachment to sensory objects but this is a dogma I shall not go into.

Zen, a philosophy now popular in the United States, descends from Gautama's teaching.[27] Alan Watts calls it one of Asia's most precious gifts to the world. Like Buddha's sermon at Benares and Lord Krishna in the Gita, Zen aims to release men from sensory bondage to inconsequential matters and give them serene adjustment. The way to this goal is easy, Zen says. When you stop liking and disliking, then you will be ready to let the light flow in.

The chief difficulty with these dogmas lies not in any error or impracticality they possess but in the way they are phrased. The advice they offer is difficult to understand and hence to apply. There is a reason for this. The conceptual maneuvers they prescribe cannot be given in operational, one-two-three detail. Many writers have made fresh translations or written copious commentaries

[27] Alan W. Watts, *The Way of Zen* (New York, 1957); D. T. Suzuki, *An Introduction to Zen Buddhism* (London, 1949); Sohaku Ogata, *Zen for the West* (New York, 1959).

IROQUOIS UNCONSCIOUS IMPULSES AND PERSONAL ADJUSTMENT

Huron and other Iroquoian-speaking Indians whom Jesuit missionaries studied in the seventeenth century believed that the soul experiences inborn desires concealed from consciousness. Wishes well up from the depths of the soul and make themselves known through dreams. If these deeply rooted desires are satisfied, the soul stays at rest. If they are denied gratification, the soul becomes angry and deprives the body of happiness, causing illness or death.

The Indians carefully noted their dreams so that they could provide what the soul required. Some men, more enlightened than others, could penetrate to the depths of the soul not only by interpreting dreams but in other ways, too, thereby revealing the soul's desires. Once these wants were revealed, the individual, his friends, and relatives tried to gratify them.

At certain ceremonies and in time of illness Indians made special provision to gratify the soul. People obliquely announced their unconscious desires, into which they had gained insight. A person intimated that he wanted beads, a special food, or coitus with a woman not his wife. Sometimes men and women dramatized their dreams in charades. War captives provided men and women a chance to act out hostile dreams against actual victims with real violence. Aggressive dreams involving in-group members could only be enacted symbolically.

Gratifying one's dream wishes, even if only symbolically, doubtless contributed to personal well-being. As one might expect, however, such periodic catharsis could occur only in a social system pervaded by a sense of freedom and in which external restraints were weak. The Huron and other Iroquoian-speaking Indians disliked any suppression of individual autonomy. Later Iroquois culture rejected psychotherapeutic release and adopted a goal also found in mid-twentieth-century psychiatry. Emphasis was put on renouncing impulses rather than on gratifying them cathartically.

Anthony F. C. Wallace, "Dreams and the Wishes of the Soul: A Type of Psychoanalytic Theory among the Seventeenth Century Iroquois," *American Anthropologist*, 60 (1958), 234-248; "The Institutionalization of Cathartic and Control Strategies in Iroquois Religious Psychotherapy," in Marvin K. Opler, ed., *Culture and Mental Health* (New York, 1959).

---

rephrasing the teachings in what they hope are clearer terms. Some years ago a philosopher, F. S. C. Northrop, found a fresh way of giving the essence of these Oriental teachings.[28] All determinate things, he says, like flowers, people, human passions, and even scientific laws, are fleeting. They arise out of a changeless background of pure experience that is verbally indescribable. Northrop calls this background the undifferentiated aesthetic continuum. Liberation, personal adjustment, or, in Zen terms, letting the light flow in means to merge oneself with the undifferentiated aesthetic continuum, to become one with all-transcending pure experience wherein ego is obliterated. Can one attain this state of mystically informed being without leaving the

[28] F. S. C. Northrop, *The Meeting of East and West* (New York, 1946), chaps. 9-10.

world? The Bhagavadgita says that one can by adopting a sufficient degree of nonattachment to everyday life.

Popular philosophies of the Hellenistic age also sought for a more satisfactory life.[29] They strove to liberate people from worldly turmoil and disentangle them from a social system that had ceased to inspire respect. Stoics echoed ideas of Hinduism and Buddhism when they said that it was enough to act without becoming ego-involved in results. One should work diligently but always remain indifferent to success and failure. Cynics, the most radical school, promised adjustment to anyone willing to abandon his claims to possessions, friends, and loved ones. Free from attachment, man would also be spared pain produced by losing what he loves. These philosophical outsiders sneered at social conventions and prejudices practiced by a collapsing society. Apart from freedom and self-control few conventional ideals claimed their respect. Masturbation was one with sexual relations attained with the most beautiful woman, they declared, for both served the same physiological end.

A similar policy of cultivated disillusion and revolt against conventions is manifested by Camus and other writers of revolt, those who purport to speak for the Beat Generation and the Angry Young Men.[30] Significantly, these iconoclasts are searching for new values to recommend to others. Sheer negativistic disillusion seems to be insufficient. It provides only a perilous state of adjustment, which explains why such doctrines survive only a short time. But their perennial reappearance must also be explained. Periodically thoughtful persons become satiated with optimism and disgusted by unwarranted smug content in an imperfect society. They perceive little promise of basic improvement beyond, perhaps, a steadily climbing standard of living.

FURTHER READING

Anthropologists have critically examined early theories alleging small-scale exotic people to possess inferior mentalities. In the process they cite interesting material about exotic thoughtways. See Alexander Goldenweiser, *Early Civilization* (New York, 1922), part III, and Alfred M. Tozzer, *Social Origins and Social Continuities* (New York, 1934), pp. 17-34, 53-83. An important recent study of values is Clyde Kluckhohn, "Values and Value-Orientations in the Theory of Action," in Talcott Parsons and Edward Shils, eds., *Toward a General Theory of Action* (Cambridge, Mass., 1951). Célestin Charles A. Bouglé, *The Evolution of Values,* trans. Helen Stalker Sellars (New York, 1926) remains a fine examination of the social role of values, and Solomon E. Asch, *Social Psychology* (New York, 1952), chaps. 12-13, discusses values in relationship to their situational context.

The essence of science is given in James B. Conant, *On Understanding Science*

[29] Robert Eisler, "Cynics," in *Encyclopaedia of the Social Sciences* (New York, 1931); Edwyn Bevan, "Hellenistic Popular Philosophy," in *The Hellenistic Age* (Cambridge, 1923).

[30] John Cruickshank, *Albert Camus and the Literature of Revolt* (London, 1959); Judith N. Shklar, *After Utopia* (Princeton, 1957).

(New Haven, Conn., 1947). See also his "Foreword" in J. B. Conant, ed., *Harvard Case Histories in Experimental Science* (Cambridge, Mass., 1957). In this chapter I disagree with V. Gordon Childe who regards technology as rudimentary science. See his *Magic, Craftsmanship, and Science,* The Frazer Lecture delivered at Liverpool, November 10, 1949 (Liverpool, 1950). Alexander Vucinich writes on "The Ethos of Soviet Science," *The Pacific Spectator,* 9 (1955), 332-344.

Cultural Patterns and Technical Change (Paris, 1953), edited by Margaret Mead, contains numerous illustrations of how social systems standardize attitudes to time, and Edward T. Hall, *The Silent Language* (Garden City, N.Y., 1959) gives close attention to both time and space. Two studies treating myths as repositories of the past are James K. Feibelman, *The Theory of Human Culture* (New York, 1946), chap. 2, and David Bidney, *Theoretical Anthropology* (New York, 1953), chap. 10. Chapter 2 of John R. Seeley, R. A. Sim, and E. W. Loosley, *Crestwood Heights* (New York, 1956) describes the meaning of space in a suburban Canadian community. Admirable introductions to the comparative significance and use of property have been written by E. Adamson Hoebel, *Man in the Primitive World,* 2nd ed. (New York, 1958), chaps. 25-26, and M. J. Herskovits, *Economic Anthropology* (New York, 1952), part IV. Eleanor Leacock, *The Montagnais "Hunting Territory" and the Fur Trade,* Memoirs of the American Anthropological Association, no. 78, 1954, interprets the fur trade as an agency that encouraged private ownership of land among northeastern American Indians. African land tenure and problems created by changing rules of tenure are treated with insight in T. R. Batten *Problems of African Development. Part I., Land and Labour,* 2nd ed. (London, 1954), chaps. 2-4. See also Austin Kennett's explanation for a lack of land cases among the Bedouin in *Bedouin Justice: Laws and Customs Among the Egyptian Bedouin* (Cambridge, Eng., 1925), chap. 9.

Nobody has examined the tenets of the personal world view as well as Lucien Lévy-Bruhl. He has received a poor hearing, largely because he at first insisted on grounding the personal world view in a prelogical mentality that distinguished "primitives" from modern men. Later (1949) he abandoned the idea of two kinds of logic. See his books *Primitive Mentality,* trans. Lilian A. Clare (New York, 1923); *How Natives Think,* trans. Lilian A. Clare (London, 1926); and *Les Carnets du Lucien Lévy-Bruhl* (Paris, 1949). Concerning evil eye see Helmut Schoeck, "The Evil Eye: Forms and Dynamics of a Universal Superstition," *The Emory University Quarterly,* 11 (1955), 153-161. I recommend Bernard J. Siegel and Alan R. Beals, "Conflict and Factionalist Dispute," *The Journal of the Royal Anthropological Institute,* 90 (1960), 107-117, as a promising theory with which to compare witch-finding and the pursuit of Communists and fellow-travelers. Works on Unani medicine in South Asia are not too satisfactory. Government of India, Ministry of Health, *Report of the Committee on Indigenous Systems of Medicine,* 2 vols. (New Delhi, 1948) contains pertinent papers by Inayatullah Shah, "The Place and Scope of Indigenous Medicine in New India," and M. H. Shah, "Memorandum on Constitution of Medicine." Edward G. Browne, *Arabian Medicine* (Cambridge, Eng., 1921), is also appropriate. In *Man Takes Control* (Minneapolis, Minn., 1961), chap. 3, Charles J. Erasmus discusses forms of medicine competing in a social system expanding in scale. Meyer Fortes, *Oedipus and Job in West African Religion* (Cambridge, Eng., 1959), writes on the notion of fate and how cultures prescribe means for escaping the threat of destiny.

Most topics of this chapter are treated in greater detail in John J. Honigmann, *The World of Man* (New York, 1959), chaps. 34-37, 39.

11

Exploiting the World Through Art

Any expression of emotion—and all human behaviour is, in one aspect, expressive—must be both a more or less successful piece of material manipulation and an expression of intrinsic quality. . . .

Art is the expression of the intrinsic qualities men find in reality—in things, persons, events or life as such. . . . the artist is concerned to bring out the flavour of the universe.

Godfrey and Monica Wilson[1]

THE MEANING OF ART IN CONTEXT

At times people pay special heed to what they do. The hostess arranges a variety of colorful and tasty dishes in especially attractive patterns and sees to it that candlelight brings out the subdued whiteness of her damask tablecloth. Consciously or unconsciously the woodcarver chooses his bright colors to accentuate the beaked nose, gross, flaring mouth, and cavernous eyes of the wooden mask. The storyteller takes advantage of moonless dark to add drama to his tale. Draft follows draft into the wastebasket; still the poet fights for the precise image that will express his potent but elusive conception of love. These are all artists calculatingly bending their skills in order to express and, hopefully, arouse emotion. The media they control vary: food, light, wood, color, spoken words, and images expressed through words on paper. To these the potter adds clay, sculptor stone, gardener flowers and shrubs, dancer her own body, musician his instrument, and orchestra conductor dozens of instruments and players. Whatever other purposes motivate them, they all share a

[1] *The Analysis of Social Change* (Cambridge, Eng., 1945), pp. 76-77, 79.

concern with feeling. Each employs his ability to control some refractory or renitent medium, so that he may reveal his feelings with what he gauges to be his maximal effectiveness. At times art stops short of communication and autistically concerns itself simply in relieving dammed up feelings. More usually, though, artists create to excite the emotions of others, whatever other aims their work implies.

True there are less deliberate ways of expressing feeling. Examples include the hopeful expressions with which a Kaska hunter departs from camp, the expectancy of Hopi as they watch the rain clouds pile up, the hurriedly murmured prayer that a Muslim carpenter utters as he begins to work, and the tension of students entering an examination room. But without calculated thought given to deepening or communicating these feelings I cannot visualize art occurring.

Art makes do with slight things in the world: an arm movement, a walrus tusk, driftwood, or a rose. More than once I rode behind a Pathan bus driver as he negotiated twisting, narrow mountain roads leading to Swat. A rose between his teeth or on the dashboard added a startling quality to the trip and contrasted with the grim, hot, dusty ordeal.

Art is twofold. It is a process that relies on movement, tone, words, or rhythm and it is the object on which an artist has left a permanent imprint. To understand art it is well to be clear whether you are going to attend to process or, where possible, to product. If it is the latter, will you approach the object guided by your own tastes and the meaning it has for you or will you perceive it in terms of the cultural context from which it has strayed? For art objects diffuse and acquire new meanings in the culture that receives them. A pear-shaped hand-ax that an Old Stone Age hunter 200,000 years ago fashioned out of a lump of flint arouses our admiration.[2] But who knows if the manufacturer attached any more emotional significance to his tool than we attach to a potato masher? We possess a grubbing culture that rewards archeologists who bring back remainders of the past. Objects that strike our feelings responsively, we then prize as more than facts. In living room and museum we proudly display them as art. In the same spirit we enjoy rewritten folktales which an editor has pared of repetition and incomprehensible references. Such reinterpretations are commonplace in any large-scale culture.

Wisely, though, we ought to be alert to the significance that these objects held or still hold for their primary owners. The most difficult task in studying any art is gauging its existential meaning. We are fortunate if persons can elucidate the symbols they paint on their bodies, the intricate gestures that constitute their dance, or the carved temple images before which they set down offerings. Sometimes our informants only say that the music, dance,

[2] Henri Breuil, "Die aeltere und mittlere Altsteinzeit," in Fritz Kern, ed., *Historia Mundi,* erster Band, *Fruehe Menschheit* (Bern, 1952), p. 286.

THE CONTEXT OF ART NEUTRALIZED

(*Heraclion Museum, Crete*)

Museums can be traced back to Alexander's time but on their present scale they are a Renaissance product. The era of discovery and exploration opening in 1492 nourished museums abundantly.

Not everything that later generations find worth preserving fits into a museum. The Colosseum in Rome, the Parthenon at Athens, and this Minoan ruin, the Watch Room of Knossos in Crete, attract their admirers outdoors.

Behind railings, velvet cords, and glass, we neutralize the context in which the captive art secured its original meaning. On exhibition, art is reinterpreted in a new culture for a different audience.

painting, or weave is beautiful, religious, or enobling—as we could have guessed from context. Any fuller, more explicit meaning eludes them. The vacuum tempts us to impose our technical meanings which derive from some theory of color, form, or unconscious symbolizing. But the implicit meanings that informants themselves fail to verbalize are nevertheless there as part of the context. Perhaps if we stay with the people long enough and participate in their life sufficiently, we too will learn the feelings that their art expresses and informs. Even then, describing what we have learned in another medium —words—may prove an insurmountable obstacle and prevents us from communicating our awareness to others.

The outstanding features of the stick game, primarily an occasion for gambling among the Kaska Indians, are swiftness, excitement, and ceaseless distracting movement. One team aims to hide a token while its members keep their hands under cover. The men then straighten up. The leader of the opposing team tries by gesture to guess which hand holds the token. Once he has pointed, the players fling out their hands in glee, especially if the guess has been wrong! And all the while the drummer maintains a relentless rhythm to which the players chant "tch-tch, tch-tch" and sway their bodies. The stick game blends gambling, music, dancing, and miming. Art and play are combined in this occasion.

Anything in culture becomes art if it fulfills the conditions of art, that is, if control is exercised to express or arouse emotion. Body painting, social intercourse, sexual intercourse, cuisine, advertising, and, of course, so-called creative tasks like painting, music, sculpture, or embroidery are eligible to meet these conditions. Obviously all social systems don't draw art from the same techniques. Kaska Indians neglect cultivating social intercourse as an art. They don't take pains to express gracious hospitality or to make the visitor feel a relaxed and welcome guest. In contrast, upper-class men in Swat attend vigilantly to this art. Negro Africa and Melanesia emphasize sculpture in the round but, like many small-scale communities, ignore representational painting. With increased social scale more and more areas of life become involved in the task of bringing out and influencing feelings. In large-scale communities arts fuse so that they blossom in concert. Opera offers a good example in the way it fuses instrumental music, singing, acting, painting, stagecraft, lighting, and costume. This merging of many skills is carefully calculated and intended to arouse a desired emotional response. In a large-scale culture art, like most areas of culture, becomes a relatively specialized activity. Specialized artists devote much time to evolving constant originality within the confines of tradition. When the time comes, they pioneer in fresh new styles.

Cultures that diverge greatly in their conventions of expression exchange little art. Most westerners find Chinese music or Indian movies unintelligible or pointless. The language barrier also effectively stops us from sampling Asian poetry, except occasionally in translation. At home, in a stimulating large-scale atmosphere of variety and ceaseless originality, tastes also clash. Proponents of divergent styles remain steadfastly loyal to their preferences. Each style of art enlists its partisans who can't see value in another mode of expression. Puritans fear art that appeals too frankly to the senses; authoritarians distrust art because it resists totalitarian control. Censorship defining obscenity narrows the artist's permitted range of expression.

Originality encounters resistance when for some reason it goes too far. With the most catholic sympathy I have honest difficulty understanding what an artist wants to express in too untraditional a way. Conflict of this sort can be exciting but it also distresses painters, writers, and sculptors whose work critics indignantly reject or ridicule. Yet, firm adherence to comfortable tradition also brings strong protest and vigorous iconoclasm. Avant-garde protest movements that rely on shock to achieve expression, like futurism, dadaism, Beatnik poetry, and the theatre of Ionesco, go to such extremes that their professors have been called anti-artists.

THE DIFFERENCE IT MAKES

Why art? One might at the same time ask why anything in culture apart from activities which satisfy biological needs, like food-getting, eating, sleeping, and building for protection from cold. No matter how modest its content, every known culture contains more than behavior that is simply a response to elemental survival needs. Each culture includes a playful, expressive side that exceeds man's minimal needs. People don't merely eat, they eat with manners; they dress colorfully; they talk with gentleness or sternness; they paint their bodies, cave walls, or pieces of canvas, and make music to sing or dance to.

The answer to why art, or why any other intrinsically oriented activity, involves recognition of man's fertile imagination. And partly these acts originate in man's low tolerance for monotony.[3]

Apart from providing a vehicle of pure expression, art achieves functions of considerable importance for individual, society, and culture. Art like ritual (the two are often combined) brings men to terms with their emotions. With his palette of color, a painter captures a sunset that overwhelms him. An artist controls emotion in order to achieve, through dancing, poetry, or music, some *measured* form of expression. Art allows men to face up to and vicariously resolve life's problems. Through art they also confess their passive surrender and helplessness. Art gives vent to protest. With a few brilliant strokes of his pen a satirist exposes sham. Sharp characterization enabled proletarian novelists in the Depression to demolish capitalists subjectively. Art relieves the creator's insecurity. It promises or earns him fame. Through the painfulness of creation it also stirs in him a painful mixture of despair and frustration.

When the artist shares his expression with others he arouses more or less the effect he aimed for in his painting, musical composition, dinner party, or ritual. In doing so he may, like the movie-makers, offer his audience fantasy to relieve stringencies in their lives. We see fantasy made concrete among Indians of the British Columbia coast who possessed an insatiable appetite for rank. Their folktales are perfect examples of wish-fulfilling fantasies telling of poor men attaining outstanding prestige. Or an artist's enobling view of life provides people with renewed hope and fortitude. It may offer simply a new perspective with which to adjust in a troubled age. Gratified audiences respond intangibly as well as, at least in a market economy, tangibly. The fact that a storyteller is repeatedly visited or a potter's designs are praised is sufficient proof of gratification received. Our professional artists are out for bigger gains. We reward some of them generously for their skill in amusing us or selling cigarettes and canned tomatoes. In a large-scale mass society a thoughtful artist beams his efforts toward a certain portion of the social spectrum. He deliberately plans to gratify mainly the tastes of certain people; others he shrugs off. This is done through the kind of music a conductor selects, the complexion of his orchestra, and his style of conducting. Before the eighteenth century an author wrote for his peers, a small upper-class, sophisticated group that spoke his "language." Then came the industrial revolution and popular education to expand his market. Some artists, like Stendhal, ignored the enlarged opportunity. Others, like Walter Scott, aimed for the mass market as did Mark Twain generally. The masses loved Twain when he postured as a cracker-barrel, humorous philosopher.[4]

---

[3] For a discussion of how behavior is affected by monotony, see Woodburn Heron, "The Pathology of Boredom," *Scientific American*, 196, no. 1 (1957), 50-56.

[4] Dwight Macdonald, "Mark Twain: An Unsentimental Journey," *The New Yorker*, 36, no. 8, (April 9, 1960), 160-196.

Religious art secures the vitality of sacred concepts thereby reinforcing whatever moral values the concepts embody. Raphael's Madonna. (*The Bettmann Archive.*)

Peace, bitterness, anger, amusement, gustatory titillation, and many other sensory or feeling states get aroused through art. In the process art accomplishes a variety of other functions. When employed in the service of kings and corporations it celestializes the ruler and projects the image which the public is supposed to perceive. Art keeps the economy going. Art educates, as in explanatory myths that transmit the story of creation. Gruesome tales of cannibals and incest warn of danger that deviant behavior brings on. Hero tales, in which a brave man struts through one adventure after another, reinforce the positive values attached to exemplary behavior. Religious art impresses spectators with the vitality of sacred concepts and symbols as well as with the moral values that those concepts embody. On a more mundane level, the popular song teaches the teen-ager what to think about love. Confession magazines (I realize that you have never before considered work of this genre

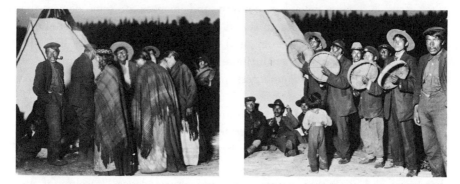

Rhythm dominates in the purely secular tea dance of these Cree Indians photographed in northern Alberta in 1914. (*Geological Survey of Canada; photographs by Francis Harper.*)

to be art) reinforce moral convictions held by a slightly older generation. The teacher uses art in his craft, too, in order to transmit feelings (the logicalness of mathematics, the value of tolerance) with facts or to make his facts more palatable.

But with so much talk about the differences art makes, what happens to the notion that art, like recreation, consumes human energies as an end in itself? So it does. An artist may create purely for the sake of expression. Functional analysis assumes that we understand art better when we trace its ramifications in the life of a people. True, art bakes no bread. The volume of art and the time spent in artistic expression can increase only when a social system produces enough to feed the artist. He then feeds the eye and soul, as Edman says.[5]

TECHNIQUE, CONTENT, AND STYLE IN THEIR SETTING

How does art make its impact? Devices vary from one art to another. Always, however, there is the basic unit of artist working through his medium, that is, basically we have technique. The medium need be no more than a dancer's disciplined plastic body; but even then surrounding space, light, and shadow contribute to the feelings aroused and to the art's functions. Other artists work directly with inanimate media, with pen, brush, ink, paint, paper, or canvas. Others release their creativity through the intervening medium of a machine that they expertly control. They produce thousands of books or packages, each identical with the other. Each when bought and used provokes feeling.

Depending, then, on craft, the impact of art is achieved, first, through what I shall call evidence of technique. Line, color, composition, rhythm, melody,

[5] Irwin Edman, *Arts and the Man* (New York, 1939).

pitch, tone, harmony, metaphor, lighting, and imagery are some devices that express the artist's intention and, functionally speaking, make the difference. The writer's words, whether strong and filled with feeling or weak and cold, together with his syntax also contribute to the process. The sculpture's size, a flower bed's health and vigorousness, play of light and shade on a house are evidence of effective technique.

Whatever mirrors life inevitably distorts reality as perceived by the senses, but for effect art also at times deliberately fosters extreme distortion. In this process experience is intensified far beyond what is normal. Take Kafka's novel, *The Trial*. It is like no trial ever was; yet, in another sense it is all trials. Freshness and originality, within limits, are also evidence of technique and help create an emotional impact. But some cultures, Balinese, for example, reject originality completely and only copy and recopy past tradition.

In some arts the tchnical attributes I have mentioned convey a content. The music, epic, or novel tells a story; the poem contains more than rhyme and rhythm, its words are about something; the painting offers a scene, person, or still life; and vestments are embroidered with symbols. This art achieves its impacts through content symbolism as well as through evidence of technique. This poetic evocation of an elementary school classroom arouses dormant feelings:

> Our sour cream walls, donations. Shakespeare's head
> Cloudless at dawn, civilized dome riding all cities.
> Belled, flowery, Tyrolese valley. Open-handed map. . . .[6]

But these lines are meaningless for a reader lacking actual or vicarious experience to reconstruct the setting in his mind. How empty Wordsworth sounds on a Pakistan student's lips who has never seen a cottage or churchyard! A Madonna evokes different emotions in spectators who attend predominantly to its religious significance rather than to its historic significance. Content stirs up unconscious reactions as well. The evil woman in fairy tales, psychoanalysts say, often stands for the child's repressed image of its cruel mother. The Balinese witch play reenacts a childhood trauma.

Content normally conveys far richer explicit and implicit meanings than these paltry examples indicate. The Papago Indians have a humorous song that you won't understand until you know the meaning Papago attach to clouds.

> The iron wagon hither runs.
> The iron wagon hither runs.
> Over it a cloud is lying.
> Oh! It's only the smoke.[7]

[6] Stephen Spender, "An Elementary School Classroom in a Slum," in *Ruins and Visions, Poems 1934-1942* (New York, 1942), p. 138.

[7] Ruth M. Underhill, *Papago Indian Religion* (New York, 1946), p. 311.

TWO CONCEPTIONS OF FEMININE BEAUTY

(*Soprintendenza alle Antichità di Roma*)

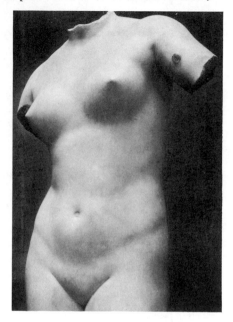

(*Museum of Fine Arts, Boston*)

The heavenly being to the left, a Yakshi, represents Indian sculpture. The sculptor unquestionably succeeded in conveying his ideal of femininity, but very differently from the more sensuous Greek artist who produced the Aphrodite of Cyrene.

Try further to compare the two female figures and discover how difficult it is to capture and express styles of representational art in prose. Hence, a camera is invaluable to study visual art objects comparatively.

B. Rowland, *Art in East and West* (Cambridge, Mass., 1954), pp. 16-20.

The last line breaks with sharp disappointment. In a Papago's world of meanings clouds possess strong, positive emotional significance. To these desert farmers clouds mean rain bestowed by guardian rain beings living in the four directions. Anything over which a cloud hangs has entered the divine aura of these beings. Is the train also divine? The punch line clears up the doubt—"It's only the smoke."

Color and geometric elements used in weaving, painting, and embroidery can also possess symbolic properties at the same time that these elements are expressive purely in themselves. Color on Hopi Katchina masks possesses explicit meaning. It reveals whence the Katchina has come. If the mask is black, he is one of the nether Katchinas; if red he derives from the south or southeast, and so on. Other emblems on the mask stand for stars, moon, rainbow, friendship, or corn and further identify the being whom the false face represents. Among the American Plains Indians the matter is complicated. Women explain that their designs stand for referents like "reflection on water" or a buffalo. But anthropologists turn up the same designs with other women ascribing different symbolism to them. Such designs bear names but don't measure up to being true symbols.

Much art achieves its appeal without programmatic elements. The "purity" of a symphony or nonobjective painting, however, limits the extent to which such expression can function in society. Didactic teaching, for example, is hard to accomplish through pure art.

Art makes its impacts through technical attributes, content symbolism, and also through what I will call the total setting wherein it occurs. A garden party conveys different sentiments than a formal dinner does, even if both celebrate the same occasion. The theater adds dramatic overtones lacking in a printed play. The book's binding and typography enhance its content, as the warning against judging by cover indicates. Restaurants that pay attention to setting make eating more exciting. Diners show their appreciation by paying extra for this amenity. Churches amplify the spirit of their dogmas through architecture and decoration. A Friend's meeting room contrasts severely with a Gothic cathedral.

The manner and form with which any art is produced in a particular social system are what we attend to when we speak of style. By style we recognize the end of one period of art and the start of a new one. The sculpture of Melanesia manifests a style different from that of West Africa, but our records are too scarce to perceive period differences in either area. Of course, style may spread from one culture or period to another. Henry Moore confesses he has been influenced by ancient Middle American sculpture.

This raises the question of whether the period differences in at least fine arts invariably reveal progression through three steps: formative beginnings, classic mastery, and flamboyant roccoco exhaustion. Anthropologists and art historians have seen this sequence repeated where cultures developed into civilizations.

Along with style we may consider all relevant habits with which an art is executed: the number of people directly involved in the artistic act (is it in-

A PLAINS INDIAN TRIBE INTERPRETS ITS DESIGNS

Arapaho decorative art has no fixed system of symbolism. Figures like those on this rawhide bag are interpreted in a personal and arbitrary manner that partly depends on context. The two large triangles at either end of the lower portion of this rawhide bag "are" tents. The four obtuse triangles along the sides have been painted red and "are" mountains. Small yellow triangles enclosed by them "are" again tents. Double blue lines surround the entire pattern and they "are" mountain-ranges. The small rectangles in the border "are" lakes.

A. L. Kroeber, *The Arapaho,* Bulletin of the American Museum of Natural History, no. 18, 1902-1907, p. 115; see also 144-145.

tended for a few or is it truly popular?); the artist's relationship to his audience (is it formal like at Carnegie Hall or informal like in American Negro folk singing?); the artist's physical behavior, especially if he performs in public; technical attributes or evidence of technique; symbols together with their socially assigned meanings; purposes that motivate the art; how the art is learned and transmitted, and any physical media or instruments involved.

Armed with a description of style and a knowledge of function we are ready to gain additional perspective by comparing art. Let's take folk singing.[8] American white folk sing solo style; the group sits and listens in silence, though sometimes it sings refrains in poor unison. The singer holds his body tightly; his expression remains masklike; his voice is rigidly pitched, somewhat higher than his normal speaking tone. The song tells a story, perhaps one that

[8] Alan Lomax, "Folk Song Style," *American Anthropologist,* 61 (1959), 927-954.

points a moral or seeks to instruct. The mood sometimes is melancholy, nostalgic. In contrast American Negro singing is mainly choral, the group being cued into the song at various points. The singer moves his body sinuously. His expression changes almost line by line with the mood of the song. His voice is his normal speaking pitch. The purpose may be to enliven worship or work. Songs openly express sex and, through satire, aggression, and aim at combating racial injustice.

ART AND CULTURE

At practically every point arts reflect the culture in which they are at home. Eskimo folktales describe how a strong hunter arrogantly bullies a small band of hunters and their families until unexpectedly a weak, poor, despised boy breaks the tyrant's power. An Eskimo food-gathering band, possessing no political authority or police, was vulnerable to such an asocial, perhaps psychopathic bully. What could members do if they feared their tormentor? The folktales reflect their predicament, but in manageable proportions. This is much the way a mystery story generates terror which, because it isn't full-fledged, is actually pleasant. What I wish to emphasize here, however, is not that fantasy relieves strain but rather the way folktale themes reflect cultural conditions.

Art is related to culture by more than content. Technical resources available in a culture inevitably channel art. True, artists occasionally prefer to work in techniques that everyday life has discarded, like pottery; but they cannot very well create with instruments or media not part of their cultural repertory. Almost equally apparent is the link between art and cultural values. Puritanism ushers the naked human form out of painting and sculpture. Gregory Bateson dealt with more implicit values when he described art in the middle Sepik River area of New Guinea as emphasizing male sureness in the same way that other elements of culture reflect strong prohibitions on passivity and stress masculine potency.

Painting reflects the manner in which a social system prefers to approach experience.[9] Lin Yutang, the Chinese scholar, says that to an Oriental a western painter always seems to have painted an object from the outside. An Oriental paints objects from within, with feeling and identification. Chinese painting attends to experience that is immediately apprehended, the way I can apprehend a blue sky without concerning myself about what makes blueness. I attend to blueness itself and become one with it. So the Chinese painter tries to capture pure experience without reference to common sense or other concepts which in day-to-day thought envelope the objects of experience. Knower and object are continuous in a realm of feeling or pure experience.

[9] F. S. C. Northrop, *The Meeting of East and West* (New York, 1946), pp. 317-318.

A NEW ART STYLE EMERGES

(Kaj Birket-Smith and the Danish National Museum)

(National Film Board of Canada)

From contact between Arctic Eskimo culture and the Europeanized outside world of Canada a new art style emerged. The "woman in boots," to the left, belongs to the Thule period of Eskimo culture, which flourished prehistorically across the length of Arctic North America and Greenland. The figure is about 600 years old and was found in eastern Canada. At the right is an example of modern Eskimo, soapstone sculpture, the kind made to be sold in Ottawa and Montreal. Sculpture is traditional in Eskimo culture but, as you see, the current style is new.

Around 1949 James Houston, an artist, went north and taught the Eskimo of Hudson Bay to carve marketable art work. He is chiefly responsible for stimulating a new form of art, one that has brought money to needy Eskimo. Today a Canadian Government manual teaches Eskimo how to make such carvings.

Department of Northern Affairs and National Resources, *Canadian Eskimo Art* (Ottawa, 1955); Edmund Carpenter, review of *Eskimo-Plastik aus Kanada*, *American Anthropologist*, 62 (1960), 346-348.

Chinese painting differs from much western painting in which the artist screens experience conceptually. In the same way western thought emphasizes experience made palatable by concepts and theory. Chinese thought is more

ART REFLECTS ITS CULTURAL CONTEXT — PAINTING ON BARK

(C. P. Mountford)

Northeastern Arnhem Land

Western Arnhem Land

Painters attempt to cover nearly the whole bark surface. The artist provides a framework for the painting that is independent of the boundaries provided by the length and breadth of the bark. He shapes his design within this framework. He employs considerable detail and crams as much as possible into the background. He seems to abhor blank space, filling it with crosshatching. Primarily through contrast in color he makes figures emerge from their background. The central design is carefully attended to. Each clan and linguistic unit possesses its particular designs.

In the upper rectangle is a bark hut occupied by two women and a newborn child. The serpent thrusts his head inside and swallows the child. Then he returns to his well.

No attempt is made to cover the complete bark surface with designs. There is no framing. The artist selects a relatively few features for illustration. He prefers open spaces and concentrates on the main figure or figures, rather than on their setting. Detail is subordinated to main design.

The man Gradau, covered with long hair, spears a wallaby. Note the spearthrower flying from his hand. The wallaby furnishes a good example of x-ray art.

attracted to approaching the world of experience directly, in a personal, non-verifiable manner.

The soaring spires, vaulted ribs, and pointed archs of a Gothic cathedral

CULTURAL CONTEXT

Northeastern Arnhem Land	Western Arnhem Land
Involvement is the keynote of the culture as of the art. Moieties are divided into clans, each of which is associated with several linguistic units (tribes). Each of these is made up of several patrilineages. Crisscrossing kinship ties are like the cross-hatching in bark designs. The linguistic units and clans are associated with numerous totemic beings and concepts, each of which possesses its own symbolic meaning and is known in different contexts. The situation parallels the enormous detail found in the bark paintings and the avoidance of open spaces. People like repetition. Clans and linguistic units share myths and associated rituals in sections but these sections often duplicate one another. Life is arranged in a series of ritual steps from birth to death. Religion is the permeating force of life. The use of language leaves much to be made clear through context.	The culture is as relatively straightforward as the art. The linguistic units, or tribes, are divided into moieties and phratries. People recognize a great variety of totemic emblems (more than in the northeast) but they appear in fewer ritual contexts. Totemic elements are not bound up with as much detail and reiteration as in the northeast. Life from birth to death is not arranged in a series of ritual stages as in the northeast. Religion though important permeates life less. Songs, which possess plenty of repetition, are more succinct. The use of language is more specific and better avoids misunderstanding.

R. M. Berndt, "Some Methodological Considerations in the Study of Australian Art," *Oceania*, 29 (1958-1959), 26-43. See also C. P. Mountford, *Records of the American-Australian Scientific Expedition to Arnhem Land, I., Art, Myth and Symbolism* (Melbourne, 1956), and A. P. Elkin, R. M. Berndt, and C. Berndt, *Art in Arnhem Land* (Melbourne, 1950).

offer another lesson in the relationship of art to culture. In the first place, this monumental edifice testifies to the piety of the men who paid for and built it. Cultural conditions in the twelfth and thirteenth centuries, such as a peaceful political situation and rising economic prosperity, made the cathedrals possible. So did growing knowledge of working in stone masonry and of roofing large structures. The vitality and upward soaring movement of the Gothic cathedral expresses the Age of Faith. Compare this architecture with the auditory churches that England built in the late seventeenth and early eighteenth centuries. Like Protestantism in general, these churches are plain and severe. Some resemble theaters. They allow everybody to see and hear the minister deliver his sermon from a conspicuous pulpit which has replaced the altar as the congregation's focus.

For all the proof we have that art works in tandem with other parts of culture, it must be acknowledged that art possesses a degree of autonomy. Lyric poets ignore war, missiles, and atomic armament in order to perpetuate tradition. Occasional American Indians still drum rhythmically on skin-covered tambourine drums but make music in contexts that have changed drastically from the past. The fact is, the autonomy of art or, put another way, the artist's imaginative power, is precisely what allows us to escape from our space and time bounds. In that lies the essence of art and a major reason for its universality.

FURTHER READING

Alexander Goldenweiser reviews several problems of art pertaining particularly to small-scale communities in *Early Civilization* (New York, 1922), chap. 9. The general reader is apt to find Leonhard Adam, *Primitive Art,* rev. ed. (Harmondsworth, 1949) more satisfactory than Franz Boas' volume of the same name (Cambridge, Mass., 1927). For further enlightening discussion see E. R. Leach, "Aesthetics," in *The Institutions of Primitive Society* (Oxford, 1954); Raymond Firth, *Elements of Social Organization* (London, 1951), chap. 5; and Ruth Bunzel, "Art," in Franz Boas, ed., *General Anthropology* (Boston, 1938).

George T. Mills discusses "Social Anthropology and the Art Museum," *American Anthropologist,* 57 (1955), 1002-1010, and Herta Haselberger "Method of Studying Ethnological Art," *Current Anthropology,* 2 (1961), 341-355. Anti-art is considered in Basil Taylor, "Art–anti-Art," *The Listener,* 62 (1959), 819-822. Several studies by anthropologists have examined movies and their psychological function. Especially see Martha Wolfenstein and Nathan Leites, *Movies, A Psychological Study* (Glencoe, Ill., 1950). Another significant book is Siegfried Kracauer, *From Caligari to Hitler* (Princeton, N.J., 1947). Also in the context of contemporary popular arts, "westerns" are reviewed by Martin Nussbaum in "Sociological Symbolism of the 'Adult Western,' " *Social Forces,* 39 (1960-1961), 25-28, and popular songs are the subject of S. I. Hayakawa, "Popular Songs vs. The Facts of Life," *ETC: A Review of General Semantics,* 12 (1955), 83-95. Hugh D. Duncan speaks on the celestialization function of art in "Sociology of Art, Literature and Music: Social Contexts of Symbolic Experience," in H. Becker and A. Boskoff, eds., *Modern Sociological Theory in Continuity and Change* (New York, 1957). Jane Belo takes up the question of how much originality art demands in "Balinese Children's Drawing," in Margaret Mead and M. Wolfenstein, eds., *Childhood in Contemporary Cultures* (Chicago, 1955). See also Margaret Mead, "The Role of the Individual in Samoan Culture," *The Journal of the Royal Anthropological Institute,* 58 (1928), 481-495. For the concept of style see Meyer Schapiro, "Style," in A. L. Kroeber, ed., *Anthropology Today* (Chicago, 1953), and A. L. Kroeber, *Style and Civilizations* (Ithaca, N.Y., 1957). R. R. Sellman offers a short comparison of Gothic and postreformation church architecture in *English Churches* (London, 1956). See also H. L. Short, "Changing Styles of Nonconformist Architecture," *The Listener,* 53 (1955), 471-474. Jiri Kolaja and Robert N. Wilson examine an art in its cultural context taking up "The Theme of Social Isolation in American Painting and Poetry," *The Journal of Aesthetics and Art Criticism,* 13 (1954), 37-45.

12

Limits to Diversity

> For Right is only an abstract name for the multitude of concrete demands in action which others impress upon us, and of which we are obliged, if we would live, to take some account. . . .
>
> Social pressure is but a name for the interactions which are always going on and in which we participate, living so far as we partake and dying so far as we do not. The pressure is not ideal but empirical, yet empirical here means only actual. It calls attention to the fact that considerations of right are claims originating not outside of life, but within it.
>
> John Dewey[1]

DIVERSITY, VALUED AND DISVALUED

Man has achieved remarkable success in controlling his environment by technical means. Also his ability to organize large numbers of people so that they can act in concert and support one another inspires admiration. But despite some ingenious social inventions man has proven to be very ineffectual in controlling behavior that periodically destroys social stability.

Every social system tries to limit the range of behavior in which it permits members to engage. Individuals who exceed the range of permitted variation discover that their acts are no longer condoned. Notice, I don't say that all differences are outlawed. That would be impossible. Certain kinds of diversity are necessary for social life. Women's roles complement men's; the priest's specialties move and heal his appreciative congregation; the potter, carpenter, and barber rely on exchanging their products and services for different goods. Also we value diversity in the form of originality. We line up to borrow a new novel or see a new movie, play, or musical. We applaud an original rendition of an old musical masterpiece. But we value differences that remain

[1] *Human Nature and Conduct* (New York, 1922), pp. 326, 327.

within limits. If the potter turns out too thin or poorly fired ware he hears complaints. His diversity then exceeds the tolerable and is disvalued. A new interpretation of the Eroica must not deviate from accepted standards of performance. If it does it will be repugnant. In brief, a social system thrives on diversity as long as diversity complements existing needs and values. Or else, new needs and standards must be promoted to facilitate acceptance of deviance.

Deviance is culturally relative in the sense that this good-humored Eskimo woman could not publicly smoke her pipe in a U.S. community. Her tonsure might also send eyebrows skyward and the identification tags, by which the Canadian government keeps track of its Eskimo, don't rate with us as socially approved ornaments.

There is another aspect of distressful diversity. It is exemplified by mental illness and other impairments that prevent human beings from adequately fulfilling expected social roles. In this chapter I will be little concerned with unwelcome deviance of this sort.

SOCIAL CONTROL

Man's biological nature prompts nearly everyone to exceed limits of acceptability occasionally. To understand deviance from the vantage point of biology, consider, first, that human beings generate quite enough energy to explode their society through acts like cruelty, rape, and murder. Then, too, biologically most individuals are capable of rich ideological fertility. Occasionally some persons develop this endowment and their new insights, plans, and ethical codes are welcomed into the stream of culture. At other times man's capacity for original thought also leads him into heresies that contradict important values. He innovates forms of expression so fresh that they shock traditional sensibilities. Also individuals are by their human nature susceptible to error. Occasionally we are all a bit careless or slipshod. We can't avoid all mistakes. Errors are annoying, costly, and even devastating transgressions that can echo with long-range consequences. Finally, human organisms periodically go awry, become sick. The direct financial costs of illness, its indirect costs, and the emotional pain it engenders furnish reason enough for trying to control this biological proclivity.

Unacceptable diversity also arises because there are social imperatives. Every social system must maintain some degree of harmony within diversity. Man cannot give up differences, but the differences must complement each other. Diversity run riot makes it impossible for a social system to survive. Hence in every social system means are found to limit diversity that inevitably occurs. Furthermore, man's commitment to social living requires not only that he maintain complementary differences but also keep to some widely shared values. Blunt questioning of these common values or any behavior that flagrantly contradicts them is unwelcome and hence curtailed. Also social man must regulate conflict if his social systems are to survive. And, finally, every social system from family to nation recognizes social roles that must be fulfilled in a socially appropriate manner. Failure to play roles adequately frequently invites social pressure to curtail unwelcome deviance. No doubt other important social imperatives also exist but the ones I have noted illustrate sufficiently how social problems are generated by the very demands inherent in social systems. So, from the nature of group life combined with human nature arises the necessity for social control.

To understand social control in action we can examine the laxity, rigidity, and consistency with which a social system circumscribes limits of permitted variation. We can inquire about measures that prevent potential transgression of the limits. And, of course, we can investigate what happens once someone has actually exceeded the limits of permitted variation.

From one social system to another the over-all range of permitted variation varies in "width." Some communities without being normless tolerate more over-all variation than others. The Plains Indians of the United States impress me as having accommodated a variety of behaviors which, even though they were recognized as atypical, didn't disqualify a person from being socially accepted. In western history we find that the over-all range of permitted variation has varied from time to time. Our western democracies tend to draw in or to whittle down the limits during national emergencies.

Over-all tolerance is harder to measure than the way control varies from one subject matter to another. Sex and aggression, for example, are among the most tightly controlled areas of life in many communities. Obviously the intensity with which limits are drawn must vary from overt to covert behavior. Covert behavior—thoughts and feelings—is difficult to control. Nevertheless we know that some social systems, like the Hopi Indians and certain contemporary revolutionary nations, do in fact try to reach into the mind. Psychotherapy, too, is a highly skilled way of trying to contain covert behavior between approved limits of variation.

We are all familiar with steps taken to prevent illness. In analogous fashion communities use foresight to prevent other behavior from exceeding bounds of tolerance. Most commonly preventive social control relies on enunciating clearly what mishaps or punishments will follow certain kinds of transgression. We do this through codifying legal norms and then advertising the code. A similar though less formal process operates when people are given to understand the consequences of illness, or shirking responsibilities, or failing to measure up to standards. Modern states attempt to prevent certain behavior by monopolizing force and preventing ready access to weapons, alcohol, and drugs—instruments that are perceived to instigate intolerable forms of diversity.

I have emphasized *deliberate* forms of prevention. Actually, many aspects of culture work preventively. Lifelong socialization, for example, conveys norms and sanctions that govern behavior. Ritual periodically renews paramount values, thereby restraining contradictory values from making headway. Ideas about how the universe is organized may forestall unwelcome diversity. For if individuals believe that aggression, incest, or hate can disturb the earth, arrest rain, or keep animals at a distance, won't the awareness lead them to inhibit such dangerous behavior?

SOCIAL PRESSURE

One of the commonest means of maintaining complementary forms of diversity in social relations is through pressure exerted by individuals on one another.[2] By no means is this only physical pressure, that is, force or corporal punishment. I exert social pressure when I correct someone's misstated fact, his conclusion erroneously drawn, or his identification wrongly made. To do so I may rely on reasoning, bitter sarcasm, blunt ridicule, as well as physical chastisement.

Social pressure checks behavior that bursts the limits of acceptable diversity.

[2] Godfrey Wilson and Monica Wilson, *The Analysis of Social Change* (Cambridge, Eng., 1945), pp. 28, 49-58.

It intends to prevent recurrence of the deed by letting others know that the deed is intolerable. It also has a ritual side. The public circumstances in which a guilty party hears his sentence or purifies himself of evil impresses everyone. All acknowledge the gravity of his offense. The prominence of the scaffold on which the condemned man hangs expresses ceremoniously the community's repugnance for murder or treason.

But social pressure should not be too narrowly identified with law. Law is merely one avenue utilized to check undesirable diversity. To deter mistakes and avoid the consequences of unwise conclusions men also reason with one another. Against other offensive behavior we bring the sanctions of shame and ridicule. Neighbors break off relations with someone who persists in behaving intolerably. The more intensely groups or individuals in a society interact, the greater the pressure they exert on each other. Each group presses for its own safety, rights, or advantages, for its own moral, intellectual, or religious standards. Colonialism, the conquest of remote national frontiers, and stepped up international cooperation and world organization all bring about intensified social pressure that is often unwelcome. Precisely its unwelcomeness may inspire a group to resist being incorporated more tightly in a larger social system. So it clings to states' rights or to national sovereignty.

Social pressure is exerted only through some activity. The pressure is not in the norms, ideals, written laws, and unwritten constitutions, but in the way those norms, legal and nonlegal, are actually imposed in social relations. We know social pressure when we see it in operation: a mother reasoning with a delinquent boy, a policeman arresting a housebreaker, elders in a village fixing guilt, a critic pointing to flaws in a novel, or strikers trying to paralyze a corporation.

RESTRAINT THROUGH AUTHORITY AND POWER

Social pressure succeeds when it is backed by authority and power. Power may be physical or intangible. The power to excommunicate a believer is no less potent than coercion used by police. One Kaska Indian trying to convince another to leave a married woman alone converts whatever authority he has into power. He exerts his power in a moral matter. The princely ruler of Swat bestows part of his authority on three judges who constitute the realm's central religious court. Because of his religious training each of the three jurists possesses further authority in his own right. Their authority backs up their judgments and supports their power to command obedience. If necessary, though, they can also rely authoritatively on physical force; state police stand prepared to compel a defendant to obey court orders. Remember what I said in an earlier chapter: naked power, power that isn't backed by authority, is uncertain. It is harder to apply naked power effectively than power that derives from authority.

Even objects possess authority that can be used to maintain complementary diversity. Suppose a friend points out that "judgement" is spelled incorrectly. You dispute the point. Neither party accepts the other's authority with respect to how the word should be spelled. Fortunately both acknowledge the dictionary's authority. And that object resolves the issue in favor of either variant, for two acceptable ways exist of spelling "judgment." Printed books exert more authority than mimeographed papers. Hence publishers speak of the "authority of hot metal."

That political administration frequently exercises considerable social pressure is far from coincidental. Even in a social club elected leaders have the task of deciding what to do when behavior exceeds limits of tolerable diversity. By relying heavily on political officials social systems take advantage of already established authority to implement social pressure. They avoid the difficulty of creating independent agents of social control who might rival political authorities. Of course, everybody in a group possesses some authority and power. By their disapproval the masses keep even administrators in line. Some countries arrange things so that nearly everybody who is of age regularly exercises his authority, for example in elections. Dictatorships prefer to recognize no other source of legitimate power than the governing body's but even they must bow to rampant indignation.

LAW IN ACTION

We can say that law is present when by general consent physical coercion or restraint predictably follows on the heels of a transgression. The community arrests, whips, or executes the wrongdoer. It may compel him to pay a fine under penalty of imprisonment or insist that his wealth be destroyed. By no means is all physical force equivalent to law, only that which the community sanctions. And all transgressions don't fall under the purview of law. Normally failure to dress in up-to-date fashion doesn't call forth the hand of law. However, during a revolution outlawed garments can land a person in jail; dress then becomes legally controlled.

Every community recognizes norms that people can safely predict will be legally enforced. In Swat shopkeepers must report their earnings honestly so that a tax can be assessed. A shoe dealer or spice merchant knows—or has good reason to fear—that if he deliberately neglects to make an honest return he will be arrested, tried, and then fined or jailed for his omission. An aboriginal Kaska Indian who committed murder knew he faced the victim's vengeful kin. They would demand that he pay them blood money; otherwise they would kill him. Such retaliation met the community's approval; it was law. Note that even though the Kaska lacked police, courts, and jails they had law.

Behind law is a body of more or less clear norms. Because they will be enforced by approved coercion or physical restraint they are called legal norms. Such norms may be unwritten. The important point is that people living under legal norms can predict that conformity to the norms will be insisted upon, even to the point of physical force. I prefer not to call legal norms themselves law. Law is process. It is what happens once legal norms are broken. Modern nations have converted even individual rights into legal norms. Government must defend those rights by force if necessary. Holding its big legal stick in reserve some governments try to accomplish other ambitious tasks, like banishing heresy and hastening the dawn of utopia. But just as these goals may seem, law and justice are far from equivalent. Justice is a ceremonious way of referring to law.

Dispute arises when law must be applied in a given circumstance. Modern legal codes try to be highly specific in defining an offense. Nevertheless, one situation never precisely resembles another. Hence courts must decide whether a legal norm covers the case before it. Lawyers for the defendant argue strenuously that the norm doesn't apply; the prosecution maintains equally firmly that it does. The point is, the legal process involves discovering whether an act committed or omitted was really illegal.

Small-scale exotic communities face the same problem, though they solve it in a less complex and more informal fashion than we do. Many such communities lack agencies specialized for law. A politically unorganized community leaves enforcement of legal norms largely up to an offended party and his kin. This is apt to work hardship. A powerful offender whose kin group is large can escape punishment. Or a murderer may resent the sanction which an aggrieved party seeks to impose on him. Hence he strikes back, compounding murder with further killing. Matters have gotten out of hand. The two parties have become involved in a feud that may persist for generations.

Many communities with rudimentary political organization came to realize the uncertainty and precariousness of law left solely in the hands of an aggrieved party. Desiring stability they sought a more effective form of law. One fairly simple solution calls for men with dignity and authority, say village elders, to assume responsibility for discovering whether a legal norm was indeed violated and, if it was, fix punishment. The elders rely on their knowledge to find the facts and on their prestige to convince the guilty party to accept judgment.

How can anyone prove that a legal norm was violated? Suppose I complain that my neighbor killed my cat and he denies it. How do we discover if he is guilty or innocent? Modern courts prefer witnesses and other empirical evidence. Legal norms govern procedures used by police and courts to obtain such evidence. They detail the kind of evidence that may be considered or that

LAW IN ACTION — THE CASE OF THE HOTELKEEPER'S RESPONSIBILITY

The three religious judges (qazis) listened carefully as the hotelkeeper and his guest, Abdul, told their stories.

Abdul had given the hotelkeeper Rs. 55 (about $11.00) for safekeeping. This happened in the remote mountainous portion of Swat where hotels are very plain, lacking both private rooms and locked doors. Knowing the risk his guests ran, the hotelkeeper had asked Abdul for his money lest the guest be robbed.

On the following morning Abdul's companion, Salim, came to the hotelkeeper and asked for part of the sum that Abdul had entrusted to the host's care. Salim argued persuasively that he had Abdul's approval. The hotelkeeper obeyed. Later when the hotelkeeper met Salim in the bazar Salim asked for the rest of Abdul's money and the hotelkeeper again obliged him.

Now Abdul asked the court to compel the hotelkeeper to pay him Rs. 55. The hotelkeeper protested strongly. He already paid the money back in good faith. He gave it to Salim, believing that Salim was telling the truth.

Naturally the court asked where Salim was. It turned out he had gone to Karachi. The judge who conducted the case proposed a postponement until Salim returned. Abdul protested this suggestion. The court asked the hotelkeeper if he would swear on the Quran that he had indeed given the money to Salim in good faith. (According to Muslim law, which is practiced in Swat, an oath may be employed in lieu of witnesses.) The hotelkeeper said he would so swear. (The court assumed that if he swore falsely on God's word then God would punish him drastically.) However, no oath was actually administered.

Protracted discussion followed between the qazis and other persons present, including the hotelkeeper and Abdul. Words flew too fast for my interpreter to keep up. My information indicates that the court was trying to decide what in this particular instance the law should be. The qazis were reviewing past cases and relevant legal principles in order to decide if the hotelkeeper should be forced to pay back the money. The court knew it had power to force repayment, or at least they could order prison for the hotelkeeper if he refused to obey their order.

Finally the three learned men reached their decision. The hotelkeeper had won his case by virtue of the oath he was willing to take. He no longer had any responsibility. He had in good faith turned the money over to Salim who, he thought, was Abdul's representative.

---

can have no bearing on the question of guilt or innocence. Probably no legal system will omit witnesses should any be available. But beyond that, the concept of satisfactory evidence varies. Islamic law used in the courts of Swat allows an oath taken on the Quran or at a saint's tomb to substitute for a witness in some kinds of cases. Also, when witnesses contradict one another the court in Swat gets at the truth by asking one side to swear. Obviously truth is a matter of agreement or convention; outsiders may well doubt that such methods really get at the truth.

Another manner of ascertaining truth is divination. "If such and such is the case," the court or community says, "then let the poison oracle kill the fowl."

A dose of poison that does not invariably produce death is publicly administered to the innocent chicken. Should the hapless animal die, then it is apparent that "such and such" is indeed the case. The guilt of an accused has been demonstrated.[3] Closely related to divination is the ordeal. Here the accused himself must publicly prove his guilt or innocence by some dangerous or painful feat. Among Arabs of the Egyptian desert and Sinai peninsula he licks a hot spoon.[4] A seared tongue proves his guilt; a clean tongue indicates innocence. We don't know how the ordeal allows some men to escape unhurt. Perhaps the person holding the spoon presses it more or less firmly on the tongue. But a better hypothesis is that guilty parties will confess rather than go through the frightful ordeal; and so the ordeal serves a useful purpose.

WHERE LAW IS ABSENT

The Brazzaville African artist in this ceramic design has illustrated a diviner preparing a "bath of truth." Into boiling palm oil he plunges a red hot iron. An accused person who is innocent will be able to retrieve the iron without the slightest injury to his skin. But a guilty man's palms will be atrociously burned. (*Esther van Loo, "Artisans de Brazzaville," Géographia, no. 76 (January, 1958), 15.*)

Law is never a wholly satisfactory system of social pressure. It sometimes finds the innocent guilty and punishes them callously. It fails to reform many guilty persons even though they spend long terms in prison. It doesn't deter heroic people with principles so firm that they cannot be deflected by legal punishment. Nor does it manage to reconcile the ideals of such heroes with community norms.

Yet, modern nations rely heavily on law to maintain the smooth flowing interdependence of corporations, other groups, and individuals on which our specialized society depends. What is the other extreme? Is there any community in which practically no norms are legal? Strange to say, reports claim there are. The Caribou Eskimo living in the treeless Barren Lands west of Hudson Bay are largely "lawless."[5] "In case of dispute, I rather would run

---

[3] E. E. Evans-Pritchard, *Witchcraft, Oracles and Magic Among the Azande* (Oxford, 1937), pp. 258-351.

[4] Austin Kennett, *Bedouin Justice; Laws and Customs Among the Egyptian Bedouin* (Cambridge, Eng., 1925), chap. 11.

[5] Geert van den Steenhoven, *Report to the Department of Northern Affairs and National Resources on a Field Research Journey for the Study of Legal Concepts Among the Eskimos in Some Parts of the Keewatin District, N.W.T. in the Summer of 1955* (1956), mimeographed.

WHERE IS LAW?

Pongalak ranks as Public Enemy No. One among the Caribou Eskimo living in the moss-covered, rocky country northeast of Ennadai Lake, Northwest Territories. In one camp consisting of three tents lives Auledyut (the man shown here). Forty-three years old, he is the quiet, acknowledged leader of a peaceful, cheerful, and well-integrated social system containing 20 souls.

Another camp, lying one day's distance from Auledyut's, is Pongalak's. Fifty-five years old, Pongalak is a man of strong character; he is a good craftsman and a reputed shaman. He lives with his wife, three sons, and one daughter-in-law. A *Life* magazine photographer says that unlike Auledyut's camp, in Pongalak's he heard no laughter.

Around 1920 Pongalak married Auledyut's widowed mother. Shortly afterwards, the Eskimo say, he starved her to death along with one of her sons. Fortunately an uncle had taken Auledyut and another son away from the woman at her request shortly before her death. Nothing happened to Pongalak for allegedly killing his wife.

In 1950, people say, Pongalak abandoned a 14-year-old orphan boy on the winter trail, letting him freeze to death. By luck a man suspicious of Pongalak's story explaining the boy's absence traced the youth and rescued him. Nothing happened to Pongalak for this behavior.

Auledyut accuses Pongalak of having slandered him. Pongalak is also charged with having stolen foxes from another Eskimo's traps. Pongalak hasn't been tried or punished for these acts.

Auledyut detests Pongalak as do other Ennadai Lake people. But nobody feels the community should proceed against the unpopular man. "The Eskimos don't tell him what they think," Auledyut explained, "for they are scared of him as an evil man. The Eskimos would not punish him but keep away from him."

What would Auledyut do should Pongalak come and live in his camp? Auledyut was sure he would move away.

Geert van den Steenhoven, *Report to the Department of Northern Affairs and National Resources on a Field Research Journey for the Study of Legal Concepts among the Eskimos in some Parts of the Keewatin District, N.W.T. in the Summer of 1955* (1956), mimeographed. See also *Life*, 40, no. 9 (Feb. 27, 1956), 80-91.

away than fight," an Eskimo said. Again and again Caribou Eskimo insisted they would not proceed against a man who had persistently transgressed norms, although they might move camp to avoid him. If a troublemaker were starving, other people would even offer him food. Occasionally the community might kill an intolerable nuisance but the unpredictableness of this extreme sanction robs it of the right to be called law. The camp is far more likely to move away passively from the nuisance. Blood revenge practiced by these Eskimo is strictly private. The community takes no legal interest.

The counterpart of the Eskimo's anarchic absence of law exists in modern international society. Some political scientists would argue that an international law governs the world's free and independent nations. I find this use of the term law mystifying. Of course there are rules of warfare, a law of the high seas, and solemnly concluded conventions and treaties between nations. But where is the predictable power that can enforce these codes with the general consent of international society? Has the International Court of Justice really sufficient authority and power to enforce decisions? The United States stipulates that the World Court shall not decide any question affecting this country unless we give it permission. What kind of a court is it in which a defendant must give his consent before the court can adjudicate? The essence of law is prediction. I can predict with fair accuracy that if I steal and get caught I will be punished. Such predictions cannot yet be made in international relations.

FORCE OF REASON

Gifted above all creation with a unique capacity to reason, man employs reason as a device to check disvalued diversity. The pressure exerted by logical argument in social control is less punishing and more reforming than any other form of social pressure. Unfortunately it is also limited. Some people can't be touched by appealing to basic principles which their behavior unwittingly violates or by pointing to undesirable consequences which they in effect invite. Even more serious is the difficulty of using reason to control behavior when the deviant does not accept the principles which underlie the reasoning process. I cannot successfully convince a non-Christian Kaska Indian that his custom of wife-lending goes against the will of God. The principle of a moral God opposed to wife-lending has no place in Kaska theology.

Reasoning cannot succeed unless two people share some relevant common value. If you and I agree that spelling in accordance with Webster is desirable and if we both accept Webster as having authority, then I can successfully convince you to correct your spelling. Reasoning is effective when applied by a person who possesses authority in the area under dispute. A physician's reasoning with respect to health is usually more weighty than a TV repairman's. But I would respect the repairman's criticism of the way I use my set. Reasoning works so casually that we may not recognize it in our own behavior. We rarely have to state our premises explicitly; we take them for granted whenever a community of understanding obviously exists. It is enough for a Hopi Indian to admonish a worrier by saying, "Keep a good heart." Much is compressed in that statement. It implies the premise that hostility and unhappiness are unhealthy. Understood is the unspoken assumption that man is linked with nature so intimately that even his thoughts and feelings affect life beneficially or adversely.

Reasoning sometimes works reflexively as when, in the form of conscience, it restrains our behavior. In the absence of social pressure a person reviews in his mind what he is about to do or has done. If the deed contradicts principles in which he believes or invites consequences he would rather avoid, then he will inhibit or determine to reform his conduct.

THE STING OF PUBLIC OPINION

Shame is one of the most potent forms of social pressure. Merely by our tone of voice we signify disdain for some unwanted deviance. More biting is open ridicule as we confront another person with the intolerability of what he is doing. But as with law and reasoning, shame doesn't work all the time. Like reason it is ineffectual when the other person scorns our opinion or holds standards of what is good, true, and beautiful which vary grossly from ours. In a community divided into social classes, lower-class people are unlikely to hold standards after which middle-class people will model their behavior. On the other hand, a stockbroker's ridicule will sting a person who is about to make an unwise investment. The broker has authority and power in this situation; his opinion is respected, especially if he combines his ridicule with a little positive reasoning.

Social systems with only rudimentary legal systems and small communities in which everyone knows everybody else rely heavily on public opinion. Derision, spontaneous or incorporated in formal song-duels, is much used as a sanction among central Canadian Eskimo. Such communities socialize children to be extremely vulnerable to shame. Investigators in Hopiland asked Indian children ages 8 to 18 to tell when they had been much ashamed.[6] A similar test was also given to midwestern U.S. children. Comparing results showed Hopi children to be much more concerned than midwest children with having appeared to others in a bad light. Their sensitivity to shame remains active all through their lives. It produces that over-disciplined self

[6] Robert J. Havighurst and Bernice L. Neugarten, *American Indian and White Children* (Chicago, 1955), chap. 3; Richard B. Brandt, *Hopi Ethics* (Chicago, 1954), chap. 4 and pp. 67-72.

GUILT AND SHAME ARE RELATIVELY DISTINCT SANCTIONS

Children of several American Indian communities took the Emotional Response Test. Only responses given to questions concerning shame are reported here. Children were asked: "Sometimes people are very ashamed. Have you ever been very much ashamed? Can you remember when you were very much ashamed? Tell me about it." The last question was asked three times. Midwestern schoolchildren of about the same age answered similar questions but wrote down their replies.

Replies were analyzed to see if the child's discomfort arose from guilt (the presence of other people not being a necessary part of the feeling) or from embarrassment due to the presence of others.

Here are some results:

| | Percent of Responses Indicating: | | |
	Guilt	Embarrassment	Neither (Ambiguous Response)
Hopi	26	59	15
Zuni	12	81	7
Navaho	3	96	1
Sioux	30	63	7
Midwest	46	42	12

Robert J. Havighurst and Bernice L. Neugarten, *American Indian and White Children* (Chicago, 1955), chap. 3.

which cautiously limits many desires, emotions, and even ambitions. Although shame is internalized, it should not be confused with guilt. Guilt works in a person whether or not others know that he has done wrong. Midwest children compared to Hopi youngsters are more guilt- than shame-ridden.

BREAKING OFF RELATIONS

Every community depends on exchanging goods and services. At its simplest, a wife performs certain tasks and her husband provides other satisfactions through his goods and services. In Swat more complex specialization is added to division of labor by sex. Another type of reciprocity is gift-giving, a custom that periodically intensifies the sentimental bonds connecting certain kinsmen or other individuals. Among Hopi Indians periodic gifts validate the social ties created at a baby's naming feast. The father's female relatives, particularly his mother, visit the house where he lives. They bring quilts or blankets for the new mother and her extended family. Thereby the father's kinfolk become privileged to name the child. In return for his name the youngster assumes a lifelong obligation to help his father's relatives. A girl offers them household services; a boy makes them presents of rabbits and other game, brings them salt from the mountains, and provides them with field assistance. Cooperative work parties illustrate a common form of reciprocity, one common in Africa. A work party assembles when agricultural or building tasks are too big for one family to manage alone. Neighbors, relatives, and friends are invited to help. In their turn the hosts will reciprocate by joining a neighbor's work party.

Exclusion of a person from any such circuit of reciprocity constitutes a forceful weapon with which to control his intolerable behavior. Exclusion from reciprocity is not only economically costly but it implies social rejection by relatives, friends, and neighbors—persons whose opinion matters a great deal in a small-scale community.

SATYAGRAHA—PHILOSOPHICALLY GROUNDED SOCIAL PRESSURE

Under the inspiring leadership of Mahatma Gandhi Indians have developed boycotts into an elaborate, philosophically grounded technique of exerting determined social pressure.[7] In satyagraha they combine social pressure with positive action in an attempt to reform behavior that has exceeded the limits of acceptability. Satyagraha means "firm adherence to truth," but it is also translated as "soul force."

Satyagraha has been used several times against government itself. True it is costly and also illegal, but it has the incalculable virtue of being safer than armed resistance. Naturally it is used only when a government can't be moved by first proceeding through the courts. Satyagraha has developed from several traditional modes of resistance and persuasion that are deeply rooted in Indian history. For example, there is *dharna*, meaning to hold out. A petitioner sits at his opponent's door until wrongs done to him are redressed. *Dharna* carries a note of revenge that is lacking in another traditional technique of social control, fasting, which aims to move an opponent through pity. Here we have an attempt to combine purely negative social pressure with some positive action capable of correcting intolerable behavior. *Hartal* is again more negative. The word signifies stopping work and business on a wide front. A whole city closes its shops, often at considerable self-sacrifice, to compel some kind of official action. Gandhi recognized deficiencies in all

[7] Joan V. Bondurant, *Conquest of Violence* (Princeton, N.J., 1958); Mohandas K. Gandhi, *Satyagraha in South Africa*, 2nd ed., trans. Valji Govindji Desai (Ahmedebad, 1950).

these traditional techniques. All rely too much on trying to compel somebody to change his mind. They are coercive and not sufficiently reformative.
In satyagraha Gandhi hoped to fuse both forms of social pressure.

A campaign of satyagraha is carefully planned. Initially leaders negotiate
directly with the opponent. Perhaps a mutually satisfactory solution can be
reached through arbitration. If this attempt fails the people are readied for
more direct action. Meetings are held. Discussion and a critical examination
of motives are in order to be sure that no action is taken out of hate. Followers
are reminded of the rules of discipline governing satyagraha.

Harbor no anger but suffer the opponents' anger without returning violence.
Submit to no order given in anger.
Refrain from insults.
Protect even opponents from insult or violence though it be at the risk of your own
    life.
Do not resist arrest or attachment of your possessions.
As a prisoner behave in an exemplary manner.
Obey the satyagraha leaders or resign in event of serious disagreement.
Do not expect guarantees that your dependents will be maintained while you are
    engaged in satyagraha or in jail.

In the next stage propaganda and agitation arouse the followers' emotions
and reinforce their commitment to the campaign. Songs, slogans, mass meetings, and public prayers build up morale. Then an ultimatum is issued to the
opponent. Candidly, steps about to be taken are described. People will withhold all cooperation until the government reforms. The ultimatum is not a
threat. It is a last effort at securing agreement and goes out in such a way that
an opponent can still capitulate without losing face. If the ultimatum brings
no satisfactory response noncooperation begins. It starts mildly. Men resign
their titles and offices and in other ways refuse to serve government. Later
they boycott schools and other public institutions. In time carefully selected
legal norms are deliberately violated. Leaders select norms that symbolize
their aims. Should relief still not be forthcoming the campaign becomes even
bolder and usurps government functions. A parallel system of government is
set up, somewhat like a wartime government in exile, except that the satyagrahis extend the greatest possible amount of cooperation to the other
government.

It would be too much to expect that satyagraha always succeeds. At times
Gandhi had to call off civil disobedience because his followers could not
discipline themselves sufficiently and resorted to force. But cases of successful
campaigns are on record. One occurred in a South Indian town where
Untouchables formerly had to take a long, circuitous road in order to avoid
passing in front of a castemen's temple. Satyagraha lasting from the spring of
1924 to the fall of 1925 succeeded in eliminating this obnoxious obligation.
Government supported the orthodox Hindus and erected a police barricade

on the forbidden road. The satyagrahis stood opposite the police and tried persistently to reason with the orthodox Hindu leaders. For months the parties remained deadlocked, each inflexible, until finally the orthodox opponents changed their values. Recently Americans saw a version of satyagraha applied by sit-in and other demonstrators working for Negro rights in the South. These campaigns, too, have largely succeeded.

MORE DEVIOUS PATHS

Sometimes social pressure achieves its way more deviously. For example, take sulking. Proust, the French novelist, remained in bed a fortnight in protest against the fuss made over his more highly favored, heterosexual brother's marriage. Anthropologists have studied societies in which an insulted person "assaults" his opponent by sulking. In the most extreme form of sulking the victim of an injury takes his own life in revenge. Psychologists will perceive that such acts deflect aggression inward, against the self rather than against the aggressor.

When a community believes some individuals to be specially gifted with an inherent capacity for evil, the possibility of being so identified and branded as a witch acts as a powerful factor in circumscribing behavior. Individuals then guard against deviating from the norms. They even take care not to farm too successfully or accumulate too many possessions, lest they be suspected of practicing evil witchcraft. Hopi Indians are apt to regard any eccentric, aggressive, or unusually daring person—anybody who shows marked individuality, including someone insane—as a witch. A village chief fears lest anything go wrong in his village because then he too might be branded. The much vaunted Hopi attitude of moderation, the individual's habit of decrying his abilities, his profession of humility, his fear lest he excite envy, and his reluctance to seek high office actively are all at least partly determined by the dread of being suspected of witchcraft. However, as Laura Thompson argues, to put too much stress on the negative sanction is like ascribing our conformity to traffic regulations entirely to fear of the policeman. Negative sanctions are generally supplemented by more positive considerations in maintaining social control.[8]

WAR AS CONTROL

We recognize war as a legitimate, though deplorable, means of limiting international diversity. All war, like all force, isn't social pressure. Pirates fight simply for plunder, head-hunters go on the warpath to secure victims,

[8] Laura Thompson, *Culture in Crisis* (New York, 1950), pp. 119-120, 124-126.

and Plains Indian men formerly sought fighting for the prestige it brought.

In the absence of international law or other forms of social pressure capable of curtailing intolerable behavior between nations, force may be employed on a grand scale, for the magnitude of military force keeps pace with size of a population. War also keeps pace with social organization. Underorganized food gatherers, like the Kaska Indians, engage only in small raiding parties in which each man is pretty much on his own. The number of killed and injured is small and so is the amount of destruction; hostilities are brief. Some food gatherers, like the Central Arctic Eskimo, lacked war completely though they well knew individual combat. As social organization effectively coordinates more people, wars become greater. In constant readiness the nation supports well-trained, standing armies provided with the most deadly weapons technology can build.

Leopold Kohr argues that war grows likely from the moment national leaders believe they control greater power than a prospective adversary.[9] International power comes not merely from men under arms, ready missiles, or nuclear warheads but also from a high level of national morale, heavy production of wealth, and allies. To reduce the magnitude of modern war, Kohr suggests, we must diminish the size of nations. Bigness leads to devastation. Summation has brought us to hell. Division, he claims, is the road to future progress. Whether Kohr is right or wrong, the world is unlikely to reduce the scale of nations in order to end the threat of destruction. Largeness confers too many advantages for it to be abandoned.

REFORMING THE DEVIANT

I have mentioned social pressure that proposes to heal a breach or reform a deviant rather than simply to punish him. The South African Lovedu make reconciliation and compromise fundamental objectives of their "legal" system.[10] Their court is not a court in our sense because its prime concern is not fixing penalties. Lovedu procedure aims at settling disputes through engineering friendly adjustments. There are several tiers of courts, culminating in the court of the queen herself. Trials are usually held at a defendant's court. Here men publicly hear the case under informal circumstances. One case will illustrate proceedings. A son in anger stabbed his father who had intervened in a fight between him and his wife. The court ordered father and son to become reconciled through a traditional ritual known as begging pardon. Family courts in the United States attempt reconciliation and the same object governs our arbitration procedures.

[9] Leopold Kohr, *The Breakdown of Nations* (New York, 1957).

[10] E. Jensen Krige and J. D. Krige, *The Realm of a Rain-Queen* (London, 1943), chap. 11.

Occasionally our prisons and reformatories try to reeducate. For example, group psychotherapy may be used. Convicts or delinquents take part in group sessions which are directed toward giving the group members insight into motives behind their deviance. The sessions explore the individual's attitudes toward society and encourage him to substitute law-abiding values for the value which he hitherto lived by. However, in many cases prison rehabilitation fails due to the very fact that it is enforced. The artificial prison environment also limits the extent to which an inmate can reorient himself to outside society. Fellow inmates constantly reinforce the convict's value system in contrary directions. Furthermore, lower-class prison inmates are unlikely to share the reformers' values. A study done in Boston, not in jail but in a guidance clinic, shows how little we can accomplish in the way of reform even when we are willing to try. Nearly 9 out of 10 delinquent boys referred to the clinic continued misbehaving.[11]

Occasionally tolerance is broadened in order to reform a wrongdoer. We temporarily tolerate even offensive behavior in the belief that by accepting the deviant and showing him every consideration we will induce him to adopt approved behavior standards. This technique is often used with the unruly adolescent or the returning war veteran unable to settle down to the tempo of peacetime living.

A dramatic, large-scale experiment in positive social pressure has been launched in mainland China. Revolutionary reeducation, aiming at thought reform, has successfully reoriented attitudes in a number of individuals. But the Chinese experiment is heavily tinged with fear and coercion, especially when it occurs in prison.

BEYOND CONTROL

Some kinds of diversity are intrinsically difficult to control, especially those founded on radical differences in value and belief.[12] If such behavior involves a violation of legal norms, the person violating the norms neither fears nor respects the court's authority which, therefore, is shorn of power. Even if he is punished he or others continue to carry out their deeds through genuine conviction that they, not the courts, are right. If the dispute involves religious questions, priests cannot touch the deviant believer. He rejects their principles as they reject his.

A radical divergence in values may be hard to discover. It underlies countless breeches of legal norms, logical premises, and conventions. Courts are kept busy, rival parties argue back and forth on many controversial issues,

[11] Sheldon Glueck and Eleanor Glueck, *One Thousand Juvenile Delinquents* (Cambridge, Mass., 1934); William Healy, Augusta F. Bronner, and Myra E. Shimberg, "The Close of Another Chapter in Criminology," *Mental Hygiene*, 19 (1935), 208-222.

[12] Wilson and Wilson, *op. cit.*, chap 5.

and the community is kept seething with constant disequilibrium. The law cases and controversies are all symptoms of the underlying implicit conflict which no one recognizes because it is never voiced directly.

As social systems grow in size radical opposition also increases in intensity and perplexity. After the Middle Ages much of western Europe began to writhe in a centuries-long dispute over rationalism and traditionalism, a dispute few men at the time recognized for what it was. It erupted into acrimonious religious conflicts, it led parliamentarians to challenge kingship, and it inspired heated controversy over the relative priority of science and religion.

In contemporary Pakistan a similar underlying conflict expresses itself in questions about whether a man is justified in marrying as many as four wives and whether divorce can occur simply at a husband's will or must be sanctioned by a court.[13] Intertwined with such questions is a dispute over which brand of Islam shall prevail or, to put it in different terms, how Muhammad's teachings and the God-given Quran shall be interpreted in the twentieth century. Traditionalist Muslims in good faith affirm that tenets of Islam found in the Quran or obvious from traditions about what the Prophet said and did are for all time. They are not subject to revision as culture changes. Polygyny and the free right to divorce are in this category; they are scripturally sanctioned customs in which no man and no legislature has authority to interfere, nor should they be abused for licentious or selfish ends. Less traditional, revisionist Muslims demur. These Muslims continue to acknowledge Islam as the true religion but affirm that a democratic government must from time to time create legally enforceable norms and render illegal customs that have become obsolete. They claim that the Quran contains mostly general injunctions. Its generality allows it to be interpreted anew in different ages. Although the Muslim president of Pakistan in 1961 decreed that polygyny and divorce could be restricted by government authority, he did not bring the underlying controversy between rationalists and traditionalists to an end. Furthermore, as is customary in radical opposition, the same individual in Pakistan unhappily finds himself in opposed camps, thoroughly muddled. He perceives that unregulated divorce can lead to social problems in an impersonal, modern, urban setting. He recognizes the advantages of free inquiry, of thought unrestricted by religious dogma, and of untrammeled scope for research. Simultaneously, however, the fixity of tradition and the sanctity of God-given principles that are free of doubt also attract him. So, when radical opposition prevails in a community not only do radically opposed parties contest each other's view but turmoil is reflected in the individual personality itself, lending to all of life a lack of coherence, stability, and consistent meaning.

[13] John J. Honigmann, "Radical Opposition in National Culture: A Case Study," *Davidson Journal of Anthropology*, 1 (1955), 169-180; "Culture Change and Personal Law in Pakistan," *West Pakistan*, 1, no. 9 (1958), 12-17.

FREEDOM FOR DIVERSITY

Every social system undoubtedly values some degree of individual freedom. Yet no community can avoid putting limits on diversity. Reconciling freedom with control is a perennial problem that has engrossed many philosophers. One answer contains a grain of truth. To restrict freedom is actually to protect everybody's freedom. For if everybody had untrammeled liberty then nobody's liberty would be safe. Such a general formula, however, is no help in particular questions. A law restricting what an editor can print restricts his freedom then and there. He is not concerned with the more abstract, general freedom it supposedly protects. Hence society is left with a challenging problem, one growing ever more acute as our interdependence intensifies. How can we maintain firm limits to disruptive diversity and yet maximize everyone's real freedom to innovate, to act spontaneously, to live by conscience, and to act creatively? Inevitably such freedom will occasionally lead to conflict. What can we do to make a wide range of diversity bearable?

I assume that value exists in incorporating in society as wide a range of diversity as possible. Good reason exists for advocating such breadth of tolerance. Unique genetic inheritance and unique individual experiences guarantee that every individual will be different. Therefore, suppressing individual differences will cause suffering and invite rebellion. In the end, to seek too much conformity increases the difficulty of maintaining stability either in or between social systems. Can we, somewhat like the Plains Indians, accommodate a wide range of temperaments and interests in our social life? They valued war but allowed pacifically inclined men to carry on without disgrace in women's roles (but not as homosexuals). Contrarily, a manly-hearted woman could win prestige through her not fully approved forthright sexuality. They safely incorporated individuals who could potentially threaten social equanimity. They converted the potentially illicit into something acceptable.

FURTHER READING

On the relationship of deviance and social structure see Richard R. Korn and Lloyd W. McCorkle, *Criminology and Penology* (New York, 1959), chap. 7; Talcott Parsons, "Illness and the Role of the Physician: A Sociological Perspective," *American Journal of Orthopsychiatry*, 21 (1951), 452-460; and Talcott Parsons, "Definitions of Health and Illness in the Light of American Values and Social Structure," in E. G. Jaco, ed., *Patients, Physicians and Illness* (Glencoe, Ill., 1958). An important work pointing up the relativity of deviance between different cultures is Ruth Benedict, "Anthropology and the Abnormal," *The Journal of General Psychology*, 10 (1934), 59-80. Considerable data indicate that persons possessing less prestige in a society are not strongly expected to live up to ideals. For example, see Maurice Freedman, *Lineage Organization in Southeastern China,* London School of Economics, Monographs on Social Anthropology, no. 18, 1958, p. 28; S. Dube, *Indian Village* (London, 1955), pp. 139-140, 145-146; and Allison Davis, Burleigh B. Gardner, and Mary R. Gardner, *Deep South* (Chicago, 1941), pp. 17-18, 499, 507, 520.

K. N. Llewellyn and E. A. Hoebel examine *The Cheyenne Way* (Norman, Okla., 1941) of resolving disputes through law. Other pertinent contributions by Hoebel are *Man in the Primitive World,* 2nd ed. (New York, 1958), chap. 27, and the *Law of Primitive Man* (Cambridge, Mass., 1954). L. T. Hobhouse reviews a large volume of literature on maintaining complementary behavior through law in "The Simplest Peoples. Part II. Peace and Order Among the Simplest Peoples," *British Journal of Sociology,* 7 (1956), 96-119. Geert van den Steenhoven examines *Legal Concepts among the Netsilik Eskimos of Pelly Bay, N.W.T.,* Northern Coordination and Research Centre, Department of Northern Affairs and National Resources, no. NCRC-59-3, 1959. Culture change in relation to law is a well-covered topic. See A. St. J. J. Hannigan, "The Impact of English Law upon the Existing Gold Coast Custom and the Possible Development of the Resulting System," *Journal of African Administration,* 8 (1956), 126-132, and A. Phillips' comprehensive examination of "Marriage Laws of Africa," in A. Phillips, ed., *Survey of African Marriage and Family Life* (London, 1953). John J. Honigmann's "Culture and the Courts: A New Field for Applied Anthropology," *Social Problems,* 3 (1956), 154-160, examines strains between legal procedure and other customs. For what happened among the Kwakiutl after they could no longer use social pressure to protect rights in titles and associated privileges see Ronald L. Olson, "Black Market in Prerogatives Among the Northern Kwakiutl," *Papers of the Kroeber Anthropological Society,* 1 (1950), 78-80.

On the limits of law consult Roscoe Pound, "Jurisprudence," in Harry E. Barnes, ed., *The History and Prospects of the Social Sciences* (New York, 1925); Norman Marsh, "Personal Freedom and Legislative Power," *The Listener,* 61 (1959), 975-976; and John J. Honigmann, "Value Conflict and Legislation," *Social Problems,* 7 (1959), 34-40.

Turning to other forms of social control, Ralph Piddington considers "closed-circuit" reciprocity in *An Introduction to Social Anthropology,* 2 vols. (Edinburgh, 1950), vol. I, pp. 271-275. In "Mental Disorder and Self-Regulating Processes in Culture: A Guatemalan Illustration," in *Interrelations Between the Social Environment and Psychiatric Disorders* (New York, 1953), Benjamin D. Paul describes rejection used against a girl evading feminine role behavior. The complex motives entering suicide among the Trobriand Islanders are analyzed in Bronislaw Malinowski, *Crime and Custom in Savage Society* (London, 1926), pp. 77-78, 94-98. Studies showing how fear of being accused of witchcraft restrains behavior include Clyde Kluckhohn, *Navaho Witchcraft,* Papers of the Peabody Museum of American Archaeology and Ethnology, Harvard University, vol. 22, no. 2, 1944; Max G. Marwick, "The Continuance of Witchcraft Beliefs," *The Listener,* 55 (1956), 490-492; Max Marwick, "The Social Context of Cewa Witch Beliefs," *Africa,* 22 (1952), 120-135, 215-233; Monica Wilson, "Witch Beliefs and Social Structure," *American Journal of Sociology,* 56 (1951), 307-313. For the theory of war as related to cultural and social complexity see Arthur Gladstone, "Some Cultural Factors in Primitive Warfare," *Bulletin of the Research Exchange on the Prevention of War,* 4 (1956), 99-103.

Problems encountered in moving from punitive social pressure to "correctional therapy" are detailed in Richard R. Korn and Lloyd W. McCorkle, *Criminology and Penology* (New York, 1959), chaps. 23-24, and Donald R. Cressey, "Contradictory Theories in Correctional Group Therapy Programs," *Federal Probation,* 18, no. 2 (1954), 20-26. Robert Jay Lifton describes another kind of positive social pressure in *Thought Reform and the Psychology of Totalism* (New York, 1961). In *Patterns of Culture* (Boston, 1934), chap. 8, Ruth Benedict shows why it is important to incorporate in society as wide a variety of human types as possible. H. L. A. Hart restates the problem of reconciling control and liberty in "Immorality and Treason," *The Listener,* 62 (1959), 162-163.

13

Coming of Age

... one man in his time plays many parts.
His acts being seven ages. At first the infant,
Mewling and puking in the nurse's arms.
Then the whining schoolboy with his satchel
And shining morning face, creeping like snail
Unwillingly to school. And then the lover,
Sighing like furnace, with a woeful ballad
Made to his mistress' eyebrow. Then a soldier,
Full of strange oaths and bearded like the pard,
Jealous in honor, sudden and quick in quarrel,
Seeking the bubble Reputation
E'en in the cannon's mouth. And then the justice,
In fair round belly with good capon lin'd,
With eyes severe and beard of formal cut,
Full of wise saws and modern instances;
And so he plays his part. The sixth age shifts
Into the lean and slipper'd pantaloon,
With spectacles on nose and pouch on side;
His youthful hose well sav'd, a world too wide
For his shrunk shank, and his big manly voice,
Turning again toward childish treble, pipes
And whistles in his sound. Last scene of all,
That ends this strange eventful history,
Is second childishness and mere oblivion—
Sans teeth, sans eyes, sans taste, sans everything.

William Shakespeare[1]

AGES OF MAN

Life is continuous, each interval unfolding into the next from beginning to inevitable end. Culture, however, erects mileposts on the journey from conception to old age and marks the transitions from callow recruit to seasoned sergeant major, from teaching assistant to emeritus professor.

[1] *As You Like It,* Act II, Scene 7.

Kaska Indians count mileposts after birth. For the first three years a baby remains in a stage of nonreason. Then he graduates to a level of partial reason that lasts until around age 7. There follows a youthful period, from 7 to 12, when people assume he can think for himself. This interval prepares him for early maturity, a stage extending from 12 to 17. Marriage promotes him to responsible adulthood. In due time the growing maturation of his children ushers him into a phase of respectable seniority. Finally, biological decline brings him at last to unenviable old age.

Like other small-scale exotic people, until recently Kaska Indians kept no track of birthdays. They measured progress through the life cycle by their seven ages of man or, more accurately, they followed growth by the degree of responsibility they could entrust to an individual. Each age carried different expectations and brought appropriate rewards.

ACCOUNTING FOR WHAT HAPPENS IN THE WOMB

The world holds mixed ideas about how life is established, which is not strange considering the microscopic elements responsible for conception.[2] Still, to profess total ignorance about the biological facts of life is exceptional. Otherwise observant Trobriand Islanders, who live in the Southwest Pacific, have startled anthropologists by outrightly denying that the husband is physiologically the father of his children.[3] They claim that copulation merely opens the vaginal passage and thereby allows a tiny spirit child to enter a no longer virgin woman. Probably the Trobrianders have been misunderstood. Perhaps they mean to say that life consists of inherited spirit that could scarcely derive from a mechanical act of fertilization but which spiritual agencies send from beyond. Even this belief reduces the father's importance in procreation to paltry insignificance. But this is quite congruent with the way Trobrianders socially overlook the father when they matrilineally assign children membership in unilinear descent groups.

Many social systems do not go as far as the Trobrianders and invest spiritual beings with only partial, but still substantial, responsibility for starting new life. Hopi Indians on Third Mesa correctly appraise sexual intercourse but then supplement biology with a female deity from whose fecund womb babies issue.[4] However, this supernatural mother does not release all babies born.

[2] Clellan S. Ford, *A Comparative Study of Human Reproduction*, Yale University Publications in Anthropology, no. 32, 1945, pp. 34-42.

[3] Bronislaw Malinowski, *The Father in Primitive Psychology* (New York, 1927); M. F. Ashley Montagu, *Coming into Being Among the Australian Aborigines* (London, 1937).

[4] Fred Eggan, *Social Organization of the Western Pueblos* (Chicago, 1950), pp. 47-48; Pearl Beaglehole, "Notes on Personal Development in Two Hopi Villages," in Ernest Beaglehole and Pearl Beaglehole, *Hopi of the Second Mesa*, Memoirs of the American Anthropological Association, no. 44, 1935.

Some births are direct reincarnations of children who lived briefly once before but died before they could be initiated. They receive another chance as they reenter the same matrilineal household where they had previously visited.

Another plausible theory maintains that more than a single sex act is required to build life in the womb. Repeated coitus makes a child. This theory thoroughly involves the father in a process from which Trobrianders almost completely exclude him.

All such ideas enable people with little exact knowledge of physiology to explain troublesome biological facts, like the fact that some marriages remain childless for years. What small-scale people don't suspect is that the woman might be mating with a sterile partner or that perhaps she herself is barren. It is also a fact that not every sex act "takes" in the sense of being followed by pregnancy. Hence communities that allow premarital sex relations rarely run into complications due to girls conceiving before marriage. Physiologists have even a better explanation for adolescent infertility, one unknown to most of the world.[5] Sexual relations early in puberty tend to be ineffective because a young girl's organism remains unprepared to bear a viable fetus. Physiologists have coined a somewhat misleading term, "adolescent sterility," to designate the interval between onset of physiological puberty and the point some months later when the girl's more mature organism allows full-term pregnancy. By then many girls in small-scale exotic social systems will very likely be having sex relations with their husbands.

We must not exaggerate. Most cultures in some way causally associate sexual intercourse with pregnancy. They even recognize that pregnancy fundamentally depends on the fluid which a man contributes during coitus. Therefore, people are quite able to conclude that if they wish to avoid or space children they must either remain continent—for normal adults a formidable restriction—or perform intercourse while taking proper precautions. If initiative is up to a man, he can forestall conception by calculatedly withdrawing in time to ejaculate well outside the vagina, thereby preventing sperm from reaching the uterus. The symbolism of contraceptive magic is much less cumbersome and, at least immediately, far less frustrating than these maneuvers; it also is more common. Convenient mechanical methods, in which a diaphragm blocks entry into the womb during intercourse or a condom safely shields the penis, enjoy popularity in Europe and America largely because they provide minimum interference with the mechanics or pleasure of coitus. India, Japan, and the Arab world have long known mechanical and even chemical modes of birth control, though common folk in these lands hardly employ them. Rarely do small-scale exotic communities know how to forestall

[5] M. F. Ashley Montagu, *The Reproductive Development of the Female*, 2nd ed. (New York, 1957).

conception mechanically. Only by prohibiting sexual intercourse for some months after birth or during nursing years do they achieve some spacing of births.

BIOLOGICAL BIRTH

A baby is born twice, first when it is delivered at home or, increasingly even among small-scale people, in an aseptic hospital or professionally staffed maternity home. Its second, social birth doesn't come until several days or weeks later when a baptismal rite gives the child a name or some other passage ritual incorporates him into the social world.[6] Among the Hopi a rite that introduces him to the sun acknowledges his social personality. Closely allied passage rites at this time separate mothers from impurities surrounding birth and safely reintegrate them into normal life.

If childbirth were easy and painless, then so many cultures would not include in their repertory preliminary observances designed to facilitate birth, to make it safe, and to avoid spontaneous abortion. Pregnancy observances frequently require strict attention to diet. A Kaska woman avoided numerous foods and her husband sympathetically observed equally pointed dietary rules. On the mother's part, food taboos by reducing calories may well have contributed to the well-being of the mother and helped to secure an uncomplicated delivery, though women didn't carry out the rules with this in mind. Fulfilling taboos gave women as well as prospective fathers a feeling of being in control of an uncertain biological process. The magic enabled them to circumvent some measure of anxiety and heightened their sense of security.

A personal world view allows a man to be as responsibly involved in pregnancy and birth as the mother herself. Hopi illustrate this nicely. During a woman's pregnancy her husband avoids injuring any living creature lest the infant be born deformed, scarred, or dead. If necessary, he can counteract danger he inadvertently roused by smoking the dead animal's skin while praying for the unborn child's safety. He dare not tie a hobbling rope around any beast's neck; otherwise, the umbilical cord would choke the emerging infant. And to make white prayer sticks would bring an albino into the world.

Experienced, confident hands of elderly women, who themselves have borne several children, assist in delivery. Fairly commonly a woman goes home to her parents to give birth, at least to her first child, and the familiar setting probably further relieves her anxiety. People like the Kaska, who dread the contamination that birth brings to men, build special parturition shelters in secluded places. Even with birth taking place at home, unnecessary people are commonly excluded. Sexual modesty is sufficient ground for barring men. Excluding the husband from the painful scene spares him from sharing his

[6] Ford, op. cit., pp. 43-74.

wife's suffering. In general, limiting visitors reduces the high risk of infection which women in labor normally run.

Delivery techniques vary. Assistants hold the Kaska and Hopi parturient under her arms while she squats and forces out the child. Other people provide a pole which a kneeling woman clenches to support herself. Most unusually does the mother recline, though professional staffs in modern hospitals find that position very convenient for assisting delivery. In some parts of the world a husband symbolically takes to his "confinement" bed, simulates labor, and accompanies his wife in giving birth. Perhaps the couvade, as this custom is called, compensates him for the magnified attention going to his wife. Quite possibly it provides him with a means to quell his anxiety concerning both wife and child. In place of helplessly awaiting an uncertain outcome, the couvade takes up slack time and gives him something to do. The fact that the couvade occurs in areas as remote from one another as South America, northern Japan, and the Pyrennes Mountains makes it logical to assume that here is a custom with material adjustive value. Apart from preliminary magical precautions and prayerful or magical petitions, small-scale exotic communities are powerless should delivery become abnormally complicated. If pelvic deformities severely narrow the bony canal through which the child must pass, Caesarian section may save its life and one East African tribe is known to have practiced this complex form of surgery.

Considering all the pains taken with pregnancy and the attention lavished on birth itself, how strange that parents with no sense of wrongdoing should ever kill a newborn infant. Infanticide is rare and always selective. Among Eskimo girl babies occasionally (hardly invariably!) are done away with in order to hasten the advent of a boy, a future provider. One or both twins are killed where twins threaten misfortune or, being of different sex, are deemed guilty of an incestuously close, uterine relationship. To destroy deformed babies is felt to be wise where institutions can't foster their lifelong care. Infanticide immediately after birth leaves the mother no chance to become deeply attached to her child. Note, too, that infanticide also occurs well before social birth, that is, before ceremonies enroll the baby as a full-fledged community member.

BABIES TAKE PRIORITY

Because they are utterly helpless babies survive only through adults' care.[7] Because child care especially involves a woman it inevitably limits the sphere of feminine status. To reduce inroads which child care makes on a woman she may employ a full-time nurse and, later, a governess. Israeli kibbutzim, committed to the principle of sexual equality, use nurseries and professional

[7] Ford, *op. cit.*, pp. 75-85.

staffs to rear children so that both parents may work. In many cultures partly grown children or a woman's sisters are available at home to help with a child while the mother carries on her other duties. American Indian women find some kind of portable cradle or other carrying devices very useful in order to work and yet keep their babies with them. In traveling a woman simply swings the cradled infant across her back. At home or outdoors she props the cradle against a wall or hangs it from a low branch nearby where she can quickly respond to the baby's needs. By the time healthy growth makes a child too heavy to be packed about it can partly support its weight clinging to the mother's body or toddle alongside her. Another artifact that aids child care is the nursing bottle, which makes a baby independent of the mother's breast. The mother can be gone all day without engaging a wet nurse or starving her infant. The glass allows her to watch and measure nourishment flowing out to be sure that the baby gets enough to eat. Where female vanity is pronounced, bottle feeding somewhat offsets the risks of maternity by preventing a woman's breasts from losing their alluring firmness.

Hopi infants spend much time lashed to cradleboards like this one. The experience does not restrict their development. (*Southwest Museum, Los Angeles.*)

The purpose, meaning, and timing of child-rearing routines vary considerably among cultures. To be sure, broad generalizations can be made that hold for many small-scale exotic communities. For example, in many places mothers are taught to wait a day or two before breast feeding a newborn baby. Undoubtedly this custom is related to the fact that a new mother's breasts yield only colostrum, a harmless, mildly laxative substance, but one noticeably different from milk and one which many people deem to be unfit for food. Kaska Indian women sometimes massaged their breasts to get rid of it quickly. Another generalization holds wherever people are not time conscious, which means in practically all of the earth's small-scale communities. Here women nurse babies whenever youngsters show sign of discomfort; they don't wait four hours from the last feeding. But these are superficial resemblances. They miss the underlying, existential tissue of motivation which gives contrasting emotional color to similar forms of child rearing.

Swaddling illustrates how superficially similar behavior reveals unique aims and significance when viewed cross-culturally.[8] In European Russia parents

[8] Ruth Benedict, "Child Rearing in Certain European Countries," *The American Journal of Orthopsychiatry*, 19 (1949), 342-350.

claim that swaddling is absolutely necessary to keep a baby from hurting itself through its own violence. They also admit that it is easier to carry a swaddled than an unswaddled infant. Polish women don't fear violence but worry about a newborn infant's fragility; it will snap in two if not firmly bound. Then, too, although swaddling may be unpleasant, Poles feel it is good because it hardens the child just as suffering hardens an adult. East European Jews swaddle to keep the child warm and snug and to make its limbs grow straight. Swat Pathans don't think of swaddling as unpleasant but stress the comfort it affords a baby.

Back-packing of children occurs among many of the food-gathering and trapping Indians who live in Canada's North, between Labrador and British Columbia.

Where the clock doesn't govern feeding, one of the earliest contest of wills between adult and child occurs over weaning. A child is attracted to other foods but he also wants to continue nursing while his mother proposes to discontinue the habit. Culture contains three tried techniques for promoting weaning. In some places parents send a child away for a time, perhaps to grandparents where he will forget about nursing. A more definitely punishing way converts the breast, hitherto so richly gratifying, into an unpleasant, frightening object. The child tastes something bitter on the nipple or is terrified by its coating of soot. In the gentlest way of all, a mother gradually reduces her readiness to nurse, using various forms of distraction to induce a youngster to relinquish his breast claims. Pressure to wean a child is intensified where a mother must abstain from sexual gratification during the many months over which nursing normally lasts. A polygynous husband, on the other hand, usually finds no difficulty avoiding intercourse with one wife.

TRAINING FOR ADULT RESPONSIBILITY

When the time is right, new group members begin to be trained in skills, provided with suitable ideals, and endowed with grounds for making proper discriminations.[9] Most exotic communities appear more satisfied with their relatively unsystematic, traditional mode of education than we are with our

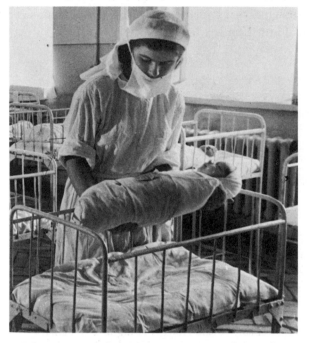

The nurse in this Moscow maternity home shows how easy it is to handle a stiffly swaddled Russian baby. (*Sovfoto.*)

professionally staffed, multimillion-dollar school system. The custom of having individuals spend 8, 12, 16, or more years in classrooms getting ready for independent maturity grew up in our western world relatively recently as a response to the growing volume of basic skills and facts needed to cope with modern industrial culture. Despite its importance, the system we have devised works only imperfectly. Many children resist learning, the knowledge they are taught doesn't always fit them for life, and methods of teaching modern subjects are practically medieval. In the junior grades the youngest members of school population reject many things whose relevance they can't appreciate. In a slowly changing, homogeneous community, on the other hand, children see their future daily. In life around him the child perceives the relevance

[9] George A. Pettitt, *Primitive Education in North America,* University of California Publications in American Archaeology and Ethnology, vol. 43, 1946.

A CONTEMPORARY ARTIST RECORDS THE EARLY AZTEC LIFE CYCLE

On the following two pages: At the top (left) a father instructs his 7-year-old son in using a fish net while a girl (right) learns spinning from her mother. Below, at age 8, both children weep when they are threatened with punishment by thorns. Threats are not enough. The 9-year-old son and daughter have been disobedient and are severely punished. When children are 10, parents use clubs to chastise them. Still more severe punishment follows when the boy and girl, now 11, are obliged to inhale pungent smoke, or at age 12 a boy is made to lie in mud.

Remaining scenes show a mother overseeing her 12-year-old daughter sweeping the house. At 13 a boy is big (and disciplined?) enough to fetch wood from the mountain and bring in reed grass by canoe to use at home. His sister grinds meal and cooks. Both work under their like-sexed parent's direction. A 14-year-old boy takes the canoe out alone for fishing and his sister receives instruction in weaving. Note the emphasis on admonition in these scenes. "Parents always talk to children," modern American Indians are likely to say. The whole or partial discs in each drawing indicate a child's daily tortilla allotment. Each cake actually measured about a foot in diameter.

Edward King Kingsborough, *Antiquities of Mexico*, 9 vols., (London, 1830-1848), Vol. I, pp. 59-60; George C. Vaillant, *The Aztecs of Mexico* (New York, 1941), chap. 6.

of all he learns. The content of basic knowledge is small enough so that parents and other kinsmen, availing themselves of example, discipline, formal instruction, and dramatic ritual can transmit everything that experience has proven young people should know. A limited number of kinsmen are obligated to provide education. Parents, certainly are; first the mother and later, toward puberty, primarily the like-sexed parent. The matrilineal Hopi Indians never rely much on the father for discipline but rather on the mother's brother, who belongs to his nephew's or niece's unilinear descent group.

Human beings' urge to grow and extend their area of responsibility underlies education. On the other hand, biological facts, like the child's utter dependence and his inferior strength give parents at least physical power over children. Whether incentives from within or from without will dominate learning depends on arrangements in particular cultures. In Swat adults enforce strict discipline over their pupils. Among Kaska and many other North American Indians a highly indulgent relationship prevails between mentor and tyro. The vivid personal world view prevailing among them enables Indians to use supernatural sanctions more than physical coercion to back educational goals. Among the Hopi, until children reach an age where they can detect mummery, terrifyingly masked and benevolent Katchinas enforce some kinds of learning. Parents with recalcitrant children secretly notify

Katchinas where to pinpoint their attentions. Many communities praise a child's every significant gain in independence and dexterity. Kaska Indians celebrated a youth's first game with a feast and a Hopi youngster hears applause when he manages to bowl over a target with toy bow and arrow. Praise does not mitigate the educative value of shame. Keen sensitivity to ridicule instilled in children makes shame the predominant, lifelong sanction. The constantly fresh names which American Indians bestow work like other forms of praise and shame. A ridiculous sobriquet painfully sticks until by good performance a child overcomes it and wins a more praiseful name.

American children's large assortment of toys familiarizes them with a cross-section of adult culture, including furniture, telephones, literature, American Indian lore, and the value of personal possessions.

Neither the form or activities of so-called African "bush schools" much resemble arenas of learning as we know them. They push boys and girls of proper age to maturity under forced draft. In them education is advanced first by separating the novitiate from his parents, wrenching him from his familiar home environment to which his behavior hitherto was suited. Then, in a religiously charged atmosphere, new disciplinarians teach him secret myths, the hidden meaning of rituals, and the most highly endorsed values. The attendant ceremonies literally push him into adulthood. Youth villages are one people's exceptional way of inducting boys into full-scale responsibility.[10] Each generation, among the East African Nyakyusa, boys about 10 or 11 years old leave home. They move onto unoccupied land where they build small huts. About a dozen youths suffice to start a new village but more join before settlement closes. When the boys are about 25 years old they marry and bring home their brides. From now on instead of cultivating their fathers' fields they grow their own food. They build full houses in which they rear their children. The young men still haven't gained full independence but soon older men relinquish governing responsibility that their sons take over. In turn, sons of this generation grow up and establish new youth villages. Nyakyusa justify such villages in terms of decency and propriety. Living by

[10] Monica Wilson, *Good Company* (London, 1951).

themselves boys are protected from hearing lewd talk between their parents. Physical separation makes it easier for them to manifest correct ritual reserve whenever they encounter senior men. It removes danger that as the young men mature they will be tempted to purloin the sexual favors of their polygynous fathers' young wives. Also, the Nyakyusa say, youth villages allow young men plenty of opportunity to enjoy each other's congenial company.

Since many children's games imitate or employ adult activities, their function, too, is educational.[11] They extend a child's familiarity over adult tech-

This Eskimo boy's play foreshadows paddling of the kayak he will someday steer in this same water.

niques which he masters at least to his own satisfaction, techniques like snaring birds, catching them with small nets, dressing dolls, cooking with mud, using a model telephone, or releasing destruction from toy weapons. Real life and play, however, are not always as far apart as they are in western culture. If children enjoy developing through using toy utensils and by imitating adult tasks, why shouldn't they also find pleasure doing real things, as far as they lie within their capacity? Work and play then run closely together and the child's role becomes an economically useful one, as it is in Austrian Bauer families where children delight in doing some farm tasks, like driving a tractor.

Verbal games, riddles, schoolyard jingles, jokes, and coined slang develop covert skills. Even a modest level of proficiency enables a child to test and bend his language and to explore the surprising, many faceted meanings of a

[11] S. Culin, *Games of the North American Indians,* Annual Reports of the Bureau of American Ethnology, no. 24, 1903.

word. "Riddle me this," asks an African girl, "the chief entering a crimson pool?" What is it? Obviously, the sunset. And the heart full of muck? An orphan. Pleasure comes from controlling the rhythm and rhyme of words:

> Never let your braces dangle,
> Never let your braces dangle.
> Poor old sport
> He got caught
> And went right through the mangle;
> Went through the mangle he did, by gum,
> Came out like linoleum,
> Now he sings in kingdom-come:
> Never let your braces dangle, chum.[12]

Elements of surprise and thrill underlie children's as well as adults' play. Uncertainty and not-too-extreme risk build up delectable tension. Coasting downhill on sleds, running races, wrestling, ball games, and even pulling cat's cradles contain their quota of excitement. Who will win? What will happen next? Irresolution mounts to a bursting climax beyond which the end comes swiftly. Socially destructive acts contain another kind of excitement. Boys pit themselves against adults with whose values they don't identify and whom they are determined to outwit and hurt. In games conforming to rules, a young child at first believes the rules to be transcendental, eternal, and sacrosanct. Gradually he perceives them to be man-made conventions and thus learns something of the power inherent in social organization.[13] Thrill, important as it is in children's games, doesn't always depend on defeating one's opponents. Stress may simply be on winning, not on also beating another person.

Like so much else in culture, play systematically fits into the rest of a way of life. Children in hunting groups play with bows and targets, in the United States with guns, toy autos, tanks, and, more recently, space helmets. Attitudes children seriously invest in games parallel values adults hold toward illness, competition, discipline, sex, Communists, or whatever. Sometimes adult values are too joyless to be imitated. On one Southwest Pacific island, Manus, adolescents and adults thoroughly hated the social roles they unwillingly assumed.[14] Youngsters perceived this distaste. They took no pleasure imitating the onerous, if striking, social relationships incumbent on their elders. Manus children identified closely with their fathers and absorbed the men's sense of adult life as overly exacting and unduly coercive. Once they held those feelings they weren't drawn to enter adult provinces vicariously in play. After the second world war the Manus transformed their culture,

---

[12] Iona Opie and Peter Opie, *The Lore and Language of Schoolchildren* (Oxford, 1959), p. 18. By permission of the Clarendon Press.

[13] Jean Piaget, *The Moral Judgment of the Child,* trans. Marjorie Gabain (Glencoe, Ill., 1948), chap. 1.

[14] Margaret Mead, *New Lives for Old* (New York, 1956), pp. 364-370.

Early induction in work that suits the child's capacities takes the place of formal schooling in many peasant communities. (*Pakistan Embassy.*)

going far to make their lives easier, more relaxed, and more fully satisfying. Today children more enthusiastically attend to adult affairs (which an outsider, anyhow, finds have become a bit duller). The relaxation of adult life has also freed children's imagination. Their spirits, which the sense of an undesired and unfree future formerly depressed, are now unbound and more fully released in play.

SIGNS OF PUBERTY

Semen production in boys and menstruation in girls signals that physiological puberty has arrived. Many social systems at this time confer an increasing number of adult privileges as well as responsibilities on young people so that puberty brings a fairly sharp break with the dependence and freedom of earlier years.

In a number of communities a boy all during his early life expects some day to pass through an initiation ceremony. He hears much about the rite even though its secret details are guarded by elders. He knows that he can expect painful hazing from his seniors and that his sisters and his mother will be rigidly excluded from the ceremonies. Although some cultures include parallel, if less highly featured, ceremonies for girls, boys' rites fall into a special category, as I will show. Ceremonies for boys tend to be most dramatic in those cultures where an emotionally intense relationship fuses mother and son during early childhood.[15]

The custom of mother and baby sleeping together for a time after birth, excluding the father, is a mark of such emotional closeness. Theory says that sharing his mother's bed and her body's closeness builds up in a boy exceptionally strong, lasting feelings of dependence. Initiation ceremonies energetically break into that attachment. They curtail his lingering dependence on his mother and thrust him into the company and roles of men. Obviously, no comparable responsibility faces girls, however extensive their puberty rites may be.

Male initiation ceremonies have a second, closely related function. They counteract the boy's animosity toward his father. The older man long ago resumed his legitimate place by his wife's side, displacing his son. But the boy retains a smoldering, unconscious envy and challenging rivalry. As a powerless child he reined those feelings. With maturity comes physical strength to match his father's and the hostility now threatens open conflict. The initiation rite by welding the boy to the ranks of men promotes a close emotional identification with his father. Becoming-a-man ceremonies, then, do considerably more in the life cycle than ritually signaling maturity. As this theory and earlier remarks concerning their educational nature indicate, they promote children to new stages of growth. It doesn't make too much difference that they are frequently celebrated for boys who still have some years to go before reaching physiological puberty.

Physiological and social puberty more often coincide in girls than boys because menstruation is so conspicuous, far more so than involuntary seminal emissions. Few peoples concern themselves with inventing explanations for menstruation. Those who do either ascribe it to the moon, whose phases neatly correlate with menstrual periodicity, or else, somewhat surprisingly, claim that sexual intercourse initiates menstrual bleeding.[16] The latter explanation obviously visualizes girls having sexual intercourse early, even before they reach puberty. No doubt, observation that rupture of the hymen starts bleeding analogically justifies the view that initial intercourse brings on menstruation.

If we can judge from limited available information, menstruation doesn't usually cause pain or bring distress. However, women may fear these periods

---

[15] John W. M. Whiting, Richard Kluckhohn, and Anthony Albert, "The Function of Male Initiation Ceremonies at Puberty," in Eleanor E. Maccoby, Theodore M. Newcomb, and Eugene L. Hartley, eds., *Readings in Social Psychology*, 3rd ed. (New York, 1958).

[16] Ford, *op. cit.*, pp. 9-19.

because they then become more vulnerable to supernatural attack. In some cultures menstruation is also believed to spread contamination to others, particularly to men, and this is one reason why in those cultures women prophylactically seclude themselves during each monthly period. Very frequently men are warned to avoid sexual intercourse with menstruants. Whatever the purpose underlying such caution may be, men who heed the injunction avoid a risk of bacterial infection. But in fact they don't always obey the rules. Among some American Indians, the menstruating girl safely secluded beyond the ken of her parents was sure to attract adventurous adolescent boys whom she didn't always warn to keep their distance. Rules forbidding menstruating women to cook, handle food, and move around freely, effectively prevent menstrual blood from coming into contact with things and people. Pads of leaves, moss, cloth, or other material to collect menstrual blood for easy disposal also prevent contact. A woman provided with some convenient means of collecting and concealing menstrual blood has less need to remain secluded or to avoid domestic roles she ordinarily performs. Hence, when collecting devices come into use, restrictions on the activities of menstruants lift.

SOCIAL RESTRICTION OF SEXUAL BEHAVIOR

Nothing illustrates more strikingly the penetrating reach of social standardization than the fact that an affair as private as sexual relations, even in puritanical cultures where frank discussion of sex is avoided, should conform to norms. Therefore sexual behavior varies. The "perversions" of one culture may well be accepted practice in another. Still, we can't overlook that most cultures decisively ban some erotic activities, notably homosexuality, masturbation (at least in adults), sexual masochism no less than sadism, and coitus with animals (known as bestiality). Although human sexuality is phylogenetically continuous with the sexual activities of other animals, cultural patterning makes it unique.[17] Man drenches sex in moral evaluation. He restrains this powerful drive to conform to social expectations. Reflecting on his erotic behavior he elaborates it into an art, stresses the amatory side of sex, and invents new techniques and exciting circumstances to augment the sexual act's intensity.

The notion that sex is always more unbridled in small-scale cultures than in European and American civilization is a carry-over from early anthropologists' judgments that their exotic contemporaries in Africa, Polynesia, and Melanesia possessed evolutionarily primitive ways of life. "Savages," nineteenth-century scholars believed, still stood close to mankind as he had been during the remote, hypothetical period of "primitive promiscuity." Anthro-

[17] A. I. Hallowell, "Psychosexual Adjustment, Personality and the Good Life in a Non-Literate Culture," in Paul Hoch and Joseph Zubin, eds., *Psychosexual Development in Health and Disease* (New York, 1949).

pologists today reject the idea of cultures or customs surviving like rock-bound fossils. Highly discerning field studies carried on all over the world have demonstrated that every social system regulates sexual relations and some small-scale exotic communities do so extremely strictly.

A community can get by doing little to restrict sexual activity apart from shaping an approved style of expression and prohibiting persons in certain statuses to become sexual partners. Nearly everywhere incest rules bar sex relations between parent and child, brother and sister.[18] Often intimacy between aunts and nephews and between parallel cousins also comes under ban. At an opposite point of extreme severity stand communities that place the sexual aim itself under heavy restrictions. In the process, of course, they very much enlarge the range of persons with whom sex is forbidden. Highly restrictive cultures puritanically proscribe sex as an avenue of pleasure. Veiling erotic behavior in shame and danger, making it synonymous with immorality, they confine sex to marriage and to the limited end of procreation.

We have indices with which to measure and compare sexual leniency and stringency between cultures. For example, we can examine the indulgence or severity of the training children undergo with respect to masturbation, heterosexual play, and immodesty.[19] Individuals acquire lifelong sexual attitudes from early training in these areas, so as cultural measures they would seem to be quite significant.

Lenient social systems regard these practices with extreme tolerance and permissiveness. Alor in Indonesia, for instance, earns 19 out of a possible 21 points for being highly indulgent toward masturbation. Adults freely pacify Alorese infants by stimulating their genitals and allow older children to masturbate publicly. In the handling of masturbation our American middle class receives a leniency score of 10; it falls below the least indulgent of the 15 small-scale exotic communities on which we have information.

From a combined rating covering all three sexual practices we can gauge over-all sexual leniency. A comparison of such ratings reveals the Marquesans, a Polynesian people, to be sexually most indulgent to children; they receive 19 out of 21 possible points. Permitted sex play here goes on regularly from earliest years. Children readily learn sexual techniques by watching uninhibited sexual intercourse as it occurs during periods of ceremonial license or at home. In comparison Hopi Indians earn only 11 points on indulgence and fall a bit below the median.

We turn now to measures of severity. In the strictness with which parents inculcate sexual disciplines we find, as expected, the Marquesans among the lowest. They score a mere 8 points on severity. Apache Indians stand near the maximum of severity with 17 points. Hopi Indians fall in the middle. The

---

[18] George P. Murdock, *Social Structure* (New York, 1949), chaps. 9-10.

[19] John W. M. Whiting and Irvin L. Child, *Child Training and Personality* (New Haven, Conn., 1953), pp. 77-91.

15 points scored by our American middle class reflect considerable over-all sexual severity. The frequency with which Oceanic communities located in Polynesia and Melanesia rate high for indulgence and low for severity has special significance. These people provided major examples to support the nineteenth-century anthropologists' conclusion that small-scale exotic people tolerated unlimited sexual freedom.

Another index of sexual leniency or strictness simply checks off whether or not premarital sex relations are allowed. Why is this a significant index? Because puberty arouses the sex drive to intensely pressing levels and young people are strongly motivated to find sexual satisfaction without waiting for the social sanction of marriage. A social system that will not tolerate sex relations before marriage must exercise the most careful surveillance if it is to prevent premarital sexual contacts from occurring. Chaperonage and keeping girls in restrictive purdah even prior to adolescence (as many Muslims do in Swat) are two means by which adults control the budding sexual impulse. On the other hand, a social system that allows young people to experience coitus sympathetically appraises the nearly inexorable force of the newly awakened sex drive. A good portion of the world turns out to be quite sensible. Out of a sample of nearly 250 social systems, 65 freely permit premarital sex relations, 20 more give qualified consent, and 54 forbid it.[20] For the rest the sources provide inadequate data.

In the Polynesian Samoans we have one of the best-known cases of institutionalized premarital sexuality. Margaret Mead's classic description of them, Coming of Age in Samoa, demonstrates the decorum with which unmarried Samoans exercise premarital freedom. She also points out that the high-ranking taupo, or village princess, does not share the opportunities that other girls possess.

Americans, of course, strongly oppose unmarried adolescents' experimenting with sex relations. Not only do parents, schools, and churches stress the immorality of sex acts, but, despite highly perfected mechanical contraceptives, they emphasize the danger of unwanted pregnancy. And to show that we mean what we say, we treat unwed mothers with exemplary harshness. Ignoring the newly awakened sex drive can't banish it from existence. Young people do have sexual relations before marriage. However, they don't do so to the same degree in all social strata. Men who have been educated only through eight or fewer school grades much more often than college graduates report that they gratified sexual tension through premarital coitus.[21] We can safely assume that young men experience an equally powerful sex drive regardless of social level. How, then, do adolescents on higher social levels deal with sex tension? The college population more frequently than its grade school con-

[20] Murdock, op. cit., p. 5.
[21] A. C. Kinsey, W. B. Pomeroy, and C. E. Martin, Sexual Behavior in the Human Male (Philadelphia, 1948), pp. 374-383.

AZTEC MARRIAGE

Marriage occurred when a girl was 15 and a boy 20. This scene shows the betrothed couple on a mat, their clothes knotted to symbolize unity. Between their heads fumes of incense rise to the gods. The square figure above the incense burner represents the family hearth. Food has been set out below the couple's mat. On one side two old men deliver a discourse to the boy; on the other side, two old women exhort the girl.

Edward King Kingsborough, *Antiquities of Mexico*, 9 vols. (London, 1830-1848), Vol. I, p. 62.

temporaries reports gratification obtained through masturbation. Also college boys occasionally achieve sexual climax in the course of intense petting, something that is rare in the culture of youths who only attended grade school.

Turning to American women who report premarital sex relations, those with only grade or high school education begin premarital intercourse 5 or 6

SOCIAL LEVEL AND THE UNMARRIED MAN'S SEXUAL BEHAVIOR BETWEEN 16–20

School Grades Completed by Informants	Percent of Total Sexual Outlet Achieved Through		
	Solitary Acts (Masturbation and Nocturnal Emissions)	Heterosexual Acts (Intercourse and Petting-to-Climax)	Homosexual Acts
0– 8	34	58	7
9–12	44	45	11
Over 13	82	15	2

A. C. Kinsey, W. B. Pomeroy, and C. E. Martin, *Sexual Behavior in the Human Male* (Philadelphia, 1948), p. 378. A small proportion of outlet obtained through animal contacts has been omitted.

years sooner than women who receive graduate training.[22] Earlier and longer sexual experience, incidentally, is only one reason why girls with less formal education more frequently become pregnant in their teens.[23] Earlier marriage for girls with minimum schooling soon frees them from the difficult problem which other American girls continue to face in handling sexual impulses. On upper social levels too, we find masturbation increasingly resorted to in the years while they wait for marriage.[24]

Young people who find sexual gratification through solitary masturbation must put up with a variety of dire, if fictitious, alarms. Many imaginary horrors are ascribed to this biologically innocent, resourceful means of meeting sexuality in the long period between puberty and marriage. Paradoxically, our sexually stringent culture not only prohibits premarital coitus but contrives to block any direct means of reducing sexual tension in the unmarried. Some advisers recommend that young people sublimate sex in religious devotion, study, and physical exercise. It is very doubtful if sex drive can be transformed like physical energy and converted into "higher" things or that it can really be relieved by physical exercise.

THE VARIETY OF SEX

It is far from clear how kinds of sexual behavior become socially standardized. Yet, of course, they do. Otherwise why should many of the world's men

[22] A. C. Kinsey, W. B. Pomeroy, C. E. Martin, and P. H. Gebhard, *Sexual Behavior in the Human Female* (Philadelphia, 1953), pp. 293–294, 333.
[23] P. H. Gebhard, W. B. Pomeroy, C. E. Martin, and C. V. Christenson, *Pregnancy, Birth and Abortion* (New York, 1958), p. 46.
[24] Kinsey, Pomeroy, Martin, and Gebhard, *op. cit.*, p. 148.

MASTURBATION VERSUS INTERCOURSE IN BOYS BELOW 15

School Grades Completed by Informants	Percent of Total Sexual Outlet Achieved Through:	
	Masturbation	Heterosexual Intercourse
0– 8	52	36
9–12	59	25
Over 13	80	3

A. C. Kinsey, W. B. Pomeroy, C. E. Martin, *Sexual Behavior in the Human Male* (Philadelphia, 1948), p. 378. Total outlet does not equal 100 because other sources of satisfaction have been omitted.

remain unexcited by what American men regard as a most potent source of erotic arousal, the naked female breast? It is not too difficult to guess how boys learn the breast's erotic symbolism. Other things are less clear, like the fact that a far greater variety of sexual stimuli arouse college-educated American males than affect men with only a grade-school education. One thing is certain: college classes don't train students to respond erotically to sexual fantasies, to both pornographic and "good" erotic literature, and to descriptions of sado-masochistic behavior.

The problem of social standardization extends to how Americans from one social status to another learn to prefer different modes of coitus. Nearly 90 percent of college-educated men report that they have sexual intercourse while nude but only 43 percent of those men who never got beyond grade school admit this habit.[25] And how does it happen that preliminary to marital coitus college men more frequently have oral contact with their wives' genitals than men with less schooling? And why is occasional reversal of the common European-American coital position twice as common in the upper-social level?

I can deduce one illuminating principle from these data, though it doesn't really answer the questions I have asked. Apparently the variety of sexual acts tends to increase with social scale. College men, larger in scale than men with less formal schooling, are sexually more given to variety. Civilizations like China and India, we suspect, also incorporate more diverse sexual forms and varieties of erotic stimuli than small-scale or middle-range people like the Kaska or Hopi. What we see in sex parallels what we have already witnessed

[25] Kinsey, Pomeroy, and Martin, *op. cit.*, pp. 366-374.

in culture as a whole: variety keeps pace with social scale. To be sure, in large-scale communities sexual variety is not indiscriminately distributed. College-educated or middle-class men (assuming that social-class position coincides with educational level), who are relatively large in scale manifest a wider range of sexual behavior than their peers on lower-social levels. From a functional viewpoint, variety is a way of increasing stimulating experience. It also enables a social system to accommodate a wider range of temperaments and personalities which are not all required to fit into a single, common mold.

SEX AND CULTURE

Several studies have tried to demonstrate that involvement with sex rises or falls with other things in culture. Unwin's theory holds that sexual restraint, as manifested in premarital chastity, releases additional human energy which a social system then uses to build an elaborate culture and extend its reach of political power.[26] His thesis falls down under examination. In rejecting his conclusion Ruth Benedict astutely remarks that "any thesis, no matter how unlikely, can be upheld by a suitable rearrangement of cultural facts from different social systems."[27] Unwin's economical attitude with regard to sex parallels Freud's reasoning. The founder of psychoanalysis claimed that human energy is limited.[28] What a man spends upon women through sex he withdraws from culture. To accomplish great things he must apportion his libido wisely. To which somebody replied, then how did the great painters, men who also loved liberally, find sufficient energy to create their masterpieces?

Another theorist, Richard Mohr, views a culture's preoccupation with sex to be the consequence of a world view which visualizes a magical, dynamic, life-giving power pervading everything.[29] This life force especially inheres in the genitals and endows sexual acts with magical potency. Therefore sex relations, marital and premarital, and sexual rites become magically fortifying and enable people to live more effectively.

Sexual restraint enforced on children probably doesn't contribute to building civilizations and empires. But in America's middle class it does strengthen adults' power and authority.[30] Prohibiting premarital sexual relations is one

[26] Joseph D. Unwin, *Sex and Culture* (London, 1934); *Hopousia; or the Sexual and Economic Foundations of a New Society* (New York, 1940).
[27] Book review in *American Anthropologist*, 37 (1935), 691-692.
[28] Sigmund Freud, *Civilization and Its Discontents*, 3rd ed., trans. Joan Riviere (London, 1946).
[29] Richard Mohr, "Wertungen und Normen im Bereiche des Geschlechtlichen," in J. Haekel, A. Hohenwart-Gerlachstein, und A. Slawik, eds., *Die Wiener Schule der Voelkerkunde* (Wien, 1956).
[30] Jules Henry, "The Social Function of Child Sexuality in Pilagá Indian Culture," in Hoch and Zubin, *op. cit.*

of a large series of demands which middle-class parents impose on children. These demands clearly demarcate the boundary between two statuses of un-equal authority. Sexual restraints help adults produce that well-disciplined, conformist, middle-class personality valued by our age.

"SPECTACLES ON NOSE AND POUCH ON SIDE"

With or without previous opportunity for heterosexual experience, nearly everyone marries. Marriage, it is logical to conclude, promises more than sexual satisfaction. That it serves many other aims is even more apparent from the way adult relatives frequently concern themselves with finding proper mates for children. Marriage, they know, is too important a matter to entrust to inexperienced youngsters. Exhausted sexual attraction rarely constitutes sufficient grounds for divorce. Everywhere major effort attempts to hold together a marriage that shows signs of breaking up, particularly after children have been born. Most of this book deals with the adult's activities up to the scene where he puts "spectacles on nose and pouch on side," so let's turn to the closing portion of the life cycle, noting the special problems that attend old age.

After a certain number of years our vigor and resistance to disease steadily decline until something kills us; the inevitable biological process, aging, has set in. Lengthening the life-span through diet and medicine, though welcome, brings no escape from later-life's adjustment problems. In fact, adding to the proportion of people who survive until old age confronts a social system with special problems whose solution proves costly for those still in the prime of life.

Advanced age diminishes not only an individual's biological vigor but also his power and prestige, unless he retains control of economic resources or com-mands enhanced magical sanctions. By those means an oldster sometimes manages to maintain dominion over grown sons even though they inwardly seethe with frustrated rebellion. Where the old are visualized as about to join their ancestors, deified supernaturals who at every turn determine the welfare of the living, there too, they very likely enjoy continuing respect. In many social systems, however, prestige suffers once an individual must relinquish more energetic economic roles and no longer has young children to rear and train. Often he finds retirement hard to face. No wonder the Hopi say, the less one thinks of old age the better off he is.

In western industrial nations, where jobs constitute highly significant status markers, social standing becomes anomalous for anyone who reaches the birthday at which, regardless of ability, he must retire. The job he had to wait 30 years to win is taken from him 35 or 40 years later. Yet, physiologists believe, a certain amount of work may actually help stave off premature marks of aging. Compulsory retirement is only one way in which our culture betrays its implicit orientation to youth and leaves the old out of things. The nuclear family isolating itself in a house or apartment, firmly independent of both sets of the children's grandparents, also reveals the emphasis we put on the younger generation.

With curtailed roles and withering prestige old folks must learn, as gracefully as possible, to find new satisfactions. Partial compensation may come through religion. In Hindu India increasing age ideally brings increasing retirement from worldly things until at last the old man or woman completely withdraws from the everyday world's distractions. He calmly retires to seclusion where he exclusively practices poverty and meditation. A ceremony of transition honors people who actually take this final step.

Life's end comes either voluntarily or involuntarily. Food gatherers, who depend on mobility for survival, are reluctantly prepared to sacrifice an infirm oldster unable to keep up with the search for food. Gerontocide is never carried out harshly nor does it spring from callous disregard of human life. Surrounded with cut wood the kinsman is left behind, others firmly intending to return if and when resources permit. But by then it will be too late. Under some circumstances social systems admire suicide, especially when it is altruistically motivated to bring victory in war or save lives. But even then, kinsmen may try to dissuade the victim who proposes to sacrifice himself. In a more masochistic vein, suicide serves as drastic punishment for a grievous offense against the victim. Kaska Indians content themselves with a threat of suicide dramatically announced. It suffices in its aim, which is to bring prompt reassurance from friends and relatives. This happens only during intoxication for at other times Kaska adults resist betraying any sign of dependence.

A corpse is a noxious object that sooner or later, in one way or another, must be gotten rid of. Records of ground burial go back to the Paleolithic Age, and our well-kept cemeteries testify that this is still a favorite means of disposal. Details vary. The deceased rests on his back or on his side, knees straight or flexed. Or he sits up in his grave, knees drawn close to his chin. In Swat graves have a niche that goes off at an angle from the main shaft. Tombs, more or less analogous to abodes of the living, are built only where time, wealth, and technical resources permit. Ancient Egypt went to great lengths to provide the dead with luxurious accommodations and rich accompaniments, which first thieves and, much later, archeologists found well worth plundering. Stratified social systems perpetuate inequalities of wealth, power, and prestige in their treatment of the deceased. Flamboyant royal burials steeped in treasure contrast with far ruder graves of commoners much more sparingly furnished. During the Bronze Age, Europe favored cremation, the world's second favorite means of disposal of the dead, and one for which Hindu India is noted.

Whereas the Egyptians through mummification sought to preserve the corpse from dissolution and keep it as close to its living form as possible, Parsis in India and Pakistan invite quick destruction without putrefaction. They expose their naked dead to hordes of screaming, scavenging kites and vultures that sweep out of the sky down upon the massive, stone Tower of Silence. By no means rare are two or more steps taken to get finally rid of a corpse. Huron Indians in northeastern North America waited as long as 10 years between the great ceremonies that accompanied exhuming and reburying their deceased.

FURTHER READING

Accounts of the life cycle in different cultures inevitably overlap with more explanatory works describing personality and its formation, subjects of the next chapter. A few outstanding books predominantly concerned with growth and development under exotic cultural conditions include Inez M. Hilger's two monographs, *Chippewa Child Life and Its Cultural Background,* Bureau of American Ethnology, Bulletin 146, 1951, and *Arapaho Child Life and Its Cultural Background,* Bureau of American Ethnology, Bulletin 148, 1952; O. F. Raum, *Chaga Childhood* (London, 1940); Laurence Wylie's perfect *Village in the Vaucluse* (Cambridge, Mass., 1958); Hamed Ammar, *Growing Up in an Egyptian Village* (London, 1954); and Margaret Read, *Children of Their Fathers* (London, 1959). Autobiographies provide an existential insight into the growth process as it is experienced in other cultures. See, for example, Hazari, *An Indian Outcaste: the Autobiography of an Untouchable* (London, 1951); Paul Radin, ed., *Crashing Thunder, the Autobiography of an American Indian* (New York, 1926); and Leo Simmons, ed., *Sun Chief, the Autobiography of a Hopi Indian* (New Haven, Conn., 1942). There are many, many more good life histories.

Literature on reproduction is also extensive. Basic books include Clellan S. Ford, *A Comparative Study of Human Reproduction,* Yale University Publications in Anthropology, no. 32, 1945, and Clellan S. Ford and Frank A. Beach, *Patterns of Sexual Behavior* (New York, 1951). Robert F. Spencer has written a comprehensive review of "Primitive Obstretrics" for *Ciba Symposia,* 11 (1949), 1158-1188. Other pertinent readings include: Warren R. Dawson, *The Custom of Couvade* (Manchester, 1929); Herbert Aptekar, *Anjea, Infanticide, Abortion and Contraception in Savage Society* (New York, 1931); George Devereux, *A Study of Abortion in Primitive Societies* (New York, 1955); and H. Berkusky, "Der kuenstliche Abort bei den Naturvoelkern," *Sexual-Probleme,* 9 (1913), 458-467, 556-567. For more specific works see M. Lucia Van der Eerden, *Maternity Care in a Spanish-American Community of New Mexico,* Catholic University of America, Anthropological Series, no. 13, 1948, and Flora L. Bailey, *Some Sex Beliefs and Practices in a Navaho Community,* Papers of the Peabody Museum of American Archaeology and Ethnology, Harvard University, vol. 40, no. 2, 1950.

Franz Boas looks at education in Chapter 8 of *Anthropology and Modern Life,* rev. ed. (New York, 1932), and so does Robert H. Lowie in Chapter 9 of *Social Organization* (New York, 1948). All of S. N. Eisenstadt, *From Generation to Generation* (London, 1956) is pertinent in this connection. Vernon Brelsford deals with "Some Points of Contrast Between Primitive and Civilized Theories of Education," *Colonial Review*, 3 (1944), 150-151. George D. Spindler, ed., *Education and Anthropology* (Stanford, Calif., 1955) contains many papers by anthropologists viewing education cross-culturally. "Mutilations" is the special topic of the *Ciba Symposia*, 8, no. 7 (1946). On the same subject see A. Dembo and J. Imbelloni, *Deformaciones intencionales del cuerpo humano de carácter étnico* (Buenos Aires, 1938), and H. H. Ploss, "Die operative Behandlung der weiblichen Geschlechtstheile bei verschiedenen Voelkern," *Zeitschrift fuer Ethnologie*, 3 (1871), 381-397.

More than glimpses of sex life are offered in Thomas Gladwin and Seymour B. Sarason, *Truk: Man in Paradise*, Viking Fund Publications in Anthropology, no. 20, 1953, pp. 100-117; Géza Róheim, "The Western Tribes of Central Australia: Their Sexual Life," *Psychoanalysis and the Social Sciences*, 5 (1958), 221-245; and Bronislaw Malinowski, *The Sexual Life of Savages*, 3rd ed. (London, 1932). For the "Sexual Behavior of University Students in the Arab Near East," see L. Melikian and E. T. Prothro, *The Journal of Abnormal and Social Psychology*, 49 (1954), 59-64, and Ira L. Reiss for *Premarital Sex Standards in America* (Glencoe, Ill., 1960). Social level factors related to sexual behavior based on the Kinsey Reports are brought out in several papers published in Jerome Himelhoch and Sylvia F. Fava, eds., *Sexual Behavior in American Society* (New York, 1955). George P. Murdock's "Family Stability in Non-European Cultures," *The Annals of the American Academy of Political and Social Science*, 272 (1950), 195-201, briefly examines divorce in cross-cultural perspective.

An early review of death customs is Waldemar Sonntag's *Die Todtenbestattung* (Halle, 1878). See also E. Bendann, *Death Customs* (London, 1930). Contemporary Euro-American practices are discussed in C. J. Polson, R. P. Brittain, and T. K. Marshall, *The Disposal of the Dead* (New York, 1953). Embalming is examined in *Ciba Symposia*, 6, no. 2 (1944). J. Wisse writes on *Selbstmord und Todesfurcht bei den Naturvoelkern* (Zutphen, 1933). Altruistic suicide is taken up by Alexander H. Leighton and C. C. Hughes, "Notes on Eskimo Patterns of Suicide," *Southwestern Journal of Anthropology*, 11 (1955), 327-338.

14

Personality in Culture

The vulgar are apt to carry all *national characters* to extremes; and having once established it as a principle, that any people are knavish, or cowardly, or ignorant, they will admit no exception. . . . Men of sense condemn these undistinguished judgments: Though at the same time, they allow, that each nation has a peculiar set of manners, and that some particular qualities are more frequently to be met with among one people than among their neighbours.

David Hume (1748)[1]

FOCUS ON PERSONS

In 1934 Edward Sapir remarked how little anthropology concerned itself with the gradual and groping process by which a child discovers culture.[2] Two years earlier he had made another, related point. Anthropology, he noted, limited itself to studying culture as an impersonal group phenomenon, a description skimmed off the behavior of real persons. Despite their basic importance for culture, individuals themselves rarely got into the anthropologist's report. The traditional approach to culture obscured persons, who are the active carriers of culture, and ignored how every individual reinterprets portions of culture which are relevant for him. In Sapir's opinion it was time to take personality into account. For richer understanding he urged combining the study of group behavior with simultaneous attention paid to individuals who actually make a social system work. Like the psychiatrist, let's focus on people, seeing them from childhood as they interact in the full context of human relation-

[1] "Of National Characters," in David Hume, *Essays Moral, Political, and Literary,* 2 vols., new impression, eds. T. H. Green and T. H. Grose (London, 1898), vol. I, p. 244.
[2] Edward Sapir, "The Emergence of a Concept of Personality in a Study of Cultures," *Journal of Social Psychology,* 5 (1934), 408-415; see also his "Cultural Anthropology and Psychiatry," *Journal of Abnormal and Social Psychology,* 27 (1932), 229-242.

ships. Let's pay special regard to how an individual's ideas and feelings are nurtured through social relationships and how they mature. Sapir held up psychiatry as a model for a richer understanding of culture. Psychology was too impersonal and too much given to fragmenting individuals into processes like learning, memory, intelligence, and emotion to be useful for the kind of understanding Sapir wanted. Psychiatrists focused on whole persons and always saw them as they adapt and adjust in social relations.

I would exaggerate if I claimed that Sapir started a new movement in anthropology. In the first place, Sapir's precise vision has never been fully realized. He urged autobiographical or at least intensive studies of discrete individual personalities, regardless of whether they were typical of their social systems. Instead his successors emphasized *types* of personality belonging to different social systems. And then, too, Sapir wasn't first. Margaret Mead had already published results she obtained on a remote Samoan island studying the lives of adolescent girls and their younger sisters.[3] And even before Mead's field trip, a psychoanalyst, Géza Róheim, had approached cultural understanding through personality, this time among aboriginal Australians. But trends take time to flourish. Sapir brought to an end the hatching period of what has become an exciting if contentious field, culture studied in the locus of individuals. "Culture and personality" remains the somewhat cumbersome title bestowed on this approach.

Culture and personality research ambitiously asks a variety of questions which can be answered by working with a relatively small number of persons whom one gets to know very well. What does any culture mean to those individuals who through their day-to-day behavior keep it alive? How does anyone learn to conceive and carry out the roles of his culture? In what circumstances, how deeply, and how meaningfully does he learn sentiments like dependence on ancestors, respect for a flag, or obedience to tradition and authority? What is there about Kaska, Hopi, or Swati culture which, when adequately communicated to a child, leads him to become a Kaska, Hopi, or Swati in his general orientation to life? More importantly, how does such communication transpire? What are personality adjustment and maladjustment within the context of a particular culture? Are culture patterns like war, science, competition, prostitution, or corporation management better suited to some personality types than to others? What fate befalls deviant individuals who won't conform to demands of business, war, or schooling?

In one popular way of answering at least some of these questions the field worker delineates a characteristic personality type (or national character) associated with a social system and explains how each generation of children renews that type. What is Great Russian, Kaska Indian, or Hopi Indian personality like? National character is an old idea. Contemporary anthropology

[3] Margaret Mead, *Coming of Age in Samoa* (New York, 1928).

has refurbished the concept and subjected it to zealous application to test its usefulness. Glib generalization must be avoided in defining the personality that characterizes a social system.

Personality types can be best perceived by living closely with people and getting to know them with the aid of personality theory, for example, psychoanalysis. It is indefensible to leap blithely from what people do in day-to-day behavior to the inner core of their personality, thereby seeing the motives and percepts that govern activity as direct reflections of what people say and do. It is unwarranted to conclude that because Hopi culture ideally endorses peaceableness and strongly rejects even a flicker of hidden animosity Hopi Indians never harbor hostile wishes. They may not, but that must be established by independently learning about their motivational life.

PERSONALITY AND CHARACTER STRUCTURE

Personality is a word with many meanings. In one context it engulfs everything an individual does, thinks, and feels: it inclusively embraces his total system of overt and covert behavior. When a psychiatrist studies a "whole" personality he is usually more selective than this. For example, he ignores the exact way a millworker performs at his spindle, at least until he learns that in a particular case this information might be a significant clue to an inner state. The psychiatrist pays strongest attention to emotion-revealing responses which his patient makes, responses that reveal dependence, high or low self-esteem, insecurity, or confidence. He notes carefully how the individual reports having handled those most powerful of human impulses, sex and aggression. From such knowledge unhurriedly acquired the psychiatrist infers covert behavior: motives, percepts, and feelings.

An anthropologist, though he works with mentally healthy people, uses both definitions of personality but often prefers to emphasize behavior that reveals emotion, acts through which it is possible to plumb the inner, motivational, and perceptual life of people, that is, the core of their personality. Inner life and outer life constitute a single system. This behavior system over a period of time remains in some degree stable or relatively invariant. In his inner and outer life an individual carries something over from one point of time to another.

At the risk of being somewhat overconcrete in describing what is, after all, a very abstract phenomenon, I will differentiate between peripheral and nuclear regions of personality. The nuclear region contains an individual's central needs and interests. Here I locate the broad organizing feelings and beliefs by which he perceives the world and which enter into many specific responses constituting day-to-day behavior. The more specific responses which are based on the feelings and beliefs of the nuclear region make up the personality's peripheral region. The nuclear region or, as I will also call it, character structure, includes the highly generalized world view and self view, percepts according to whose terms an individual interprets his experience and appraises his capacity to cope with the world as he perceives it.

Nuclear world and self views operate partly through a process called projection. Sioux Indian children provide an instance of projection at work.[4] After showing them some rather indefinite pictures of human beings, an interviewer asked them to make up stories about the characters. The children saw individuals who like themselves were uncertain, who lived in an insecure environment that provided little guidance, and who confronted a bleak future. The children's characters reflected the story-tellers themselves; both were failing to attain desired objectives. The children projected their own, rather bleak, world and self views into the indefinite pictures. In this manner, by projection, character structures carry their fate with them. The way a person sees the world is also the way he responds to it and that response, in turn, quite easily forces from the world the very reaction which the individual anticipates! Character structure is self-fulfilling; it condemns an insecure person to spend his life in a persistently hostile environment while secure people live serenely through what, objectively speaking, appear to be very similar conditions. Doubtlessly character structure may change. Intensive psychoanalysis is one way of accomplishing characterological change. But the long time required for thorough analysis indicates how firmly nuclear attitudes are anchored in personality.

Persons reared under relatively common cultural conditions such as mark an enduring social system come to possess a relatively distinct, common personality. In talking about a personality that is characteristic of a total social system I propose to use the term social personality. The nuclear component of social personality, then, can be called social character or, when speaking of modern nations, national character. The Hopi Indians, Kaska Indians, Americans, Germans, and Japanese all have definable social personalities or social characters. To see a culture as it gives rise to and expresses a social personality is one way of following Sapir's suggestion that we see culture as it is rooted in individuals. To accept the assumption of social personality in no way denies that every individual remains unique in his psychological makeup. A social personality is a type which no specific individual will match perfectly. Still it is likely that everyone, except possibly the most subnormal and marginal members of a social system, will in some degree reveal many of the traits that compose the type.

Within a community distinctions in social personality coincide with various statuses. Women in their role play out a stable reactive system different from men; corporation executives make decisions and give orders differently than

---

[4] Gordon Macgregor, *Warriors Without Weapons* (Chicago, 1946), chap. 14.

CHARACTER STRUCTURES AT WORK

An identical stimulus, the picture reproduced on the facing page, was shown to two young men living on Truk, an island in the western Pacific Ocean. Each perceived the scene guided by his own private world of meanings.

Sam	Roger
(Both parents alive; he is 13, relatively self-confident, and with no unusual anxiety about hostility or aggression.)	(Both parents dead; he is a relatively anxious youth of 17 who lacks self-confidence.)

Sam

(Both parents alive; he is 13, relatively self-confident, and with no unusual anxiety about hostility or aggression.)

In response to the card he said: "This man and his wife are up in their garden; these are all their breadfruit trees. They are through with their work and are going home. They went home, cooked their bread-fruit and bananas and ate. The next morning, they went out again, went back and ate, then went out again. He climbed this tree and cut some breadfruit, and came down again, and she picked them up under the tree. They are just alone on their land; they have no children, and live alone in their house. They married, and their mothers and fathers are dead. They have no children, for the man has a bad disposition, and is angry every day. His wife does not look at him, for she is afraid he will hit her and kill her. This is her property [trees on left] and this his [trees on right]; first he cut some breadfruit from her trees, and now he has come down from cutting fruit from his tree. They are going to eat from each of their trees. They are going home, and will not come back; they will eat. But he stays here, because people have been stealing from their garden all the different kinds of food that are there."

Roger

(Both parents dead; he is a relatively anxious youth of 17 who lacks self-confidence.)

In response to the card he said: "These two are married. The man had said to the woman, 'Let's go inland and look for some food. We are hungry.' So they went. He cut some breadfruit, and then she went and got some bananas. Then he said, 'Let's go to our house and eat it.' They went to their house, and broiled the breadfruit. Then she cooked the bananas, and when they were done, she called her husband and said, 'Let's eat.' They ate and ate, and when they were through, he went out and cut some coconuts. But he fell out of the tree when he was cutting coconuts. His wife came to him, and said, 'Why did you fall out of the tree?' He said, 'I don't know.' She took hold of his leg, which was broken, and he cried out. She asked him why he cried out, and he said, 'Because it hurts terribly, so that I am almost dead.' Then she cried, hard. He said, 'Don't cry. If you cry and cry, I will be dead.' But she could not stop crying so he died. That's all."

Thomas Gladwin and Seymour B. Sarason, *Truk: Man in Paradise*, Viking Fund Publications in Anthropology, no. 20, 1953, pp. 291-296, 300-306, 579, 584.

generals; and middle-class people exhibit a personality that is pretty intolerable in a lower-class neighborhood. Let's call the personality type associated with a given status, status personality or, when dealing with the status personality's nuclear region, status character.

LEARNING TO BE A PERSON

Socialization makes out of each normal individual the kind of human being who more or less perfectly measures up to his community's expectations. It channels an individual's unfolding capacity to adopt ever more complex forms of behavior. It directs those capacities into directions that his community values and in doing so creates social personality. Socialization utilizes social pressure but it involves much more than simply correcting behavior that exceeds permissible limits. And it is not limited to childhood but continues through practically all of a person's life. Even the aged must modify their activities, thoughts, and feelings.

Any kind of socially standardized experience can be the instrument through which socialization operates, provided that it induces children or adults to modify their behavior lastingly. Some socially standardized experiences affect practically every person in a social system. They lead practically all individuals to modify their behavior durably in the same direction, say, to withhold any explosive show of hostility. Other socially standardized experiences are less prevalent. They may affect only individuals of the same age, sex, social class, or occupational status. Such restricted socializing experiences give rise to status personality.

Socializing experiences are manifold and often reinforce one another from situation to situation. All their lives Americans encounter experiences that teach them that nature can be controlled by human will and intelligence. Hopi Indians, on the other hand, are socialized consistently to conceive of man adapting to nature rather than opposing his will to nature. A Hopi character structure emerges that is wary and disciplined lest man through rash acts unleash serious trouble. Much in Hopi culture—much that a Hopi does— expresses this fearful conception of nature; similarly, much that an American does expresses his confident certainty that nothing unsatisfactory need re- remain as it is.

Young Hopi girls must stay close to home and help with housework. They have less freedom than their brothers and not until late in childhood are they finally aroused from their simple, walled-in existence. (*U.S. Public Health Service.*)

People mediate the bulk of socialization. Parents, teachers, and other persons deliberately attempt to shape behavior, although sometimes they are unaware of the influence they unintentionally exert on developing personalities. A Hopi parent quite deliberately tells children about Katchinas who will reward or punish them. Occasionally Katchinas themselves make a dramatic appearance at the child's home, either to reward his good behavior with gifts or frighten him for wrong-doing. Unintentionally these masked figures sow in even a young child some germ of the notion that life is dangerous. Whether they are aware or unaware of their influence, agents of socialization in a given social system tend to resemble one another in certain attributes. Many Hopi mothers hold out to their children the same conception of the world, the same standards of conduct. To some degree they act alike in transmitting these traits to their children. As a result, Hopi children nearly all undergo relatively

A Samoan youth returns to his village from spear fishing. The round houses on stone platforms are usually open at the sides. They help to condition little fixation on privacy. (*Official U.S. Navy Photo.*)

the same socialization and acquire practically the same social personality. Things are a bit more complicated in a heterogeneous community, in which families are separated into social classes or castes. Here socialization practices vary somewhat from one category of people to another. These variations bring into being distinct status personalities, but within some degree of over-all order. Even in a heterogeneous community, some social experiences undoubtedly impinge on nearly the whole population, at every social level. These common socializing experiences enable individuals, regardless of their social level, to grow up possessing common attributes.

Apart from people, socially standardized artifacts also mediate socialization.

Airplanes quite recently and in a direct way altered our conceptions of time and space. More indirectly, by dissolving a social system's isolation they open the way for new social experiences to pour in and alter personality. Where people can read, fiction and nonfiction books do their part to set a common style of behavior. Motion pictures also have an influence. The plots of films made in this country, for example, emphasize winning. This traditional motive is stressed each time an audience sees some determined hero, after a tough, unrelenting struggle, succeed in reaching his goal.

Socialization limits or channels persons' potential range of overt and covert behavior. Therefore, it represents learning, the process that psychologists with the collaboration of mice, rats, and monkeys have studied so successfully under controlled laboratory conditions. However, we must not conceive of a pupil as passive during the molding process of socialization. He is not. Always he responds actively, sometimes reaching out eagerly to what promise to be gratifying experiences and sometimes resisting his teacher's challenge. I saw the active side of socialization among Eskimo, where children in a variety of ways are impressed repeatedly with the importance of sharing. A child who comes home clutching a few candies is told to share his prize with all other children present. Frequently his mother sends him to other tents with gifts of meat and fish or to beg tea and flour. Thus he learns that people share. Furthermore he hears his parents condemn niggardly neighbors. Up to about the age of 7 he does not easily assimilate either the value or practice of sharing. He clings to possessions and even fights for things. In time he masters his feelings so that more gracious attitudes prevail in his personality, though they don't prevail equally in everyone.

SOCIALIZATION BY VIRTUE OF BELONGING

Socialization is accomplished in and by the aid of groups. As members of a national group citizens learn to shape their self-image to conform to the image they receive of their fellow nationals. Within a nation, say the United States, each generation is socialized in still smaller groups, like a Hopi Indian pueblo. In such a group people respond to socially standardized influences that are relatively distinct from those that their contemporaries encounter in another group, for example, a Spanish-American village. Sometimes such groups isolate themselves resolutely in a determined effort to exclude stimuli from the larger social system to which they belong. They are trying to monopolize their members' socialization by keeping out influences which, they fear, would lead to undesirable modifications in personality. Throughout the world the family is the earliest and most profoundly influential group for socialization. The family transmits to young members expectations that originate in the wider social system in which these youngsters will someday play roles. Peer groups, consisting of friends and playmates, and schools also contribute to social personality in childhood, and ceremonial groups, like a church or synagogue, bear further responsibility for social learning. In later years task-oriented work groups, like an office, factory, or air force squadron, contribute their pressure on personality. An individual in a middle- or large-scale community belongs to several groups, each of which provides him with somewhat different socially standardized experiences. In a heterogeneous community many of these groups partly reinforce one another as they contribute to the unfolding social personality. Some, however, discordantly inculcate behavior that conflicts with expectations held out by others.

Socialization occurs in and through groups but in the last analysis it is interaction between members of a group that promotes socialization. Feeding, love, punishment, and religion involve each parent in interaction with his children; through such interaction in the family group the child is led to make enduring modifications in his behavior. He acquires a portion of his basic world and self view and it may last for the rest of his life. Play and aggression bring each child into interaction with his age mates; through such interaction he acquires further modifications of personality. Work, play, sex, politics, commerce, and countless other topics involve adults in interaction with other people. Such interaction, too, contributes to develop or maintain social and status personality.

NATURE AND NURTURE

Any personality trait appears through the joint action of heredity and environment. In other words, personality results from both nature and nurture.

Let us talk about heredity first. An individual incorporates potentialities to grow and behave in certain ways. He inherits these potentialities in his chromosomes. Each chromosome is a package of microscopic chemical units called genes. At conception half of these chromosomes came in his mother's egg cell and half in his father's sperm cell that fertilized the egg. It is the union of these two cells, ovum and sperm, that mark the beginning of new life. A person's heredity, then—meaning his potentialities to have brown hair or blonde, to be tall or short, and to assume the roles demanded by his social system—depends on the genetic endowment which he draws from both parents. Every individual, except identical twins, starts life with a unique hereditary potential (identical twins, because they both develop from a single fertilized egg, always inherit precisely the same genes). We may view the chromosomes as packages of instructions, genetic instructions, which parents transmit to children. Sometimes the instructions are strict and uncompromising; they can be carried out only in one way. Much more often there is broad latitude in the way the instructions can be carried out, life experience and environmental conditions bending the action of the genes.

In any case, whether the commands are strict or whether they operate within broad limits, genes always exercise their in-built instructions in conjunction with the action, first, of a prenatal and, later, of a postnatal environment. But any environment, no matter how favorable, can influence development only as far as the genetic instructions allow. In discussions of heredity, environment is a word that includes the full range of geographic, chemical, nutritional, and social factors that impinge on an individual. It includes the mineral content of soil and water, potentially harmful radiation, whether man-made or not, accidents that maim or cripple, and teachers who drill their pupils in school. When we observe differences in behavior from one culture to another it becomes obvious that man does much to control heredity by varying the environments in which life develops. But environment doesn't therefore transcend the importance of heredity. Which is more important, the heat of the potter's furnace or the potentialities of whatever clay the potter shapes? The one-time sharp debate over whether nature or nurture is more potent has been settled by the formula: nature *and* nurture. For certain kinds of questions it makes more sense to consider the work of the chemical units rather than experiences a person encounters in growing up. Hair color, eye form, hairiness or its absence, blood type, hemophilia, albinism, diabetes, and the normal physiological reactions of the body are all better understood as stemming from hereditary potential than from specific conditions of environment. Nevertheless, in the course of development environment does become implicated and allows these potentialities to express themselves. On the other hand, heredity is not the place to dwell if one wants an explanation of social personality. To understand the genesis of social personality we study socialization. But we cannot deny that even here a hereditary potential of which we know next to nothing is also at work.

AS THE TWIG IS BENT

Socialization is part of a larger biological process, development. Each individual develops from a single fertilized egg cell (zygote) and in time is transformed into an adult organism. Development begins in the uterus. Experimental evidence very clearly demonstrates the prenatal environment's importance for development. For example, minnow eggs that develop in ordinary sea water produce minnows with two eyes. In sea water that contains a slightly higher concentration of magnesium salts minnows are born with only one eye, though the hereditary potential for two eyes remains unaltered. The human embryo (as we call the organism up to eight weeks of age) is similarly dependent on its intrauterine environment. However, the degree to which socially standardized experiences—culture—guide human prenatal development has only begun to be explored.[5] We know that a mother's diet determines the fetus' nutrition. That explains why fetuses of mothers of low socioeconomic status remain smaller and have a higher mortality rate. Prenatal nutritional deficiency also affects postnatal development. It is also known that stress in pregnancy affects prenatal development, for example, helping to produce children with cleft palates or highly sensitized nervous systems. But we don't know how a mother's established personality influences her unborn child during the 266 days of gestation. Therefore, in culture and personality we confine our interest predominantly to postnatal development as it guides personality formation.

Development can be summed up in three principles. First, personality as it is manifested in any situation—nursery, classroom, combat, or retirement—depends on all previous events in a person's life which were existentially significant for him. I am saying a bit more than that a person's response stems from how he perceives his situation. The principle of cumulative influence, to give this first principle of development a name, maintains that an organism's total capacity to behave in given ways is shaped by all its significant previous experiences. Popular speech rephrases this principle in pithy phrases like, "The child is father to the man," and Alexander Pope's often quoted words, "As the twig is bent the tree's inclined." To understand why Eskimo, Hopi Indians, or Great Russians are the kind of people they are, we must find out the successive steps in their socialization plus the significance which specific socialization practices possessed for their developing personalities. No one incident in socialization by itself constitutes a complete explanation of later behavior. Unfortunately, we cannot always judge how given events become significant for an individual or even how obviously significant events influence his later behavior. Growing knowledge of socialization in different cultures is needed to remedy this serious deficiency.

Used improperly, the principle of cumulative influences can be misleading. You cannot account for an individual's school performance solely in terms of his previous life history. It would be ridiculous to ascribe a Hopi Indian's world view entirely to his rearing. No matter how significant some event was in the past, it is relevant for understanding current behavior only if it continues to be active in the person's current situation. The past is relevant only as far as it exists dynamically in the present. Hence we must imagine persons in the course of development internalizing significant earlier experiences. Such experiences manage to persist in the individual, either as living memory or in his unconscious. Any bit of the past lives in us, however, only as it has been worked over by subsequent experience.

To account for behavior we need to know the significant steps in the cumulative process through which a social personality is forged. Some re-

[5] M. F. Ashley Montagu, *Human Heredity* (Cleveland, 1959), chaps. 5-6.

GUILT FEELINGS AND TECHNIQUES OF PUNISHMENT

Do children who are punished by threats of ostracism, by denying them love, or by depriving them of rewards, grow up with strong guilt feelings? We hypothesize that they do.

A

6 social systems that put *little* importance on love-oriented techniques of punishment put much emphasis on holding a patient responsible for his own illness. Strong guilt feelings are thereby indicated, contrary to the hypothesis being tested.

B

10 social systems that put *much* importance on love-oriented techniques of punishment also put much emphasis on holding a patient responsible for his own illness. Strong guilt feelings are thereby indicated, just as the hypothesis predicts. (The Hopi Indians are in this category.)

C

11 social systems that put *little* importance on love-oriented techniques of punishment also put *little* emphasis on holding a patient responsible for his own illness. Weak guilt feelings are thereby indicated, just as the hypothesis predicts.

D

8 social systems that put *much* importance on love-oriented techniques of punishment put *little* emphasis on holding a patient responsible for his own illness. Weak guilt feelings are thereby indicated, contrary to the hypothesis being tested.

The answer to the question raised above is a qualified yes. Strong guilt feelings (as measured by the degree to which a social system attributes illness to a patient's own acts) do tend to occur more often in those cultures that use love-oriented techniques of punishment in socializing children. Conversely, where such techniques are unimportant, signs of strong guilt are also not pronounced. The relationship is better than could have been expected to occur through chance alone, but it is not perfect. Boxes A and D contain cases that do not conform to the prediction being tested. It is reasonable, then, to suspect that in addition to love-oriented techniques of punishment, other conditions can also engender a sense of personal responsibility for getting sick or, to read below the surface, are responsible for strong guilt feelings.

John W. M. Whiting and Irvin L. Child, *Child Training and Personality* (New Haven, 1953), pp. 220-246. The authors analyze their data statistically through a t-test and discover that t has a value of 1.77. There are less than 5 chances in 100 that a value as high as this could have occurred by chance alone.

search, however, successfully ignores this injunction. Instead of working with cumulative influences, some studies single out one discrete event of early life in a sizable number of different social systems to see if it is followed predictably by the same later-life condition. Is it true, as psychonanalysts have asserted, that guilt follows when children in the course of development are threatened with ostracism, are punished by withholding love from them, or are deprived of rewards for wrongdoing? Cross-cultural examination shows that the expected condition, guilt, does follow use of such "love-oriented techniques of punishment" in a sizable number of communities, though not in all that were examined.

THE CRITICAL YEARS

The second principle of development amplifies the first principle of cumulative influence. It maintains that all life-history experiences do not possess equal significance for a developing individual. Some experiences, possibly because of the age of the individual or the circumstances in which they occur, exert greater force than others on subsequent behavior. Difficulty lies in discovering just what postnatal experiences in different cultures are most critical for social personality. More about this later.

Kaska Indian children after they are 3 or 4 years old receive more warmth from grandparents than from their own parents. A mother, particularly, withdraws emotionally from a 2- or 3-year-old baby and becomes remote and affectionally neutral. Such emotional isolation traumatizes a child. He responds by himself developing an emotionally constricted personality.

The third principle says that the younger an organism, the more likely it is to be seriously affected by its experiences, particularly by disturbing conditions. In keeping with this principle many students of socialization, particularly those influenced by psychoanalysis, concentrate their attention on the child's early years and on painful or frustrating childhood events.

A great, unresolved difficulty confronts us when we try to interpret the meaning of early childhood experiences. How can we know what happens on the covert level of personality during the first few months of life in the infant's earliest social relationships? I raise the question though I don't deny that something probably does happen and that what actually transpires probably is relevant for personality development. Emphasis on early years does not, of course, imply that they are most important for *all* aspects of personality or that even critical early events can't be offset by later experiences. Bear in mind that regardless of any critical importance attached to childhood, socialization endures as a lifelong process. Especially in a rapidly changing social system

PERSONALITY RESEARCH BEGINS ON THE LEVEL OF DIRECT OBSERVATION

	C Earlier Life-History Events	D Later Life-History Events
A Level of Direct Observation (Overt behavior)	How early socialization occurs. These socialization events are observed in their relevant cultural context and with a view to understanding their existential meaning. Such overt data are interpreted to yield information like that shown in box 3 and also, when relating later and earlier life history, to information like that shown in box 4. 1	What people do and say, including the form or quality with which overt behavior occurs. Responses to psychological tests are included here. Interpretation of such overt data yields information like that shown in box 4. 2
B Level of Inference (Covert behavior)	Motives, fears, world view, self view, and other covert percepts inferred from overt behaviors. Included here are the meanings that early socialization events have to individuals being socialized. 3	Motives, fears, world view, self view, and other covert percepts inferred from overt behaviors. 4

Personality research always starts with what people say and do, including how they execute overt behavior (level A). The observer infers covert personality (level B), including nuclear traits of character structure. To study socialization in the critical years we begin with box 1 and then infer what those events mean to the individuals involved by how children react to them. A researcher also asks how later overt and covert behavior (column D) can be traced back to childhood socialization (i.e., back to column C).

like our own, but to some extent in all communities, persons continue to modify their behavior even after they retire from the active period of adult life.

THE MORE DELIBERATE SIDE OF SOCIALIZATION

At times socialization proceeds quite systematically and deliberately. At other times experiences mold behavior in a less deliberate manner. In deliberate, highly systematic socialization parents, teachers, and others hold out explicit inducements or drive home formal lessons to more or less attentive subjects. A factory foreman explains the machine and offers himself as a model operator for the new employee to imitate. In some schools a child is trained to inhibit aggression and to recite each multiplication table unhesitatingly. At home he is scolded for failing to share a gift with his siblings. In such direct fashion individuals acquire a substantial repertory of behavior, including ways of showing emotion; attitudes to aggression, authority, and sharing; toilet habits, signals for driving, and the etiquette for serving tea, kava, or cocktails.

Techniques for accomplishing such relatively direct learning vary from one social system to another and even in the same social system from one situation to another. Balinese make considerable use of kinesthetic communication to mold a child's ability to dance or play a musical instrument. The pupil sub-

Balinese make considerable use of kinesthetic channels to train a child to dance and to play musical instruments. (*Indonesian Embassy; photograph by Scherpenhuyzen.*)

mits almost plastically to another's attentive, manipulating hands. Balinese bodies become suited to this kind of learning. They are normally relaxed, maintaining for years that fetal and neonatal flexibility which in most communities disappears soon after birth. Rote learning in a Swat classroom contrasts with a school that expects children to learn by themselves while being aided to discover practical solutions to problems. American Indians rely on imitation for socializing the young. A boy for several years sees his father or older brother guide the dog-drawn toboggan. One day they ask *him* to take charge while the older person runs ahead to test the river ice. They assume that he has learned what to do. A small girl who has watched her mother build many fires is told, without further explanation, to build one herself. If she succeeds she is praised lavishly. Naturally such a teaching method can be used only when activities are fully open to the pupil's observation.

An active desire to learn, please the teacher, or master an intrinsically rewarding technique motivates socialization. External sanctions also insure that culture and the appropriate cultural character will be transmitted successfully. Positive sanctions take the form of praise, gifts, gold stars, the first seat in the first row, pay raises, and promotions. Negative sanctions are offered both in threat and actuality, including scolding, corporal punishment, withdrawal of privileges, and withdrawal of signs of love. The balance between positive and negative sanctions varies from one culture to another. Observers have for a long time commented (sometimes disapprovingly) on the American Indian's disciplinary laxness and his passion for indulging his children.[6] There is no place for punishment based on inflicting bodily pain in a culture that places a premium on being able to bear pain unflinchingly. When American Indians chose to make stoicism a virtue they logically ruled out employing pain as an adjunct of socialization. In some tribes the American Indian child's closeness to the supernatural world from which he has recently been reincarnated further limits harsh discipline toward him. Other tribes believe that a child is so loosely attached to life that he will be frightened off by bad treatment, a belief made plausible by high mortality during childhood years. Robert H. Lowie perceives "almost a direct ratio between rudeness of culture and gentleness with children."[7] Is it that the huge mass of civilization that we have to transmit allows us too little time to be patient with youngsters particularly those slow in learning? Mode of socialization does depend on the rest of culture. As values like stoicism and beliefs about the supernatural give place to others and as a culture becomes less "rude" socialization practices also alter and so do those traits of personality which arise nondeliberately through the very nature of such disciplines.

A LESS DELIBERATE SIDE OF SOCIALIZATION

A person learns not only from what he is taught but also from how he is taught. He modifies his behavior as he responds to the conditions in which his development occurs. From the way he is taught multiplication, has his body plastically molded in dance, or is encouraged to compete in games or for grades, he, mostly unknowingly, adopts social meanings and attitudes as a firm part of his makeup. Some of the things he learns in such nondeliberate socialization belong to his more nuclear personality. They include motivating conceptions, like the notion that he has free will, feelings of individualistic resourcefulness and self-sufficiency, and the conviction that ends transcend in importance almost any means used to attain them. Of course, such concepts may also be deliberately fortified through explicit teaching. But some

[6] George A. Pettitt, *Primitive Education in North America,* University of California Publications in American Archaeology and Ethnology, vol. 43, 1946, pp. 6-9.
[7] Robert H. Lowie, *Are We Civilized?* (New York, 1929), p. 167.

deeply held attitudes are never communicated explicitly.

The less deliberate side of socialization relies on what Cora Du Bois calls absorptive discipline.[8] Enduring traits of personality are assimilated by a kind of contagion. An anthropologist himself experiences the force of such learning after he has spent time living under exotic cultural conditions. He comes to identify so closely with the people that he begins to imitate their habits and share their values. In the same way boys and girls grow up becoming increasingly aware of whatever value the social system places on male or female roles or of sentiments associated with food, flags, and religious symbols.

Under the less deliberate side of socialization I put the lasting impression left on a population by some historic events—for example, a depression or a great war. The impression need not vanish when the generation that was involved dies; instead, it is transmitted to future generations in the guise of fears and hopes. History contains more than cataclysmic events. The U.S. attitude that class is something to overcome and a challenge to upward mobility—an attitude acquired anew in each generation—was forged during those decades when millions of European immigrants, confident and eager to make their fortunes, landed in the New World. Then the idea of an unlimited future belonging to every man was forged into the American dream. A few historians have concerned themselves with the historical roots of character structure but anthropologists can be justly criticized for having neglected the subject.

The success with which a Samoan girl passes unscathed through adolescence, escaping the storm and stress that make this period enormously difficult in America, largely stems from the quality of her socialization. According to Margaret Mead's now classic work, *Coming of Age in Samoa*, the Samoan girl finds growing up easy and simple in a social setting where casualness pervades the whole way of life.[9] Socialization imposes no strong or deep attachments to a few persons that would prevent her from readily substituting more satisfying relations for ones that occasionally fail. She is spared those poignant situations that arise whenever a child must make weighty choices between equally dazzling alternatives. Furthermore in this slowly changing culture she doesn't face bewildering conflicts between half-dozen equally demanding standards of morality. She learns to regard sex as a natural, pleasurable experience. No rival groups, philosophies, or religions compete for her allegiance. Biologically speaking, the Samoan adolescent girl closely resembles her American age mate. Yet adolescence comes out differently in the two communities. Nobody wills it that way. The reason lies in the way growing up impinges on individuals in both places.

[8] Cora Du Bois, "Attitudes Toward Food and Hunger in Alor," in Leslie Spier *et al.*, eds., *Language, Culture, and Personality, Essays in Memory of Edward Sapir* (Menasha, Wis., 1941).

[9] Mead, *op. cit.*, chap. 13.

ATTENTION TO MEANING

An individual responds actively to events that happen to him in the course of his socialization. The conscious or unconscious interpretation he makes of those events motivates his response. What counts in socialization is not so much what happens or even how it happens, as the construction a person puts on his experiences or the significance they possess for him at a given level of his development.

The meaning of any event in a child's life obviously depends on his ability to differentiate and perceive simuli. We assume that even an infant finds food and warmth significant but his perception of these things in early life hardly compares to the meaning which they later acquire. The individual's psycho-

Guns are objects of engrossing interest for Kaska Indian men and boys.

biological state at the time when specific socialization events impinge on him also influences their impact. A child chronically hungry or at a loss for persons with whom to identify experiences socialization differently from a more thoroughly satisfied youngster. A child must find it very difficult to inhibit masturbation when at the same time that this learning is required of him he must also take the large step toward greater independence, weaning himself emotionally from his mother. The dramatic intensity with which experiences descend on a person—for example, the climax of impressive becoming-a-man rituals—also affects the traces the experiences leave. Then, too, the kind of relationship a person enjoys with teachers tinctures his perception of what he accepts from them.

It would be a mistake to ignore the explicit meaning which a socializing experience possesses to the community at large. Although part of this meaning, say of an initiation ceremony, may fail to be transmitted fully, understanding it helps to gauge how the experience is perceived. Obvious misinterpretations, like mistaking ritual scolding for its genuine counterpart, will be avoided. Knowing with what attitudes socializers regard their pupils also helps to gauge how pupils perceive socializing acts. Clinical research has shown a close relationship between maternal attitudes and children's behavior. Naturally a child can't directly perceive his mother's covert attitudes. Her frame of mind motivates expressive acts to which the child responds.[10]

In the course of socialization individuals perceive some experiences as symbolically equivalent to others. The pleasure Kaska Indian children find in guns stems from unconsciously equating weapons with power or strength. However, as yet only a paltry bit of evidence supports the psychoanalysts' conclusion that people in different cultures attach similar symbolism to experiences which they share.

EARLY LIFE

Few people would deny that the early years are critical for personality formation, though far from exclusively so. J. W. M. Whiting and his associates have experimentally tested the assertion that particular ways of early feeding, weaning, sexual disciplines, and anal, dependence, and aggression training predictably occur in conjunction with certain adult behaviors.[11] For example, in 17 different social systems where the circumstances of nursing and weaning are such that they predominantly provoke oral anxiety rather than oral gratification, people center their worries about health around the body's oral zone. They conceive that illness is caused by eating or drinking or that it can be brought on through an evil magician's verbal incantations. Conversely, adults in 13 communities where feeding and weaning induce considerable oral gratification (Hopi Indians fall in this category) show little inclination to explain illness in oral terms. They focus their health worries elsewhere than on the mouth. Though such findings can't be wholly ignored, their meaning remains equivocal. Correlation between a childhood experience and an adult mode of behavior doesn't prove that the adult behavior grew out of that specific childhood event. Furthermore, Whiting's careful statistical measures often buttress a cumbersome and shaky framework of assumptions. Can we really take the fact that people offer oral explanations for illness as evidence that for them anxiety actually centers on the mouth? Once we question this assumption, Whiting's correlation loses much of its usefulness for predicting the critical significance of early socialization.

There is another way in which early handling of the child may be used for

[10] Robert I. Watson, *Psychology of the Child* (New York, 1959), chap. 7.
[11] John W. M. Whiting and Irvin L. Child, *Child Training and Personality* (New Haven, Conn., 1953).

understanding personality formation. Bathing, feeding, and weaning babies, play between mothers and fathers and their children, and similar early experiences testify eloquently to certain emotion-laden attitudes that adults hold toward children, attitudes too implicit to be verbalized readily but operative in guiding personality formation. For example, the Sioux Indian mother won't allow her child to suck colostrum, the substance that precedes the flow of breast milk. For one thing she deems it poisonous. But also, she wants to spare her infant the wasteful effort of sucking useless, watery material from which he will obtain nothing beneficial. This attitude reveals that she perceives her baby sympathetically and feels that it deserves rich, unearned gratification. Other Siouan child-rearing practices carry out the same theme of babies deserving abundant indulgence.

Even pregnancy customs together with ideas about prenatal development furnish clues to socializing attitudes. A pregnant Yurok Indian woman rubs her abdomen to keep the fetus awake. By such means these California Indians attempt to accelerate a baby's development, pushing it forward, even before it is launched in the world. Acting on this clue, we inquire whether Yurok children are urged toward quick independence and self-reliance. We discover that this is indeed the general character of early Yurok socialization.

The richer the information we obtain about adults' covert perceptions, goals, and feelings toward children, the better we can judge the impact of early experiences. Emotionally tinged attitudes toward infants also provide a baseline against which to note when new, more severe expectations come into action. Of course, parental attitudes expressed in action will induce a child to modify his developing personality only when they are actually expressed toward the youngster.

FIVE PRIMARY SYSTEMS OF BEHAVIOR

Theory predicts that a child lastingly modifies his behavior in response to stimulation he receives in five primary areas of behavior.[12] Cues come to him from his oral zone, that is, in the way he is fed and weaned. From the way he is forced to control his sphincters his attention is drawn to his body's anal zone. Sexual behavior inevitably comes under social purview. He cannot avoid responding to stimuli that channel behavior in the area of dependence or that limit and guide aggression. Child rearing in every system includes attention to these five critical areas but each social system attends to them in manifestly different ways as well as with varying attitudes.

The most important messages from the surrounding world to an infant probably reach him through his mouth and lips. Eating literally gives the baby his

[12] See *ibid.*, chap. 4; E. H. Erikson, *Childhood and Society* (New York, 1950); John W. M. Whiting *et al.*, *Field Guide for a Study of Socialization in Five Societies* (Cambridge, Mass., 1954), mimeographed.

earliest taste of life. His first opportunity to develop either trust or distrust in himself and his environment comes with this experience. Subsequently many things may happen that lead him to revise or that reinforce his earliest picture. There is a striking contrast between the Arapesh mother of New Guinea nursing a passive baby generously and immediately upon the first sign of discomfort and the way an Iatmul mother living nearby expects her baby to demand the breast and thereby to make his earliest self-assertive responses. Arapesh children grow up to be passive people while adult Iatmul, consistently enough, are notably self-assertive. But note, nursing alone doesn't instigate passivity or aggression. Nursing is merely the first medium through which adults communicate their expectations of passivity and self-assertion. It alerts us to look for other channels communicating similar expectations. In appraising early oral behavior in any social system for its clue value and meaning for a child, we note the degree of indulgence it provides, interview adults for their conception of suckling, observe with what frequency nursing occurs, and note whether it comes at the child's demand or by the adult's schedule. We attend to whether a nursing mother must perform duties in the field or market that conflict with wholly devoting herself to the baby. We watch for the age and leniency with which a child is weaned—that is, makes his first move toward independence—and inquire into how adults' perceive weaning. Whiting and Child find that weaning typically occurs at about 2½ years in world culture as a whole. Longer nursing, then, indicates oral indulgence while earlier weaning suggests deprivation that a child finds painful.

Psychoanalysts assert that anal behavior provides a child with early practice in making responses to the world, like holding on and letting go, responses that can please or displease people. Toilet training is further significant because it compels a youngster (usually when he is between 1½ and 2½) to terminate in some degree his earlier anarchy. In learning to manage his sphincters he acquires some conception of what duty, obedience, and compliance mean. His first experience with shame may occur with regard to anal behavior. This channel of learning also informs him about adult attitudes of meticulousness, compulsiveness, or flexibility. It hardly seems necessary to say that bowel training itself doesn't suffice to perpetuate these complicated attitudes from one generation to the next. It merely provides an early occasion for learning about them.

The sexual behavior system offers children an opportunity to gratify their own bodies and thereby may contribute to a developing sense of personal resourcefulness. Where sex play or masturbation are forbidden as immodest or sinful children receive an early lesson in shame or guilt together with more information about self-regulation and self-discipline. An important part of a child's conception of his parents is learned through sexual disciplines, particularly when these disciplines accompany clear-cut pressure on the boy to become increasingly independent of his mother. The conjunction of sex and independence training is what psychoanalysts point to in part when they speak of an oedipal situation.

The child starts out being dependent. But even without deliberate encouragement to grow increasingly self-reliant, a normal child would hardly remain content with dependence for the rest of his life. Social systems vary with respect to the age when they expect independence. In the world as a whole such teaching begins typically at about 3½ years but U.S. mothers start at least a year earlier. Progress toward independence implies that a child learns to orient himself toward achievement, self-reliance, obedience, responsibility, sociability, and dominance. All are significant traits as far as a personality system is concerned.

With increased growth an individual's aggression system comes under increasingly tight control, in some social systems more severely than in others. The most rigorous attempt to suppress aggressive acts fails to eradicate covert hostility. Dreams, fantasy, fiction, games, or drunken behavior offer evidence that such feeling exists. To the degree that a culture expects to eliminate all trace of hostility from personality it probably makes an unreasonable demand on human nature. In such a case the irrepressible upsurge of disallowed hostile impulses will generate alarming anxiety.

Now for a general hypothesis covering all five primary systems. Early indulgence of any of these systems, theory predicts, will heighten that system's capacity to evoke satisfaction in later life. For example, early oral indulgence by encouraging positive fixation on the mouth endows that body zone with a powerful capacity to evoke subsequent satisfaction. People will be drawn to seek gratification through the mouth. For reasons which I shall omit, such a theoretical expectation need not be entertained as seriously as the next statement of the theory. This maintains that early punishment or frustration encountered in any primary system of behavior heightens that system's likelihood to generate anxiety and conflict in later life. Behavior connected with the system will in certain circumstances evoke feelings of anxiety and guilt. For example, persons who experience severe, early sexual disciplines grow up to experience conflict over the propriety and wisdom of sexual behavior. They can't enjoy sex as naturally as they enjoy other pleasures. In a world-wide sample of communities Whiting and Child find evidence showing this prediction of negative fixation to be supported.[13]

GOING BEYOND THE FIVE PRIMARY AREAS

Early socialization revolves around more than five systems of behavior. It is impossible to list all the significant experiences that enter into the developing

[13] Whiting and Child, *op. cit.,* chaps. 8-10.

personality or, like early feeding and anal training, offer clues to adult attitudes and percepts that govern personality formation. A large number of people engaged in nurturing an infant, for example, suggests a highly nurturant underlying attitude toward children. Swaddling indicates characteristic adult attitudes in some cultures. Games in later childhood draw out selective responses that become fixed, including cooperation, aggression, or individualism. Stories told to children embody conceptions of world and self, conceptions that a youthful audience incorporates. Different kinds of fear are emphasized in different cultures: fear of one's own impulses, fear of the punitive effects of conscience, fear of external threat and danger. Fear may be directly communicated by bodily contact from adult to child and can be a device by which adults circumscribe children's initiative. Some cultures rely more on the feeling of shame to control behavior; others on an implanted feeling of guilt. If shame is predominant, then fear of social rejection becomes crucial for restraining wrong-doing. With guilt, however, an individual himself well knows the nature of sin, regardless of whether his deed is public knowledge.

To study how a personality forms, we also observe how in his relations with parents and siblings a child more or less effectively struggles for independence, learns rivalry or jealousy, comes to accept or reject his own sex, and acquires certain attitudes toward authority. Culture change among the Sioux Indians deprived adult warriors and hunters of their formerly meaningful and prestigeful roles; hence it also deprived boys of figures with whom they could satisfactorily identify and upon whom they could model their behavior. The way a child is urged to respond to his mother's succorance (the Arapesh baby with passive dependence, the Iatmul with self-assertion) or to parental dominance (in the U.S. with slight submission) contributes to the growth of enduring behavior patterns. Some parents, in Great Britain, for example, present themselves in an essentially exhibitionistic manner, encouraging spectatorship in the child. In the U.S. roles are reversed. Here children exhibit their gains for a parental audience that does not always understand the full significance of those achievements. Through encouragement given in family situations an individual learns when and in what degree to show dominance or submission, succorance or dependence, exhibitionism or spectatorship, aggression or passivity. He learns whether to respond to a show of dominance symmetrically, that is, with more dominance on his part, or asymmetrically, with submission. Family and other relationships encourage, sometimes unintentionally, yielding, negative, or destructive behavior in a child. Many interpersonal relationships teach a youngster how to handle emotional expression, whether freely, as in Italians, or more constrictedly and with greater reliance on fantasy, as in the Irish. From his adult models an individual learns how to defend himself against threatening situations. Kaska Indians, who greatly value individual resourcefulness, characteristically defend against illness and other threats by denial. Perhaps their response would be different if medical facilities and financial means to employ them were more available. We have also to observe how work and industriousness are introduced in an individual's life and whether the learning situation frequently invites failure or encourages a sense of inadequacy by posing demands that a child cannot meet.

Agents of socialization who succeed parents, like priests or teachers, may consistently demand the same responses which an individual learned earlier. Or inconsistency may confront the pupil. Later socialization may reverse earlier experiences and inculcate different traits of character. Navaho Indians as infants and children receive a maximum amount of protection and gratification. Yet they develop into anxious adults, because later experiences conflict with the earlier.[14] The first serious trauma occurs when the Navaho child, calm and poised, leaves home for school. At the end of a year he returns nervous and tense. Another kind of disjunction occurs in class- or caste-divided communities, particularly for those children who grow up in a category that the community stereotypes unfavorably and on which others bestow low prestige. These children soon gain knowledge of their unfavorable status and this knowledge colors their status personality. A U.S. lower-class child experiences a sharp dilemma when he enters a middle-class dominated school and encounters standards of behavior radically different from those of his family or neighborhood group. He may endorse the new standards, thereby taking the first steps out of his class, or he may rebel against them violently but at severe cost to his social adjustment.

PROVING THE POINT

How do we know whether the statements we make about socialization in a particular community are correct? After all, it is very hard to verify such conclusions by experimenting with human beings. Nobody can legitimately keep some Hopi children away from certain early experiences that their fellows enjoy and then step back to observe what differences will follow. The answer is that we first adopt a plausible theory of personality formation by which to draw conclusions and then logically check our conclusions against the theory. If too frequently what we discover contradicts the theory, then that theory must be discarded and a new and better one constructed.

Culture and personality theory is eclectic. It draws ideas from a wide variety of other theories, including psychoanalysis, psychology, child development, social psychology, and anthropology. In this chapter I have sketched the framework of a theory for understanding personality formation. Now I want to examine the meaning of proof in general.

[14] Dorothea Leighton and Clyde Kluckhohn, *Children of the People* (Cambridge, Mass., 1947).

Any theory specifies what phenomena to look for and predicts the kind of order to be expected in those phenomena. Our theory deals with social personality and its formation. It spells out how socialization leads individuals to modify their behavior lastingly. We test our conclusions concerning the power of any experience to modify behavior very much the way a historian accounts for the occurrence of an event, say a war. Judiciously he points to particular prior conditions which his very eclectic theory (much of it is based on common sense) predicts can be influential enough to plunge countries into battle. He cannot in a laboratory duplicate those earlier conditions to see if they do regularly create turmoil and bloodshed. That kind of proof, prized by the experimental scientist, is barred to students of history, society, and culture. A good historian can only present his evidence, his carefully garnered facts, and then argue as cogently and logically as possible, in terms of his theory, to demonstrate that the prior events indeed acted to bring on war. Proof always remains evidential rather than experimental. So it goes in much culture and personality research. Events that according to theory create social personality are observed and described with all relevant detail. The adult personality is carefully portrayed. The influence of the early conditions on development is cogently and logically argued. Naturally any conclusion always remains open to a better interpretation.

A related problem occurs when covert behavior or social character is inferred from what persons overtly do and say. How do we know if our interpretation of the covert states is correct? For one thing, instead of being undisciplined guesses such inferences are guided by a plausible theory. But no available theory can guarantee accuracy. Proof of our conclusions when we proceed from the known to the relatively unknown levels of personality comes from whatever degree of plausibility and consistency our final interpretation possesses. What people in a social system say and do must be theoretically consistent with the picture of their character structure that we infer. Any seeming incongruity between the two sets of data must be systematically and logically accounted for. We should take no interpretation of character structure as final. Additional knowledge about personality dynamics when it becomes available will doubtlessly lead to different ways of accounting for the same overt facts, ways that will be more convincing and plausible.

FURTHER READING

For introductions to comparative personality study see John J. Honigmann, *Culture and Personality* (New York, 1954); Margaret Mead, "The Cross-Cultural Approach to the Study of Personality," in J. L. McCary, ed., *Psychology of Personality* (New York, 1956); Margaret Mead, "National Character," in A. L. Kroeber, ed., *Anthropology Today* (Chicago, 1953); Abel Miroglio, *La Psychologie des peuples* (Paris, 1958); Mikel Dufrenne, *La Personalité de base* (Paris, 1953); and

S. Kirson Weinberg, *Culture and Personality* (Washington, 1958).

Collections of papers on various aspects of culture and personality research have been issued, including Douglas G. Haring, ed., *Personal Character and Cultural Milieu,* 3rd rev. ed. (Syracuse, N.Y., 1956); Bert Kaplan, ed., *Studying Personality Cross-Culturally* (Evanston, Ill., 1961); and Francis L. K. Hsu, ed., *Psychological Anthropology* (Chicago, 1961), a work that contains a survey and assessment of work done in several world areas. Sapir's papers are reprinted in *Selected Writings of Edward Sapir in Language, Culture, and Personality* (Berkeley, Calif., 1949).

A useful theory of personality is given by O. H. Mowrer and Clyde Kluckhohn in "Dynamic Theory of Personality," J. McV. Hunt, ed., *Personality and the Behavior Disorders,* 2 vols. (New York, 1944), vol. I. In speaking of the individual as constituting an active force in learning I incorporate a part of the psychology that views learning as more than drive reduction. For a résumé see Robert W. White, "Competence and the Psychosexual Stages of Development," in Marshall R. Jones, ed., *Nebraska Symposium on Motivation 1960* (Lincoln, Neb., 1960).

A modern synthesis of heredity and environment is provided in John L. Fuller, *Nature and Nurture* (Garden City, N.Y., 1954). Frank A. Beach and Julian Jaynes have cooperated in a comprehensive review of the "Effects of Early Experiences upon the Behavior of Animals," *Psychological Bulletin,* 51 (1954), 239-263. I have found Robert I. Watson, *Psychology of the Child* (New York, 1959) an excellent guide to child development and socialization. For a statement of what is significant in a child's world of meanings see G. P. Meredith, "The Space, Time, Language and Intellect of the Young Child," in Kenneth Soddy, ed., *Mental Health and Infant Development,* 2 vols. (New York, 1956), vol. I. Karen Horney describes how the past of an individual is refurbished in development and not mechanically perpetuated in *New Ways in Psychoanalysis* (New York, 1939), chap. 2. Gregory Bateson touches on the less deliberative side of socialization in an appendix to an article by Margaret Mead, "The Comparative Study of Culture and the Purposive Cultivation of Democratic Values," in *Science, Philosophy and Religion, Second Symposium* (New York, 1942). Evidence of cross-cultural similarities in unconscious symbolization is provided by Clyde Kluckhohn and William Morgan, "Some Notes on Navaho Dreams," in George B. Wilbur and Warner Muensterberger, eds., *Psychoanalysis and Culture* (New York, 1951). The shame and guilt dichotomy is appraised in Gerhart Piers and Milton Singer, *Shame and Guilt: A Psychoanalytic and a Cultural Study* (Springfield, Ill., 1953). Socialization in a modern heterogeneous cultural setting is the subject of Margaret Mead's "Character Formation and Diachronic Theory," in M. Fortes, ed., *Social Structure* (Oxford, 1949).

For the truth value of anthropological propositions see Robert Redfield, "Relations of Anthropology to the Social Sciences and to the Humanities," in A. L. Kroeber, ed., *Anthropology Today* (Chicago, 1953), and A. L. Kroeber, "Concluding Remarks," in Sol Tax *et al.,* eds., *An Appraisal of Anthropology Today* (Chicago, 1953). The comparative method of testing as used in culture and personality is described by John W. M. Whiting in "The Cross-Cultural Method," in Gardner Lindzey, ed., *Handbook of Social Psychology,* 2 vols. (Cambridge, Mass., 1954), vol. I. In their article, "The Interpretation of Data: Puberty Rites," *American Anthropologist* 64 (1962), 463-485, Edward Norbeck, Donald E. Walker, and Mimi Cohen critically examine procedures Whiting and his associates have used.

15

Nature of Culture

Mass is both a condition to, and a result of, organization.

Herbert Spencer[1]

VARIETY AND GROWTH

Magic, religion, family, subsistence activities, political organization, art—these and many other subjects fill people's lives. Just as a cotton print is more than a varied collection of colors poured on at random, culture is no haphazard collection of artifacts, activities, thoughts, and feelings. Color lies on the cloth harmoniously; it forms designs that grew out of an image in the mind of the designer.

Cultures as a rule have no designers but neither do they add whatever new thing comes along. A social system ungovernably adopting everything its members thought up at home or envied in the life of a neighboring community couldn't survive for long. Activities would compete for the same worker's time and energy; ideas would contradict each other; bride and groom couldn't reside with both his and her parents simultaneously; and uncoordinated deities would mix up their adherents so badly that worship might cease. Sometimes, to be sure, behaviors do clash. But confusion would be terrible if all trace vanished of the selectivity that governs admission of traits to a way of life.

Without question, some cultures include considerably more variety than others. To put it figuratively, they have more content or a larger mass. The culture of the Hopi Indians has more parts than Kaska Indian culture. In Swat culture is still larger than for the Hopi. True, no person participates in every part of the content of a rich culture.

Several conditions govern degree of cultural elaboration. The size of a culture's inventory depends on the number of windows on the world that a social system has open. In other words, a community with many, far-flung contacts

[1] *The Principles of Sociology*, 2 vols. in 5, 3rd (Westminster) ed. (New York, 1885-1896), vol. I–i, p. 11.

encounters many opportunities to borrow additional forms of behavior and artifacts. Links with the past serve the same end. People with wide and far-reaching memories preserve much behavior from bygone generations. When contacts with the past grow dim, doctrines, sagas, spells, and heroes fade away and the culture content shrinks. With more people doing things together in a social system, variety also increases; sheer size of population influences cultural variety. One hundred adults are severely limited in what they can do; after all, they can devote only about 1,600 hours to a waking day's activities. Ten thousand adults have 160,000 hours, time enough for some to grow food, bargain with the miller, develop new knowledge, cultivate knowledge from the past, paint pictures, play, and worship. Another potent factor closely linked with cultural variety is a food supply sufficient to allow men to do more than procure subsistence. Food gatherers like the aboriginal Kaska Indians can't afford to retire any man from actively pursuing subsistence. A single hunter can comfortably support only about four other persons and even they must help secure food. Agriculture, on the other hand, particularly when it is executed with a plow, frees some persons from food production and through them encourages cultural florescence.

No matter how small or large a culture's content, items within it hold unequal significance. One or more topics engross the community's interest and attention. The Kaska focus on trapping, the Hopi on agriculture and ceremonies that promote fertility, and Islam is a focus in Swat. A large social system, with its several ethnic groups, occupational specialists, and clearly defined, administrative nerve center, has many foci. Farmers in Swat devote their lives to agriculture, traders to trade, and administrators there focus on coordination.

Human culture in its half-million or more years of recorded existence has grown enormously in appliances, forms of social organization, ideas, entertainments, and in those fundamental skills that have steadily increased man's control over his environment. War, plague, or plain weariness have on occasion arrested the growth process. Catastrophe sometimes even reversed growth. The cultural mass ran out like sand and life became simpler in a particular community. Cultural decline is rare and so far culture as a whole has never taken this direction. Nuclear warfare, if it cannot be sufficiently controlled, might some day give surviving anthropologists an opportunity to study general cultural decline amidst the rubble of bombed cities, rusting rails, buckled asphalt, and weed-infested pastures.

SOCIAL INTEGRATION

The activities that men perform span a social system like a web and join one social system to others. Goods and services, whether rendered freely or exchanged, bring groups and individuals into relationships that are both harmonious and mutually rewarding. The parts of the system support one another much as organs of the body cooperate to maintain life. At other times cultural activities like aggression, exploitation, and power bring individuals or social systems into relations that seethe with dangerous opposition.

I have already given instances of culture integrating social systems. For example, ceremonies in a Hopi village belong to ceremonial groups in which representatives of several families cooperate to benefit the whole pueblo. Kaska Indians are a less tightly organized social system because they lack the binding link of religion, or any corresponding focus, to draw families and individuals together.

Economic transactions illustrate social integration nicely. From the plowman in Swat flows grain to support manufacturers of pottery, clothing, and other goods. It also supports merchants in the bazar who through the medium of money exchange grain for the products of local and foreign industries. Bankers take a share of the grain (or its monetary equivalent) in return for furnishing credit to manufacturers. Town restauranteurs also benefit from the money earned by farmers, bankers, and manufacturers. Government draws its support from the plowman and other specialists, claiming a share of their wealth in taxes. This tax money, or raw grain paid by farmers, is redistributed to administrators, police, road workers, and militia. The relationship is not as one-sided as I have described. All benefits don't originate with farmers. In return for grain, manufacturer and merchant provide clothing, additional foodstuffs, and other goods for the peasant family to enjoy. For taxes paid, government maintains conditions that allow everyone to work and to enjoy the fruits of his work. If I stop at this point and omit references to how farmers, merchants, and administrators in turn relate to religious leaders, transport workers, house servants, prostitutes, I obviously leave an oversimplified picture of social integration in Swat. But I think that I have made my point, namely, that culture is the cement through which members of a social system are held in relationships to one another. Social integration, after all, is no new concept. I touched on it in Chapter 4 when I discussed roles. For roles simply represent culture allocated to individuals of requisite birth, sex, age, and training. One new point deserves emphasis. Integration is not always a matter of harmonious cooperation. War integrates a society as intensely as trade, holding men in a web of mutual awareness and participation. And, conversely our obligations to kinsmen may carry a strong current of antagonism and suspicion.

Alter a culture's content and the bases of social integration must also alter. Persons and groups will then have to turn out new goods and services, find new skills, and employ new bases of evaluation. They will have to master new topics on which to preach or to teach.

CULTURAL INTEGRATION

Cultural integration implies a different idea. By this concept I mean that the traits comprising a way of life come into some kind of adjustment with each other so that a culture constitutes a system.

To demonstrate any culture as a system we can start with some sector of behavior and, using it as a hub, show how other behaviors and artifacts are conditioned to it and to each other. Many traits in the life of Swat, for example, are shaped by the people's profession of Islam. Meat is eaten only when freshly killed, pork and carrion are avoided, women avoid showing their faces to unrelated men, if the family is literate the Quran occupies an honored place in the house, calendars show scenes of Muslim holy places, Thursday night has special significance, and Friday is at least a half holiday when business shuts down. Even the conception of greatness is a consequence of Islam; the Prophet and saints are ideals upon whom one should model conduct.

We can understand cultural integration by examining the place of industrial mass production in the texture of American life. Industrial mass production underlies our view of greatness. Successful entrepreneurs like Ford and the senior Rockefeller have joined the ranks of heroes. We think of our sons' and daughters' careers in terms of opportunities created by modern industry. Long, hard, formal education is prerequisite for most of those careers and our school system is designed to help fill them with qualified persons. Mass production with powerful machines has pared down the contrast of poverty and wealth. We no longer even believe that poverty is necessary. Industrial production shapes our conception of work; work in industry is something done with machines. Purely manual labor generally carries very low prestige. Everywhere in our culture we see what industrial mass production has accomplished. The wide-scale ownership of cars, radios, television, kitchen equipment and other house furnishings, books, and sports equipment is a conspicuous feature of American life that we owe to industry. In the process of adopting industrial production, fitting ourselves into its careers, and using its products we have even altered our personalities. For example, we have come assiduously to "need" up-to-date material amenities. Without these needs our machines would cease and our factories collapse. We have changed from being inner-oriented to other-oriented conformity and compatibility. A closely geared modern industrial civilization requires only few staunch, principled individualists. Ability of men to oblige one another is more valuable and dominates the hiring of key personnel, not only in business but even in churches, schools, and universities. So we see that many sectors of life are conditioned by industrial manufacturing or are geared to support thriving industrial production. Change any part of the cultural system and corresponding alterations can be expected in linked areas. Should these secondary changes lag, then dislocation will ensue in culture and disturbances in the personalities of the culture's carriers.

Naturally, all references to culture as a system and to one area being interdependent with other areas must be understood metaphorically. Life is a flow of behavior undivided into areas. No mechanically causal nexus exists between machines humming in Detroit and Americans' conception of greatness. Culture is behavior executed by individuals who enter into organized relations with one another. They wisely design their behavior to reduce ambiguity and conflict and to heighten consistency. Through such wisdom social and cultural integration both arise.

ETHOS

Every culture's content has far-flung origins: our alphabet derives from the ancient Middle East, timepieces from medieval Europe, and parts of our cuisine from France, Germany, Hungary, India, and Latin America. In time traits lose their foreign cast. Discordant notes between elements of divergent origins are shed. These component elements of a system become transformed as they become integrated so that a qualitatively coherent, self-consistent whole appears. We recognize a culture as a distinctive whole through its over-all qualities.

One way a culture achieves coherency and wholeness is through many of its parts being infused with a common ethos. Not every discrete artifact, act, thought, or feeling need reveal the ethos with the same sharpness. Some parts in a cultural configuration express the quality more definitely than others. An ethos of puritanical wariness stands most starkly revealed in a people's sex behavior. But it also colors their use of leisure and domestic routines like cooking, dressing, and child rearing. An ethos of life lived fully, recklessly, with litle regard for moderation or safety is reflected in situations that involve risk or even death. But it would indeed be surprising if the same ethos didn't pervade the home where the young cathect it early. Despite the popularity of terse expressions to sum up over-all cultural qualities, I see no reason why it must be expressible in one or two words. Nor need ethos always be quite as unitary as in the examples I have used. In some cases the unitary cast of a culture will follow from dual ethoses—ethoses of men and women or nobles and commoners—balancing each other or will arise from people weaving several emotional strains into their way of life. In any case, a culture's ethos is abstracted by noting not so much what people do but how they do it. It derives less from cultural content than from manner of performance.

Insoluble difficulties are created if instead of seeing ethos as secondary, as something we abstract from culture, we make it primary and treat it as though

Some of the elements in this scene from the annual Gallup intertribal festival are out of the American Indians' past. Others, like cloth, glass beads, metal balls, and foreign designs, are imported. Woven together they make a newly styled whole. They belong to a pan-Indian culture that is partially designed to appeal to tourists. (*Santa Fe Railway; photograph by Frank E. Meitz.*)

it were the soil, culture then being treated as the plant growing as the soil dictates. Ethos cannot be dependent on race and therefore transmitted in the genes from one generation to another. If that were true, then ethos would remain constant as long as population makeup remained unaltered. We know, however, that the cast of life changes independently of race. The Plains Indians donned their militaristic venturesomeness after they received the horse and not after an infusion of new genes. If the theory of racial soul were true then an ethos would change as soon as sufficient immigrants bred into a population. By no means does such a change follow inevitably; many times the hosts' ethos captures the immigrants and persists.

HOLISTS AND ABSTRACTERS

Holists are people who don't care to see the trees apart from the forest. They emphasize to a maximum that culture is a system. They expect that just as any two individuals differ even when they share many apparently identical traits, so two cultures will be distinct. Just as the same mink stole fits differently on

Mrs. Brown and Mrs. Smith, any trait will possess a unique identity in two distinct cultural systems. The system makes the difference. The only way of understanding any bit of culture, holists assure us, is to see it in its fullest cultural context. War was quite different in the life of the Plains Indians than in the modern world even though many elements, like killing, plunder, taking prisoners, and sending out scouts, occur in both cases. So with swaddling, a practice that occurs among the Kaska Indians, Hopi Indians, and Pathans of Swat. Apart from variations that creep into swaddling in each place, the act itself forms part of vastly different cultural systems. In each it is done under markedly different circumstances and by mothers who have quite diverse attitudes toward the swaddled child. Hence, holists advise, don't go too far in comparing swaddling in different cultures. The mere act is not much when the total contexts in which it occurs contrast so greatly. Holism obviously possesses considerable truth. Common sense tells us that roast turkey is scarcely the same when it is served at breakfast, at a regular family dinner, and on Christmas day.

Many anthropologists remain undismayed by these strictures of holism, which they regard as primarily philosophical and somewhat impractical. With great confidence they compare things like swaddling in various cultures quite without regard to context. They simply abstract similar traits—sorcery, monotheism, war—and treat them as though they were the same, regardless of qualitative variations and local color.

AUTONOMOUS PARTS OF THE SYSTEM

Your own experience undoubtedly convinces you that various sectors of culture indeed depend on one another and that cultures are systems. But probably you can also recall instances when one sector of life changed while in other activities you carried on as before, even though the discordance between the two sets of behavior was as obvious as unmeshed gears. Perhaps you had such an experience when you went off to college and clung to previous attitudes rather than assuming more independent habits of thought. Or perhaps you went abroad and failed to adopt the etiquette of an exotic culture because you felt more comfortable with your own. Or, like many people, do you bless the abundance brought by mass production but wish that life wasn't so standardized and that everything on the job wasn't so regimented?

Everything in a way of life isn't harmoniously adjusted to everything else. Culture *is* a system, but to say that and no more ignores important facts. More accurately, culture is a system of more or less autonomous parts. Spheres of life and traits of culture possess varying degrees of independence that in unequal measure leave them untouched by one another. For this reason among others, change is often uneven in a way of life.

Language has a particularly high degree of autonomy. Hopi Indians who have left the reservation to serve in the armed forces or to work in southwestern cities alter their way of speaking Hopi very little, though they may change their attitudes to time, change their dress, and even learn a second language. Hopi culture has absorbed many innovations since the Spaniards first introduced fruit trees, cattle, sheep, and horses and the U.S. government brought schools and public health clinics to the reservation. But the phonemes comprising Hopi and the grammatical rules for using the language underwent no comparable change. To be sure additions appeared in vocabulary. Vocabulary in any language is highly responsive to changes in other sectors of culture and therefore is far less autonomous than, say, the grammatical structure itself.

The degree of autonomy possessed by separate areas of culture grows as cultural variety increases. In modern civilization it is quite customary for people in one sector of life, say, business, to do things incompatible with values enunciated in other sectors, say, in church. Also specialists and organized groups, like capital and labor, pull in independent directions and limited concord marks the values of social classes.

DISSECTING THE SYSTEM

All except confirmed holists recognize that it sometimes helps to break down portions of a cultural system into constituent traits. Take, for example, the Kwakiutl Indians of coastal British Columbia and Vancouver Island.[2] Their large wooden houses facing the sea contained many possessions, all strictly owned. Even the land and sea were owned by groups of kinsmen and passed down to all descendants of a group. Kin groups owned clam grounds, hunting territories, and berry tracts on which they forbade trespass. Songs, names, titles of nobility—all were private property and heritable. When a person assumed a title of nobility he also assumed the greatness of all the ancestors who had ever borne that title. No title could be taken on unless validated by a potlatch, a distribution of wealth, in which mats, baskets, skins, blankets, canoes, shell money, and etched sheets of natural copper that possessed value higher than anything else were given away. Elders in the family accumulated such wealth for a child who prepared to assume his first title of importance. They loaned him goods with which to potlatch. Recipients of the potlatch later repaid with interests the gifts they had received. The child in turn repaid with interest those who had financed him, pocketing a margin of difference. Considering that a person of any importance changed titles like a snake changes its skin, the excitement of potlatching occurred pretty constantly among the Kwakiutl.

[2] Ruth Benedict, *Patterns of Culture* (Boston, 1934), chap. 6.

A Kwakiutl village facing the sea. The photograph was taken in the 1880s. (*American Museum of Natural History.*)

A man potlatched at marriage, when his daughter or granddaughter came of age, or simply to challenge a rival man of influence. The whole life of an important man consisted of laboriously potlatching himself up a ladder toward ever enhanced prestige measured against the prestige acquired by his rivals. Titles plus prerogatives that the titles carried, like rights to a song, dance, or a canoe name, were the ladder's rungs. Each succeeding rung had to be fought for by first accumulating and then distributing wealth. In this atmosphere of rivalry competition was open and unmitigated. A big man even destroyed wealth in order to shame his rival. So magnificent a gesture brought him no return except the ineffable feeling of having once again beaten his rival.

Now let us see how some of the elements of Kwakiutl culture can be cut loose as it were and presented like individual bricks in a way of life. Counting even negative traits (if one can imagine counting bricks that a cultural edifice lacks!), the total list of elements in Kwakiutl culture amounts to 1,797 items. But this number could easily be increased or decreased simply by making finer or grosser divisions. In the following list the left-hand column lists the traits and the right-hand column gives information about each for two out of 7 Kwakiutl local divisions. A plus sign shows the trait was present, a minus sign indicates absence, and no sign shows that information on the particular element could not be secured.

	Koskino	Kwexa
Privileges owned	+	+
Personal names	+	+
House names	+	+
Canoe names	+	+
Songs, dances	+	+
Territorial rights owned	+	+
Fishing places	+	+
Hunting grounds		
Berry and root grounds	+	—
Titles [subtraits eliminated]	+	+
Skins as wealth	+	+
Trade blankets as wealth	+	+
Loans made	+	+
For potlatching	+	+
At interest	+	+
Fixed rates	+	+
Short term: 50 percent	+	+
Long term: 100 percent	+	+
No fixed rate	—	—
Potlatches at life crises	+	+
Birth	+	+
Girl's puberty	+	+
Marriage	+	+
Face-saving potlatches	+	+
Competitive potlatches	—	+
Property destroyed	—	+
Names assumed at potlatch	+	+
Privileges assumed at potlatch	+	+

SOURCE: Philip Drucker, *Culture Element Distributions: XXVI Northwest Coast*, University of California, Anthropological Records, vol. 9, no. 3, 1950, pp. 220-221, 231-233.

Such lists can't be read for pleasure. But they are useful to compare cultural systems.

CULTURE, IDEAL AND MANIFEST

Like an iceberg, part of culture is apparent for all to see. Greetings, games, pregnancy and puberty customs, feasts, cremation practices, and material elements like houses, ornaments, and deliberate bodily deformations correspond to the iceberg's overt part. Covert culture includes the motives with which people act, the meanings their actions and artifacts possess for them, their conception of the world, and their ideas of man's place in the world.

The covert side of culture includes ideals according to which people intend to shape their lives. Many anthropologists have had the experience of asking individuals how they carried on in some social relationships only to be given an answer that didn't jibe with readily observable facts. People were responding in terms of how they were supposed to act, not in terms of their manifest day-to-day behavior. Ideal and manifest were in contradiction. I secured a neat example of such contradiction among the Kaska Indians. There, you will recall, menstruation was especially dangerous to a man because it threatened his ability as a hunter. To avoid contamination, a menstruating woman was secluded. A young Kaska lady told me that seclusion might fail in its purpose. Boys visited an unmarried girl in her menstrual camp heedless of the danger that could accrue to them. Of course, she described a relatively recent period of Kaska Indian culture, when the old way had begun to break down. When a culture is in flux, great discrepancies between ideal and manifest can be expected. In fact, conflict is likely to occur between ideals themselves, new standards of conduct being absorbed in the stream of culture before everyone abandons incompatible old ones.

Ideal and manifest need not be in conflict. People may keep their overt acts in line with

A titled Kwakiutl girl holding a partially destroyed copper plate. The corner has been cut away in defiance of her father's potlatch rivals. (*Smithsonian Institution, Bureau of American Ethnology; photograph by Franz Boas, 1895.*)

their standards. Such a culture is in Edward Sapir's words, a "genuine culture." If it builds magnificent churches it does so to symbolize a deep and vital religious feeling. Like the Plains Indians of an earlier day, a genuine culture weaves war into every significant fiber of life rather than confusing ideals of preparedness and disarmament. A genuine cul-

---

IDEAL AND MANIFEST DISPARITY IN PUEBLO CULTURE

" . . . no more glaring discrepancy can be found anywhere between theory and practice than among these Pueblos. On the one hand, they exalt sweetness and light: tribesmen must collaborate, they must suppress urges toward self-assertion, must refrain from quarreling, lest the gods in disapproval of dissension withhold the all-important rain. A Shipaulovi chief declared that the tranquillity reigning in his village brought heavy rains during a festival, whereas clouds stayed away from the discord-cleft Walpi. On the other hand, there is an undeniable record of constant gossiping, altercation, and literal schism."

R. H. Lowie, *Robert H. Lowie, Ethnologist* (Berkeley, Calif., 1959), pp. 73-74.

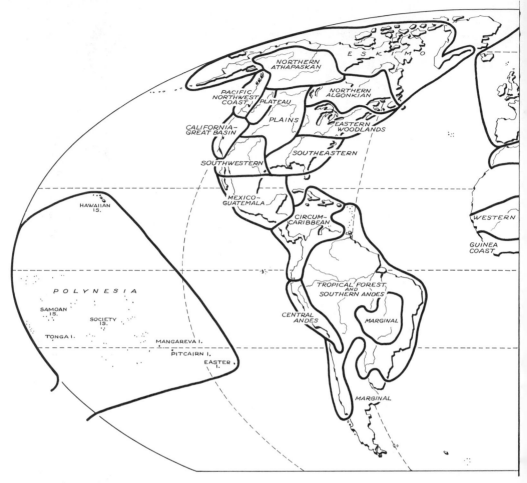

The world's main culture areas. After *Elizabeth Bacon, "A Preliminary Attempt to Determine the Culture Areas of Asia,"* Southwestern Journal of Anthropology, 2 *(1946), 117-132; Melville J. Herskovits, "The Culture Areas of Africa,"* Africa, 3 *(1930), 59-77 (also see G. P. Murdock,* Africa *[New York, 1959]); Raoul S. Narroll, "A Draft Map of the Culture Areas of Asia,"* Southwestern Journal of Anthropology, 6 *(1950), 183-187; Clark Wissler,* The American Indian,*3rd ed. New York, (1938); Raymond Kennedy,* Islands and Peoples of the Indies,

ture "is not a spiritual hybrid of contradictory patches, of water-tight compartments of consciousness that avoid participation in a harmonious synthesis. If the culture necessitates slavery, it frankly admits it; if it abhors slavery, it feels its way to an economic adjustment that obviates the necessity of its employment. It does not make a great show in its ethical ideals of an uncompromising opposition to slavery, only to introduce what amounts to a slave system into certain portions of its industrial mechanism."[3]

[3] Edward Sapir, "Culture, Genuine and Spurious," *American Journal of Sociology,* 29 (1924), 401-429.

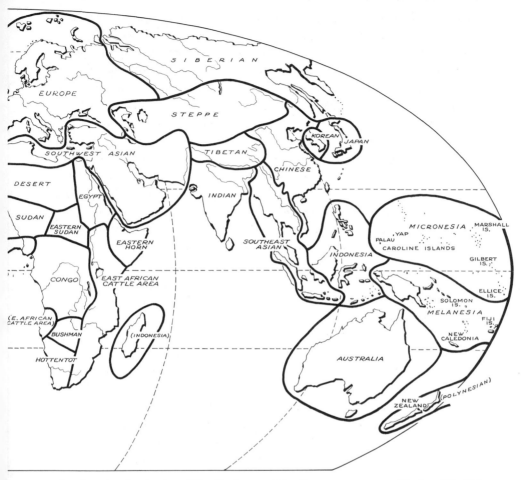

Smithsonian Institution, *War Background Studies, no. 14, 1943; Herbert W. Krie-ger*, Island Peoples of the Western Pacific: Micronesia and Melanesia, *Smith-sonian Institution, War Background Studies, no. 16, 1943; J. E. Weckler, Jr.,* Polynesians—Explorers of the Pacific, *Smithsonian Institution, War Background Studies, no. 6, 1943; Julian H. Steward, "South American Cultures: An Interpre-tative Summary," in Julian H. Steward, ed.,* Handbook of South American Indians, Vol. 5, The Comparative Ethnology of South American Indians, *Bureau of Amer-ican Ethnology Bulletin 143, 1949; with additions.*

CONTINUITY

Imagine looking back into the corridor of history. What you see is culture starting as a very thin stream some half a million or more years ago and con-stantly expanding, faster and faster, with time. The stream can be divided into periods, each marking a relatively sharp break with tradition. Other divisions could be made to show where one contemporary culture leaves off and another begins. Ignoring oceans and inhospitable areas on the earth's surface, culture is continuous in space as it is in time. Spatially speaking, culture forms an imaginary sheath girdling the earth's surface almost from pole to pole.

When Europeans began to explore the world's continental areas, the world's culture sheath could be divided into about 40 major areas. In each of these culture areas life followed characteristic directions, bents, and interests. For example, in North America's Eskimo realm winter hunters secured seal and other game through the ice, dressed in fur garments, and traveled by dog-drawn sledges. South of the Eskimo came the caribou area. Here hunters and fishermen, like the Kaska Indians, traveled across the snow's powdery surface aided by snowshoes. Further south came the bison hunting Plains Indians living in what is now North Dakota, South Dakota, Montana, Wyoming, and points south. Pueblo Indians like the Hopi are often taken as representing the typical culture of the American southwestern area. And so on, covering other culture areas into which South America, Africa, Asia, and Oceania are divided.

Within any single area the culture sheath is further divisible into less sharply distinct phases. Modern southern culture, for example, with its grits for breakfast and attitudes toward the Negro, is a distinct contemporary phase of twentieth-century North American culture. Pathan culture is a phase found mainly in northwestern West Pakistan. Phases again break down into purely local varieties that sometimes correspond to integral social systems. *Plantation County,* a book by Morton Rubin, interprets one variety in the southern phase of American culture. In *Blackways of Kent* Hylan Lewis sympathetically reports his understanding of another southern cultural variety. A single social system may embrace several varieties of culture. Swat, for example, includes the cultures of valley-bottom Pathans, higher-dwelling, pastoral Gujars, and mountain people who live beyond the range of Pathan conquest.

THE SOURCES HERE AND NOW

At each moment every culture remains closely involved with three sets of conditions that lie outside of itself: the human organism's biological nature; the number of human beings in society, their age, sex, and other characteristics; and, finally, the landscape in which those persons live or which they exploit. These three interdependent groups of conditions constitute a single organized system, the cultural field. Relations between culture and field are such that a change in the field—for example, an increase in population or erosion of top soil—spells a difference for that way of life. Conversely, man through culture alters his culture field.

Man possesses a capacity for culture that is part of his biological nature. By himself, of course, no individual can manage to bring a culture into being. People—young, old, and healthy and organized in groups—are required. Also geographical conditions enter a way of life. What causes culture: biology, a plurality of organisms, or environment? None of these things alone. Each component is involved with the others in whatever culture we study. Culture has no direct cause but is maintained by, at the same time that it helps to maintain, an interactive field of phenomena.

Erosion, at times a man-made condition of the cultural field, has prompted many efforts by man to restrain its continuing, devastating action. (*U.S. Soil Conservation Service.*)

To understand culture in any social system—whether a business office, Indian pueblo, or modern nation—it helps to know relevant conditions existing in the cultural field. But steer a wary course! Many wise people have gone astray trying to explain all of culture in terms of some specific noncultural condition, like race or climate. Beguiled by their personal version of the "nothing-but" fallacy they overlooked everything else but what they regarded as the master key. Keep in mind that biology, numbers of people, and landscape are by themselves powerless to evoke any behavior for which the culture is not already prepared, for which people lack requisite knowledge, tools, organization, or inclination. Ultimately it is a people's view of their cultural field that determines how they will respond to its components. What our industrial culture has done with the anthracite coal fields of Pennsylvania is unthinkable for the culture of the Indians who lived in the same region during pre-Columbian times. The anthracite was there but as an inert part of the landscape that couldn't determine for man what his culture would be.

ONE HUMAN SPECIES

One component of the cultural field, the human organism, remains basically the same all over the world. Furthermore, as far as we can tell man hasn't changed significantly for thousands of years, perhaps for hundreds of thousands. True, this single human species shows abundant racial variety, but racial differences enlighten us very little about human culture. We get no help in understanding Kaska or Hopi culture by learning that these Indians belong to two distinct breeding groups within a larger Mongoloid race called the Amerindian. From a cultural point of view it isn't very significant that the darkly pigmented Negroid people of Africa, with their frequently spiral hair, everted lips, and high frequency of blood types A and B, can be set off from the hairy, white (i.e., Caucasoid) Mediterraneans of North Africa, southern Europe, the Middle East, and northwestern Pakistan (Swat) who possess prominent noses set in small faces and only a moderate frequency of blood types A and B. These racial peculiarities explain none of the vast number of differences between African cultures and, say, the cultures of desert nomads in the Middle East. Yet, in some multiracial communities, like the southern United States, it is very hard to shake people loose from their belief that intelligence, morality, and achievement are inherited in the same direct way as skin color, blood type, and other racial attributes.

Anthropology's conclusions concerning race are worth bearing in mind. Race has long served scientists as a classifying device, one that happens to make use of heritable, physical characteristics. Distinctive physical characteristics appear in a population after it has remained isolated for a relatively long time. Through frequent inbreeding the isolated population in time comes to differ physically from other breeding populations. It becomes a race. But human isolation always remains far from complete, even when laws try to keep it so. As a result the world's races shade into one another or are mixed. Speaking from a biological point of view, no certain evidence has yet come to light showing that race mixture is either beneficial or harmful. Even hybrid vigor, should it occur through race mixture, is not necessarily good. On the other hand, advantages and disadvantages following from miscegenation are clearer from a social point of view. Race mixture can be socially very beneficial if it reduces the visibility of a population that has been discriminated against. Individuals are spared from undignified special treatment once they blend into the total population. However, crossing one race with another will not be socially beneficial in a social system that discriminates harshly against offspring of racially mixed unions.

Difficult as it is for a few people to accept, mankind's innate capacity for intelligence appears to be distributed quite independently of racial differences. Hard as doubters try, to date they have failed successfully to contradict this conclusion. As soon as home environments and educational opportunities for races approach equality, high and low IQs occur irrespective of racial lines. These points are worth emphasizing because they cut the ground from under people who justify racial discrimination by insisting that some races are less favorably endowed than others.

FURTHER READING

For theories of culture, see A. L. Kroeber, *Anthropology*, new ed. (New York, 1948), chaps. 7-8, and Robert Redfield, *The Little Community* (Chicago, 1955). The outstanding study of cultural integration is still Ruth Benedict's *Patterns of Culture* (Boston, 1934), of which chaps. 2-4 are especially worth reading in the context of this chapter. Laura Thompson's concept of logico-aesthetic integration carries configurational thinking about as far as any contemporary theorist. See her book *Toward a Science of Mankind* (New York, 1961), chap. 10, and the paper "Logico-aesthetic Integration in Hopi Culture," *American Anthropologist*, 47 (1945), 540-553.

To show the integration of culture, I at one point contemplated using Darwinism as an integrating hub of western culture. Pertinent literature developing this idea includes J. M. Drachman, *Studies in the Literature of Natural Science* (New York, 1930); Leo J. Henkin, *Darwinism in the English Novel, 1860-1910* (New York, 1940); Richard Hofstadter, *Social Darwinism in American Thought*, rev. ed. (Boston, 1955); Lionel Stevenson, *Darwin Among the Poets* (Chicago, 1932); and Conway Zirkle, *Evolution, Marxian Biology, and the Social Scene* (Philadelphia, 1959, chap. 5

For more about Kwakiutl culture see Franz Boas, *Kwakiutl Culture as Reflected in Mythology*, Memoirs of the American Folk-Lore Society, vol. 28, 1935, and Helen Codere, "The Amiable Side of Kwakiutl Life: The Potlatch and the Play Potlatch," *American Anthropologist*, 58 (1956), 334-351.

Kroeber goes over the theory of culture-area classification critically in "The Culture-Area and Age-Area Concepts of Clark Wissler," in S. A. Rice, ed., *Methods in Social Science—A Case Book* (Chicago, 1931); see also Kroeber's textbook, *Anthropology*, pp. 261-265. Reviews of world culture areas will be found in that book, pp. 732-764, 768-771, 785-792, as well as in Ralph Piddington, *An Introduction to Social Anthropology* (Edinburgh, 1950), vol. I, chaps. 2-3, and Harry H. Turney-High, *General Anthropology* (New York, 1949), chaps. 13-16. My concepts of phase and variety are derived from Philip Phillips and Gordon R. Willey, "Method and Theory in American Archeology: an Operational Basis for Culture-History Integration," *American Anthropologist*, 55 (1953), 615-633.

Further information is available summarizing many continental areas shown on the map. For South America see Julian H. Steward and Louis C. Faron, *Native Peoples of South America* (New York, 1959); G. P. Murdock is mentioned in the map caption for his book, *Africa* (New York, 1959), which radically revises the cultural map of the African continent as it is now drawn; Simon and Phoebe Ottenberg have introduced Africa as a whole in *Cultures and Societies of Africa* (New York, 1960), a collection of papers; Raymond Kennedy, *The Islands and Peoples of the South Seas and Their Cultures,* Jayne Memorial Lectures, American Philosophical Society (Philadelphia, 1945). The European continent has been mapped by prehistorians and in folklore atlases but I know of no attempt to delineate full-fledged culture areas for it. In addition many summaries are available for particular culture areas, for example Fay-Cooper Cole, *The Peoples of Malaysia* (New York, 1945) for Indonesia and A. G. Wenley and John A. Pope, *China,* Smithsonian Institution, War Background Studies, no. 20, 1944. Other culture area maps are to be found in Robert F. Spencer and Elden Johnson, *Atlas for Anthropology* (Dubuque, Iowa, 1960).

My concept of cultural field is similar to John Gillin's idea of the cultural situation in *The Ways of Men* (New York, 1948), chap. 10. Material on the topic is further developed in *The World of Man* by John J. Honigmann (New York, 1959), chap. 11. Biological factors entering into culture are treated at length in Gillin's *The Ways of Men,* chaps. 7-8, 12-13. In *The Human Animal,* Weston La Barre (Chicago, 1954) also examines the manifold relations of human culture and biology, using the latter word in its broadest sense. Bronislaw Malinowski views culture as primarily a response to basic biological needs. Out of this response secondary needs develop. See his book, *A Scientific Theory of Culture and Other Essays* (Chapel Hill, N.C., 1944), chaps. 8-11. Stanley M. Garn provides a convenient summary of *Human Races* (Springfield, Ill., 1961). A simple account of blood types is *Races and People* by William C. Boyd and Isaac Asimov (New York, 1955). Unesco organized a conference to formulate a consensus of informed opinion about race. It is reported in *The Race Concept: Results of an Inquiry* (Paris, 1952).

Change and Cultural Momentum

Actual social change is never so great as is apparent change. Ways of belief, of expectation, of judgment and attendant emotional dispositions of like and dislike, are not easily modified after they have once taken shape.

John Dewey[1]

FOR COMFORT AND SURVIVAL

Ours is a civilization packed with unparalleled, constant, and deliberately fostered change. Hopeful designs for altering people's behavior in predetermined directions are not drawn up only in totalitarian and underdeveloped countries. Each session of Congress passes social legislation aiming to reform Americans' behavior. Applied psychologists design environments in which they and their employers hope we shall be tempted to work more productively. Advertising agencies profitably work at arousing new desires or maintaining unflagging expectancy in old ones. And always there are new forms of transportation, weapons, and life-saving drugs that put intense pressure on us to up-date our diplomacy or to tamper with habits as personal as reproduction.

Some change is utterly essential in order to survive. By altering his behavior from time to time and from place to place man has succeeded in adapting himself to practically every kind of habitat, from beyond the Arctic Circle to the Equator. As far as survival is concerned, change is the most important thing in the world. Yet, although change is widespread and at times indispensable for survival it is not always welcome. Counterbalancing change is a momen-

[1] *Human Nature and Conduct* (New York, 1922), p. 108.

tum in human behavior—a "force" Sapir called self-preservation—that keeps culture headed resolutely in whatever directions it has been following. Put negatively, in many areas of life we resist change that threatens to deflect us from customary paths. This conclusion applies even in a lively civilization turning over as rapidly as ours.

FROM DRIFT TO REVOLUTION

We are not unique, only different in the rate and magnitude with which our lives are changing. In a small-scale, isolated community change proceeds so gradually that culture seems to be standing still. Once a population swells or after isolating barriers collapse culture change speeds up. Today the day of slowly changing culture is at least temporarily finished. Following A.D. 1400 the Great Age of Discovery and then the late, unmourned era of colonial expansion succeeded in bringing the whole world into contact with western merchants, missionaries, and administrators. As a result European and American civilization are everywhere in the process of actively infiltrating small-scale lifeways.

Ultimately all culture change is man-made. As population increases more minds and hands become available to create new ideas and translate them into actions and objects. Natural modifications in geography trigger people to modify customary behavior. The sea threatens to cover a beach and man responds by building a breakwater to safeguard his hotels and clean white sand. Brilliant human achievements also have power to set in motion devastating geographical changes that people never intended but to which they must adapt. Guns all but exterminated American bison. Plows carelessly used quickly erode fertile topsoil. Large-scale irrigation systems, indispensable if man is to farm in arid zones, waterlog the earth and draw ruinous salts to the surface so that planting becomes impossible. Such consequences clamor for further change. As a matter of fact, any change is apt to confront people with the need for more change. Space-leaping inventions like the airplane and nuclear weapons have brought new dangers that compel us to find ways of maintaining international relations. Still we must be careful not to make it all sound too logical. Human creativity may indeed perform best in response to crises but sheer restlessness, fancy, and sportiveness have also contributed their share of ingenious inventions and salient discoveries.

Examples of culture change include improvisations like a new poem or novel, clarification about the sources of biological evolution, or the advent of colored telephones. These are improvisations in existing patterns. Individually each hardly disturbs the pattern itself. But then we recognize other innovations that severely jolted tradition, like agriculture, the wheel, gunpowder, printing, wireless, the theory of evolution, the steam engine, and the discovery that atomic fission releases vast energy. Even where precise evidence is lacking, we are safe in concluding that all these great discoveries came gradually. Small improvisations in knowledge and practice built up, one after the other. The improvisations drifted along until a new pattern emerged. Step by step American women altered their traditional status. The trend started even before girls regularly began to attend college in the first part of the nineteenth century. Then college-educated women stepped into prominent roles in public affairs, though still not able to do much when it came to elections. In 1920 women won the vote in all states and claimed at least a foothold in practically all occupations. Once a woman could smoke a cigarette in public while sitting on a speakeasy barstool like a man, the new pattern was nearly complete. In the same determined fashion, American labor climbed step by step to reach the stupendous revolutionary power which union leaders today wield.

Such drift, Melville J. Herskovits points out, is not haphazard but shows direction.[2] The leaders who promote women's rights or labor's power are committed toward these goals. Culture change shows direction even when there aren't resolute feminists or labor leaders determined to keep changes on the track. The half-century of French poetry following 1850 exhibits a trend toward symbolism that is as clear as labor's determination to expand its influence. From the first hand-axes in the Old Stone Age down to present-day community development programs in underdeveloped countries, man has kept up a trend as he step by step expands his control over the forces and vagaries of nature.

There is nothing mystical about change adhering to certain directions. Certainly no in-born, instinctual urge drove women to gain what influence they could. Basically people have to agree on the directions change is to follow. Explicitly or implicitly we accept certain goals as worth pursuing. Once the goals are decided on, clever minds start working to find ways of reaching them. Selection is then made from the spate of innovations constantly thrown up by human creativity, restlessness, and sportiveness. People readily adopt and perpetuate changes compatible with their goals, reject changes that threaten the things they want to achieve, and are passive toward those that seem neutral.

Not all change is basically cumulative, made up of small innovations selected either because they adhere to a direction in which some segment of the society is headed or because they are neutral. We can't ignore the fact that from time to time social systems spurt toward goals that until then they pursued in a slow, drifting fashion. In a spirit of radical exuberance leaders urge their enthused followers to jettison old goals, break with tradition, and adopt a brand new, more promising set of standards. Then change achieves the magnitude of an explosion. A revolution shakes the culture. It upsets established political authorities inflexibly committed to the old way and reforms nearly every department of life, including clothing, alphabet, and calendar. The sanctions of priests yield to the more persuasive authority of scientists or to the inspired convictions of men heading monolithic parties. Outright confiscation hastens redistribution of wealth. Forceful efforts bring about rapid industrialization. The French, Russian, and Chinese revolutions fit this order of change. So do other known social upheavals whose historical remoteness obscures their details. Also in this category of change are the nonviolent British social revolution that hurried in a welfare state and our own New Deal. It must be admitted that revolutions begin much more ambitiously than they finish. The need to establish internal stability as quickly as possible and to resume normal foreign relations causes leaders to modify the noble resolution with which they started out to establish the perfect culture.

THE INNOVATOR AND HIS CULTURAL MILIEU

Change starts when somebody someplace originates something. Few things are completely new but we need not get into the question of deciding how to recognize originality, a problem that the Patent Office also finds difficult. For our purpose an origination occurs when a scientist in his laboratory, a person out in nature, a philosopher in his study, or a medical man in the clinic discovers what he takes to be a true and original addition to belief or knowledge. Quite possibly he is wrong or somebody may already have made the discovery before him. Some ancient Greeks perceived the earth and planets to revolve around the sun but a rival theory won out. Credit for the heliocentric theory goes to Copernicus who only rediscovered it 18 centuries later. The stubborn iconoclasm of the Beat Generation is not new. In several ways it resembles attitudes entertained by the Greek Cynics. Origination also occurs when somebody invents a solution to a practical problem. The telephone, penicillin, and psychotherapy are familiar inventions. Just as highly original inventions are apt to embody the contributions of several previous generations of discoverers so they lend themselves to further tinkering and combination. The steam engine combined with anciently invented wagons and ships produced the railroad engine and steamship. Electric motors are applied to drive clocks, phonographs, and a hundred other things. Originations are by no means confined to technology. They occur in philosophy, religion, government, art, and recreation. But somehow original contributions in those areas more easily pass unnoticed. We stress technological innovation because business profits, greater leisure, and even national survival depend on it.

Since origination is important it is worth asking about the circumstances which encourage or endanger creativity. A rich and unflagging ability to conceive bright ideas is the most important guarantee of sustained creativity. It is true that not everybody possesses this capacity equally. Yet experience proves that encouragement and training can develop the ability to be bright in more people than currently show it. The innovator endowed to think creatively must also *want* to generate bright ideas. Motives that inspire origination vary.

UNITED STATES POSTAGE

SAMUEL
F.B.MORSE

2¢

The fame they acquired earned several U.S. inventors a place on postage stamps. (*U.S. Post Office Department.*)

The inventor may be driven by a conscious desire for wealth, fame, or whatever other benefits patents and certificates of authorship guarantee him. He may be impelled by something as ignoble as resentment of a colleague's renown. Some originations are due to agitating conflicts of an age that trouble innovators. A person sees a conflict between science and the Bible or Quran. The coexistence of poverty with abundance distresses him. Southerners are torn between their traditional adherence to segregation and the need to obey federal law that forbids teaching Negroes and non-Negroes separately in state-supported schools. Some people feel these conflicts more keenly than others and it is they who look for a means to resolve their predicament. They become the originators of a new philosophy transcending science and religion or propose new social legislation. In Virginia segregationists originated the idea of independent schools which would be operated through private funds and in which, they hoped, segregation would be legal. Once more, we must not make it all too purposeful. Some originators are motivated by nothing more definite than curiosity to know more about something. Sheer creativity urges a composer to write music. A prophet receives God's word in a vision or dream and communicates it. If others heed the words a new religion is born.

Individual incentive is not enough to insure a steady stream of originations. Cultural conditions also favor originations to the degree that they are present in a social system. Just as soil is unequal in its capacity to support plants, so cultures differ in their power to foster discoveries and inventions. It is inconceivable that the Kaska Indians could rival Russia or the United States in productivity of innovation. Not that inherent ability is proportionately rarer among those marginal people. The Kaska couldn't survive in their rigorous setting unless they were able to learn from experience. So biological factors can't explain why some communities don't originate new items of culture to the same extent as others. Conditions under which origination thrives have been thoroughly studied by Homer G. Barnett.[3] A really thriving creative milieu, he points out, depends on a richness of cultural possessions. The more a culture contains in the way of things, processes, and ideas, the greater the number of possibilities available to originators to combine and recombine them into novel forms. The wider a man's cultural horizons, whether he is a trapper, farmer, pharmacist, historian, or physicist, the more resources he has to work with and the richer his creative output can be. Without the resources of chemistry and physics laboratories and unaided by modern mathematics, nuclear fission could never have been discovered. A country possessing well-equipped, comfortably endowed research institutes, each well equipped with books and apparatus, offers its highly qualified scientists the most favorable opportunities for creativity. Countries that can't afford to equip laboratories or libraries will also lack resources needed for adding to science. But perhaps conditions in those countries are favorable for pioneering in other kinds of innovation, like religious concepts or new forms of political and social action. Well endowed with imagination and intellect some West African people have conceived of cosmological theories so intricate and well organized that they make Genesis an elementary child's tale. Such conceptions require no intricate laboratory facilities, indexed reports of earlier experiments, or complex mathematical formulas.

A cultural climate which favors equally all kinds of origination precludes any authoritarian control over what an investigator may study. Scholars must be free to inquire into whatever excites them, free to share with others what they discover. External control, however, narrows origination to only a few problems for which many investigators will inevitably lack aptitude and interest. Modern history demonstrates how an official biology or state enforced styles of art stifle creativity. Soviet physics remains quite as free as physics in the United States. It is far more productive than Soviet biology, in which a prescribed party line determines what research shall be conducted.

Of course, practical considerations curb everybody's creativity. Problems that confront a social reformer limit him to a degree at the same time that they stimulate him to thought and action. The scientist's very theory is a ceiling. He can't fly higher than his theory permits. The assumptions that belong to an age, the *Weltanschauung,* are shackles that confine even the growth of theory. Only the rare genuis occasionally succeeds and overcomes such limits. He takes a really tremendous, pace-making step forward pushing the boundaries of his discipline to undreamed of new limits. But his contemporaries may not be able to accept so daring a break with tradition. When we say that a genius is ahead of his time we mean that his innovation is so adventurous that his culture can't assimilate it.

Innovators benefit from social arrangements that get ideas into circulation

[3] Homer G. Barnett, *Innovation* (New York, 1953), chaps. 2-3.

periodically, transmitting them to interested persons. Conferences on child development or on the Napoleonic era, annual meetings of zoologists, engineers, and copywriters, and the thousands of published professional and trade journals all perform this function. As a result one man's discoveries quickly enrich the experience of his colleagues who are working on similar tasks. This is genuine cooperation freely given. A poor scholar need not even subscribe to the journals; he can read them in a large library. Universities know well the importance of periodically infusing stimulating new ideas in their faculties. Hence they pay the expenses of their professors to attend scholarly meetings. Universities are also alert that the library receive important books and journals, most of which mean little to the typical undergraduate. Furthermore, each year the massive volume of published material is broken down by indexing. The index will disgorge the exact references that enable a researcher to work toward a major breakthrough. Working only by himself he might never come up with the precise combination of facts he needs. While origination thrives under the modern world's comprehensive system of publishing, indexing, and storing ideas, we owe these facilities themselves to an invention of basic significance. Originating some 6000 years ago, writing enabled scribes to anchor ideas in tangible form. Impressed on clay, leaves, bark, or paper, ideas were bound fast and could be stored as though they were bricks or boxes until such time as someone chose to re-examine them.

Some men doubtlessly work better alone than in teams but nobody who is cut off from social contacts can steadily originate new ideas or appliances. And so it is with social systems. Isolated, the Kaska Indians and other small-scale communities could confine their creative abilities only to the limiting stock of whatever they had at hand. Between two communities, the one with more windows open on the world will be the most creative. Even a language changes more rapidly if the speakers have intensive contacts with speakers of other languages. A dense population also stimulates rapid change. A large-scale community, one whose written records reach deeply into the past and whose living contacts range far in space, is very well situated to produce a large number of diversified innovations.

To be deprived of something essential or good provides another condition in which origination thrives. When wars cut off imports they set up a frantic search for substitutes. Nobody wants to surrender comforts to which he has become accustomed. And so innovators get to work to preserve as far as they can the momentum which had been established.

Having dealt with cultural conditions favorable to sustained origination, we ought to note the circumstances that work to the contrary. Affluence and other kinds of well-being depress certain kinds of innovation. In our time such blessings contribute to a climate in which potential kinds of change—for example, experiments in economics and social welfare—are inhibited. Cultural momentum is encouraged. Our contemporary devotion to conformity and renewed interest in conservatism grow out of what Carl Sandburg calls "fat-dripping" prosperity. Affluence simply deprives people of that condition from which some of the most relentless problem-solving springs—unmet basic needs for food, clothing, shelter, and less tangible forms of physical security. Well-being makes us resigned to many deficiencies. After all, things are going prosperously well, so why do anything drastic? Perhaps de Tocqueville had something like this in mind in 1835 when he wrote that "a kind of virtuous materialism may ultimately be established in the world which would not corrupt but enervate the soul, and noiselessly unbend its springs of action."[4]

Poverty also depresses innovation. Food gatherers living at the very margin of subsistence have little time to devise new ways of hunting and fishing. So it is with marginal farmers. Yet they need improvements more than the prosperous cultivators who possess enough land to experiment adventurously with new seeds and methods. Underdeveloped nations that most need technical change if standards of living are to increase have the least scope to innovate. They can't afford to send trainees abroad who will return to improve existing procedures. They can't reward or equip researchers to look for more efficient means of production. If new ways become available, underdeveloped countries can't themselves find capital to switch over.

SIMULTANEOUS ORIGINATION AND CROSS-CULTURAL PARALLELS

From 1835 to 1858 Darwin uncertainly pondered his theory that species survive by inheriting characteristics which bestow on them special fitness or adaptability. Nature selects the strong and swift but leaves the weak and slow to perish. Until 1858 Darwin confided this theory to only a few friends. Then he received a manuscript from a naturalist, Alfred Russel Wallace. Like Darwin, Wallace had traveled a great deal and what is more had read the same books that inspired Darwin's vision on evolution. Wallace too had observed that some animals are better adapted than others for survival and came to the conclusion that evolution proceeded through selection of the fittest. Naturally, Darwin recognized the similarity between the theory he had been mulling over for 20 years and the one Wallace had "independently" originated. He showed Wallace's letter to his friends. Goaded by them, at long last he took courage and prepared to publish *On the Origin of Species*.

What happened between Darwin and Wallace is no isolated case. Simultaneous originations are more common than we think. It is easy to cite a

[4] Cited in C. J. Radcliffe, *The Problems of Power* (London, 1952), p. 124.

RESTRICTING COMMUNICATION TO SLOW DOWN PROGRESS

As atomic physicists moved closer to the atomic bomb they decided on a move that amounted to a new chapter in the history of science. Among them was Leo Szilard, a Hungarian who had immigrated to the U.S. His vivid imagination perceived with shocking clarity a possible international race in the production of highly destructive atomic armaments. He proposed to Enrico Fermi that the scientists should voluntarily censor their work. Fermi, who had just escaped from Italy where secrecy and censorship crippled intellectual endeavor, refused. For centuries science had fought for the free exchange of ideas. How could scientists ever support the opposite principle? But fear of what the German dictator, Adolph Hitler, might do with atomic bombs increasingly gripped physicists in the U.S. In 1939 P. W. Bridgman announced regretfully that henceforth he intended to forbid scientists from totalitarian countries to enter his laboratory. Very few voices were raised against this break with tradition and even Fermi at last agreed to voluntary self-censorship.

Didn't the scientists go far enough? Some years later Werner Heisenberg, a German physicist said: "In the summer of 1939 twelve people might still have been able, by coming to mutual agreement, to prevent the construction of atom bombs."

Robert Jungk, *Brighter than a Thousand Suns*, trans. James Cleugh (New York, 1958), pp. 72-75, 81, 92-97.

couple of dozen classic instances like the nearly simultaneous discovery of the North Pole, photography, steamboats, anesthesia, sunspots, and nuclear energy. In cases where only one author of a discovery is known, other simultaneous originators probably remain forgotten simply because they failed to publish or establish their claim.

Does this mean that certain originations, like photography or nuclear fission, are inevitable? It is better not to explain simultaneity by crediting it to a superindividual force. But simultaneous originations do prove that something more than equally endowed minds are at work. Something in a way of life inspires men to limit and concentrate their thought, focusing it on specific problems. Restless, intelligent, creative contemporaries are led to struggle with the same stubborn problems and challenges. Cultural momentum is operating. The social system is eager to move in certain directions: toward cheaper transportation, conquest of an obstinate disease, an explanation for some puzzling regularity, or to penetrate a still remote corner of the globe that fascinates explorers and their backers. Facing common problems originators utilize the same new tools or pieces of apparatus as soon as they appear; avidly they scan the same literature and attentively show up at the same meetings and conferences in which new links in the chain of discovery are publicly communicated. Assuming that the searchers are also about equally alert, well-trained, and intellectually endowed, then what is more likely than that at nearly the same moment two or more of them should duplicate the same momentous origination?

Similar traits in two or more cultures, like pyramids in Egypt and Mexico, agriculture in Old and New Worlds, fire-pistons in France and Indonesia, can't be explained in terms of cultural momentum. Parallel cultural elements are also often too widely separated in space or time to believe that they were carried from one center of origination to the other areas. Then how can cross-cultural parallels be explained? In the first place, when similar traits in two regions are closely examined they sometimes turn out to be far from true parallels. Egyptian pyramids, once served as tombs whereas the truncated Mexican structures provided mounds for temples. Truly parallel traits coincide both in form and purpose. Oars, for example, possess similar forms all over and also fill an identical purpose.

Two explanations account for true parallels. One claims that because human beings are all basically alike they will often come up with similar behavior in similar situations. This principle cannot always be applied. Many exceptions deny the rule that similar situations are met similarly. People construct round houses as well as shelters with parallel sides; they build on the surface of the ground, underground, and on stilts. There are dozens of ways to dispose of dead bodies and women give birth in several positions. No doubt choices are limited but that can only be because more than psychic unity is at work.

A somewhat broader explanation, the principle of limited possibilities, often serves us more satisfactorily. Cross-cultural parallels, this theory explains, arise out of a combination of similar conditions. The problem in each case is the same. Let us say river folk in two social systems wish to propel a boat. The available material with which means of propulsion can be fashioned is also similar, wood. Now a limit is set on what can be done, given the problem, resources, and, let us add, available tools. In addition, the strength of the typical adult who will propel the boat is similar in each community. Though each group may start from somewhat different beginnings, their efforts converge as, through trial and error, they discover the most efficient shape and size for the oar and the boat.

Parallels similar from the start require no convergence. Trial and error never led to convergence in such things as circumcision in becoming-a-man ceremonies or in the custom called couvade, which requires the father to lie-in and restrict his customary activities when his wife gives birth. These customs are found among too many, widely separated people to assume that they were derived from a single center of origin. They are due to independent, parallel origination. Let us try to explain one of these instances of parallelism. Circumcision in initiation transforms a youth into a man. All cultures probably associate the penis with the adult masculine role. This makes it a very likely organ on which to emblemize the youth's newly achieved status. I don't offer this as an explanation of all circumcision. It obviously doesn't cover hygienic circumcision, but only truly parallel instances of circumcision in becoming-a-man rituals. Before the couvade can be explained in these terms it would be well to ascertain that in form and purpose the couvade really is identical between cultures.

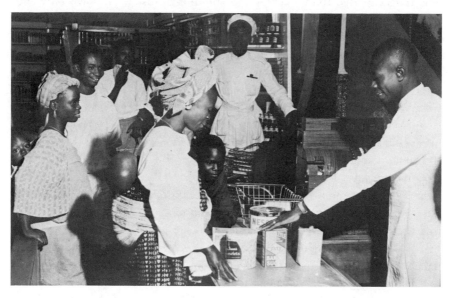

Markets have been held for a long time in West Africa. The packaged foods, cash register, and physical layout of supermarkets represent a wholly new pattern of marketing, one that is still diffusing around the world. (*National Cash Register Company.*)

LAUNCHING CHANGE

I have described how innovations are born but that completes only the first step in culture change. An innovation becomes a real change only when it has been launched successfully in the stream of culture. To count as change it must become more than one man's prized discovery or the brilliant breakthrough achieved by a research team.

The image of ripples spreading in a pond is often drawn to illustrate how an origination spreads as it is adopted by an ever-increasing number of persons. It is a good image, though it conceals much of the complexity with which innovations are launched. Ripples spread in all directions from a splash. Innovations don't diffuse so evenly. The image of the ripples fails to show that innovations are often blocked from diffusing. To make the image reflect what really happens some ripples should disappear almost as soon as they leave the splash. Others would reach shore only in corners of the pond but not all around. A textile mill in South India reached out for laborers and readily attracted Untouchables. They became involved in the newly diffusing pattern of factory labor. It took longer and proved more difficult to persuade members of higher castes to apply for mill work.[5] Revivalistic, millennial religions appeal readily to relatively dispossessed persons but others with more security scorn such faiths. The image of the ripples indicates no difference between new traits exported from a center and stimulus diffusion in which only suggestions of the traits themselves ripple through society. Many social systems that adopted writing ignored the letters of whatever alphabet they imitated. Rather they took over the principle of writing signs that would represent the significant units of sound (phonemes) used in speaking. Impressed by this principle originators applied themselves and developed a new writing system. Communities themselves reach out to borrow time-tested, fragmentary traits from many cultures. These they then combine into unique forms to fill their needs. India's Constitution derives from the written or unwritten constitutions of Britain, Canada, and Ireland, and our own Bill of Rights inspired those sections that cover fundamental rights.

Every culture owes a great deal to other cultures. Despite this fact, time having erased all record of the borrowing that took place, people often believe that they themselves originated their customs. Or else they credit supernatural beings with having originated their way of life. Soap, shaving, razor, compass, paper, printing, coins, pottery, wheelbarrow, kites, suspension bridge, gunpowder, and alphabet are common traits of non-American origin. A surprising portion of our basic heritage derives from Asia, including the religions professed by Jews and Christians. Ralph Linton once estimated that no culture owed more than 10 percent of its total stock to originations made at home. When highly coveted know-how is prevented from diffusing freely, circuitous ways are found to get at it. The mystery of rearing silkworms was smuggled out of China along with the insect's cocoons. Recently espionage helped to spread secret data concerning military uses of nuclear energy.

REINTERPRETING THE INCOMPATIBLE

Successful diffusion is never automatically accomplished. Innovations diffuse when they meet certain conditions and diffusion promptly slows down or ceases when other conditions exist. Anthropologists who have studied what lies behind the spread of culture stress the importance of compatibility. Diffusion speeds up whenever an origination is congruent with strategic features in the receiving culture. Every propagandist knows that he can't impress

[5] V. S. Parthasarathy, "Caste in a South Indian Textile Mill," *The Economic Weekly,* 10 (August 16, 1958), 1083-1086.

DIFFUSION OF AN INNOVATION

Vehicles furnished with solid wood wheels originated in Mesopotamia in the fourth millennium. Two thousand years later they reached Europe whence they were carried to America.

Date (B.C.)	Vehicles with Solid-Disc Wheels Known in:
3250–3000	Lower Mesopotamia (Iraq)
3000–2700	Turkestan (Soviet Central Asia)
2500–2000	Indus Valley (West Pakistan)
2400–2000	Syria; North Caucasian Area and southern Ukraine (U.S.S.R.)
2200–1800	Crete and Hessen (Germany)
1750–1250	Lower Austria and North Italy

Note: Spoked wheels originated after 2000 B.C. and diffused more rapidly than the solid discs. They reached Egypt around 1600, mainland Greece around 1550, Crete around 1450, and the Baltic countries and China around 1300.

V. Gordon Childe, "The Diffusion of Wheeled Vehicles," in H. Kothe and K. H. Otto, eds., *Ethnographisch-archaeologische Forschungen*, no. 2 (1954).

people who hold ideas or values exactly opposite to those he wants to spread. Tooting the horn for socialism is time wasted at a meeting of the National Association of Manufacturers. In the same way schools are ridiculously incongruent with Saharan nomads' wandering lives. Compare these two examples with the way Soviet scientists avidly read American scientific journals or the enthusiastic reception fashion-conscious American women give to the latest Paris creations.

Patience, ingenuity, plus a strong longing for something new can overcome incompatibility. Exporters or importers may remake an innovation so that it will fit easily into a way of life. France wanted Saharan children to go to school; therefore educators experimented with mobile desert schools. But such reinterpretations are costly or require more ingenuity than men can muster. It is easier to take an incompatible trait and spontaneously reshape merely its meaning to make it congruent. A clock is converted into an ornament, a compass becomes a charm against storms, and an ascetic saint is made over into a virile culture hero by people who don't know how to tell time, read a compass, or appreciate self-denial. Another way of adopting an incompatible trait in a culture is to change the existing way of life, not the novelty. This occurs when people are convinced that they want the promised benefits of an unalterable innovation. Kaska Indians who wanted to enjoy more amenities than they could carry around with them on their wanderings, settled down. When men trap and hunt, women and children stay at home in cabins that are equipped with stoves, tables, beds, and washtubs. For the sake of an innovation devoid of all promise people will scarcely modify familiar ways of living. The Alaskan Eskimo didn't see enough in herding imported reindeer to give up the sociability of village life for the isolation of herding camps.

Timely reinterpretation enables a community regularly to refurbish its cultural heritage of laws and customs in the face of other changes that have penetrated its life or modified its physical environment. Such change is a way of keeping up with the times. The Supreme Court's 1954 decision outlawing segregation in publicly supported schools reinterpreted the existing law of the country. It did so in the light of recently established evidence that American Negroes were suffering psychologically under segregation legally enforced in southern states. The court's decision brought custom into line with national public opinion which had come to believe that legal discrimination was contrary to constitutional guarantees. The Court's decision brought the Constitution up to date, much to the distress of many southerners who could not reinterpret their traditional values that flexibly.

Not only the t-shirt, wrist tag, and uniform cloth diffused to these Samoan dancers while American Samoa was under Navy jurisdiction. Notice also the stripes on the lavalavas and the U.S. Navy insignia. At present Samoa is administered by the Department of Interior. (*U.S. Navy.*)

LEARNING TO WANT

For diffusion to occur speedily and with minimal resistance many individuals must eagerly want change. Like the steel ax or gun, the innovation must promise to solve one or more needs immediately and better than anything people already possess. Few changes launched in culture show promise as readily as did the steel ax and gun. More often before anything diffuses an incentive to change must be deliberately cultivated in a population. The job of persuaders on Madison Avenue and of experienced missionaries consists of creating such incentives. They seek to stimulate overwhelming longings that their products will satisfy. Missionaries who dwell on the perils of damnation also instill a need to escape from these; their religion satisfies that need. Galbraith in *The Affluent Society* points out that U.S. economic growth depends on maintaining a constant state of dissatisfied wanting in people who already live at a standard of living never before so widely equalled. Citizens of underdeveloped lands, too, will adopt schools, vaccination, screens, latrines, seed for a new type of wheat, covered wells, or stud bulls only if wants exist for these improvements. Leaders directing culture change in underdeveloped countries are themselves attracted to the new elements of life. Through strenuous propaganda, precept, and example they attempt to arouse a desire for them in others. When leaders become impatient they resort to more desperate pressure. Instead of appealing, they threaten and levy punishments to coerce people to change. The peasant who keeps his child home from school or away from vaccination is fined. A village is forced to build a drainage ditch. Too much force, however, heightens social instability and may provoke violent resistance.

It helps if someone with great authority and prestige can be induced to be first in adopting an innovation. After all, people are accustomed to taking their cues from persons with authority. Hence when such a person adopts an innovation his followers, if they can afford it, are likely to emulate him. Yet experience indicates that even the man of greatest distinction cannot push seriously unpopular changes without losing authority. A king of Afghanistan lost his throne in 1938 partly through trying to force on Muslim subjects western customs that conflicted with their religious values. On the other hand, Kemal Ataturk of Muslim Turkey used his authority zealously to promote a cultural revolution that secularized his land. The big difference between Turkey and Afghanistan lay in Turkey's initial readiness to change. Enough people possessed an inclination to westernize and a readiness to alter their traditional religious outlook. Then, too, the government was not reluctant to use coercion to punish religious leaders who showed counterrevolutionary tendencies.

Just as prestige constitutes a lever for change so whatever promises to equalize existing prestige differences is likely to encounter intense resistance from persons whose favored positions are threatened. They resort to their authority and power to induce even the most disadvantaged classes to resist the abominal innovation. Highly placed families in India feared the equalizing effects of land reforms designed to dissolve big estates. Upper Indian castes at one time deplored the way education was being extended to low caste children thereby removing a traditional basis of social distinction.[6]

Teachers and farm extension agents have learned the value of a demonstration in launching change. Showing an innovation in action proves what it can do. Everyone who visits the farm demonstration plot with his eyes open can see the merits of a new variety of wheat or corn. A new medicine quickly proves its power by curing sick babies. Demonstration sells new traits by showing them in the hands of persons who count.

[6] D. N. Majumdar, "Rural Life and Communication," *Eastern Anthropologist,* 11 (1958), 175-188.

An origination hard to demonstrate has a hard time. Miracle drugs have swept around the world because their effectiveness is easy to see. In Swat I watched a busy bazar curer for 15 minutes as he injected one patient after the other with penicillin drawn from one of several cartons of the drug at his elbow. He is part of a world-wide trend away from folk remedies to new medicines that have demonstrated their effectiveness. The value of innoculation and other forms of preventative medicine is far more difficult to demonstrate. We seek innoculations and practice sanitation because we understand germ theory and other principles on which public health is based. But people who lack knowledge of those principles are hard to convince of merits in preventive medicine.

COMMUNICATING FROM ASSUMPTIONS UP

Demonstration is a form of communication. Some kind of communication is essential to diffuse new culture traits and, if it is to be successful, it involves more than speaking the same language. Individuals or groups communicate effectively when the intellectual assumptions and emotional values underlying what a speaker says also form part of his listener's background. Conversely, communication fails when a listener perceives information with values that the speaker doesn't dream exist. An American military mission that gave airspeed computers to Turkey assumed they would be issued to pilots and used as quickly as possible.[7] The Turkish officers in charge of equipment had a mania for thrift and saving. They careful stored the computers, reasoning that the instruments might get lost if pilots used them. No doubt the Turks understood they had a valuable flying device but they held a point of view unexpectedly different from that of the American military mission.

Even in science inaugurating a radical new theory becomes highly cantankerous when scholars argue from mutually unacceptable assumptions. Freud's psychoanalysis, Rhine's parapsychology, and Lysenko's biology are examples. Proponents stress the advantages of the new position, arguing with assumptions belonging to the theory whose cause they advance. They have no alternative; surely they can't employ arguments based on the opposing theory, which they believe has outlived its usefulness. The opponents are men who still favor the old theory. They draw on its assumptions to argue against the new position. Each side uses a vocabulary intelligible to the other but because both start from unshared assumptions neither succeeds in convincing the other. They can't experiment to compare the value of the respective theories because they dispute the fundamental assumptions by which the experimental results are to be interpreted. The dream that convinces a psychoanalyst of the devious way in which the patient's id operates has quite another meaning for

[7] Hal Lehrman, "Bargain in Turkey," Fortune, 41, no. 3 (March, 1950), 59-60.

a psychiatrist who rejects the assumption of an unconscious id that motivates behavior. Statistical findings given in support of extrasensory perception are ignored by a psychologist who assumes firmly that communication can only occur through a specific medium; thoughts can't travel unaided.

Much frustration and ill-tempered bickering are avoided if agents with the job of transmitting culture from one way of life to another remain aware of communications barriers and recognize the many ways diffusion becomes blocked. For this reason missionaries, technical assistance experts, health educators, and colonial officials are trained in anthropology. But more than technical training is called for. Men and women who are arrogantly convinced of the superiority of their own way of life, who become anxious when confronted by stark cultural differences, and who cannot teach by taking advantage of what their pupils already believe, never make good intercultural agents. Careful selection is needed for the job of intercultural communication. I read recently that a prominent U.S. brewery hires as salesmen amiable, middle-aged men who can josh customers in taverns and bear up under the drinking they must do. Much cultural diffusion is still entrusted to persons not half as thoughtfully chosen or prepared for their responsibilities as a beer salesman.

MARGINALITY

In addition to psychological and cultural factors diffusion is arrested by the physical inaccessibility of communities. Without efficient, year-round transportation or dependable means of communication regions like Arctic Canada remain marginal to more highly developed parts of North America. An older way of life tarries there. Central New Guinea, some coves in the Allegheny Mountains, and valleys in the far Hindu Kush Mountains also evade the modern world. Nowadays roads and military installations together with aircraft, jeeps, and radios are rapidly penetrating the world's marginal pockets.

THE MAP THAT PROTECTS ITSELF

Self-conscious awareness and careful strategy are needed if culture change is to succeed and overcome the counterbalancing tendency of culture to persist. To describe one way culture maintains itself I will use the image of a map. Culture acts like a map by predicting what will happen if men adhere to recognized lines of behavior. Some cultural maps specify that religious contemplation brings the good life; others show the good life much nearer at hand, in fighting, competition, individualism, technological efficiency, headhunting, or a combination of things. Lines of conduct left off the map are nearly inconceivable. As William James said, "We feel neither curiosity nor wonder concerning things so far beyond us that we have no concepts to refer

344 UNDERSTANDING CULTURE

them to or standards by which to measure them."[8] How can tribesmen who find proof of manhood in head-hunting see anything in pacifism to commend it? They adhere to the map with the consequence that their aggressive custom persists.

As we have several times said, cultural momentum limits change. The most brilliant inventor can conceive nothing which is utterly different from all he knows. That's why the most imaginative science fiction only exaggerates twentieth-century times. The future we work toward grows out of the present, and the present itself is a product of what we did in the past. We carry our past into our projection of the future when we design cities to accommodate heavy automobile traffic without knowing what the prevailing mode of transportation will be in 1980. Of course, by planning along certain lines we sometimes make sure that the future will conform to our current expectations. The results can be tragic. Our colleges train students for a world in which economics, international relations, and domestic politics will be as they now are. With such an orientation, isn't it likely that in these realms the world will remain as imperfect as we know it? What people regard as impossible usually turns out to be at least quite difficult. How effective a way to discourage original problem solving! Culture is a map that fulfills itself.

To see how the cultural map suppresses alternative lines of conduct take the Hopi Indians' belief in witches. Why don't the Hopi discover something so obvious to us, that witches exist solely in their own minds? We might suppose that accused witches could repeatedly prove that they didn't send an illness or cause an accident for which they are blamed. By furnishing exonerating proof of innocence once, twice, and a third time, they would throw doubt on the portion of the map specifying witchcraft. It doesn't happen. Rarely among the Hopi can anyone successfully prove his innocence of witchcraft because, as Mischa Titiev tells us, normally nobody is ever openly accused of the crime.[9] According to the Hopi map, to forthrightly recognize anyone as a witch is tantamount to inviting dreadful misfortune and even death. Obviously people don't want to bring dire consequences on themselves and so they practically never openly accuse neighbors or relatives of witchcraft. In other words, the Hopi way warns Indians to stay clear of the very behavior that might in time undermine their belief in witches. People who are suspected of malevolent witchcraft and talked about behind their backs can rarely clear themselves of suspicion because they are not directly accused. As long as the Hopi remain fairly isolated there is little danger that they will discover evidence which challenges the accuracy of their map.

But communities rarely remain perfectly isolated. In these times especially,

[8] William James, *The Principles of Psychology*, 2 vols. (New York, 1890), vol. I, p. 110.
[9] Mischa Titiev, "Notes on Hopi Witchcraft," *Papers of the Michigan Academy of Science, Arts and Letters*, 28 (1943), 549-557.

people of different faiths, conflicting traditions, and opposite beliefs brush against one another. Alternatives to behavior come up frequently and challenge cultural maps. As a result grave crises periodically confront formerly integrated, self-reliant communities in which many generations had worked out balanced and coherent views of man, nature, and the cosmos.

Fortunately, and sometimes unfortunately, cultural maps are merely highly resistant, not impervious, to change. Events march on and the inadequacy of conventional wisdom becomes exposed. Or else people repeatedly see some novelty that their theory tells them can't succeed but which easily demonstrates its efficacy. There comes a point at which the map encounters so many contradictions to its view of reality that a grave crisis is signaled. Something is seriously wrong. People no longer trust their old map because its predictions don't work as they should. Something like this happened in the United States during the great depression. Business failures, mass unemployment, and economic stagnation indicated a gravely defective economic system, one that did not behave as it was supposed to. In response the President asked Congress to originate drastic social legislation to correct the malady. Another blow to our confidence in our map came when a few U.S. prisoners of war in Korea defected. Indoctrination of some of these young men with communist ideology came as a shock that at first we tended to explain away by crediting the Chinese communists with marvellously powerful drugs. We speak of brainwashing, a metaphor that pictures the captive as passive in his captor's hands. More recently the challenge of Soviet science caused some harried worrying about whether our education system was adequately prepared for atomic- and rocket-age survival and whether we were becoming a "second best" power. But even such jolts to the map never sweep away all commitment to tradition.

UNEVENNESS, A CALL TO CHANGE

The course of change never runs smoothly. Change would be much less troublesome if every innovation promptly and evenly spread to all those people whom it concerned and if at the same time incompatible hangovers from the past were promptly shed from culture, like a ptarmigan's white coat in spring. The invention of a drastic weapon ought at once to pry officers loose from adherence to older forms of fighting and incur compatible new attitudes of responsible statesmanship. In that way the whole way of life would gracefully and quickly adjust to the new trait's challenge.

Unfortunately for us and everybody else caught in the century's maelstrom of change, change is far from even. For one thing, it takes time to adjust all parts of culture or all groups in society to an innovation. Persons insist on clinging to traditional customs, nostalgically ignoring the way they complicate the use of costly machines or interfere with rational production methods. Capital investment and other kinds of vested interest perceive strong threats in change that some groups in a social system welcome. American railroads can't afford to risk investments by experimenting with radical forms of rail transportation. In the same way I hesitate to trade in my still serviceable hi-fi speaker merely because an improved version has come along. Labor-saving devices in industry are to be expected but labor resists them when they promise lay-offs.

As a result, new and old exist side by side without matching too well. The

What evidence of uneven change in material culture can you discern in this photo? (*National Film Board of Canada.*)

airplane, telephone, and telegraph have helped to shrink the world; ever more powerful weapons constantly increase every country's vulnerability to destruction. But the old ideal of national sovereignty persists tenaciously. Nations make no headway in learning to trust one another and shrink from trusting themselves to a true international organization. What would happen to our economic well-being if we became one with the rest of the world? The threat of cheap labor and fear of a market flooded by cheap products terrify us more than the prospect of nuclear war. Take another example of uneven culture change. Health workers in underdeveloped areas are far less able or inclined to induce people to limit offspring than they are able to prompt them to swallow life-prolonging medicines and adopt higher standards of sanitation. In one year India allotted 14 million dollars for malaria control while the whole Second Five Year Plan, from 1956 to 1961, budgeted only 10 million dollars for family planning—2 million dollars a year. India is solving one grievous problem while aggravating another, namely, the pressure of population on resources.

Unevenness occurs when some people adopt modern ideas while their neighbors lag, clinging to beliefs little changed since grandfather's day. Such divergence makes for disharmony. Citizens with traditional value scorn their modern contemporaries as sinful, vain, or simply troublesome. In turn the modernists scorn the traditionalists for staying backward. On some issues—like segregation—tension between people affected unevenly by change explodes violently.

Uneven change demands further change to close the gap between the disharmonious segments of the population or the incompatible traits in culture. Unevenness presses relentlessly for measures that promise to restore harmony or integration. In this way the agitating conflicts of an age stimulate origination and encourage diffusion.

At the same time that unevenness acts as a compelling drive to further, healing change, it constitutes a drag on innovation. A population largely without formal education holds back industrialization championed by a few. American Indian schoolgirls study home economics but in substandard homes, where parents prepare traditional meals rather than meals balanced in nutrients, they can't practice all they have learned. At this point a revolution will have advantages for overcoming pronounced drag. Through a combination of aroused enthusiasm, dedicated leadership, and, perhaps, coercion everybody comes to participate intensively in change—at least for the time being. Contemporary China is a case in point. Individual shirkers and lagging culture patterns receive swift, unsympathetic attention in an effort, never fully realized, to accomplish a complete transformation of cultural materials which will affect the entire population.

FURTHER READING

Recommended general books on culture change include Homer G. Barnett, *Innovation* (New York, 1953); William F. Ogburn, *Social Change* (New York, 1950); and F. R. Allen, H. Hart, D. C. Miller, W. F. Ogburn, and M. F. Nimkoff, *Technology and Social Change* (New York, 1957). Charles J. Erasmus, *Man Takes Control* (Minneapolis, Minn., 1961) considers the dynamics of change from the goal of technical development.

Melville J. Herskovits writes on culture drift in *Man and His Works* (New York, 1948), chap. 34. A good analysis of revolutions appears in A. L. Kroeber, *Anthropology*, new ed. (New York, 1948), pp. 408-411. C. D. Tuska, *Inventors and Inventions* (New York, 1957) emphasizes the importance of creative imagination for origination. Discovery, invention, and convergence are intelligently treated in A. Goldenweiser, *Anthropology* (New York, 1937), chap. 8. The same author has written most perceptively on convergence in "The Principle of Limited Possibilities in the Development of Culture," *Journal of American Folk-Lore*, 26 (1913), 259-290. For examples of convergence see Kroeber's *Anthropology*, chap. 14. Interesting accounts exist of originations that made important contributions to human culture. See O. T. Mason, *The Origins of Inventions* (London, 1905), and Leslie Spier, "Inventions and Human Society," in H. L. Shapiro, ed., *Man, Culture and Society* (New York, 1956).

Ralph Linton, ed., *Acculturation in Seven American Indian Tribes* (New York, 1940), chaps. 8-9, offers illustrations of diffusion and reviews its principles. For further treatment of the concept see A. L. Kroeber, *Anthropology*, chap. 12-14; Clark Wissler, *Man and Culture* (New York, 1923), chap. 7; and John J. Honigmann, *The World of Man* (New York, 1959), chap. 15. In the early part of the century controversy raged over the relative significance of diffusion and invention in culture building. The arguments are briefly given in G. E. Smith, B. Malinowski, H. J. Spinden, and A. Goldenweiser, *Culture, the Diffusion Controversy* (New York, 1927).

Psychological factors underlying persistence of behavior are discussed in Gardner Murphy, *Human Potentialities* (New York, 1958), chap. 6. Franz Boas also considers conservatism in *Anthropology and Modern Life*, rev. ed. (New York, 1932), chap. 7. In the last century Edward B. Tylor analyzed some factors underlying the tendency of culture to endure through time; see his *Primitive Culture*, 3rd ed., 2 vols. (London, 1891), vol. I, chap. 3. That even drastic change may occur in conjunction with persistence is demonstrated by S. N. Eisenstadt, "Sociological Aspects of the Economic Adaptation of Oriental Immigrants in Israel. A Case Study in the Problem of Modernization," *Economic Development and Cultural Change*, 4 (1956), 269-278. The conditions under which adherence to traditional medicine weakens are described by Charles J. Erasmus, "Changing Folk Beliefs and the Relativity of Empirical Knowledge," *Southwestern Journal of Anthropology*, 8 (1952), 411-428.

Godfrey and Monica Wilson develop the concepts of uneven social and uneven culture change in *The Analysis of Social Change* (Cambridge, Eng., 1945), especially chap. 5. See also Honigmann, *The World of Man*, chap. 16. The drag of unevenness is discussed by Margaret Mead in *New Lives for Old* (New York, 1956), pp. 445-450.

Novels furnish fine perspectives for perceiving the impact of change on individuals. Some I would recommend are Oliver La Farge, *Laughing Boy* (Boston, 1929); Philip Woodruff, *Call the Next Witness* (New York, 1946); and two works with the industrialization of rural Wales as their subject, Geraint Goodwin, *The Heyday in the Blood* (London, 1936), and Richard Llewellyn, *How Green Was My Valley* (London, 1939). Two papers by anthropologists in *The Yearbook of Education—1954* (London, 1954) provide especially timely studies of modern change; they are "From Tribalism to Modern Society" by Kenneth Little and "Resistance Factors in the Transformation of African Society" by O. F. Raum.

17

Helping Change Along

Men account what is ready to hand as more precious than the chance of future possession and prefer ease to exertion. . . .

Abū 'l-Fazl (c. 1599)[1]

The science of constructing a commonwealth, or renovating it, or reforming it, is, like every other experimental science, not to be taught *a priori*. . . . that which in the first instance is prejudicial may be excellent in its remoter operation, and its excellence may arise even from the ill effects it produces in the beginning. The reverse also happens; and very plausible schemes, with very pleasing commencements, have often shameful and lamentable conclusions.

Edmund Burke (1790)[2]

FROM BIRTH CONTROL TO THE MILLENNIUM

Any social system that builds and maintains research laboratories in universities, government, and industry helps change along. A corporation management that hires consultants to redesign the business along more efficient lines isn't waiting for the slow change that comes only when somebody on occasion unravels snags in the work. So, too, when an underdeveloped nation invites foreign technical assistance in the form of experts, teachers of teachers, road builders, and big dam engineers—instead of waiting for its own citizens to venture abroad for training and then to trickle back and put their knowledge to use—the less developed country hastens change by speeding up diffusion. On the local level, in thousands of underdeveloped villages the same hurried pace is carried on through programs that aim at modernizing village life. At

[1] *Ā'īn-i Akbarī*, 3 vols., trans. H. Blockmann and H. S. Jarrett (Calcutta, 1939-1949), vol. III, p. 4.

[2] "Reflections on the Revolution in France," in R. J. S. Hoffman and P. Levack, eds., *Burke's Politics, Selected Writings and Speeches of Edmund Burke* (New York, 1949), pp. 304-305.

times, to better chances of success, these ambitious attempts at social reconstruction seek deliberately to utilize what social science knows about culture
change. More commonly, an intensely dedicated social visionary relies on his
charisma to swing followers behind his program; or a farm extension agent is
mindful only of the hybrid corn that, having been tested under experimental
conditions, he believes is bound to produce higher yields. Enthusiasm and
impatience sometimes blind these men to vested interests threatened by the
changes they propose as well as to other factors that support existing customs.
Higher yields indeed may be desired, but not flour that tastes unfamiliar or
that doesn't make good tortillas.

Popular demand makes modern governments increasingly eager to help
change along. Their enterprises range from promoting birth control to per-
suading people to dedicate themselves unselfishly to the millennium. We will
better understand what is involved in any large-scale program of directed culture change after examining a few such ventures. I propose studying three:
an attempt to engineer utopia in nineteenth-century America, contemporary
community development in South Asia, and revolutionary reeducation in
Communist China.[3]

UTOPIAS UNLIMITED

Communitarian socialism is the name given to some of the nineteenth-
century experimental communities that started up idealistically between 1840
and 1850 at the rate of one every three or four months. Few lasted more
than about three years. The decade's enthusiasm for utopias is a bit hard to
understand because similar ventures during preceding decades had met no
spectacular success. But perhaps that is exactly why idealistic communitarians
persisted. Failure only made them more intent to demonstrate that their designs to perfect society could work. Once this demonstration was made, they
felt that other people would hardly be able to resist adopting the model.

Robert Owen was one of the earlier communitarians. An Englishman of
great humanitarian sympathies he started his career as a cotton manufacturer.
Idealism led him to form a profit-sharing community of mill workers. He
formulated a still more ambitious scheme to end economic inequality, the
basis of which would be workers established in small, self-supporting communities. But a Parliamentary committee showed disappointingly little interest when Owen stood before it to propose his idea. Thereupon he behaved
as dedicated men often do when an idea to which they are intensely committed is rejected or fails to work. He became more convinced than ever that a
new world could be planned with almost the same mechanical perfection as
manufacturing plants and railroads in early nineteenth-century Britain.

[3] I have relegated many sources to the end of the chapter.

Owen became a propagandist. Like the French philosopher, Rousseau, he declared that bad cultural practices, particularly in the field of education, had perverted mankind's innate goodness. Fortunately, culture was man-made. Therefore, it could be improved substantially and permanently through application of human reason. Europe, however, was not a suitable place to make a fresh start. Owen saw more hope across the Atlantic and in 1825 he sailed for the United States to put his ideas into practice. His plan called for a self-governing, economically self-sufficient community made up of one or two thousand dedicated persons. Members would produce all they needed without landlords, middlemen, or capitalists to absorb any profit. Free of these exploiters of human labor, each man would need to work only three hours daily. The newly designed social system would also get rid of money. One hour's worth of labor would be the only unit of exchange. With each man's roughly equal capacity to work everyone would be truly equal.

Owen realized he might have trouble creating an ideal community out of people drawn from a considerably less perfect way of life. Therefore, in the fashion of many revolutionary programs, he gave much thought to improving future generations of members through better forms of child rearing. Years before he had written, "It may be stated that the whole success of these arrangements will depend upon the manner in which the infants and children shall be trained and educated. . . . Men are and ever will be, what they are and shall be made in infancy and childhood."[4] As one measure to prevent children from being contaminated by their parents he proposed that after the age of three every child be raised apart from his parents and communally by specially selected educators and nurses. "Scientific" upbringing in a planned environment would bring out the intrinsic goodness in human nature which improper social arrangements had so long suppressed and distorted. Marriage, anyhow, he regarded as a "monstrous evil" comparable to the selfishness inherent in the custom of private property. His "new view of society" also rejected traditional religion. From the age of 10 Owen had been captured by the deist tradition to which men like Voltaire, Rousseau, Benjamin Franklin, and Thomas Jefferson belonged. He wanted a religion that accepted only facts and nothing opposed to evidence given by human senses. New Harmony, the name of the community which he founded on the banks of the Wabash River, proclaimed freedom of religion to such a degree that everyone could preach, even lecturers who wanted the pulpit to talk on secular topics.

In western Indiana Owen purchased the property of a fairly prosperous, religiously oriented, socialist community. There he tried to launch the utopian model which, as soon as its advantages were demonstrated, would irresistably impel a good part of the world to change its manner of living. A number of

---

[4] Robert Owen, *A New View of Society and Other Writings*, Everyman's Library Edition (London, 1927), p. 280.

historians have reconstructed the story of his struggle to realize utopia. Suffice to say, New Harmony, like earlier and later ventures in utopia, failed. Quarrels led to defection. Contrary to rules, members began to speculate in private property and to distill alcohol. In two years disillusion reached such a point that a mock funeral was held to celebrate the social system's demise and the loss of $200,000 of Owen's own money. A stranger driving through this beautiful town today, where some of the founders' descendants still live, would not easily guess that here Americans and Englishmen in a small way undertook to usher in the communist age. The failure of these idealistic pioneers warns us about some of the hurdles that deliberately planned culture change must surmount.

IMPERFECT MEN AND THE PERFECT SOCIETY

Want of morale was the basic difficulty Robert Owen's community faced. It is a danger that all social systems try to avoid but one especially grievous in a community of pioneers where men must work hard. Pioneers can't afford to be apathetic. The settlers in New Harmony had suffered poverty in the industrial cities along the eastern seaboard but that didn't make them dedicated to the idealistic principles which the community was supposed to practice. Hard work held no attraction as long as it was less to benefit themselves than their children. Owen's conviction was not contagious; it didn't propagate and heighten enthusiasm. He employed as little propaganda as coercion. Compulsion, in fact, ran contrary to Owen's ideals. Later we will see how modern nations engaged in wholesale cultural transformation counteract the danger of diluted effort and deal with man's all too slight capacity for long-term self-sacrifice.

Trouble along the Wabash also came because Owen's plan was too vague and general, omitting much that was necessary. For example, he threw New Harmony open to anyone, regardless of skills. But the community needed a variety of skilled craftsmen if it was to produce goods self-sufficiently. Members with such skills came hardly at all; they were doing pretty well in the cities. Not only had the leader overlooked selecting the kind of people he needed in order to achieve his ideal of self-sufficiency, his leadership ability lacked even more. He devoted too much time traveling around the country talking about the new society and not enough to directing affairs in the group itself. His son wasn't equal to the task of management. Furthermore, some members of New Harmony didn't allow that managers had any right to give directions; wasn't this an experiment to show that all men were equal?

One handicap plagued this and all utopian and revolutionary programs. The people on whom the movement depended came from a far more imperfect society than the one they were supposed to create. The members of New

Harmony enjoyed free children's nurseries and other privileges but they didn't clamor to be made more nearly perfect. Whether perfection would really have come from following Owen doesn't matter. Men's reluctance to change radically the sentiments and goals in which they have been socialized must slow down the birth of a new society. In Herbert Spencer's words: "The machinery of Communism, like existing social machinery, has to be framed out of existing human nature; and the defects of existing human nature will generate in the one the same evils as in the other. The love of power, the selfishness, the injustice, the untruthfulness, which often in comparatively short times bring private organizations to disaster, will inevitably, where their effects accumulate from generation to generation, work evils far greater and less remediable; since, vast and complex and possessed of all the resources, the administrative organization, once developed and consolidated, must become irresistible."[5] A rare visionary who transcends the limits of his time and sees the prospect of a vastly different future isn't enough to overcome the force of cultural momentum. Most men don't heed the standard of perfection set by Christ or Gandhi; they can't or won't rise above their traditional, mediocre standard of excellence. In other words, a new culture must be built on the old. For that very reason it can't shake off the past as wholeheartedly as idealists and radicals would like. The past limits the goals of the bravest revolution at many points; it even limits the genius of the leader, however superb may be his hereditary endowment.

Not only does the past through its influence in the present limit the future but the social system whose life is to be perfected exists in a society containing other communities. Like many communitarians, Owen preferred isolation so that he could construct his model with a minimum of contamination. He even wanted self-government. But already in the early nineteenth century, the Midwest provided no real isolation. Revolutionary regimes often seek this protection from contamination by restricting their citizens' contacts with foreigners. Other countries, fearing that their nationals might be contaminated, are often glad to oblige and in turn forbid their citizens to visit the experiment under way. But Owen couldn't close his frontiers. The lack of sympathy with which other Americans regarded New Harmony didn't help to bolster members' confidence in the group's utopian goal. Furthermore, the world's industrial proletariat, whom Owen and other communitarian socialists wished to help, found other ways of improving their lives. Urban workers realized how little they shared in the prosperity which they helped to create. They were eager to secure a larger share of the growing factory product. Eventually, through labor unions and legislation to protect their rights, they did succeed in gaining power and a higher standard of living.

Owen would have liked a community in which everyone saw things as he

---

[5] Herbert Spencer, *The Man Versus the State* (London, 1884), p. 41.

did, a social system with complete "harmony" and no rebellion. Here he was unrealistic. A social system is of necessity made up of different individuals who will never think alike on all issues. A successful community recognizes this and works to balance and integrate different interest and viewpoints, not to abolish them.

WHY NOT SEX?

Again and again after New Harmony failed Americans tried to create little communities that would demonstrate ideal schemes of life. Some, like the Oneida "love colony," combined economic and sexual communism. The founder, John Humphrey Noyes, couldn't tolerate organized Christianity for what it had done to Christ's Gospel. In Oneida he proposed to implement Christ's doctrine of love. The emphasis Oneidans placed on intimate criticism of one member by another foreshadows a similar device recently launched in revolutionary China. Like the Chinese, Noyes believed that progress would be hastened by changing men's hearts not merely their social environment.

Oneida's greatest renown came from its founder's views on sex. Mankind controlled so much, Noyes observed, why not sex too and thereby spare women from the inconvenience and pain of frequent confinements. Let men control their voluntary movements in coitus so as to stop short of the final orgasm. This would make sex an act of communion more often than of propagation. It would raise sex from the brute level to the point of "amative" art. Women and their children in the Oneida community belonged to everyone. Noyes' sexual communism gave women equal rights beyond even those that Israeli kibbutzim strain for. Once again outside criticism proved more powerful than the founder's ideals and in the end economic and sexual communism gave ground in Oneida.

None of America's nineteenth-century social experiments demonstrated merit enough to inspire wide emulation. Today the world has generally given up looking for a better way through small, deliberately planned, almost self-sufficient utopias. A few idealistic communities, however, continue to operate. Idealism about improving culture survives. But today we plan for cultural transformation on a much bigger scale. Our plans call for bringing millions of people almost simultaneously into the orbit of health, prosperity, and general happiness. Are we succeeding?

RICHER LIVES FOR MILLIONS

In 1952 the largest country of South Asia, India, enlisted rural people in community development in order to raise their standard of living. Shortly thereafter India's neighbor, Pakistan, followed suit with a Village-AID program similarly dedicated to creating a richer and higher life for millions of rural men, women, and children. Many other underdeveloped countries after the second world war adopted community development as the most practical means of directed culture change.

The term, community development, has no very specific meaning. In most cases it refers to an idealistically dedicated, multipurpose drive to bring rapid progress in many areas of life. Improvement is sought simultaneously in agriculture, animal husbandry, sanitation, health, child care, education, literacy, transportation, and rural credit. In Pakistan and India the basic aim is to increase agricultural output and income in the villages, home of 85 percent of the population. An integral object of community development is to enlist the peasants themselves in planning. Culture change, developers believe, is only effective when it works at the grass-roots level with people's own felt needs. Morale will be highest when a community participates actively in solving its difficulties. However, sometimes—and here we uncover a contradiction in the idealistic philosophy of community development—it becomes necessary to help villagers discover what their "true" felt needs are.

In Pakistan and India community development hopes to popularize a spirit of self-help in place of villagers' too great passive reliance on government.[6] To arouse such a spirit and at the same time act as a guide in planning and solving problems an agent-on-the-spot takes charge of a number of villages. This young man, or, more rarely, woman, has been trained to

A village worker in Pakistan vaccinating a peasant's hens.

know something about farming, health, credit, and all the other areas of life where the national planners hope to effect improvements. In addition his training is enhanced by his social skills to work with people and promote village team work. Naturally, some village-level workers have greater social skill than others; a year or so of training isn't enough to develop expertness in half-a-dozen or more fields.

Roots of the world-wide community development movement lie partly in the United States, specifically in the U.S. Agricultural Extension Service. A

[6] Pakistan in 1961 introduced substantial modifications in this program. My description refers to the period up to that year. I also ignore the Indian National Extension Services, a more restricted attempt to promote agricultural development.

village-level worker is in some respects equivalent to the county farm agent. Experts of the Extension Service, along with rural sociologists and anthropologists, gave much advice when community development was first instituted in India and Pakistan. They also helped train the hundreds of village workers who are now in service. President Truman's famous Point Four speech in 1949 spurred strong support of such ventures abroad. Thin though it is, a basic idea links community development with nineteenth-century American communitarianism. Both movements spend major effort on small groups, like villages. Members are encouraged to work together for the common good. Community development, however, is a vaster enterprise. It is marked by efficient and detailed planning. A highly rational, bureaucratic organization coordinates programs in hundreds of villages. In South Asia blocks of 100 or 150 villages are demarcated. Each block is under an area officer's control. He in turn coordinates a number of village-level workers. Area officers bring technical specialists—veterinarians, agricultural technicians, and engineers, for example—into contact with a village that requires expert help to solve a specific problem.

Community development relies heavily on the trained village-level worker. He is supposed to be a catalyst of change, an educator in the broadest sense of the term. Sometimes he teaches through demonstration. He shows the concrete results that can be obtained through improved seed, new agricultural implements, and modern methods of plant protection. He propagates improved techniques of farming and land reclamation. He gives advice on poultry raising, drainage, and chlorination of wells. To the small proportion of peasants who can read he distributes literature. Evenings he shows films. He is also an organizer. He helps a village set up the social apparatus necessary for undertaking community-wide tasks. He arranges for exhibitions, classes to promote adult literacy (they are taught by a village schoolmaster), youth groups (modeled after 4-H clubs in the United States), and community centers. In emergencies he gives first aid and regularly he assists in mass innoculations of men and beasts. His home is a depot where the farmer calls when he is ready to try new seed or chemical fertilizer. Here the worker also keeps his demonstration implements, pedigree birds, and a breed bull. The catalyst of change has plenty of paper work. He must collect information about how development is progressing in his villages and report the facts to his chief, the area officer. From here reports go to higher centers which follow progress being made over the whole nation. India in addition has an independent body, not itself part of the community development organization, to evaluate results being obtained.

FOR THE FIRST TIME IN HISTORY

"We must embark on a bold new program for making the benefits of our scientific advances and industrial progress available for the improvement and growth of under-developed areas.

"More than half the people of the world are living in conditions approaching misery. Their food is inadequate. They are victims of disease. Their economic life is primitive and stagnant. Their poverty is a handicap and a threat both to them and to more prosperous areas.

"For the first time in history, humanity possesses the knowledge and the skill to relieve the suffering of these people."

Harry S. Truman

The New York Times, January 21, 1949.

COMMUNITY DEVELOPMENT IN ACTION

A case study will show community development at work. The citizens of Mukatpur, a small north Indian village, were troubled by a pond which during the rainy season overflowed so much that water filled the land and reached the houses.[7] "To get to the fields the owner has to wade nearly to his waist," a villager complained. "Children are always in danger of going under. It is like living in death, during the rains." In these words the village revealed a felt need.

Other ponds located in different quarters of the village also flooded and some years back the water had washed away two mudbrick houses. The hardship started 20 years before when a road and canal had been built in such a manner that they blocked the land's natural drainage into a nearby river. Deprived of its outlet, water now simply backed up and caused local floods. The villagers felt helpless to overcome their plight.

Community development officials proposed a solution. A surveyor would come, they told the villagers, and measure the land to find a slope that could serve as a drainage outlet. "Then ditches will have to be dug. With earth from the ditches, village lanes can be filled up to a higher level. If done as a whole, everyone in the village will gain." Were the men willing to do the digging so as to make their village more comfortable and safer? Mild protest greeted this question. Could not the government bring in powerful earth-moving machinery to do the heavy work? The officials replied that machines could not be spared from where they were opening up new agricultural lands needed to grow more food. Increasing the output of food grains must take priority; other-

[7] Albert Mayer and Associates, *Pilot Project, India* (Berkeley, Calif., 1958), pp. 178-181.

wise the country would have to spend precious funds abroad for food instead of for more basic goods. "When we can produce all the food needed . . . we will be able to buy the new machines and equipment which we need to build our country." Convinced, the villagers agreed to do the digging and move the earth.

If India and Pakistan succeed in helping change along, then many villagers will no longer draw water from unsanitary open wells; village lanes will not become bogs in monsoon weather; farmers will have all-weather roads over which to drive their ox-carts to the fields or market; animals will be healthier and will yield more milk and eggs; people will be healthier, not chronically incapacitated from malaria and other endemic illnesses; peasants will be able to read bulletins that report new developments in agriculture; they will have higher regard for education and send their sons and daughters to school more readily; fields of maize, sugarcane, and wheat will yield more; families will eat better; and additional grain will pour into the market to feed the growing cities.

These goals don't sound to us like the traits of utopia; they are hardly extraordinary when we read them in our technically developed, affluent United States. However, in the context of an underdeveloped social system they assume a different significance and it is in this context that they must be understood. Is community development achieving these goals in South Asia? Are increased output, income, and amenities indeed transforming the village communities of Pakistan and India? Whatever the answer may be, we expect that these experiments in community development will enlighten us, as utopian socialism did, concerning the prospects of deliberately changing culture.

THE MODERN HERESY

Community development is a relatively new approach and the movement in Pakistan and India is still learning from its experiences. The effectiveness of community development will not be fully apparent for a number of years. To date the programs have unquestionably spurred certain changes: rural folk have improved many miles of village lanes, graded approach roads to their villages, drained off rainwater from points where it collected, sprayed houses and ponds against malarial mosquitoes, and increased their use of improved seed and commercial fertilizer. Other changes which the planners hoped for came much more slowly or not at all. Farmers made little attempt to reclaim land for cultivation, build latrines, or construct new schools that the government would then take over and operate. Rather few illiterates enrolled in adult education classes. New implements for agriculture have been adopted very slowly, partly because cultivators lack capital with which to buy them.

DIRECTED CHANGE TAKES HOLD

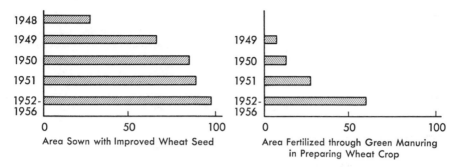

These graphs show the sometimes rapid and sometimes slow way in which Indian farmers adopt new agricultural traits. These changes took place in a district in North India where in 1948 a pilot project in peasant development began. This pilot project became the prototype for India's community development program.

Albert Mayer and Associates, *Pilot Project, India* (Berkeley, Calif., 1958), p. 246.

The villagers' selectivity in the changes they make indicates that they do not see their needs precisely the same way community development officials do. Even with respect to relatively popular changes, like adopting improved seed, all eligible peasants don't respond. In one evaluation study a quarter of the farmers remained unconvinced about the alleged superiority of the seed they were offered, lacked financial resources to buy it, found the seed to be unavailable after they called at the depot, or hesitated because they believed they lacked proper irrigation facilities for the experiment.

Far more serious has been the slow pace with which rural people acknowledged that they could help themselves to a better future. Initial enthusiasm often runs high but then popular participation in village projects falls off. Community development, of course, attaches the greatest importance to self-reliance and popular initiative, that is, to people themselves implementing their own desires for a better life. Remember that Robert Owen's dream of a new society foundered because the members of New Harmony were too little committed to the goal he held out. The members of his colony saw no point in working hard and sacrificing for future gains. That is just what community development inevitably entails. In part, South Asian villagers' reluctance to devote themselves to a future they hope will be different from the life they know stems from their deep-seated willingness to follow a traditional style of life despite undeniable difficulties which it contains. Although they complain about their difficulties, the cost of change outweighs the significance of any

MEASURING AGRICULTURAL DEVELOPMENT IN INDIA

Items	Proportion of Households Adopting Improvements to All Farm Households Sampled in Villages where Items were sponsored.	
	1954	1957
Seeds	48%	67%
Fertilizers (other than farmyard manure)	42	65
Methods of cultivation	29	57
Farms adopting two or more recommended items:		
Seeds and fertilizers	31	50
Seeds and methods of cultivation	22	44
Fertilizers and methods of cultivation	19	43
Seeds, fertilizers, and methods of cultivation	16	35

The slow pace of diffusion is indicated by these figures, especially figures on the combined adoption of two or three items. Remember, a farm adopting two or more items is likely to get a higher yield than would be obtained from single adoptions.

Evaluation Reports on Working of Community Development and N.E.S. Blocks, Programme Evaluation Organisation of the Planning Commission of the Government of India, 1958, p. 89.

results they expect for themselves and future generations.

Development officials, on the other hand, are heavily imbued with a western outlook. They are patriotically impatient for standards of comfort like those they have read about or seen during an educational tour in the United States. They have little sympathy for popular adherence to tradition and in fact don't wholly understand their own rural folk. Indeed, one part of the peasant is convinced that he should strive for such self-evident values as better health, improved physical amenities, and higher agricultural output. At the same time he hesitates to put forth the effort. Occasionally objections become a bit more coherent, as in this conversation which Santha Rama Rau overheard between an American girl and a Balinese young man. The latter is talking:

". . . even if the white man is prepared to relinquish other superiorities, he still feels that his 'way of living' is better, and he will force or cajole us into learning it. . . ."

"Don't you," Clare asked uncertainly, "need technology, medicine—?"

"Don't you," Anak Agun Anâm said, "think of anything besides making your bodies more comfortable?"[8]

He voiced quite frankly the great modern heresy.

[8] Santha Rama Rau, *East of Home* (New York, 1950), p. 292.

THE RICH GROW RICHER, THE CONTENTED DISCONTENTED

Two nearly irresolvable paradoxes face community development. Among the goals most readily accepted in rural Pakistan and India are those which benefit the farmer. But even agricultural development spreads unevenly through the village social system. Productive new methods appeal most strongly to the relatively sophisticated peasant. He being most prosperous can also best afford to adopt them. He is eager to buy improved seed and other agricultural improvements and is hungry for credit. He knows that these things will help him to raise his production to higher levels and so further increase his prosperity. The poor peasant, who would benefit much more if his income were even slightly raised, has trouble obtaining credit because he has no security. He can't buy much of the new seed or fertilizer. His limited land won't allow him to experiment with new ways of cultivation or new crops. He needs every square meter of ground for food crops which his family will eat or which he will sell in order to buy tea, sugar, and cloth. The village contains more than just farmers. Community development has more to offer the farmer to increase his standard of living than it has for rural craftsmen or laborers. As a result, the more community development succeeds in the sphere of agriculture the richer do the already well-to-do become. The poor, relatively speaking, become poorer. India and Pakistan are resolved not to unravel this paradox in the manner of some Communist countries, by eliminating more well-to-do villagers or kulaks.

Another paradox besets community development. Such movements can succeed only if they increase dissatisfaction, constantly raising new unsatisfied wants. If development is going to continue it can do so only through fresh needs continuously rising in place of those which people just managed to overcome. In one economist's words, "As a society becomes increasingly affluent, wants are created by the process by which they are satisfied."[9] The degree to which people are content, therefore, limits their ability to adopt measures recommended by community planners. Yet higher contentment is the goal of development!

It may be that democratic self-planning is not calculated to work well in small-scale, largely illiterate villages. An alternative proposal calls for more planning from on top. This approach, some anthropologists believe, is likely to be extremely disorganizing to the integrated village community. It foolishly neglects the age-old wisdom which villagers themselves gained through their own experience in a given locale. Nobody outside of that locale and apart from the local tradition will be able to plan change as well as the community itself.

Development in India and Pakistan is far from limited to villages. Reclaim-

[9] John Kenneth Galbraith, *The Affluent Society* (Boston, 1958), p. 158.

ing land, irrigation and power schemes, and industrialization are other fronts on which these lands are attacking poverty. Community development in the villages, where food and raw stuffs originate, is vital to back up or fulfill the promise inherent in these other drives. Yet a judicial appraisal of progress on all fronts in South Asia and elsewhere, leaves Gunnar Myrdal quite pessimistic: ". . . it is impossible to end with any other conclusion than that, short of a number of near-miracles, few underdeveloped countries will succeed in attaining their essential goals. The alternative to reasonable success is political catastrophe."[10]

REVOLUTIONARY REEDUCATION

"The institutions of our forefathers, erroneous as they are, must not be handled with violence, or rudely touched," said Robert Owen. "None must suffer in *person, property,* or *comfort;* all will be soon reconciled to the change . . ."[11] We know that the utopian social system he hoped for failed before it was scarcely born. Almost a hundred years later more mighty efforts began to be made to establish the proper conditions for communism. In the on-going Chinese experiment to promote this end we can observe efforts to secure commitment and maintain morale far removed from Owen's beatific confidence in the inevitable triumph of utopia. These efforts diverge radically from the approach of community development, which relies on enlisting people's voluntary cooperation.

Communitarian socialism and community development both emphasize altering the environment as the primary step in producing a better world. Get rid of private possessions in goods or wives, increase literacy, provide the peasant with better tools and seeds, make these and other repairs and social problems will be overcome. For God made man good. Only the social system is imperfect. It is unequipped to utilize human nature properly. This belief belongs to the romantic faith of the nineteenth century more than to the psychoanalytically indoctrinated twentieth century. Evidence in hand casts serious doubt on the efficacy of such a piecemeal approach to culture change. In plain words, social engineering hasn't worked as the theory says it should. Of course, it may be that we simply haven't yet learned to alter the environment skillfully enough. Today in the struggle to achieve substantial cultural change, one of the largest social systems in the world, Communist China, is applying a philosophy which candidly recognizes human evil. An evil civilization, such as China sees herself upheaving, is rooted in man's evil proclivities. To transform civilization not only external conditions need to be altered but also the internal condition of man as he has developed up to now.

[10] Gunnar Myrdal, *An International Economy* (New York, 1956), p. 314.
[11] Owen, *op. cit.,* pp. 243-244.

To help change along in China an attempt is made to reach directly into citizens' motivational life. The Chinese revolution seeks to convert people wholeheartedly to a new view of society. It tries to convince them from within that they ought to work harder toward the future. Such a method harmonizes quite well with the traditional Chinese ideal holding compulsion to be a poor alternative to moral virtue firmly instilled in human beings. Law is a bad substitute for conscience. The term "brain-washing" to describe this method of deliberate culture change grossly exaggerates its power. "Thought control" and similar terms are bitter designations likely to mislead us from the start in understanding Chinese culture. I prefer a neutral term like "revolutionary reeducation" for the process of thoroughly reorganizing an individual's whole outlook, including how he remembers the past, how he thinks of himself and his era in the present, and how he conceives of the future. Revolutionary re-education involves much more than transmission of economic and other factual knowledge. As in intensive psychotherapy, feelings—especially guilt—are deliberately aroused in order to promote the kind of basic change which is more familiar in religion than in politics. Only out of reoriented thought and feeling can a new society come. The Chinese planners view people's general reluctance to break with tradition more seriously than does community development. The Chinese realistically assume that it is a big job to deflect the course of cultural momentum.

CONVERTING AMERICAN PRISONERS

Reeducation in the outlook of the Communist revolution occurs in at least two situations: in prison and in groups like offices, communes, factories, and schools. It would be well to discuss these situations separately because different psychological dynamics operate in each.

In prison great stress accompanies revolutionary reeducation; the prisoner, whether foreign or Chinese, is under restraint and threat and feels apprehensive. Yet the aim in education is reformatory not punitive, even though it relies partially on the prisoner's apprehensiveness to achieve its aim. The prisoner's thoughts and feelings must be brought into harmony with the new social system whose ideals he transgressed. He must be convinced that his previous conduct was morally wrong. Persuasion is used to get him to admit his evil both to himself and others. There must be a true confession, that is, his confession must involve actual conviction and regret; merely to acknowledge wrongdoing verbally won't do. To achieve radical character reform the prisoner is first instructed in the Marxist-Leninist principles on which the new culture is founded. These principles, which he may hear for the first time in jail, are supposed to guide him in reinterpreting his previous conduct. The teacher also endeavors to make his pupil feel guilty about his past con-

BASIC REFORM IS ESSENTIAL

"Religious reform is essential because the traditional forms of education, political oratory, literature, and religious ceremonies have conditioned the attitudes, feelings, preferences, and spontaneous reactions of men to the old ideology. Consequently, even if one's scientific and philosophic intelligence puts old doctrines behind one, one's emotions, feelings, and habits, and even one's conscience, carry them on. It is precisely for this reason that religious conversion, as well as education, is necessary in society."

F. S. C. Northrop, *The Meeting of East and West* (New York, 1946), p. 482. By permission of the Macmillan Company.

duct. Genuine guilt, of course, is painful and adds to the prisoner's load of stress. Guilt, being painful, gives the prisoner an incentive to confess. The instructor promises additional rewards for true confession, like more favorable treatment or even release. Substantial benefits are faithfully demonstrated as each sign of ideological reform appears. The teacher becomes more accepting of the prisoner or manages to transfer him to better quarters. Such rewards are counted on to flood the man with relief and gratitude which, in turn, will inspire him to cooperate by revising his sentiments even further.

We have a frank, intimate personal document that reveals how two young U.S. citizens in a Chinese prison reviewed their earlier conduct and came to see its ignoble aspects.[12] Allyn Rickett and his wife, Adele, came to China in 1948 as Fulbright scholars. Rick had been asked by the U.S. Office of Naval Intelligence to keep his eyes open and report back to them on his return. Flattered with this responsibility, Rick agreed. The Ricketts also transmitted information out of Peiping once the Communist army occupied the city. For this activity Rick was arrested in July, 1951. Lodged in a jail reserved for counterrevolutionaries and spies, he was warned that if he broke discipline or lied to his interrogators he would be handcuffed and put in ankle chains. Should he fail to confess he would be tried and very probably shot. He was locked in a cell with Chinese prisoners, including a group leader who added his efforts to those of the security police to prompt Rick's confession. "I soon found out that the People's Government was not what I had expected," Rick wrote in 1957, after he had returned home. "They patiently explained to me that there was no need for me to die. I had committed too many crimes for them to be overlooked, it is true, but the People's Government was not out for revenge. If I were willing to change and become really a good and honest citizen, I too would be able to enjoy a happy life in the future."

[12] Allyn Rickett and Adele Rickett, *Prisoners of Liberation* (New York, 1957).

Without being really convinced of having committed any crime, Rick confessed. Immediately his cell mates warmed to him and he in turn grew more attached to them. Several weeks went by and he was transferred to a new cell with new companions where the same process of persuasion started afresh. The prisoners lodged together joined a study program in Marxism. They were encouraged to practice serious self-criticism, a task Rick found very painful because "I was not a criminal and they had no right to ask me, an American, to reform." He discovered quickly that he would not be allowed merely to parrot self-criticism but had to come to a "true realization" of himself and of what he had done. The alternative was grim; if he failed to confess and to reform, he would be tried by a military court. This court would in all likelihood condemn him to death or life imprisonment. Complete, genuine confession, on the other hand, assured leniency. Rick's awareness grew. He saw the gulf that had always divided him, an expert on China, from the Chinese people. But moral guilt came much more slowly.

Meanwhile the police also arrested Adele and made the same threat of handcuffs and ankle chains if she withheld confession. The officials actually handcuffed her when she insisted she knew nothing about espionage activities. The police quickly freed her from shackles when she decided to tell them more about her work. "I finally came to the conclusion that they would certainly force the facts out of me sooner or later if they applied torture." Note her anxiety (so far without basis). This stressful emotion helped motivate her decision to cooperate. When she confessed that she had given information to U.S. agents she took the first step toward what she describes as "total confession." From then on "I began to try to look at our actions from the standpoint of the Chinese." However, like Rick she still remained unconvinced of moral guilt and hence without true contrition.

The very ambiguity of their situation at this point suggested some kind of further cooperation. Adele and Rick really didn't know just when they could consider themselves to have been successfully reformed. How would they prove to the authorities that they had become convinced of their moral guilt? Slowly, though, the demanded degree of emotional insight came. For example, when Adele told her cell mates that she, unlike many Americans, was not racially prejudiced she also let slip her opinion that American Negroes would probably rather be white than Negro. Her companions made her realize that this belief in itself constituted an attitude of superiority. "It seemed as if everything I had always taken for granted as right was being turned upside down," including her attitude toward U.S. foreign relations. She began to worry about how she would fit into the U.S. on her return. Rick had the same anxiety when he questioned the "very foundations" of his character and discovered "the fallacy in my supposition that my espionage activities had been of service to my country. Actually, by contributing to the widening gulf between our people and the Chinese, I had been doing the United States a great disservice." Notice how, through reinterpretation, the past assumed new meaning.

In 1955 the Rickets were released separately and taken to Hong Kong on the first lap of the journey home. Reporters sneered when Adele told them that she had been justifiably arrested. An American newspaper wrote that "her mind has been twisted out of recognition." At San Francisco Navy doctors studied her body for scars. The Ricketts' convictions did not disappear back home but were strengthened and further reinterpreted. "The Christian commandment 'Love thy neighbor as thyself' and the concept that one must find his own happiness in that of the common good provide for us the only possible way to live."

IDEALISTIC CELL SESSIONS

Outside of prison revolutionary reeducation is less laden with stress. A school or factory is divided into small cells of six or seven persons. Members of a cell meet regularly to discuss revolutionary ideals. They must reveal whenever they cannot agree with those ideals or don't understand them. The objects of cell sessions are two: first, to bring members' thinking into line with revolutionary principles and, second, to keep it there. Again, genuine commitment alone suffices.

A number of factors work together in the cells to instill new convictions and sustain members' morale. The group's official nature is important along with the fact that each cell leader represents authority. He is known to report regularly to higher centers. Various kinds of social pressure also operate. For example, reason is employed to convince a doubter. Ridicule and sarcasm are still more potent. University professors in a cell find themselves confronted with their past statements or previous activities. They are challenged to admit their mistakes, to prove that they retain no shadow of doubt. To refuse may cost them their jobs. Cell members don't just listen to lectures. They criticize one another in terms of the very principles they are being taught. This gives everybody a chance to use what he has learned and so make it a firm part of himself. The idealism pervading cell sessions further contributes to the effectiveness of reeducation and so does the small group's intimacy. Each member knows the others and, what is more, learns to care about their opinions of him. Dissembling is easily spotted. Periodically, ritual expression of the new regime's values helps to lodge them firmly in place. Such ritual occurs, for example, when all China and each cell go on a Hate America or world peace campaign. Underlying all these factors at work in the cells is the profound disillusion and outright disgust that many thoughtful Chinese honestly feel for their former government. These sentiments at least free them from any nostalgic longing for the past regime.

THE NARROWING CIRCLE OF CHOICE

To evaluate reeducation in Communist China is more difficult than estimating the success of community development in South Asia. Not only are the results far from complete, but information about what is actually happening is hard to obtain. Nevertheless, testimony given by people like the Ricketts and U.S. prisoners of war indicates that conversion to new values and to new ways of seeing one's conduct does take place. What we know about social psychology and psychoanalytic psychiatry makes it quite plausible that such painstaking efforts to direct culture change at the level of the individual's motivation should succeed.

Intensive reeducation is the Chinese response to the problem of arousing conviction and sustaining morale. This difficulty, remember, contributed to the collapse of New Harmony. In India and Pakistan community development also runs into trouble trying, in accordance with its basic goal, to convince villagers that they are in large measure responsible for their own welfare. The degree to which almost clinical methods of reeducation will encourage the Chinese to dedicate themselves wholeheartedly to a new way of life is something we don't know yet. Reeducation is difficult for certain types of people, like scientists, professors, and former merchants. They are hardest to reorient, perhaps because their training and experience have left them deeply skeptical. Also they are inquiring people, broad in scale, with many windows open on the world. No doubt it is hard to convince such people of the indispensability and perfection of any one political or religious doctrine.

What about evaluating revolutionary reeducation in moral terms? We must of necessity apply our own cultural values in making a moral judgment of what the Communists are doing. Such a perspective, of course, is culture-bound. Once we adopt it we cease to regard behavior in its cultural context. But moral evaluation may well enrich our understanding of revolutionary reeducation by indicating some of its limitations. As Americans we normally tolerate propaganda, persuasion, and even education only as long as they ineffectually or only partially control human behavior.[13] An element of freedom or choice is indispensable to us in such matters. We tend to rebel when we are forced to hear advertising messages as a captive audience. We fear too adept hidden persuaders. We resent having to accept anybody's opinion. Subjectively speaking, all these things restrict our area of choice too severely

[13] B. F. Skinner, "Freedom and the Control of Men," *Perspectives, U.S.A.*, no. 15, (1956), 104-121.

and deprive us of freedom. Our standards, in other words, won't allow us to admit that too coercive or too skillful attempts deliberately to remodel human lives are ethical. They are unethical even if their goal is one that the majority wants.

Of course we are inconsistent in holding to this value. The standard itself confronts us with a dilemma as we regard the future. Very likely social science will enable man to increase his managerial, educational, and persuasive skills. Never with perfect predictability, but more and more we shall be in a position to direct culture change confidently. If we are to benefit from social science as we have benefited from physical science, won't we have to control human behavior increasingly, more and more restricting the area of free choice? As a matter of fact, isn't our freedom today already more restricted than it was a hundred years ago? What then—and this is a basic moral question posed not only by revolutionary reeducation but by every step of man's growing ability to direct culture change—should be the proper scope of the area in which choice is allowed? Or does that area, and with it our concept of freedom, vary in scope from one time to another?

If the area of freedom is variable, then how much further are we willing to have it restricted for ourselves and others? Or how much of our growing skill to direct culture change are we willing to sacrifice in order to preserve a measure of freedom?

FURTHER READING

Literature about directed culture change is still mostly narrative or confined to analysis of particular instances, like those in this chapter. Notable exceptions are Margaret Mead, ed., *Cultural Patterns and Technical Change* (Paris, 1953), and Charles J. Erasmus, *Man Takes Control* (Minneapolis, Minn., 1961). Quite a different approach is advocated in Laura Thompson, *Towards a Science of Mankind* (New York, 1961). Several articles in *The Yearbook of Education—1954* (London, 1954) reveal keen thinking on the dilemmas and problems posed in directed change, especially F. S. C. Northrop, "Moral and Ethical Implications, a Western View"; P. C. C. Evans, "Cultural Patterns and Technological Change"; and E. R. Leach, "Educational Incentives in the Field of Technical Assistance." A particularly thought-provoking book is Germaine Tillion, *Algeria, the Realities,* trans. Ronald Matthews (London, 1958). Two casebooks in directed culture change are Edward H. Spicer, ed., *Human Problems in Technological Change* (New York, 1952) and Benjamin D. Paul, ed., *Health, Culture and Community* (New York, 1955).

Writings on communitarian socialism are mainly descriptive. I have used A. E. Bestor, Jr., *Backwoods Utopias* (Philadelphia, 1950); Edmund Wilson, *To the Finland Station* (New York, 1940), pt. II; Everett Webber, *Escape to Utopia* (New York, 1959); V. F. Calverton, *Where Angels Dared to Tread* (Indianapolis, Ind., 1941), chap. 12; Arthur E. Morgan, *Nowhere Was Somewhere* (Chapel Hill, N.C., 1946). For the origins of Owen's faith see J. L. Talmon, *Political*

Messianism, The Romatic Phase (London, 1960), chaps. 1-2.

Albert Mayer and Associates tell the story of beginning Indian community development in *Pilot Project, India* (Berkeley, Calif., 1958). An anthropological field study based on the early phase is S. C. Dube, *India's Changing Villages* (London, 1958). For the role of village-level workers see the Allahabad Agricultural Institute's *Gaon Sathi, Experiment in Extension* (London, 1956). Two close-focus examinations of the Indian program in action appear in the *Sociological Bulletin,* 7, no. 2 (1958); they are Vilas A. Sangave, "Community Development Programme in Kolhapur Project," and L. N. Chapekar, "Community Development Project Blocks in Badlapur." John J. Honigmann reports on "A Case Study of Community Development in Pakistan," *Economic Development and Cultural Change,* 8 (1960), 288-303. Samuel P. Hayes, Jr., has prepared a manual *Measuring the Results of Development Projects,* Unesco Monographs in the Applied Social Sciences, 1959. A general introduction to the importance and aims of grass-roots development will be found in Gunnar Myrdal, *An International Economy* (New York, 1956), chap. 12. Also see his *Rich Lands and Poor* (New York, 1958). Several papers in Lyle W. Shannon, ed., *Underdeveloped Areas* (New York, 1957), chaps. 9-12, are pertinent.

Balanced material on Red China is very scarce. Much of the literature is either overenthusiastic, like Simone de Beauvoir, *The Long March* (Cleveland, 1958), or bitterly unfavorable, like Edward Hunter *Brain-Washing in Red China: The Calculated Destruction of Men's Minds,* new and enlarged ed. (New York, 1953). On revolutionary reeducation see Karl Eskelund, *The Red Mandarins* (London, 1959), pp. 45-46, 65; Harriet C. Mills, "Thought Reform: Ideological Remolding in China," *Atlantic Monthly,* 204, no. 6 (December, 1959), 71-77; Eugene Kinkead, "A Reporter at Large," *The New Yorker,* 33 (October 26, 1957), 114-169; William Sargant, *Battle for the Mind* (Garden City, N.Y., 1957); I. E. Farber and Harry F. Harlow, "Brainwashing, Conditioning, and DDD (Debility, Dependency, and Dread)," *Sociometry,* 20 (1957), 271-285; Theodore H. E. Chen, *Thought Reform of the Chinese Intellectuals* (Hong Kong, 1960), chap. 9; and Robert Jay Lifton, *Thought Reform and the Psychology of Totalism* (New York, 1961). *The Soul of China* (New York, 1958) by Amaury de Riencourt discusses the importance Chinese have traditionally attached to ingrained standards of conduct.

Anthony F. C. Wallace is the authority for another type of deliberate culture change, purposeful revitalization movements. See his "Revitalization Movements," *American Anthropologist,* 58 (1956), 264-281; "Mazeway Resynthesis: A Bio-Cultural Theory of Religious Inspiration," *Transactions of the New York Academy of Sciences,* 18 (1956), 626-638; *Culture and Personality* (New York, 1961), chap. 4; and "New Religions Among the Delaware Indians, 1600-1900," *Southwestern Journal of Anthropology,* 12 (1956), 1-21. Also A. F. C. Wallace, F. W. Voget, and M. W. Smith, "Towards a Classification of Cult Movements: Some Further Considerations," *Man,* 59 (1959), 25-28.

Remainders of the Past

In many a fin and reptile foot I have seen myself passing by.

Loren Eiseley[1]

PROBING PREHISTORY

One way to understand culture is to watch it, inextricably attached to its human carriers, advance down time's long corridor. All modern cultures are the fruition of bygone opportunities for growth. Historians can piece together the past as far back as 6000 years by using records left on clay, papyrus, and paper. Beyond that down the corridor, it is archeologists and paleontologists who probe among commonplace remainders of bygone ways of life to reconstruct the long span of cultural evolution and the far longer incubation period of man himself.

Paleontology, the historical arm of biology, studies biological evolution from traces plants and animals have left in rocks. Prehistoric archeology is less concerned with the record left by organisms themselves than with bygone cultures as they are revealed concretely by stone tools, remains of ancient feasts scattered on cave floors, crumbled house walls, and cooled-off hearths. For the very earliest level of culture prehistorians must be content with only tools hammered out of stone in socially standardized ways. These industries reveal very little about early man's full round of social activities. As archeology moves forward in the corridor of time, closer to the present, the cultural record becomes increasingly rich and more varied, as, in fact, culture too became. But always evidence is incomplete. The archeologist's job has been compared to the hopeless task of trying to reconstruct completely twentieth-century American

[1] *The Immense Journey* (New York, 1957), p. 24.

culture from a Sears Roebuck catalog out of which every page has been torn that depicts artifacts that themselves would disappear after 200 years burial in wet forest ground. Nearly everything that paleontologists and archeologists have learned about evolution, biological and cultural, they have discovered in the last 150 years. What a tremendous burst in scale those 150 years released for western man! Their impact on traditional religious beliefs has been particularly devastating. Before that, lacking knowledge of their distant past, men ascribed their culture to divine origin, as in Genesis or the pre-Christian Roman poet, Tibullus:

> I sing the country and its gods. They taught mankind
> to turn away from acorns (their first food),
> and they first taught us how, by joining beams together,
> to make a little home roofed with green leaves;
> they too (the legend says) first trained to servitude
> strong bulls. . . .[2]

Paleontology and archeology face a common problem: how to date with some precision facts they uncover. How old is the jawbone pried from a piece of limestone? When was the charcoal made that turns up under a rock shelter's mouldering eaves? Other sciences contribute "clocks" to answer such questions, the most common being the geological time clock. Geologists recognize an order in which strata of the earth's crust were successively laid down, Precambrian rocks followed by Cambrian, Ordovician, Silurian, Devonian, and so forth. The earth becomes a clock, its face composed of rock systems each hundreds of millions of years long. A fossil is dated by the rock system from which it has been recovered. In their turn, rock systems can often be dated by the number of millennia that have elapsed since their formation. Rock systems are classified into six paleontological eras by the kind of life they reveal (if any). Oldest of all is the Azoic or lifeless era. Then comes the Archeozoic with primeval forms of life, very early Proterozoic, merely ancient Paleozoic, middle or Mesozoic, and finally Cenozoic with modern life. Fossil evidence is very scarce or absent for the Archeozoic and Proterozoic eras. Four or more glacial episodes in the late Cenozoic era, starting a little over half a million years ago, have proven invaluable for estimating the age of early human fossils (I shall speak of these ice-age events more fully later).

Archeologists, whose data come from periods less remote in time than the paleontologists', have welcomed several promising means of dating. The most popular, radioactive carbon dating, can unlock the age only of objects that once lived. Living substances contain radioactive carbon (C-14), a substance which disintegrates following the organism's death. Fifty percent of the atoms disappear every 5500 years or so. Measuring the amount of remaining radioactivity reveals the material's B.P. (before-the-present) age, providing it

[2] Gilbert Highet, *Poets in a Landscape* (London, 1957), p. 167.

doesn't run over 70,000 years. While radioactive carbon dating cannot be applied to stone implements, charcoal from a hearth contemporary with the tools can be so dated and the age of any associated inorganic objects then estimated.

THE SLIMMEST AND SWIFTEST SELECTED

Three major kinds of theories, which do not exclude one another, have been devised to account for biological evolution. Today only one—the Darwinian—is widely applied. Its explanatory power is constantly being substantiated.

Vitalists claimed that a drive inherent in life itself impels living forms to change in order to adapt to their changing surroundings. As environment alters, the drive induces a species to develop beneficial new characteristics that allow subsequent generations to survive. Modern biologists find the vitalistic theory too mystical, meaning that it can't be supported by any tangible evidence.

The second type of theory, Lamarckism, is named after the French naturalist Jean-Baptiste Lamarck, who lived from 1744 to 1829. According to Lamarckism, experience does more than teach an individual. Use develops in him new traits—muscles, teeth, or intellectual power—that his descendants inherit. Thus experience produces evolution. The fruits of learning disappear, or atrophy, only when they become useless. This most plausible theory—after all, a similar theory in psychology explains quite a bit about habit formation—retains a surprisingly firm grip despite unflinching rejection by most biologists. Many carefully conducted experiments have over and over again failed to substantiate the claim that use or disuse transmits anything for future generations to inherit.

The third theory, Darwinism, takes its name from Charles Darwin, nineteenth-century naturalist, although it crops up earlier. Darwin himself acknowledged that Alfred Russel Wallace, a contemporary, discovered it independently. Darwinism holds natural selection to be the most important factor in evolution. Darwin sketched the essence of the theory when he said that survival among wolves depends on fleetness. The slimmest and swiftest individuals hold the best chance of surviving, and so, more often than slower animals, they have opportunity to leave offspring who inherit parental traits that make for fleetness, including slimness. Every species multiplies rapidly but not all members can survive or reproduce for the reason that each is not precisely like another. Members differ in relatively small variations, some of which, like slimness, are especially advantageous for survival under certain environmental conditions. There ensues a largely unwitting competition between individuals for a hold on life and a chance to reproduce. Individuals possessing characters that confer even a slight advantage enjoy a higher survival rate and leave more descendants than individuals lacking those advantageous variations. Less well-fitted individuals tend to die off before they can breed and reproduce many descendants. So far this theory doesn't contradict Lamarckism. Darwin said that animals successful enough to pass through the selective filter survive and reproduce their advantages. Lamarckism sought to explain how advantageous variations ever appear in a species and how eventually some traits are shed. No wonder that Darwin, when he tried to answer the question Lamarckism explains so plausibly, fell back on the same Larmarckian hypothesis.

Lamarck could not have been correct for hundreds of experiments have failed to sustain his theory. How then do the advantageous variations on which evolution depends arise? Light broke in the early twentieth century when variations that insure success in the struggle for existence were demonstrated to lie in long, threadlike chromosomes which each individual inherits from his parents. Chromosomes are made up of chemical molecules containing genetic material through which heredity is transmitted. The egg derived from the mother and sperm from the father each carry a similar set of chromosomes which are combined at conception when the egg is fertilized. Under special conditions a sudden chemical change called a mutation occurs in specific areas of chromosomes, in localities called genes. Mutations produce the small variations that appear not in the organism where the mutations occurred but in organisms that inherit the mutant genes. Most such variations hinder survival of the organism in which they appear, especially in an unchanged environment to which the species is already well fitted. Therefore they, together with the unfortunate organism that inherited them, disappear before they can be reproduced. Obviously they don't contribute to evolution. A few mutations, though manifested in new bodily or behavioral

This large scale model shows the structure of a short length of a chemical molecule containing genetic material. Mutations responsible for evolution occur in this material. (*British Broadcasting Corporation.*)

traits, apparently make no difference as far as survival is concerned. They have nothing to do with natural selection but nevertheless contribute to evolution. Then there are those truly rare mutations that confer advantages for survival and reproduction on individuals who inherit them. They are responsible for setting Darwin's process of natural selection going. In time, as small changes pile up, they result in the emergence of a new species. Along with natural selection we should also mention social selection, the poorly understood process by which members of the human species with certain heritable characteristics are selected as marital partners or are otherwise culturally elected to survive and reproduce. Social selection, too, results in evolution.

EVOLUTION, BIOLOGICAL AND CULTURAL

Biological evolution is familiar enough and evidence for it, imprinted in rocks that make up the earth's crust, is quite compelling. Its primary mechanisms, mutation and natural selection, have also been studied in laboratories. Cultural evolution is a less clear idea. Until a few years ago many anthropologists, fed up with contradictory nineteenth-century speculations of how religion, marriage, art, and other cultural features originated and developed, would hardly tolerate the idea of evolution applied to culture. They followed eagerly excavations of prehistory in Egypt, China, Europe, Arizona, and Peru but shrank from making general statements that combined the prehistory, say, of Egypt and Peru and specified how culture in general evolved. Let biologists talk about general trends in evolution; anthropologists were going to be as conservative as most historians. They would talk only of specific histories but not of human history as a whole.

Not all anthropologists wore blinders. V. Gordon Childe, Julian H. Steward and Leslie White persisted in looking for evolutionary trends in culture. Steward pointed out forcefully, marshaling accumulating archeological facts, that cultural development in remote parts of the world independently followed a parallel course. A general tendency toward increasing technical development, for example, shows up in the prehistory of China, the Near East, and the Andes Mountains, in fact, wherever small-scale cultures became large-scale civilizations. Other anthropologists pointed to parallels between biological evolution and cultural evolution.[3] Just as biological evolution in hundreds of millions of years has led the organic world to ever more elaborate forms of life—from invertebrates to fish, reptiles, mammals, and then ever more intelligent mammals, culminating in man—so it has been with cultural evolution. Culture in general, as this and the following chapter will show, has grown ever richer and in many ways more complex as it came to utilize ever greater energy. Starting with Old Stone Age cultures based on hunting, fishing, and gathering, which domesticated no animal except dogs, man moved on to agricultural and pastoral ways of life in which he benefitted

[3] M. D. Sahlins and Elman R. Service, eds., *Evolution and Culture* (Ann Arbor, Mich., 1960).

from the energy supplied by plow oxen and riding animals. Later rich, urban civilizations appeared that prospered in using vast hordes of energy extracted from waterpower, wind, coal, and oil. Whether this trend from the Old Stone Age to the Industrial Revolution and its modern aftermath amounts to true progress is a sticky matter of definition that I won't stop to debate.

Biological evolution reveals not only a general trend toward more elaborate and complex forms of life. It has also led to a sheer multiplication of forms of life. The end product consists of many diversified species each suited for survival under special conditions. We can, if we wish, study the evolution of individual species as well as the resourcefulness with which they have radiated to, and adapted in, different corners of the earth. So, too, cultural evolution through more than 5000 centuries had led to an ever greater array of stable cultures each adapted to unique geographical conditions. We have, for example, the tropical forest cultures of Africa, desert cultures of southwest Asia, steppe cultures of central Asia, modern industrial cultures of Europe and America, and highly specialized Eskimo cultures. Archeological or historical probing can define the course each of these cultures has followed and show the influences that entered its development.

Different mechanisms, of course, initiate evolution in the biological and cultural realms. Biological species change through mutation, the genetic modifications being inherited by subsequent generations. Cultures change by virtue of originations that diffuse within and between social systems. But despite these quite different sources of evolutionary change in organic life and culture, similarities in the way change works itself out mark both realms. Many mutations undergo the test of selection. If they pass the test and prove beneficial for survival they become fixed in the species. Numerous beneficial and neutral modifications end up producing a new species. Originations also undergo selection. Individuals and social systems look them over to see if they are compatible or worthwhile. Their functional capacity to provide adaptation and adjustment and to maintain the continuity of the social system undergoes a check. In time accumulated originations produce a new culture. It may be that biological selection is more imperious than selection in culture, but this indicates only a difference in degree between the two processes. So much for selection.

Both plants and animals as well as cultures that leave their original habitat must become adapted to their new environments if they are to survive. The Eskimo, for example, altered the culture they brought into the Arctic and developed a way of life closely suited to a treeless tundra. New Stone Age migrants who brought agriculture from the Middle East into Europe 6000 years ago modified their culture to make it fit the very different environment they were penetrating. Ancestors of the Navaho who moved out of the Canadian forest zone had altered their culture substantially by the time they reached the Southwest. In this process of adaptive radiation a species or culture need not exterminate previous tenants of the zone it uninvitedly enters. The whale didn't drive jellyfish from the sea and Eskimo are allowed to live in the Arctic alongside weather stations and military interceptor stations introduced through the mid-twentieth-century cold war. Taos Indians survive despite the urban artists who have moved next door to their pueblo. However, this does not mean that both parties share the environment on an equal basis. The more complex, powerful form of life usually dominates others. Mammals have taken over the world and within mammals man is lord of creation. So it is with cultures. Ways of life that control more knowledge and energy dominate other cultures which tend to emulate the newcomer. Armed representatives of an industrial culture could easily subordinate Navaho and other North American Indians as well as many African social systems. When these social systems throw off their conquerors, they do so only thanks to knowledge and implements from the conquerors' culture which they adopt.

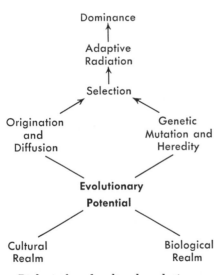

Biological and cultural evolution are similar.

Not all biological species are equally capable of further evolution. The more specialized a species, that is, the closer it is fitted into the particular environmental niche, the less it can afford to change. Hence, almost any mutation will be lethal. Animals inheriting mutant genes will die off before they can reproduce and before a new species evolves. Does a similar limitation face some cultures? Anthropologists seeking parallels between biological and cultural evolution assert that it does. As a social system comes to rely too firmly on a given way of life it relinquishes the possibility of evolving other, possibly more adaptive traits. So, present-day underdeveloped social systems, being less committed to given forms of social organization and production, have more to gain than to lose by social and technological experimentation. The underdeveloped nations of Africa and Asia, eager to reach the level of affluence current in western Europe and North America, show a high potential for evolution. Impelled by this potential and their drive for development, they may someday surpass the western nations. Their culture, whatever it may be, will then become world dominant.

The theory of evolution applied to culture is uncomfortably like the now discarded economic dogma that visualized "economic man" as helplessly subject to impersonal economic laws. About those inflexible trends man could do nothing. He simply obeyed them. Cultural evolution, too, leaves little place for individual choice. The stress it puts on impersonal forces, like evolutionary potential, selection, and dominance, is not misapplied to plants and animals but quite misses the special place of man in nature. Emphasizing the technical side of culture it ignores much else in culture and personality. The most effective techniques and energy-harnassing machines could accomplish nothing unsupported by social ties, personal morale, and ritual intensification. Until proponents of cultural evolution, with their emphasis on technological gains, recognize factors like these, the theory will remain insufficient to explain trends in human history.

STUDYING THE RECORD

Earth is about 3 billion years old and for 500 million it seems to have remained a lifeless planet. Then about 2.6 billion years ago life appeared. Actually, we lack firm fossil proof of life during early Archeozoic times. The earliest virus-like forms of life and succeeding one-celled marine organisms were not the kind of creatures able to make a fossil imprint. Hence, for those early days, proof of evolution is largely logical. The first fossil evidence—and extremely rare it is—comes from Precambrian rocks belonging to the Proterozoic era, which started 1 billion years ago. Proterozoic life still stuck to the sea but differentiation had gone far from hypothetical beginnings, paleontologists recognizing marine worms, molluscs, sponges, and limpets. I will from now on

This ostracoderm, who left the imprint of his upper and lower shields in rocks of the Devonian period, is 90 million years too late to count as an ancestor of man. Ostracoderms' ancestral role to the vertebrates earns them a picture in any account of evolution. (*Chicago Natural History Museum.*)

INTERVALS ON THE EARTH CLOCK

(To be read from bottom up)

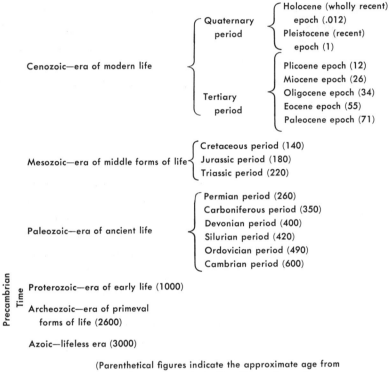

Cenozoic—era of modern life
- Quaternary period
  - Holocene (wholly recent) epoch (.012)
  - Pleistocene (recent) epoch (1)
- Tertiary period
  - Plicoene epoch (12)
  - Miocene epoch (26)
  - Oligocene epoch (34)
  - Eocene epoch (55)
  - Paleocene epoch (71)

Mesozoic—era of middle forms of life
- Cretaceous period (140)
- Jurassic period (180)
- Triassic period (220)

Paleozoic—era of ancient life
- Permian period (260)
- Carboniferous period (350)
- Devonian period (400)
- Silurian period (420)
- Ordovician period (490)
- Cambrian period (600)

Precambrian Time
- Proterozoic—era of early life (1000)
- Archeozoic—era of primeval forms of life (2600)
- Azoic—lifeless era (3000)

(Parenthetical figures indicate the approximate age from the present reckoned in millions of years.)

ignore subsequent evolution of plants and pay attention only to the record as, during ensuing Paleozoic, Mesozoic, and modern Cenozoic times, it heads toward the emergence of man, an event that concerns us because in human evolution culture is directly grounded.

Waters of the Cambrian period (consult the date chart) simply teemed with invertebrate forms of life many of which, to the benefit of paleontology, were enclosed in a shell or held together by a preservable external skeleton. We cannot clearly pick out our ancestor from among the bottom-dwellers and free swimmers of the Cambrian period, but he must have been there. Probably he rested among the starfish from whom, through many links, emerged those jawless fish of Ordovician times, sheathed in bony scales, called ostracoderms. At present ostracoderms claim the distinction of being the first fish. It is in fish to which ostracoderms gave rise that the backbone appeared in the Silurian period. The backbone rates highly in evolution. Possession of one enabled animals—we call them vertebrates—to increase vastly in size. Man is a vertebrate and therefore the earliest vertebrate counts as an ancestor of man.

By Silurian times water ceased to hold all the diversified forms of life which evolution had already created. Oxygen-making plants came to shore first and prepared the way for air-breathing invertebrates that followed. Meanwhile fish continued to evolve organs highly significant for eventual terrestrial life, like lungs, an evolutionary innovation that gave an advantage to its lucky owner for temporary survival out of water. Living African lung-fish still find lungs decidedly useful, for they live in swamps that dry up during some months every year.

Probably early Devonian lungfish found them no less adaptive, since in that period the warm seas retreated from the land. Muscular, flipper-like paired fins on Devonian fish also contributed nicely to terrestrial existence. Note that our own paired limbs evolved from fins. We owe a great deal to fishes! Devonian were busy millennia for evolution. Before the period closed it had witnessed clear-cut jaws armed with piercing teeth. Devonian fish passed on this equipment which eventually and with many modifications reached man. By the time the Devonian ends it contained a five-fingered amphibian capable of living both in and out of water. To the ancient fluid milieu of his ancestors he periodically returned to reproduce.

Seas continued to shrink in Carboniferous times as the first land verte-brates, reptiles, evolved from amphibians. Despite having achieved complete emancipation from the sea—they even deposited their eggs on land—reptiles favored warm, luxuriant swamps, the same swamps whose vegetation geologi-cal pressure converted into our rich coal seams and peat bogs. Then glaciers came, not those of Pleistocene times but the Permian ones that concluded the Paleozoic era. By then reptiles had evolved into many different forms. In fact, reptilian branches had been produced that shared both reptile and mammal-like features. In the succeeding Mesozoic era true mammals took their depar-ture from reptilian mammals.

The Mesozoic was comparatively quiet. Among its interesting products—which, however, have little connection with human evolution—are dinosaurs, reptiles which grew as long as 90 feet and yet managed to get around in bi-pedal fashion. Also noteworthy are birds that now appeared on the scene, but they likewise aren't on the track of evolutionary events leading to man. To stay on that track we have to observe what happened to mammals. For one thing, mammals unlike reptiles don't lay eggs outside the body. Generally what they do is to retain the egg in the uterus, where a special organ, the placenta, provides the embryo and later the fetus with food and oxygen and takes off wastes. The mammal, in general, is a hairy animal, though man sheds most of his downy cover before birth. Mammals are warm blooded, their fairly constant body temperature being automatically regulated. Like others in his class, man pays a high price for this internal heating apparatus. It requires a steady supply of food to keep the metabolic fire well stoked and energy flowing. One other distinguishing feature of mammals is a relatively large forebrain that augments their learning ability and in one mammalian order, the primates, makes possible culture as we know it.

With mammals evolved, we quit the Mesozoic era and enter the Cenozoic in which mammals became dominant. We still live in this era of modern life. Specifically we live in the Quaternary period, the period that succeeded the Tertiary (which, oddly enough, came first not as you might think third in the Cenozoic era). Tertiary times were restless. With great violence the earth thrust up the Alps, Himalayas, and other mountain ranges. Accompanying these spectacular geological developments, many familiar mammals evolved, like cats, bears, horses, elephants, whales, rhinoceroses, and pigs. But for human evolution it is more significant that now the primates, to whom man belongs, made their entry. Generally speaking, primates are four-handed creatures whose thumb and big toe, fitted with nails not claws, angle away from the other digits in such a way that the forward part of each limb can be used for grasping. Man has surrendered this ability in his feet, receiving in exchange an organ specialized for standing. Man's forelimbs, however, very much survive as grasping organs. Reliance on sight rather than smell and a further increase in the brain's development are other significant primate characteristics.

The earliest Tertiary primates, belonging to the Paleocene epoch, evolved from a placental, Cretaceous insect-eater, an individual resembling a modern tree shrew. One of these small, quadrupedal creatures took to the trees where evolutionary developments equipped it to rely more on sight than smell and with limbs capable of grasping food and gripping their arboreal perch. So a Paleocene primate appeared. The fact that primates promptly began to flourish is evolutionary proof that their newly acquired equipment was adaptive. Next steps toward man came with the evolution of Eocene tree-dwelling prosimians, resembling both the modern lemurs and tarsiers. What subsequent prosimian ancestor then gave forth with the two monkey lines, one in the Old and the other in the New World? We don't know. Paleontologists have no monkey fossils older than the Oligocene epoch. Oligocene monkey remains are too late to inform us of their Eocene predecessors. Eocene rocks also contain the fossil remains of apes, the next link in the evolutionary chain leading to man. The evidence is truly modest, consisting of several small jaws found in Europe, Egypt, and Southwest Asia. They demonstrate that early apes fell far short of the proportions that any living species now shows. From what ancestors did these first apes evolve? Probably from the Eocene, lemur-like prosimian of whom I spoke.

A wealth of Miocene fossils from Europe, East Africa, and adjacent Southwest Asia reveals that apes adapted successfully. It is time to name names and thereby introduce *Proconsul,* possessor of powerful jaws; *Dryopithecus,* who was about the same size as a modern chimpanzee (say 5 feet tall if male); and *Sivapithecus.* A look at their feet shows they were built to bear stresses and strains of the kind encountered in terrestrial walking. Forelimbs are not elongated; that specialization didn't come till post-Miocene times. These large primates must have spent a good deal of time on the ground. But none of these Miocene hominoids, or creatures of manlike appearance, represents our ancestor. They are all too late. Specialists now believe that man's ancestor branched off from other apes well before *Proconsul* had a chance to test his robust jaws and canines. But the Miocene hominoids give us a general idea of what our and their common ancestor looked like 26 million years ago in early Miocene times. What some features of that ancestor looked like 14 or so million years later in Pliocene times is a story told by a fossil found in an Italian coal mine. Here lay *Oreopithecus.* His chin, flat face from which all vestige of the ape's snout has vanished, and modest rather than vicious canine teeth all ally him with man. His other features are uncomfortably primitive and would better suit a creature older by some millions of years. How *Oreopithecus* will finally be classified, as man or ape, remains to be seen. Meanwhile the scholars are talking him out and hopefully consulting the crushed bones from which, somehow, the answer—man or ape—must come.

The modern ring-tailed lemur, like man, descends from an Eocene tree-dwelling prosimian. (*New York Zoological Society Photo.*)

MAN AT LAST

Oreopithecus shows us how important it is to find a working definition for someone we thought we knew well—man. Man is different things for different people. Some anthropologists refuse to acknowledge human kinship with any fossil unless proof exists that he also made tools and didn't simply pick up sticks or stones to use as implements. Other anthropologists ignore the attribute of manufacture; they define man anatomically, by the shape of his skull vault, size of his brain compartment, pattern of his teeth, presence of a chin, and whether his foot is specialized for standing. The more clearly these characteristics are present as a configuration while apelike characters are submerged, the more compelling the evidence that we have a hominid, not just a hominoid. Consulting such anatomical characteristics still leaves the problem of just when to push a fossil over the not-so-great divide between the apes and man. We can't err with living great apes (orang utan, gorilla, and chimpanzee). Their skulls' vault is low, there is little or no forehead, and the modestly spaced cranium where their small brain lodges holds only from 400 to 700 cubic centimeters. The still smaller gibbon, also an ape, accommodates only about 100 cc in his cranium. Man's skull vault is high and rounded, his forehead is a well-marked, vertical wall, and his cranial capacity averages around 1400 cc. The normal range of human brain cases, from 800 to 2400 cc, is enormous and apparently bears no relationship to manifest intelligence. This indicates that the crucial factor for human intelligence is brain potential and not size. Whereas apes' teeth are arranged in the shape of a parabola open at one end, man's dental arc resembles half of an oval. Unlike the apes', human canine teeth have shrunk to where they are only a trifle more prominent than others. Nobody skilled in anatomy would ever mistake an ape's for a man's skull. Then, too, there are foot, arm, pelvis and other traits that help in classification. The matter becomes far more difficult when groping in the dark corridor of prehistory. For there man still bears a pronounced physical kinship to apes, which have yet to evolve into the distinctive kind of creatures we see in the zoo.

Concerning the australopithecines, there is no longer any serious question about their anatomical right to be classified with man. When they hunted in South and East Africa over a million years ago, the Pliocene was finishing. Alike in some respects are *Australopithecus africanus* (the Taungs child), the eponymous type; *Plesianthropus transvaalensis* (Sterfontein Man); *Paranthropus robustus* (Kromdraai Man); *Paranthropus crassidens* (the Swartkrans remains); the most recent to join the throng, *Zinjanthropus boisei* (East Africa Man), and others. Although they all are small brained, in many other features, including upright posture, they comfortably fit hominid specifications.

Did these early Africans make tools? Well, there is hardly any question that some of them *used* tools. Heavy antelope leg bones found in close conjunction with australopithecine remains show signs of having been wielded. We have broken baboon skulls which the hominids probably broke open to

THE SKULL ASSUMES ITS PRESENT SHAPE

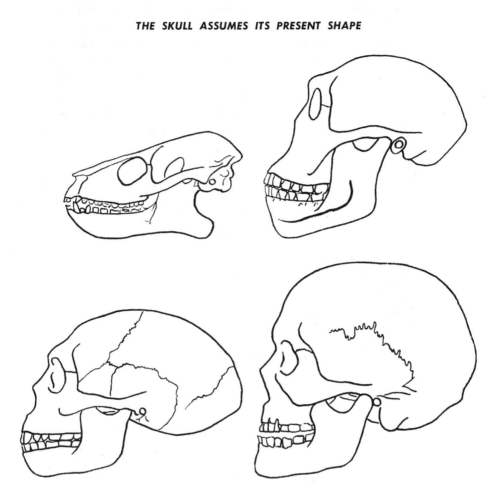

At the top left is a skull of *Notharctus,* a fossil lemurlike creature, followed by skulls of *Australopithecus,* top right, *Pithecanthropus erectus,* bottom left, and Cro-Magnon (a modern man) bottom right of the last glacial stage. The characteristic changes that occur in the skull as man's brain expands can be followed in the last three examples. Note how the face retracts and, in modern man, the chin at last appears.

Ronald Singer, "Evolution and Man," *Antiquity,* 31 (1957), 188-198. Adapted from E. H. Colbert, *Evolution of the Vertebrates* (New York, 1955), p. 278.

expose the brains. But mere use won't do; apes also employ objects, for example, to extend their reach. Did australopithecines make tools? One South African site (Sterkfontein) containing australopithecine fossils harbored stone artifacts, though not in direct contact with the bones. In type these objects fit a very early stone-tool industry called Oldowan, remains of which are known from other parts of East Africa. An Oldowan tool, really an all-purpose chopper, is truly unrefined. To copy one, find a water-worn pebble about 4½ inches long and with another stone knock off just enough flakes on both sides to provide a sharp cutting edge on one end. Did australopithecines do this? Or, as some scholars insist, do the tools belong to some other, contemporary hominid? Fresh evidence from Tanganyika provides new fuel for the debate.

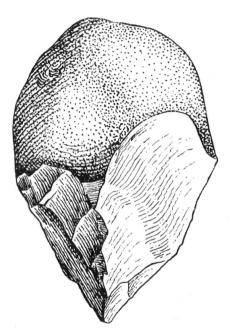

An Oldowan chopper from East Africa. (*Sonia Cole. The Prehistory of East Africa, Harmondsworth, 1954, p. 133.*)

Here in 1959 Mrs. L. S. B. Leakey found *Zinjanthropus*. Oldowan choppers turned up in the very same level with the bones. Did *Zinjanthropus* make them or did they drop from the hand of a more advanced form of man? Almost unbelievable is the age assigned to the geological stratum from which bones and tools came—1,750,000 years!

ICE AGE HOMINID EVOLUTION

Gradually climate in the northern hemisphere grew cooler. Tropical flora and fauna restricted themselves to more congenial southerly climes. Glaciers began to creep southward from icy polar regions to almost about the fiftieth parallel and down mountainsides located farther south. Four main glacial stages are popularly recognized, the first three each being broken off by a long, interglacial warm spell. Glaciers didn't directly disturb life in Africa and South Asia, though rainy (pluvial) stages that may have coincided with ice advances farther north probably did. A glacier consists of snow, snow so heavy that most of it is compacted into ice. The weighted-down mass determinedly flows where it can, like toothpaste from a tube, thrusting rocks and soil before it. In Europe the last, or fourth of the main glaciers receded between 12,000 and 10,000 years ago, though naturally ice and tundra conditions didn't vanish simultaneously all over the continent.

As far as we know, australopithecines were the only hominids extant when the glaciers began. They, remember, lived in Africa, beyond the cold. Before australopithecines disappeared from the Pleistocene epoch at least the first glacial stage had ended and another hominid type had evolved, the pithecanthropines.

Central Java maintained a balmy climate while the second glacial advance swung across most of Europe. In this comfortable Indonesian setting lived Java Man (*Pithecanthropus erectus*). He probably supported himself with tools he made, although direct evidence of them hasn't yet come forth. His brain capacity, standing at 850 cc, is at least 200 cc ahead of the australopithecines, but that needn't have made much difference in his culture. A cave at Choukoutien, 30 miles from Peiping, China, yielded remains of another pithecanthropine, Pekin Man (*Sinanthropus pekinensis*), of second interglacial age. Pekin Man's cranial capacity stands around 1075 cc, his larger brain being accommodated behind a more definitely structured forehead. In the cave was proof of his culture, including the very hearths before whose fire he had sat. It also contained his chopping tools, each a little over 3 inches long, useful for butchering and heavy work. Trimmed quartz flakes about 2 inches in length were better suited for more delicate tasks. Pekin Man preyed on his own kind. The evidence, convincing to a paleontologist even though it might not stand up in a modern court of law, consists of human skulls which the cave dweller fetched back home, presumably to pick the brains at leisure. What meaning cannibalism had to the pithecanthropines of Peiping, apart from providing them with choice morsels, we will never know.

Pithecanthropines also lived in the west. Ternifine Man (*Atlanthropus mauritanicus*) of Algeria resembles his East Asiatic contemporaries physically. Culturally, because he worked with hand-axes and not choppers, he belongs more to the west. Quartz hand-axes, flaked on both sides to give them sinuous, jagged cutting edges, are characteristic of Europe. In East Africa, they succeeded earlier Oldowan chopping tools at about the same time that Ternifine Man lived. Ternifine, a pithecanthropine like Pekin Man but with tools indicative of another way of life, provides us with an instructive lesson. Physical type places no limits on culture, neither in middle Pleistocene times or in the underdeveloped countries today.

So far we have noted preglacial, second glacial, and second interglacial men in Asia and Africa. In Africa pithecanthropines succeed earlier forms of man, the australopithecines, indicating perhaps that man originated in that continent. In Europe the second glacial (possibly even first intergla-

Hand-ax from the site of Ternifine Man. Excavated in Algeria. (*Professor C. Arambourg.*)

In time Acheulian hand-axes (right), made with more regular flaking, succeeded the earlier Abbevillian variety (left). These are finds made in France. Hand-axes persisted until the Pleistocene epoch came to an end. In later times ever more specialized stone implements—scrapers, points, and engraving tools—found their way into the craftsman's kit. (*Collection Musée de l'Homme, photograph by José Oster.*)

cial) jaw of Heidelberg Man, sketchy information though it is, points to a wide-faced, chinless hominid of the pithecanthropine type. About Heidelberg's culture we have no clue whatever.

I spoke of the chopping tools possibly made by australopithecines, Old Stone Age life at Choukoutien, and the hand-ax of Ternifine Man. Have you been waiting for me to say something about language, group life, and religion in those remote prehistoric times? I would like to, but facts from which to speak are lacking. Some anthropologists have reasoned that with the expanding brain case from australopithecines to pithecanthropines came the simultaneous growth of language, collaborative social life, ritual symbolism, and other familiar cultural features. But pithecanthropines with a cranial capacity of 700 cc had brains that fall within the range of australopithecines, whose largest cranium accommodates about 1000 cc. By the argument based on brain size, the abilities of australopithecines must have overlapped with the abilities of later hominids. Brain size isn't as important as brain potential and when it comes to that, skulls alone are mute. We can't know if the australopithecines had immaterial traits of culture, or, better put, how much culture they had. I can't bring myself to believe that these early South Africans remained apes in everything but their skeletons, especially as long as Oldowan choppers of great age dangle over my head.

RANGES IN BRAIN SIZES OVERLAP

100– 700 cc	Living apes (if the small gibbon is omitted the range of the great apes is from 400 to 700 cc)
400–1000 cc	Australopithecines
750–1250 cc	Pithecanthropines
1050–1750 cc	Neanderthal Man
800–2350 cc	Modern Man (normal range)

Brain size is gauged by measuring the cranium in cubic centimeters. Brain potential is more significant for culture than size. Apes don't rank as culture-bearing animals though a gorilla's brain falls within the australopithecine range.

Raymond A. Dart, *Adventures with the Missing Link* (New York, 1959), p. 135.

In the second interglacial stage, a time when Pekin and Ternifine men were still flourishing their choppers or hand-axes, we for the first time glimpse man about as modern looking as ourselves. Does he go further back than the second warm interlude? If he does, perhaps more of his bones will turn up in Africa, the continent which has contributed the oldest hominid remains as well as the fragment of a chinned lower jaw that is all we know of modern-looking Kanam Man. Until better data appear, it is wisest to confine ourselves to two paltry fragments of the Swanscombe skull from England. Actually the bones, from the upper part of the skull, belong to a young woman who lived along the ancient Thames, sharing the banks with elephants and rhinoceroses. Her cranial capacity hovered around 1300 cc, about what we find in a modern woman. With the bones were flint hand-axes belonging to a refined stone-tool industry called Acheulian.

On the basis of the Swanscombe fragments alone we might hesitate to trace modern man as far back as second interglacial times, when he was a contemporary of primitive pithecanthropines. But Lady Swanscombe isn't isolated. A continuous, reassuring trail of modern-looking fossil bones stretches from the second interglacial straight to the fourth glacial when, in Africa, Asia, Europe, and even America, modern forms dominate the world. For example, Germany has yielded the nearly complete Steinheim skull (of uncertain age but either second or third interglacial) and the third interglacial Ehringsdorf skull. France provides the Fontéchevade cranial bones, also third interglacial. African skull fragments assigned to Kanjera Man fit the same modern type. Pluvial and glacial stages can't be assuredly matched but it looks as though Kanjera is older than Ehringsdorf and Fontéchevade men or of about third glacial vintage.

Human evolution from the second interglacial to the last glacial stage didn't proceed along a straight line. Another type shows up during well-represented third interglacial times, Neanderthal Man. He was short; he had a large brain capacity; the back of his head protruded; he had no forehead but sported a chinless projecting face. Nowadays his ancestry is ascribed to much more modern-looking individuals in whom evolution side-tracked. Earliest Neanderthals possess a mixture of modern and pithecanthropoid characters. Progressively, in Europe, Asia, and North Africa, their appearance becomes less modern and more extreme until, with the start of the fourth glacial stage, they vanish into extinction. Why he was eliminated from survival no one knows. Poems and novels have been written about this famous hominid. William Gerald Golding's novel, *The Inheritors*,[4] imagines his life and Marijane Allen's poem pities him for his dead-ended future.

> What hunger for tomorrow had that race
> evolving deathward down an aberrant track?—
> limping to extinction without grace
> because the Breeder overlooked some lack
> unknowable to us. "Behold the jaw. . ."
> Unfutured race, I wonder what *it* saw.[5]

Neanderthal Man possessed no mean technology. Mousterian culture, replete with flint implements more specialized than any that had existed earlier, goes with Neanderthal man in Europe as firmly as kayaks, sleds, and stone pots go with Eskimo. Our vision from this distance is a bit uncertain but Neanderthalers seem to have been successful hunters. Armed with spears they killed mammoth, rhinoceros, and bison. The bola helped them bring down lighter, swifter game. And in caves where they lived they ceremoniously buried their dead, giving thought that the deceased might need tools and food where they were going.

ICE AGE CULTURE

Alongside the Pleistocene record of hominid evolution runs the Paleolithic ("old stone") record of cultural growth. The Paleolithic lasted 500,000 years or more. Paleolithic tools include, in addition to choppers and hand-axes, smaller flake implements that reveal man's growing mastery over his world. In early Paleolithic times he ceased to depend only on waste flakes and learned to prepare stone cores efficiently (by making so-called tortoise cores) in order to control the shape of the flake struck off. In some instances he further trimmed the edges of these flakes. He turned out Acheulian hand-axes of such exquisite workmanship that archeologists think he intended some of them to serve as expressive ritual objects rather than as everyday cutting

[4] London, 1955.
[5] *The New York Times,* November 15, 1956.

A SUMMARY OF ICE-AGE AFFAIRS

Pleistocene Division and Glacial Stage		FOSSILS		
		Europe	Africa	Asia
U P P E R (PLEISTOCENE)	Fourth Glacial (Wuerm)	*Cro-Magnon *Chancelade *Grimaldi	*Afalou	*Upper Choukoutien *Wadjak
	Third Inter- glacial	Neanderthal *Fontéchevade *Ehringsdorf *Steinheim	*Boskop	Solo *Mt. Carmel
M I D D L E (PLEISTOCENE)	Third Glacial (Riss)		*Kanjera (hand-ax)	
	Second Inter- glacial	*Swanscombe (hand-ax)	*crude fist (hand-ax)*	Sinanthropus (chopping tool)
L O W E R (PLEISTOCENE)	Second Glacial (Mindel)	Heidelberg	*Kanam (chopping tool)	Pithecanthropus
	First Interglacial			
	First Glacial (Guenz) ↑		Australopithecinae (chopping tool)	

*Indicates that the specimen is morphologically modern.

tools. Increasingly his implements became more specialized for cutting, scraping, sewing, piercing, and engraving. But cultural growth came very slowly. The best available explanation for the slow pace of cultural evolution in Paleolithic times is not that human brains were still inadequate. A better

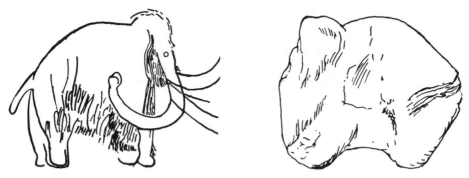

A mammoth drawn by a late Paleolithic artist. Another faces it, stylistically carved in the round. (*Baldwin-Brown,* The Art of the Cave Dweller, *London,* *1928.*)

A late Paleolithic artist impressionistically recorded a procession of reindeer. (*Baldwin-Brown,* The Art of the Cave Dweller, *London, 1928.*)

reason is that the whole inhabited world existed in the same underdeveloped state. Nowhere could Paleolithic men take advantage of diffusion and so jump forward in cultural development and elaboration. At the same time their highly restricted cultural inventory limited change. There was little from which change could start.

Archeological data are always limited but for lower Paleolithic times the record is minimal: a few stone tools made in distinctive fashion. Not till third interglacial times do we have grounds to speak of a real way of life, Mousterian. The specialized tool kit of the Mousterians (in Europe they were mostly men of Neanderthal type) included Acheulian hand-axes and D-shaped side-scrapers, the latter used perhaps for scraping skins preparatory to making clothing.

Mousterian culture lasted into fourth glacial times when late Paleolithic culture succeeded it. In Europe this was a period renowned for an amazing cultural florescence whose provocation remains as mysterious as the meaning it possessed for its creators. They were men much like ourselves, divided into Grimaldi, Cro-Magnon, Chancelade, and other races. In other words, they belong to the same modern type whose origin we have traced back to second interglacial times in the Thames valley. Tundra food gatherers, they possessed a strong artistic impulse that stamped itself in stone, bone, antler, and ivory.

Large mural paintings and relief sculpture done in remote chambers of

Observers have seen many things in this masked figure. Some perceive a man playing a flute; others see a human being masquerading ritually as a horned god. Possibly it presents a shaman charming game. Or we may be viewing a hunter armed with a bow whose disguise enables him to creep close to an unsuspecting herd of animals. Bows were probably invented in Africa near the end of the late Old Stone Age. Their presence in France during fourth glacial times ought to be better attested. (*Herbert Kuehn,* The Rock Pictures of Europe, *trans. A. H. Brodrick, Fair Lawn, N. J., 1956.*)

The Venus of Willendorf. Although the sculptor left his subject featureless, in her distended abdomen, pregnant with life, he may be expressing fecundity. The site yielding this figure dates back to about 30,000 B.C. (*Naturhistorisches Museum, Vienna.*)

caves located in northeastern Spain and southwestern France constitute the most spectacular late Paleolithic remains. Paintings include extremely lifelike polychromes done in white, black, brown, red, yellow, and mauve. Artists ground their pigments to powder and mixed them in fat or water. They painted with finger or brush, in some cases not even bothering with an outline. The painters took advantage of irregular surfaces in the rock walls to give

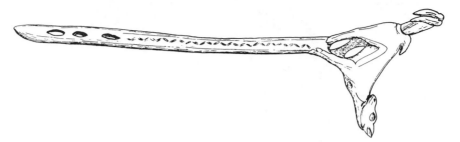

A highly ornamented, late Paleolithic spearthrower. (*Dorothy A. E. Garrod, "Paleolithic Spearthrowers,"* Proceedings of the Prehistoric Society, *21, 1955, 21-35.*)

depth to the contours of animals they represented. Did they, as nearly everyone believes, intend their works to increase and control the supply of game on which their livelihood depended? What meaning had another late Paleolithic artifact, the stone statuettes which have come to be called "Venus figurines"? The Venus is a buxom woman. Heavy breasts and conspicuous genitals accentuate her femininity. Many modern interpreters say she was a deity in charge of fecundity. As Pierre de Chardin says, if we make mistakes in interpreting some features of late Paleolithic art, we make no mistake in perceiving the artists' power of observation, their love of fantasy, and the joy they took in creation.[6]

These cold-weather hunters sewed with awls and true needles, that is, needles fitted with eyes. They employed several kinds of scrapers and engraving tools enabled them to draw on ivory and wood. Flint blades made through an original process of stone working constituted their most remarkable pieces of equipment. To make blades craftsmen detached long, fine slivers of flint by applying pressure to a core of stone with a flaking tool. With the same tool they delicately retouched the slim blade. Men of the late Old Stone Age no longer relied only on their arm to launch a spear. They employed a machine, the spearthrower, to provide them with what amounts to an extra arm joint and to increase the weapon's deadly range. Also they used harpoons of bone and antler; these were indeed developmental innovations, for they enabled hunters to hold on firmly to game once it had been struck.

Nowhere does late Paleolithic culture herald the close of the Pleistocene epoch with the same intensity as in southwestern Europe. In Pakistan-India long stone blades and an engraving tool, the burin, alone set off the later from the earlier Old Stone Age. Here in South Asia chopping-tool and hand-ax traditions met as early as second interglacial times. Choppers remained concentrated in the Himalayan foothills while hand-axes resembling European models flourished in the south.

6 Pierre Teilhard de Chardin, *The Phenomenon of Man,* trans. Bernard Wall (New York, 1959), p. 201.

An artist imagines what a campsite of late Paleolithic mammoth hunters looked like. Actual traces of these huts were excavated on the Oder River. (*Bohuslav Klíma, "Coal in the Ice Age," Antiquity, 30 (1956), 98-101; first appeared in Archelogické rozhledy, 7, 1955.*)

POSTGLACIAL FORESTS

Disappearance of the last phase of the fourth glacier in Europe ushered in a long springtime. Climatic change encouraged a radically altered environment. Birch, willow, pine, hazel, elm, lime, and oak trees colonized the former tundra and the forests in turn attracted new species of animals. In pace with the changing environment men reshaped their culture and so created the Mesolithic ("middle stone") period.

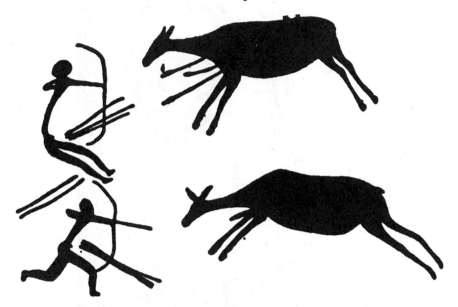

Mesolithic hunters of Spain depicted themselves pursuing deer with bows and arrows. (*Herbert Kuehn,* The Rock Pictures of Europe, *trans. A. H. Brodrick, Fair Lawn, N. J., 1956.*)

Nuts and shellfish became important adjuncts of subsistence. People fished heavily with nets and hooks, traveling over water in dugout canoes. A new machine, the bow, was a great advantage to hunters. The carpenter's adze, chisel, bow drill, and hafted ax (no more hand-ax!) show that people made considerable use of wood, though archeologists haven't seen everything

Why did Mesolithic folk paint these designs on pebbles? (*R. A. S. Macalister,* A Text-book of European Archaeology, *Cambridge, Eng., 1921.*)

PREHISTORIC ENVIRONMENTS RECONSTRUCTED AND THEIR CULTURES TRACED

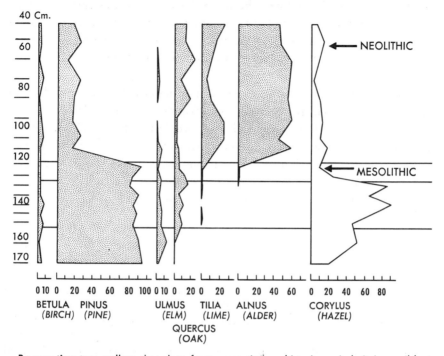

By counting tree pollens that date from successive prehistoric periods it is possible to reconstruct ancient environments. This diagram demonstrates how, following the glacial recession around 12,000 years ago in one part of Cambridgeshire, England, oak, lime, and alder replaced pine and hazel. Just before the point where lime and oak pollens become conspicuous in the peat, about 39 feet below the ground's surface, Mesolithic culture enters the scene. Note when Neolithic culture arrives (toward the top of the diagram). The graph measures the percentage of each pollen type as a percentage of total tree pollen.

John Grahame Douglas Clark, "A Microlithic Industry from the Cambridgeshire Fenland and other Industries of Sauveterrian Affinities from Britain," *Proceedings of the Prehistoric Society*, 21 (1955), 3-20; p. 5.

that Mesolithic man built. Some things puzzle prehistorians. What did Middle Stone Age hunters do with the small, skillfully shaped pieces of flint they left behind in Europe, Africa, and Asia? Some of these microliths ("small stones") may have been hafted in a handle of bone or wood to make a saw or sickle but the variegated geometric forms in which the flint was shaped aren't at all well explained by that. Also why did some European Middle Stone Age folk paint geometric designs and stylized human figures on pebbles? Problematic objects like these frustrate archeologists.

We catch glimpses of Mesolithic boudoir, kitchen, and open-air life from bone combs, amber beads, slate knives, netting needles, and sledges. No doubt sledges were drawn by the hunter or his wife, although small dogs were already being domesticated. Time permitted a little cave painting and also allowed men to engrave their tools. Small care or wealth went into burials, though the Paleolithic practice of occasionally sprinkling red ochre on a corpse continued.

Into this way of life reached a new cultural impulse that originated in the Middle East and from there first hit southeastern Europe. The new way of life was founded on farming and allowed people to settle in villages and to increase their amenities. In the far north, Mesolithic culture tarried long after the new age had begun farther south. In the same manner Eskimo stone-age culture persisted into the nineteenth century in the Arctic while the United States and Canada were becoming industrialized.

FURTHER READING

Any reader who wishes to fill in the evolutionary account of man and other primates will find it written lucidly in William Howells, *Mankind in the Making* (Garden City, N.Y., 1959) and Wilfred E. Le Gros Clark, *History of the Primates,* 7th ed. (London, 1960). The latter writer's *Foundations of Human Evolution* (Eugene, Ore., 1959) is also recommended. Juan Comas, *Manual of Physical Anthropology* (Springfield, Ill., 1960), chaps. 2, 8, gives detailed attention to particular finds and problems connected with their interpretation. Gabriel Ward Lasker has written an admirable summary of these matters in *The Evolution of Man* (New York, 1961). Many essays in Sol Tax, ed., *Evolution After Darwin,* 3 vols. (Chicago, 1960), bear in a very up-to-date way on topics discussed in this chapter.

For an introduction to paleontology see R. A. Stirton, *Time, Life, and Man* (New York, 1959) or R. Carrington, *The Story of Our Earth* (New York, 1956). These volumes were published before 1960 so the geologic dates are not the latest revised dates published, among other places, in *The New York Times,* March 5, 1960. Methods of dating are reviewed in Robert F. Heizer, "Long-Range Dating in Archeology," and Kenneth P. Oakley, "Dating Fossil Human Remains." Both papers appear in the volume edited by A. L. Kroeber, *Anthropology Today* (Chicago, 1953.)

More on mutation in relation to evolution will be found in Garrett Hardin, *Nature and Man's Fate* (New York, 1959); John Maynard Smith, *The Theory of Evolution* (Harmondsworth, 1958); and Edward O. Dodson, *Evolution: Process and Product,* rev. ed. (New York, 1960). S. L. Washburn and Virginia Avis talk less about the evolution of bodily structure and more about "Evolution of Human Behavior" in Anne Roe and George Gaylord Simpson, eds. *Behavior and Evolution* (New Haven, Conn., 1958). For recent material on the australopithecines see F. Clark Howell "The Villafranchian and Human Origins," *Science*, 130 (1959), 831-844. A compact account of South African human and cultural prehistory is J. Desmond Clark, *The Prehistory of Southern Africa* (Harmondsworth, 1959). Companion volumes are Sonia Cole, *The Prehistory of East Africa* (Harmondsworth, 1954) and C. B. M. McBurney, *The Stone Age of Northern Africa* (Harmondsworth, 1960).

Among good summaries of Paleolithic cultural growth are John Grahame Douglas Clark, *World Prehistory, An Outline* (Cambridge, Eng., 1961), chaps. 2-3; his *From Savagery to Civilization* (New York, 1953), chaps. 1-3; Kenneth P. Oakley, *Man the Tool Maker*, 4th ed. (London, 1958); and Robert J. Braidwood, *Prehistoric Men*, 4th ed., Chicago Natural History Museum Popular Series, Anthropology, no. 37, 1959, pp. 7-98. The first three chapters in Harry L. Shapiro, ed., *Man, Culture, and Society* (New York, 1956) survey evolution (Shapiro), archeological method (James B. Griffin), and the Old Stone Age (H. L. Movius, Jr.).

Guidance for Mesolithic Europe will be found in the first 48 pages of John Grahame Douglas Clark, *Prehistoric Europe; The Economic Basis* (London, 1952) and the same author's *The Mesolithic Settlement of Northern Europe* (Cambridge, Eng., 1936).

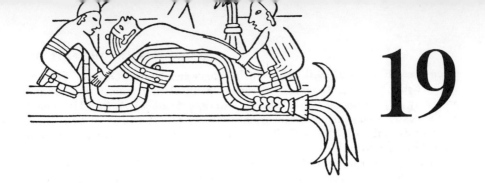

Luster of Civilizations

States are not made, nor patched; they grow,
Grow slow through centuries of pain. . . .

John Masefield[1]

THE OPPORTUNITY FOR CIVILIZATION

Domesticated animals and plants are the crucial innovations which ushered in the New Stone Age or Neolithic Period. As the name indicates, a new tradition of stone work also became dominant in this age. Grinding replaced chipping and flaking and the close-grained stone used in the newer process produced implements with longer life and higher efficiency.

Agriculture and animal domestication stand for gigantic strides in technical development. As later history indubitably confirms, they were originations holding momentous significance. For hundreds of thousands of years, starting with the australopithecines and pithecanthropines, men had followed the fashion of their food-gathering, nonhuman forebears. Their way of gathering subsistence meant frequent mobility, transitory shelters, small bands, and a simple culture. Even during Mesolithic times, strand-lopers, richly supplied with shellfish and other marine life, who settled down near beaches boasted only limited cultural equipment and lived in small communities. These men possessed brain potential capable of building a more elaborate culture but they lacked opportunity to apply it. Now that opportunity arrived.

Food production pushed man to civilization. Slowly at first and then with quickly increasing velocity agriculture harnessed to livestock initiated population explosions in different areas of the Old World. Farming allowed survival

[1] *The Everlasting Mercy and the Widow in the Bye Street*, rev. ed. (New York, 1916), p. 53.

and even luxury to more and more people who never touched their hands to a hoe or, later, a plow. They specialized in other departments of culture, like carpentering, metallurgy, pottery, trade, building construction, administration, fighting, curing, and ritual. For as social systems expanded they gave men ever added scope to rise not only by exploiting nature but by serving and conquering each other. Since farming helped culture to grow into civilization, the farmers can be visualized as paying for the new way of life.

The term civilization is not a paean of praise for the best of all possible ways of life. Civilization is life founded on domestication and including as further earmarks metallurgy, a high degree of occupational specialization, cities, and writing. A civilization is always found in a very large-scale social system where people are sophisticated or urbane as well as urbanized. The word implies achievement certified by brilliance. Accomplishments in architecture, weaving, painting, sculpture, pottery, religious ideology, and administrative coordination retain their luster through thousands of years. Hence, modern men continue to find past civilizations noteworthy.

A civilization is a culture that has risen to a level where it incorporates considerable variety, a high degree of control over the material world, and—a bit paradoxically—unique problems with which the social systems must wrestle. For example, under civilized conditions rival ethical systems come into perplexing conflict; antagonistic communities struggle with one another in hot and cold wars; political power must constantly be watched lest a few powerful persons use it to exploit the many; and rapid change churns forth novelties unpalatable to one or another sector of the heterogeneous population.

NEW DEVELOPMENTS IN SOUTHWEST ASIA

Man originated plant and animal domestication at least twice and perhaps three times.[2] The earliest Neolithic achievement in food production came in Southwest Asia about 8000 B.C. Here wheat became the focal crop and domesticated animals were chiefly sheep, goats, cattle, and later, pigs. In time the Southwest Asian Neolithic diffused to Europe, becoming the basis of western culture. Simultaneously with Southwest Asian developments a second origination of plant cultivation, focusing around rice rather than wheat, is conjectured to have occurred around the Bay of Bengal in eastern India, East Pakistan, or Burma. Perhaps it took place even further east, in Southeast Asia. With rice went pigs and chickens. However, evidence of this oriental Neolithic is woefully inadequate. Better authenticated is the innovation of agriculture—this time centered on maize with practically no domesticated animals except the turkey—that sprang up in Middle America about 7000

[2] Hermann v. Wissmann et al., "On the Role of Nature and Man in Changing the Face of the Dry Belt of Asia," in W. L. Thomas, Jr., ed., Man's Role in Changing the Face of the Earth (Chicago, 1956), p. 283.

B.C. From here farming spread rapidly northward and, somewhat more slowly, into South America. There in the tropical forest manioc was better adapted than maize and became the staple crop. In the absence of any proof to the contrary we might as well consider each of these originations to have been independent. We know the Southwest Asia Neolithic best and besides it is responsible for part of our own culture, so let's concentrate on it.

Two female figurines in clay from Tepe Sarab in the highlands of northern Iran. The figure on the right is about 1½ inches high and 8000-9000 years old. (*Oriental Institute, University of Chicago.*)

Nobody can identify the Mesolithic gatherers of wild grain who first sowed seeds, tended the ensuing plants, and then reaped a harvest in the Middle East. In what order Neolithic originations came, whether animal rearing preceded or followed agriculture, also falls beyond our ken. Definitely the earliest farmers survived with the aid of resources other than their crops—notably wild animal flesh. In fact, for a couple of thousand years they spent so much time hunting that tillage affected their lives very little. The job of tending those first gardens probably went to women, though men broke up and readied the soil for planting. If this is so, then it helps to explain the profusion of Neolithic female figurines from somewhat later centuries. They could have represented goddesses in charge of fertility. Mortars or open querns used for grinding seeds undoubtedly antedate farming. In Neolithic villages, milling flour came to take up a good share of a woman's time. Other new tools were fabricated, like sickles and ground-stone celts; celts are problematic objects that may have been hafted to serve as hoes. As life became increasingly sedentary people could conveniently accumulate a greater volume of possessions and gradually standards of comfort went up. Production of new goods—pottery, woven textiles, tools, and houses—kept pace with new wants.

Archeologists are still hopeful of locating a really early Neolithic village. All the village sites that have been discovered in the Middle East postdate by some centuries the earliest Neolithic foundations. Apartment-size Belt Cave in Iran on the shores of the Caspian Sea is such a site. Although too late to represent man's original transition from food gathering to food production, it portrays graphically the difference food production made in hunters' lives. When the archeologist, Carleton Coon, entered the white limestone cave in

1949 he found two families of dervishes there with their animals. Before they could start digging the scientists had to persuade the tenants to move from what they had hoped would be their winter haven. Underneath the cave floor four successive periods of culture were waiting to be spaded off. At the bottom were two levels of Mesolithic culture. In the first, or earliest, seal bones figure

The Dervishes had expected to winter comfortably in the haven of Belt Cave above the Caspian Sea. Below them in this picture lie cultural remains that go back 11,500 years. (*The University Museum, University of Pennsylvania and Alfred A. Knopf, publishers of Carleton S. Coon, The Seven Caves, New York, 1957.*)

prominently. In the upper Mesolithic layer, remains show hunters armed with bows and helped by dogs productively hunting gazelles. The use of seal had fallen off. The earlier layer dates from around 9530 B.C. and the second from 6620 B.C. (all are radiocarbon dates). The Mesolithic tenants left behind about 800 gazelle bones, 140 ox bones, 34 seal bones, assorted remains of sheep, goats, pigs, and other wild animals, and the burial of a 12-year-old girl. Two periods of Neolithic culture showed up, the oldest started around 5840 B.C. Excavating them revealed a radically different culture. Gazelle bones numbered a mere 5; seal bones 3. Moving from earlier to later Neolithic times, the bones of immature goats and sheep increase in frequency. What evidently happened is this: the Neolithic Belt Cavers foresightedly spared adult sheep and goats for wool and milk. They slaughtered less valuable, younger animals in which people had as yet invested little time or energy. Flint sickle blades

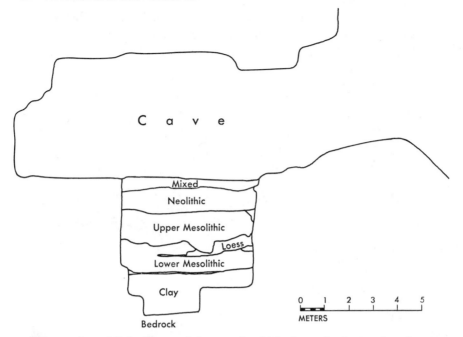

Cross-section of Belt Cave and the trench which the archeologists dug down to bedrock. (*Carleton S. Coon,* Cave Explorations in Iran 1949, *Philadelphia, 1951, p. 30.*)

point to increased reliance on cereals. With grain available, the time formerly devoted to hunting could decline. Around 5330 B.C. pottery became abundant. Some of the sherds are even decorated with painted lines. It is reasonable to conclude that the Belt Cavers did not themselves laboriously originate pottery. Its abrupt appearance in finished form testifies to diffusion.

Belt Cave lies in the highlands of Southwest Asia, precisely the region where 10,000 years ago food production began. Farming was adapted to the well-watered, hilly flanks that lie east of the Mediterranean Sea, including what is now called Kurdistan. Later, thanks to irrigation, it moved down to the more arid lowland, including the Euphrates and Tigris river valleys of Southern Mesopotamia.

THE NEW WAY STRENGTHENS AND FLOURISHES

As yields from food production grew greater and agricultural skills increased so that people could depend on each forthcoming harvest, Middle East farmers settled down. The period of incipient agriculture had ended and the stage of village communities began. Houses were built near the cultivated fields. Gradually dwellings with mud walls gave way to construction with mud brick but one or two rooms continued to suffice. Clay ovens for baking bread

THE NEW WAY OF LIFE DIFFUSES

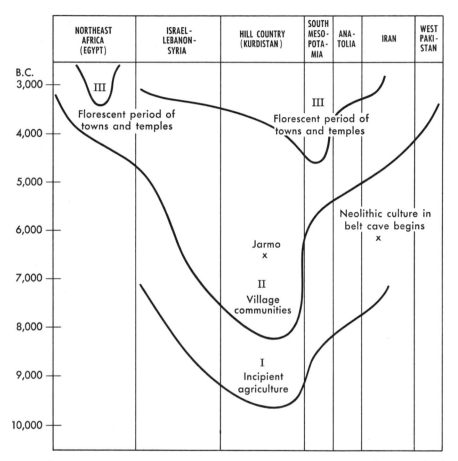

The diffusion of agriculture and other traits belonging to civilization is shown. Each of the three graph lines stands for the horizon that marks a new period of prehistoric culture. Note that the horizon is lowest (i.e., earliest) in the hill country for the first two periods shown. From the hilly lands agriculture and other formative elements diffused westward to northeast Africa (Egypt and Libya) and to Anatolia, which lies within easy reach of the Aegean and Balkan areas of Europe. Also they diffused eastward to Iran and to West Pakistan (Baluchistan). However, urbanization (Period III) began in southern Mesopotamia around 4500 B.C. From here the Bronze Age diffused westward rapidly. Note how the line moves nearly horizontally toward Israel and Egypt, indicating speedy transmission.

Reprinted from *Science* by permission.

are a distinctly Neolithic trait. Eventually they stretched from the Rhine River to Southwest Asia. A housewife fired the oven and then raked out the coals before she put the loaves in, just as Hopi Indians and Pathans in Swat still do. The family stored its harvested wheat and barley in storage pits, another feature that turned up independently centuries later in the American Southwest. The village homes contained facilities for women to spin and weave. Pins and awls beaten into shape from natural copper heralded the coming of true metallurgy. Small shrines and portable statuary reveal orientations in religion. All these traits combined mean we are witnessing the formative period of civilization. Men are learning to master new skills and to reorient substantially their energies and attitudes.

Jarmo in northern Iraq is the site of an actual, highland, Neolithic village. The time is about 6500 B.C. Twenty houses, each about as big as a small cottage, their mud walls set on stone foundations, comprise the homes of this small social system. Cultivators used flint sickles to reap their barley and two kinds of wheat. They milled the grain on querns and ate the porridge from stone bowls. Bones of sheep, cattle, pigs, and horses may still belong to wild species; the goat, however, was truly domesticated. Little clay figurines of animals and human beings (including a pregnant woman) possibly augmented the highlanders' sparse technical resources for coping with their agricultural and other problems.

Jarmo and other such Neolithic villages were practically self-sufficient. However, their inhabitants were by no means hidebound. They readily adopted new techniques and catchy styles of pottery from other villages. With small, self-sufficient villages went a compatible lack of specialization. No signs point to the agricultural outlet supporting full-time artisans or administrators. Such specialization would come only at a subsequent stage on the road to civilization.

The next batch of innovations that pushed culture to civilization occurred not in the highlands but down in the fertile river valleys of Southwest Asia. Farmers migrated into Mesopotamia, the alluvial Tigris and Euphrates plain, and began to irrigate their crops. In some places they first had to reclaim farmland from marsh through drainage schemes. To build irrigation and drainage canals demanded organized manpower. Organization, in turn, required means of firm social coordination. To supply this need political control evolved to a point where it could coordinate far more than the energies of 20 households in a small village. Political coordination began before irrigation, but the problems connected with supplying water to farmers and so assuring food for the growing population encouraged political machinery to become more complex and efficient. The administrators themselves no longer had time or talents for agriculture and stock raising. They had to be supported by taxes or tribute paid by the cultivators. Doubtlessly administrators justified such support, maintaining in one way or another that farmers were lucky to have men as astute as themselves managing things. Other specialists also had to be paid. Potters, for example, took over a task that housewives had done for two thousand years and turned out their wheelmade pots in wholesale quantities. Specialists in metallurgy reduced copper from ore and cast it into the shapes of implements. Later they discovered how to alloy copper and tin in order to obtain bronze, a stronger metal. With that step culture entered the Bronze Age period of florescence. Other specialists included professional transport workers who drove carts which utilized another timely invention, the wheel. A voluminous trade that moved on land and sea had grown since formative times.

Church and state lived in close union during the early Bronze Age. Administrators lived or worked in the temple precincts where artisans also practiced their specialized crafts. Around the temple with its shops and markets a dense

In Mesopotamian Sumer cattle, sheep, and goats were received at an official depot and paid out for religious and secular purposes. This cuneiform tablet notes the transfer of five lambs and a kid. Bronze Age Sumerian scribes recorded each such transaction. (*Science Museum, St. Paul, Minn., and Professor T. B. Jones.*)

settlement grew up. And in these most opportune circumstances the plow originated. Farmers would never have been able to feed a large, nonagricultural town population without that machine. Harnessed to animal energy the plow enabled acreage to increase without a proportionate increase in the number of cultivators.

The florescent age of towns and temples found writing a great convenience, if only as a means for keeping track of its growing wealth. Mesopotamian writing remained largely mnemonic, giving little attention to grammatical niceties, until 2400 B.C. when methodical archives turn up. At first pure pictography limited what could be written. By 3000 B.C. the pictures had been pared down to mere conventions in which we find it hard to discern the original objects. Conventionalization arose in part from a developmental innovation, the wedge-shaped stylus. In place of drawing lines freehand (always a messy business on mud), a scribe used his reed stylus to stamp lines into clay. Cuneiform writing, as this is called, saved much time in a day when bureau-

THE DEVELOPMENT OF WRITING

				Fish
				Ox
				Cow
				Barley
				Head
				Woman
				Man
				Heaven; God
				To go; to stand

Writing in the Middle East began by drawing what was meant. The first column shows the original pictograph. In the second column we see the same picture made in less time, imprinted by means of a wedge-shaped stylus. The original picture is hardly recognizable, first, because the new method of writing inevitably conventionalized the original representation and, second, because the position of the original pictograph has been altered. The third column shows each original pictograph in the position it occupies in wedge-shaped writing. In column four only stylus impressions are used. The signs have become even more highly conventionalized.

David Diringer, *The Alphabet* (New York, 1948), p. 46.

cratic bookkeeping had already grown heavy. The profesionals who employed it remembered the meaning of the signs by other criteria than their literalness. Furthermore, they drew signs that referred not only to things—men, temples, and trees—but designated more abstract concepts as well, like heaven, god, and the act of going. To symbolize such abstractions scribes invented new meanings for old pictographic signs and coined new signs. Another leap came once signs ceased to represent objects but were read as they sounded when spoken (like we read the sign 3 as "three"). Some signs stood simply for vowels. By accomplishing this, the Mesopotamian temple clerks stood at the threshold of a script in which every discrete sound unit (phoneme) comprising the language would have its own sign. But that threshold was not crossed until around 1000 B.C. when a Semitic-speaking people in the southwest corner of Asia originated our alphabet.

INTO THE LIGHT OF HISTORY

Appearance of writing means the end of prehistory and the start of history. Historians, however, often speak of a transitional, protohistoric interval sandwiched in between the first writing and the availability of enough records to permit historical work. Southwest Asia emerged into the light of history (protohistory) during the third millennium. By this time kingship and the city-state were clearly defined. Prodigious fortifications speak of the importance attained by warfare, as indeed do the empires which stumble and fall across the pages of our textbooks in ancient history. We are in the late period of the Bronze Age. Not till 1000 B.C., or a little later when iron comes into common use, can we talk of the Iron Age. These three pre-Christian millennia are the time of the classical empires of Akkad, Sumer, Assyria, Babylon, and Persia. After these the first empire to be based in Europe, the Greek, engulfed the Middle East.

The greatest days of Ur, a city reputed to be the birthplace of Abraham, belonged to this era of cyclical conquests and defeats.[3] A harbor town conveniently located near the point where the Euphrates River entered the Persian Gulf, Ur became the capital of a Sumerian empire that stretched to the Mediterranean. In the old, congested walled city, where as many as 360,000 persons are estimated to have lived, narrow streets and blind alleys set an example of unplanned urban growth that remains all too familiar. Graves of commoners, royal tombs, and house ruins have yielded archeologists a cross section of Ur's culture: chariots, weapons, gaming boards, property seals, lyres, pottery, carpentering and other tools, ornaments of gold and silver, glass and stone vessels—these are tangible proof of intense cultural elaboration. Houses had chapels and in the sacred area of the city stood an elaborate

[3] Leonard Woolley, *Ur of the Chaldees,* 2nd ed. (London, 1950).

temple where worshippers honored the moon, divine owner of all land. Here also the administrative offices were housed and farmers paid their rents. The king-emperor, god's vice-regent on earth, lived in a style that fit his exalted position. Since the moon priests couldn't know first-hand how god himself lived, what was more natural than to reproduce in the temple the magnificent manner in which his "tenant farmer," the king, lived, even to providing the divinity with a harem? The ziggurat, an impressive, artificial mountain of brick with terraces of soil deep enough for trees to grow, dominated this and other Mesopotamian cities. On top of the mound sat a shrine. Ur has captured the imagination of subsequent centuries down to the present day. After the dark ages that followed the Sumerian empire's collapse Hammurabi created a new Mesopotamian empire, the Babylonian, dominated by Semitic-speaking people, but he kept Sumerian as the temple language. A thousand years later Nebuchadnezzar took pains to rebuild Ur itself. And ever since the nineteenth century it has attracted museum expeditions which catch their first glimpse of the ruined ziggurat from the train at a station prosaically called Ur Junction.

THE NEW WAY EXPANDS

Long before the Mesopotamian city-states made conquest pay off in empires, the formative forces of agriculture, stock rearing, pottery, metallurgy, and village life began to diffuse. The process was more complex than exporting whole traits to be adopted intact, the way a Ford diffuses into foreign lands. Wherever Neolithic elements reached, they were reformed and reshaped. Prehistory in southern Asia, North Africa, and Europe uncovers many varieties of Neolithic, formative, and Bronze Age cultures. The modifications that culture elements encountered as they diffused are analogous to the evolutionary adaptations which animals undergo when they radiate from some center of diffusion into other environments.

PAKISTAN-INDIA

Let's follow the new way of life eastward to Pakistan and India before tracing its westward diffusion into Africa and Europe. Between 4000 and 3000 B.C. (if not earlier) pottery-using farmers built villages on the Baluchistan plateau above the jungle-covered Indus borderland. The plateau farmers used a little natural copper which was in time replaced by bronze. Their culture then descended into the Indus plain itself, farmers clearing away the jungle growth until, like today, it is confined close to the banks of the meandering Indus. Shortly before 2500 B.C., metropolitan centers arose at several places in the plain, cities that reached a circumference of over 3 miles. The most famous of these were Harappa (located in what formerly was called Punjab province) and Mohenjo-daro (in former Sind).

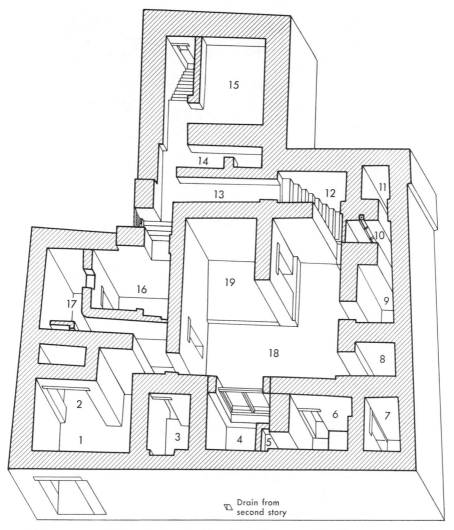

Drain from
second story

This two-story Mohenjo-daro dwelling has a frontage of 85 feet on a quiet lane and a depth of 97 feet. The walls are 4 to 5 feet thick. It is designed for outdoor living in the hot climate of the lower Indus Valley. 1, entrance house; 2, porter's rooms; 3, room with a well; 4, bathroom (drained into street); 5, bathroom; 6, chamber; 7, 8, 9, 10, 11, rooms perhaps intended for servants; 12, staircase to upper story; 13, 14, passages; 15, family living and sleeping rooms on second story; 16, guestroom (?); 17, passage; 18, paved central court open to the sky; in it is a catchment basin to collect water draining from upstairs privies; 19, kitchen (?). Other upstairs rooms were disposed around the central court, with a balcony projecting over the court. (*Adapted from J. Marshall*, Mohenjo-Daro and the Indus Civilization, 3 *vols., London, 1931*. Copyright Government of India; Permission of A. Probsthain, London.)

Over 4000 years later archeologists peeled the soil off these first manifestations of civilization in South Asia. They revealed that a central authority must

Terra cotta figurine from Mohenjo-daro. (*National Museum, New Delhi.*)

have directed the way the cities were built and planned so that their broad streets would cross each other at right angles. Efficient, covered drainage ditches carried off bath water and sewage from comfortable, fired brick dwellings. A fortified citadel dominated Mohenjo-daro. Other important buildings located in what might have been the administrative center, including a large bath and a pillared hall. Indus valley civilization had commercial ties with Mesopotamia, yet few detailed resemblances link the two cultures. The early Pakistanis drew on stimulating ideas that originated elsewhere to develop their own design for urban living.

The cities of the plain possessed writing but their script has never been deciphered. Someday it may be read. Will it then reveal under what pressure the citizens abandoned these busy centers of commerce and administration? For some reason they neglected to maintain the bunds which confined the vagrant Indus. Once the dikes fell, floods periodically overran the broad streets and houses, burying everything in deep silt. Some historians suppose that Indo-European speakers, who entered Pakistan-India around 1500 B.C. or earlier, descended on the cities and drove off or killed their population. Direct evidence neither supports nor contradicts these conjectures. In the arid hills, not far west of Mohenjo-daro, 22,000 Dravidian-speaking Brahui tribesmen live in an isolated linguistic enclave. Seventeen hundred miles separate them from the main body of Dravidian speakers in peninsular India. Are the Brahui a remnant of a formerly more dense Dravidian population that dominated the area before Indo-Europeans arrived? Brahui families who come down to the plain with their camels, fat-tail sheep, and goats to escape the winter can offer no word to solve this perplexity.

Until 500 B.C. a shadow obscures culture history in South Asia. Undoubtedly jungle-clearing went on, accompanying a steady extension of agriculture. Iron came in from Persia. We know that Indo-Europeans both fought and allied themselves with autochthonous inhabitants in the Indus and Ganges valleys. When the mist clears away, urban centers in the Ganges valley have reached a circumference of four miles. Writing, which had disappeared in the dark ages after Indus civilization collapsed, reappeared in a script definitely inspired by western alphabetic scripts. We know a fair amount of the thought which the early Ganges civilization devoted to religious and philosophical subjects. The ideas are preserved in venerated writings like the Upanishads: "The good is one thing; the pleasant is another. These two, differing in their ends, both prompt to action. Blessed are they that choose the good; they that choose the pleasant miss the goal."[4] Out of such thought grew three of the world's still living religions: Hinduism, Buddhism, and Jainism.

THE EGYPTIANS

The Neolithic thrust reached the narrow Nile valley and penetrated west and south shortly after 6000 B.C. But a new way of life unfolded only slowly. Even after Nile delta peasants had begun to cultivate wheat and barley and to raise cattle, sheep, goats, and pigs, they continued hunting and fishing. No more than early Neolithic farmers elsewhere did early Egyptians display much warlikeness. As technical proficiency in the working of stone, clay, and cold copper took hold interest canalized on fixing the dead for postmortuary careers. Dry desert sand preserved the flexed corpses reasonably well without embalming, but survivors thoughtfully provided jars of food, drink, and other goods

[4] Swami Prabhavananda and Frederick Manchester, *The Upanishads, Breath of the Eternal* (Hollywood, 1948), p. 23.

Modern bullfights in some Latin countries continue a popular ancient Mediterranean sport illustrated in this Egyptian drawing. (*J. Gardiner Wilkinson, The Manners and Customs of the Ancient Egyptians, 3 vols., London, 1878.*)

for the deceased to enjoy. Perhaps the way corpses kept when they were buried in the Nile desert stimulated attention to funerary practices. Whatever touched off the interest, by First Dynasty times (about 3400 B.C.) preoccupation with death had grown to where it manifested itself in magnificent royal tombs replete with wealth. In time out of these tombs rose the pyramids which in their turn, but well in the historic period, gave way to rock-cut tombs.

Writing in Egypt began in the fourth millennium. It developed along different lines than in Mesopotamia, whence the original impulse had probably diffused. Egyptians when they wrote on their monuments used hieroglyphs. On vegetable papyrus, using a frayed reed pen, they wrote the same signs more cursively. As in Mesopotamia the signs soon ceased to be interpreted as standing for definite ideas and objects but came to be read as they sounded.

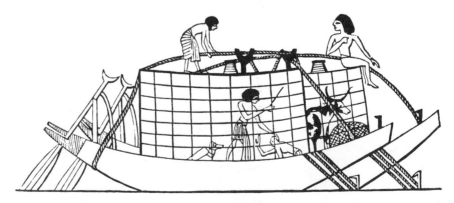

Egypt was limited to the fertile corridor that the Nile River watered. The river formed a natural traffic artery. In this cargo vessel carrying livestock and other goods, a shipmaster administers a painful beating to one of his crew. (*J. Gardiner Wilkinson, The Manners and Customs of the Ancient Egyptians, 3 vols., London, 1878.*)

As early as the end of the fourth millennium some 24 to 30 signs simply represented consonants. Despite this precocious step, for some reason the Egyptians failed to be the first people to switch over to a purely phonetic writing system.

The Nile River stimulated water-borne commerce. On land, in lieu of wheeled vehicles, the ass served for a long time as a pack animal. It is strange that wagons and chariots did not enter Egypt until historic times, long after Mesopotamia had adopted them. The historic epoch, dynastic times, brought about the full realization of civilization. It emerged from an earlier period of energetic empire building in which two kingdoms, a northern (lower) and southern (upper) had emerged as rivals. Inevitably they clashed and fused giving rise to a united Egypt under southern rule. Cities remained small during the early dynasties. Principally they were administrative nucleii hovering around the pharaoh's court. Within urban precincts craftsmen kept busy providing goods for the pharaoh to enjoy while he lived and after his death. Most people lived in houses of sun-dried brick; only royalty could afford monumental stone architecture and other luxuries.

NEW CULTURES FORM IN EUROPE

Food production with its associated elements first penetrated Europe in the southeast, the region nearest to Southwest Asian centers of diffusion. No actual evidence exists of migration from Anatolia or any other part of the Middle East into Europe. Yet the well-formed character of early Neolithic culture indicates that it must have been migrants who carried the crucial traits from which North Mediterranean civilization developed. Of course, the new way of life also diffused to indigenous Mesolithic folk. Again what occurred in Europe didn't simply copy Middle East culture. The Neolithic and Bronze Ages shaped themselves in harmony with the diverse environments that make up the European continent and in response to values held by its different social systems.

In the Aegean, an area we will return to and follow more closely than other European regions, early Neolithic settlements dating from around 3000 B.C. were small, often compounded of multiroomed houses opening off torturously crooked village lanes. In addition to cereals the farmers cultivated vines, figs, and olive trees. Farther north in the Danube basin the earliest farmers lived in what look like multifamily houses. Dwellings ranged from 30 to 130 feet in length and were from 18 to 22 feet wide. In winter the same wattle and daub houses probably protected human occupants as well as cattle and pigs. A largely self-sufficient village contained

Hafted stone axes and fire helped Neolithic farmers to clear the virgin European forests so that they could plant. This ax was found near Luzern, Switzerland, and dates from about 2700 B.C. (*Schweizer Landesmuseum, Zurich.*)

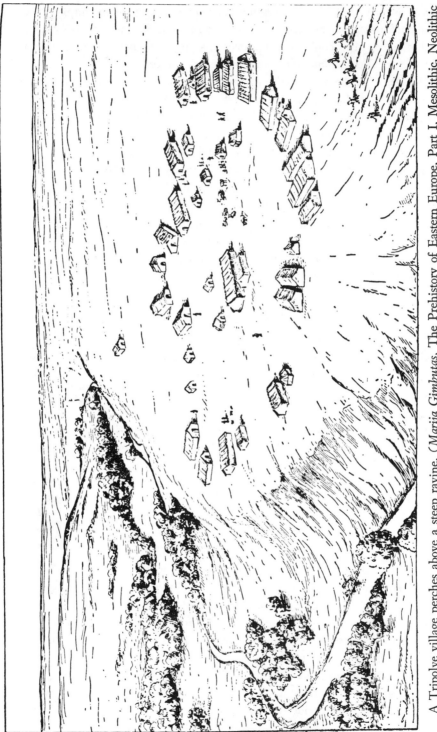

A Tripolye village perches above a steep ravine. (*Marija Gimbutas, The Prehistory of Eastern Europe, Part I, Mesolithic, Neolithic and Copper Age Cultures in Russia and the Baltic Area, American School of Prehistoric Research, Peabody Museum, Harvard University, Bull. no. 20, 1956; first appeared in* Materialy i Issledovaniya po Arkheologiyi S.S.S.R., 10, 1949.)

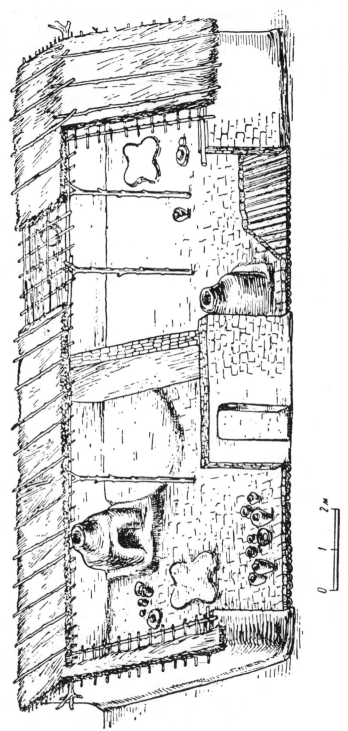

Interior of a Tripolye dwelling; notice the clay bake ovens. (*Marija Gimbutas*, The Prehistory of Eastern Europe, Part I, Mesolithic, Neolithic, and Copper Age Cultures in Russia and the Baltic Area, *American School of Prehistoric Research, Peabody Museum, Harvard University, Bull. no. 20, 1956; first appeared in* Materialy i Issledovaniya po Arkheologiyi S.S.S.R., *10, 1949.*)

about 20 such houses. Early Danubian farmers cultivated wheat, millet, barley, and flax, and made pottery in varied forms. Easily worked loess soils, not the river, attracted them and they worked these lands until the soil was exhausted. Then they moved away, cleared new lands, and rebuilt their dwellings. In addition to long houses, later Neolithic cultivators also raised smaller dwellings. Over the doors they mounted clay bulls' heads.

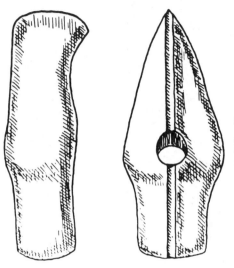

Two views of a stone battle-ax. (W. Antoniewicz, "Eneolityczne groby szkieletowe we wsi Zlota wipow Sandomierskim," Wiadomości Archeologiczne, 9, 1925, 191-245.)

    Danubian culture spread westward as far as Belgium. In Switzerland the farmers built pile dwellings at the edges of lakes. Eastward the Neolithic way of life, known as Tripolye culture, diffused around the loess lands beyond the Black Sea in southern Russia. The wheat, barley, millet, and rye farmers built their two-room and larger dwellings in an irregular circular pattern to form a village 600 to 1600 feet in diameter. They domesticated cattle, pigs, and sheep goats and horses and fished in the Dniester, Dnieper, and other rivers. Bull figurines, clay phalli, and female statuettes could all have represented religious symbols. Perhaps clay models of huts also had a place in domestic ceremonies, like modern creches set up under Christmas trees.

    Into Tripolye and Danubian settlements around 2000 B.C. moved warlike people from farther east who buried their dead in houselike structures of timber or beneath boulders covered with earthen mounds. They are called Battle-Ax folk from the weapon that accompanied their dead warriors. Perhaps these axes not only served as weapons to wield against farmers trying to defend their loess lands and villages, but symbolized the eternal struggle waged against destructive forces threatening life and security. The Battle-Ax folk probably spread Indo-European languages across the European continent.

ACROSS THE CHANNEL

In the west on the chalk downs of southern England, Neolithic colonists of the third millennium have left no signs of their villages. However, problematic hill-top causeway camps stem from a folk who introduced farming in Britain and are probably sites of their early settlement. A causeway camp consists of central space surrounded by two or more concentric ditches interrupted, or crossed, by paths (causeways). Less puzzling are barrows that reach 300 feet in length. Under them, in chambers, from 15 to 30 and occasionally more Neolithic dead lay collectively buried. Burial chambers (popularly known as giants' graves and dolmens) are an outstanding feature in the prehistory of

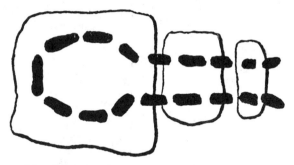

Megalithic tombs in western Europe consist of two parts, supporting stones (the solid areas of the drawing) and huge, horizontally placed table rocks (drawn in outline). Built on this basic pattern are a variety of forms. The plan shows a burial chamber into which a processional avenue leads. (*Fernand Niel,* Dolmens et menhirs, *Paris, 1958. Permission Presses Universitaires de France.*)

Atlantic Europe. Occasionally they were sunk below ground but generally the builders set up large dressed stones (megaliths) on the surface and then heaped them over with earth or stones. Where today the earth has been stripped away we see the chambers exposed. Tombs were not opened for individual interments. The confused state of many skeletons is proof that bodies were accumulated elsewhere before they or the bones were carried into the sepulcher. While British Neolithic local groups must each have been highly self-sufficient, some communities carried on an interesting trade in stone axes. Craftsmen first shaped the ax head at the quarry. Then in their permanent settlements they applied the final polish before exporting the finished products.

Continental invasions brought bronze to Britain around 1900 B.C. Soon thereafter pastoral Battle-Ax conquerors arrived. Their herds gave a new direc-

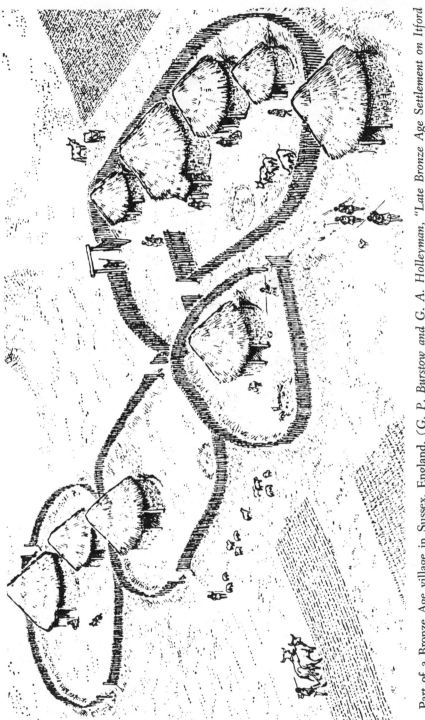

Part of a Bronze Age village in Sussex, England. (G. P. Burstow and G. A. Holleyman, "Late Bronze Age Settlement on Itford Hill, Sussex," Proceedings of the Prehistoric Society, 23, 1957, 167-212.)

The character of Neolithic culture in northern Europe differed strikingly from that farther south as this rock drawing of a man on skis from the region of the White Sea (U.S.S.R.) indicates. (*Herbert Kuehn*, The Rock Pictures of Europe, *trans. A. H. Brodrick, Fair Lawn, N. J., 1956.*)

tion to the early British agricultural pattern and their language is thought to be the first Indo-European language spoken in the Isles.

THE NEW WAY CREEPS NORTH

By 2500 B.C. the Neolithic revolution at last reached Denmark and southern Sweden but the cold, damp climate presented a severe handicap that early farmers had to overcome. They did so by concentrating on stock-raising,

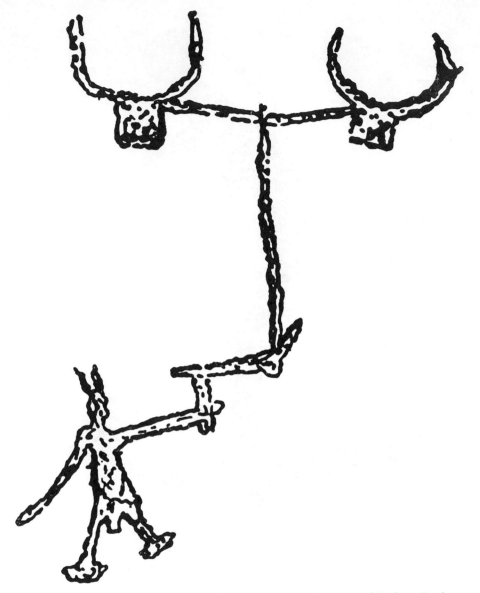

A pair of oxen drew the plow in European Bronze Age times. (*Herbert Kuehn,* The Rock Pictures of Europe, *trans. A. H. Brodrick, Fair Lawn, N. J., 1956.*)

practicing a little agriculture as a sideline. All across northern Europe pastoral tribes, known from their cord-impressed pottery and their antler or stone battle-axes, invaded and conquered in late Neolithic times. Often the Battle-Ax warriors buried their dead in chambers made of planks or stone slabs which they then covered with round or long earthen barrows. Some slipped their dead into megalithic tombs built earlier. In one or two places evidence suggests that widows destroyed themselves when their husbands died; this custom strengthens the note of male dominance in Battle-Ax culture. If these pastoralists were indeed the earliest Indo-European speakers to penetrate the northern tier of the continent, then they came nearly simultaneously with representatives of the same language family who perhaps brought widow immolation into the Ganges valley.

INTIMATIONS OF CIVILIZATION

The Bronze Age came to central and western Europe starting about 2000 B.C. It achieved no florescence comparable to the corresponding period in the Middle East or to what we will see in the Aegean region. Bronze metallurgy, agriculture with plows rather than hoes, and a modicum of specialization and trade don't automatically produce florescence. During this period many parts of Europe shipped amber, tin, copper, gold, and other products to the wealthy Aegean market, but like many underdeveloped suppliers of raw materials, the early Europeans didn't grow prosperous through such trade. Nor do we find signs of rulers concentrating religious authority, political power, and wealth in themselves; had they done so, they might have nurtured civilization more quickly. I don't mean to imply that cultural stagnation existed north of the Alps and beyond the channel. The skill of goldsmiths and the ingenuity with which bronzesmiths evolved new techniques and implements fostered unmistakable gains in cultural elaboration. European innovations like the safety pin and gold ornaments diffused even to Greece. It is a relative backwardness we find beyond the Mediterranean when we compare the area with other Bronze Age civilizations.

The Iron Age, founded on cheap and abundant iron ore rather than relatively scarce copper and tin, began to overcome

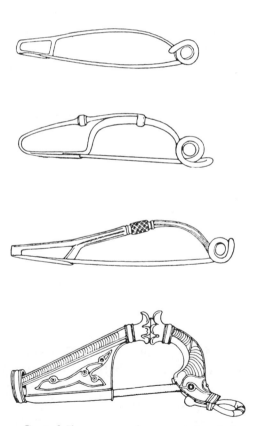

Central European craftsmen produced simple safety pins and exuberantly designed clasps. (*Hans Hahne*, Das vorgeschichtliche Europa, Kulturen und Voelker, *Bielefeld, 1910.*)

this cultural lag. Population grew and so did large fortified townships where rulers established their headquarters. Hallstatt culture (beginning about 900 B.C.) exemplifies one central European way of life in early Iron Age times. It is known mainly from cemeteries in which the Bronze Age custom of burying only after cremation gradually declines. Objects of apparel as well as ornaments went into Iron Age interments. Chariots accompanied men of valor to their graves, for the horse had just appeared in Central Europe. Absence of the potter's wheel testifies to the still limited extent of trade and specialization. On the other hand, saltworking in certain favorable places, like Hallstatt itself in Alpine Austria, employed many hands. Today the mountain rimmed tourist mecca crowded on a narrow lakeside gives no indication of what life was like below the grave fields long ago. In the subsequent La Tène period (c. 400 B.C.) Hallstatt influences spread, accompanying the hard-living Celts' expansion in Central Europe. The tribes imitated the Greeks in many ways; they even struck their own coins. Now the potter's wheel arrived and also iron locks and keys. Chariot burials continue to attest to warrior chiefs' prestige and hundreds of Celtic strongholds demonstrate that warriors found plenty of opportunity to show their mettle. Some graves include retainers and women who could have been widows for whom life without their husbands was unthinkable. A doctor's grave in Bavaria records another Celtic specialty, surgery. We have the trephining saw he used to penetrate a patient's skull and reach his brain; the snare with which he removed growths, and the wound probe that enabled him to explore below the skin. Amputation saws and needles to suture arteries are known from other late Iron Age sites. Ultimately such instruments and the doctor's knowledge derived from the Mediterranean world. They suggest some of the amenities that existed in transalpine Europe on the eve of Romanization.

AEGEAN CIVILIZATION

It was in the mountainous Aegean region, including the offshore island of Crete, that the Neolithic legacy first evolved into a full-blown Bronze Age European civilization. In the Aegean islands and on the mainland descendants of Neolithic colonists thoroughly refashioned the heritage that had originated abroad, for no similar Neolithic culture has ever been discovered in Asia. Before 2000 B.C. several significant innovations, notably the plow, potter's wheel, smelting of gold and copper, and use of bronze, had entered Aegean culture and a florescent Bronze Age had begun. The rapidity with which these developments took hold makes it certain they were borrowed ready-made and intact. Ultimately, of course, they all derive from the Middle East. Specialization grew up not merely among craftsmen but also in the roles of sailors who manned ore-propelled vessels and merchants who financed their voyages.

HEADQUARTERS OF A BRONZE AGE CIVILIZATION

(Royal Hellenic Air Force)

The Palace of Minos, at Knossos, which Sir Arthur Evans excavated in 1900 from the mound under which time had buried it, covered 6½ acres. This confusion of corridors and rooms contained the nerve center of Crete's maritime empire. By maintaining peace and safety for merchants on the high seas, Knossos with its 100,000 people attained a high pitch of Bronze Age comfort and prosperity. Actually three palaces are superimposed at Knossos. The oldest goes back to 2200 B.C., at which time Minoan civilization emerged out of a thousand-year formative period. Around 1400 B.C. a severe earthquake followed by attacks launched from overseas brought down the last palace together with the Golden Age of Minoan civilization to which it belonged.

For a plan of the palace see Friedrich Matz, *Le Monde Égéen*, trans. Jacques Boitel (Paris, 1956), Pl. 24.

Even in the early Bronze Age, Aegean sea traffic spanned the Mediterranean to reach Egypt. Overland, from central and western Europe, the Aegeans imported tin for use by their own metallurgists as well as to transship to the

Middle East, where bronzeworkers kept up a steady demand for metal. Fortified towns and plenty of weapons testify that the early Aegeans didn't attain their prosperity painlessly.

The late Bronze Age, particularly its zenith in the twelfth and thirteenth centuries B.C., is celebrated by Homer. However, since he wrote in about 700 B.C., he described a way of life that had been dead for over half a millennium. The tragedies of Aeschylus, written shortly after 500 B.C., also hearken back to what for the Greeks had become a mythical period when, with dire consequences, gods interfered in the affairs of men. In Mycenae, the mainland Bronze Age city, archeologists imagine they have dug up the tomb of Clytemnestra. She is the queen whom Aeschylus describes as having been

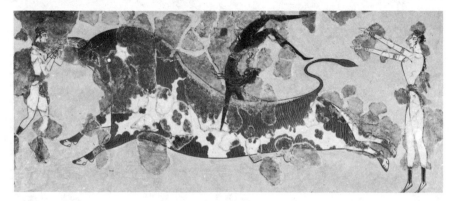

The bull possessed special meaning in Bronze Age Knossos and elsewhere in the Mediterranean. In this only partially intact fresco venturesome toreadors are grappling with one of the handsome animals. (*Heraclion Museum, Crete.*)

slain by her own son, Orestes, to avenge the murder of his father, Agamemnon. The historical value of this Iron Age poetry is limited. On the other hand, the wealthy and powerful aristocracy whom the Greek dramatists and poets describe receives archeological support in both mainland Greece and Crete. Powerful, literate cities, like Knossos and Mycenae, were the seats of monarchs who ruled in splendor. At Knossos in Crete are the ruins of three successive Minoan palaces built on a hill; even the earliest contains plumbing. Terra cotta pipes and underground channels allowed latrines to be flushed with running water. From 1700 to 1400 B.C. Crete's prosperity stemmed from her position as mistress of the sea lanes. Speedy vessels with two or three masts conveyed a heavy share of Minoan culture in the form of merchandise to other parts of the Mediterranean. The bull held a special meaning and bull-grappling was an admired skill. In preserved frescoes we see the late Minoans themselves, clean-shaven men and girls with pug noses. Both sexes have their waists compressed as thin as could be with tight belts.

Many of the Minoans lost their lives in a disastrous earthquake around

Skillful rule, localized perhaps in the throne room of the luxurious palace of Knossos, brought Crete profit from her dominant role in Aegean commerce. (*Heraclion Museum, Crete.*)

1400 and in the destructive invasions that followed. Powerful, rival mainland cities, like Mycenae, helped to destroy the power of Crete. The mainland rivals' prosperity also soon ended. Costly episodes like the Trojan war (*c.* 1184), fought not over Helen's loveliness but over trade, insured the collapse of mainland Bronze Age civilization. Dark Ages ensued out of which the Greek Iron Age rose.

This period includes the Age of Pericles and Alexander's far-flung Hellenistic empire. For the first time European power was launched in Asia. In their own minds the Greeks occupied a privileged position in the world. Their culture, heritage of the Neolithic and Bronze Ages, they exported grandly as far as Buddhist India. Meanwhile in Central Italy another urban-based, imperial civilization was growing out of Etruscan beginnings. Elements of Greek civilization abundantly present in southern Italy stimulated the rapid growth of Rome which, in turn, carried the finishing touches of civilization to the still backward regions beyond the Alps and across the English channel.

ROMANIZATION OF EUROPE

The romanization of Europe occurred largely in provincial towns that Romans built and to which emigrant Romans carried means to satisfy new wants. Enlistment in the imperial army and increasing literacy further encouraged rapid cultural transfusion. Increasingly language, housing, pottery, decorative art, and religion took on a Roman stamp. However, in the eastern part of the Roman empire—in the Balkans, for example—the stamp was predominantly Hellenistic. Roman influence did not uproot all traces of previous European Iron Age culture, no more than the westernization of Africa and Asia in recent times has utterly supplanted traditional behavior and artifacts.

Most of Europe still lagged in civilization after Roman power began to ebb. The Dark Ages constituted a new formative period in which Greek and Roman impulses were thoughtfully nurtured. But men of learning remained isolated from one another through poor communication. Division of the continent into two major language divisions—Romance (founded on Latin) and Germanic—further limited the large-scale intense interaction that nurtures civilization. Then came contact with the Arab and Byzantine worlds. Reemergence of effective government stimulated productivity. Intellectual problems stimulated thought and debate. With these stimuli there grew up after the thirteenth century an urban and urbane way of life. With the Renaissance this renewed European civilization began, for better or worse, to dominate the world.

SIBERIAN MIGRATION TO AMERICA

One area that has been heavily subjected to European civilization is the New World. In these two, vast continents several peoples had just crossed or were about to cross the threshold of civilization when the European invaders came. The Indians from New England south, whom the English encountered, remained far from any such level of culture growth. But the Aztec, Maya, and Inca, whom the Spanish Conquistadores subjugated through peerless courage and revolting cruelty, had evolved considerably further.

Not many years ago anthropologists disagreed over when the Americas were originally peopled. What can be called the late arrival theory held that the first migrations from Asia didn't occur till after the glacial age had finished. That would be when the Paleolithic period began to give way to the Mesolithic, about 12,000 years ago. After all, supporters of this position reasoned defensively, no Paleolithic-like artifacts had ever been recovered from the New World; not one early form of American man resembles Pithecanthropus or Neanderthal. Opposed were Americanists who clung to the early arrival theory. They remained convinced that the first visitors must have arrived from Siberia during the Pleistocene in Paleolithic times. They argued justifiably that it must have taken the Indian much more than 10,500 years to reach the point at which the first Europeans found him. It took him much more time to establish himself in his new milieu, diversify his languages, and in some places bring his culture to the threshold of civilization. Also they were

PERIODS OF NEW WORLD CULTURE GROWTH

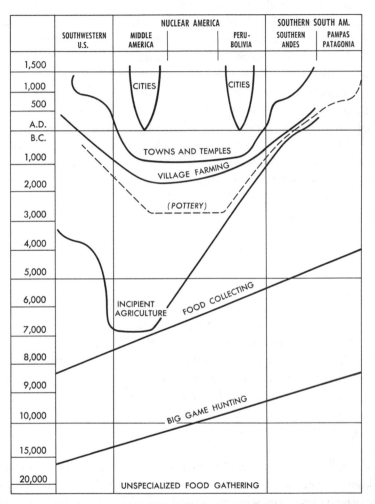

Seven major periods sum up New World culture growth. The culminating point came about the time of Christ, when cities appeared in Middle America and Peru-Bolivia.

Note the incipient beginnings of agriculture in Middle America about 7000 B.C. and its diffusion north to the southwestern United States. Although not shown on this chart, agriculture apparently entered the Southeast earlier than the Southwest. Lowland South America has also been omitted.

Gordon R. Willey, "New World Prehistory," *Science*, 131 (1960), 73-86.

convinced of their argument by traces of early culture buried in fourth glacial deposits in close conjunction with animals that no European visitor ever saw alive in this country. The early arrival theory won, though an absolute date for the original peopling of America still remains to be found. The first hunters may have crossed what is now Bering Strait as far back as third interglacial times. It seems almost positive that men lived in the New World when the last ice front descended. Whenever it was that men first came here, fresh parties of migrants continued to follow for many, many centuries. Note that I speak only of arrival from Siberia. It is unlikely that any sizable migrations eastward across the Pacific brought people here prehistorically.

It is surprising that Indians brought so little Old World Paleolithic and Mesolithic culture with them when they migrated. New World artifacts rarely parallel closely those of the Old World. Americans, as I have already said, independently invented agriculture and nurtured a large series of plants found no place else. They also invented pottery by themselves, even though another ceramic tradition probably crossed into Alaska from Asia and drifted east and south. The whole feel of prehistoric cultures in the New World contrasts sharply with that of the Old. Yet, to be sure many specific elements do link the two continents, including microliths, engraving tools, conical dwellings, semiunderground houses, spearthrower, and bow.

DEVELOPMENTS IN FOOD GATHERING

Of the cultures belonging to the unspecialized food gatherers who came here first we know next to nothing except that they survived and got as far south as Tierra del Fuego. By 7000 B.C. they had reached that dead end of southern South America. At Tule Springs, Nevada, in the Great Basin we find the site of an open-air hearth. Here a band of those early arrivers stopped to eat animals they had killed with lances, for the earliest New World food gatherers still lacked bows and arrows.

Either the same early people or subsequent migrations are responsible for the next cultural level, a period marked by the pursuit of large animals. It is best known from the U.S. Great Plains and eastern foothills of the Rockies where after 11,000 years remains of the hunters' butchered kills—mammoths, mastadons, and buffalo—still lie. To kill these beasts they made oblong, lance-shaped (lanceolate) points fitted with a channel, or flute. The flute probably helped to haft the point. Nobody can identify the precise projectile weapon that was tipped by these fluted points. Around boulder-rimmed hearths in Sandia Cave, New Mexico, these terminal Pleistocene big game hunters made themselves at home. The lanceolate points, here called Sandia, are not fully fluted but the retouching, done with a pressure tool, shows good control of flint. Along with these the cave occupants used bone points and

Sandia points. The specimen at the right shows partial fluting. (*Smithsonian Institution and Dr. Frank H. H. Roberts.*)

large, crude skin scrapers of a type distributed all the way down to the southern end of South America. Clovis and Folsom fluted points belong to this period and diffused widely in unglaciated North America. Once the last ice stage had departed, Folsom hunters moved northward into the subarctic zone, a region of abundant big game.

In western North and South America increasing aridity and a dearth of large animals pressed the big game hunters to abandon their customary habits and find new modes of subsistence. They found many, each suited to the region they occupied and all technically more developed than any earlier phase of New World culture. I call this third period Food Collecting but

Folsom points shown actual size from a Colorado site about 10,700 years old. (*Smithsonian Institution and Dr. Frank H. H. Roberts.*)

usually it is called Archaic. Neither designation goes far to distinguish it from previous modes of life. The desert phase of Food Collecting evolved earliest. In the arid west nonsedentary people lived by intensively exploiting the country for roots, rabbits, small rodents, and anything else that was edible, including seeds they ground into flour on flat milling stones. Plant fibers provided them with the material necessary to make their baskets, nets and lines. They hurled their weapons with spearthrowers. When convenient they camped in caves, stretching out on bark or grass beds under robes woven of mouse and rabbit skin. In these shelters they discarded or left for archeologists to find sandals, baskets, firedrills, pipes, nets, and mats. Altogether these make up a comfortable looking cultural assemblage, one still characteristic of surviving American desert collectors.

In the eastern woodlands, roughly from Ohio to New York, food collectors adapted somewhat differently, though they too used the spearthrower and milled seeds on stone mortars. They fished with hooks and nets and covered their homes with bark, mats, or skins. On the Tennessee River in northern Alabama shell middens testify to still another way they adapted to local resources. Here, as well as farther north, in traits like flexed corpses, separate burial of trunk and skull, and cremation we detect an exaggerated concern with death. The concern continued and gave rise to large burial mounds and other dramatic manifestations. Along the North Pacific Coast in Washington and British Columbia, sea-mammal hunting bestowed its own unique flavor on this third level of New World culture growth. In western Alaska and the by now ice-free taiga, former big game hunters incorporated in their culture microliths and burins, the latter resembling engraving tools well known in Late Paleolithic Europe.

STEPS TO CIVILIZATION

While both North and South American food collectors were taking maximal advantage of their environments, another basis of subsistence was taking shape in Nuclear America. This region encompasses the southern two-thirds of Mexico, all of Central America, Andean and coastal Peru, and adjacent areas of Bolivia. Here where civilization would simultaneously emerge in two disparate centers, food collectors learned to cultivate plants in order to reap a harvest they could count on. They domesticated gourds, beans, peppers, squash, and, most important of all, maize. Cotton was raised for textiles. From Nuclear America cultivation spread into lowland South America where manioc replaced maize as the staple.

Several millennia elapsed before practice of cultivation with relatively little reliance on hunting and collecting produced enough food to sustain village life. In the interval Nuclear Americans originated pottery and launched it in diffusion. But food gatherers in the American northeast used pottery earlier; perhaps they secured it through a separate stream of diffusion from the Old World.

Let's observe the period of Village Farming in one well-known area, namely, among ancestors of the Hopi, Zuni, and other Pueblo Indians. The sequence starts with Basketmaker Indians living in homes with scooped-out, saucer-shaped floors located both under the overhanging eaves of caves and in the open. Pit storage bins were a prominent household feature. Near them stood grinding stones for milling corn flour. Turkeys were the only animal kept for food. In time the Basketmakers constructed pithouses, their interior walls en-

Ruins of a Classic Pueblo town at Mesa Verde National Park, Colorado. (*U. S. National Park Service; photograph by Donald Watson.*)

circled by benches. To enter these one climbed down a ladder through the smokehole or else came along an entry tunnel that also served as ventilator. In these underground ceremonial chambers or temples (kivas) Indians carried on their religion. During the subsequent period of Towns and Temples, around the beginning of the Christian era. Pueblo towns grew in area. A contiguous mass of masonry rooms reached two to four stories high. Some kivas attained a width of 80 feet, although most were smaller. That was the golden or classic age of the Pueblo Indians. Rather inexplicably it didn't last long but came to an abrupt reorientation around A.D. 1300. What motivated the townsmen to abandon their well-built dwellings and disperse? Did internal dissension tax too severely their traditional way of making decisions, a way which very likely then as today demanded unanimous consent? Did the drought that stretched from 1276 to 1299 make large-scale settlements impractical? Or were their compact settlements too vulnerable to attack by marauding Indians equipped with a more archaic culture, like the Navaho and Apache? Whatever the reasons, Pueblo Indians never attained civilization in pre-Columbian times.

The growth of towns and temples took varying paths in the Mississippi and Ohio valleys, in the valley of Mexico, among the Maya, and in Peru. Among

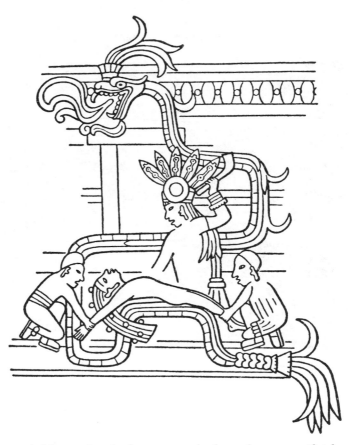

A Maya priest is about to cut the heart from a sacrificial victim. (*Reproduced from a mural at Chichen Itza, J. E. S. Thompson, The Rise and Fall of Maya Civilization, Norman, Okla., 1954.*)

the Maya, for example, mounds surmounted by temples provided a sacred focus. In Highland South America large and planned cities constituted literate nerve centers of civilization, trade depots, places in which a small, upper, administrative class showed off its luxury. Civilization in Peru rested on the cultivation of over 50 different plants. Irrigation canals helped to support a dense population, a portion of which served in a standing army. Metallurgists

WAR AND EMPIRE BUILDING IN ANDEAN BRONZE AGE CIVILIZATION

Inca culture flourished in the area around Cuzco, Peru. From here the Inca conquered the greater part of Andean territory and spread their culture. Their empire lasted about 90 years. Then the Spanish conquered. In this drawing, which a seventeenth-century Indian artist drew from hearsay in European style, Inca Bronze Age warriors are attacking a fort. Notice the cut-stone walls. One soldier is carrying a figurine, symbol perhaps of a deity watching over the army's fortunes. Defenders repulse the attack by throwing down rocks.

Felipe Guaman Poma de Ayala, *Nueva Córonica y Buen Gobierno*, Université de Paris, Travaux et Mémoires de l'Institut d' Ethnologie, vol. 23, 1936.

worked skillfully in bronze, silver, and gold, and there were many other specialists, most of whom the government employed. Andean people never originated writing but in Middle America the signs comprising a logographic script had reached the stage where scribes ignored the image itself and read signs as they sounded. They wrote on stone, stucco, and bark paper. Here metal workers knew how to work copper and gold but did not deliberately fabricate bronze. The wheel and plow remained two important Middle East traits missing from Nuclear American civilization. In fact, no animal power supplemented human labor except for the Andean lama used in transport. The Nuclear Americans were accomplished administrators capable of extending their empires. But how utterly ineffectual they proved when it came to defending their cities against the arms of Renaissance Europeans. These conquerors from across the sea terminated abruptly the growth of an independent New World civilization.

While in Mexico and Peru civilization was reaching its pre-Columbian maximum and the Pueblo Indians were striving to manage whatever difficulties plagued their Golden Age, Arctic Eskimo food collectors were orienting their efforts otherwise. They were bending their culture in an ever more specialized direction in order to live as comfortably as possible in one of the earth's most restricted environments. The "classic" phase of Eskimo culture took form in about A.D. 1500. It persisted for another 300 years, that is, until the irresistible pressure of Europeanization reached the Arctic.

FURTHER READING

Several skillful writers tell the story of civilization emerging in the Old World. Three of the best are V. Gordon Childe, *What Happened in History,* rev. ed. (Harmondsworth, 1954); Carleton S. Coon, *The Story of Man* (New York, 1954); and John Grahame Douglas Clark, *World Prehistory, an Outline* (Cambridge, Eng., 1961). V. Gordon Childe *Man Makes Himself,* rev. ed. (London, 1941) is more interested in process than simply in the record of culture growth. R. J. Braidwood gives radiocarbon dates for many sites in "Near Eastern Prehistory," *Science,* 127 (1958), 1419-1430. The same author's *Prehistoric Men,* 4th ed., Chicago Natural History Museum, Popular Series, Anthropology, no. 37, 1959, offers a quick summary of formative and later eras in Southwest Asia, while his and Linda Braidwood's "The Earliest Village Communities of Southwestern Asia," *Journal of World History,* 1 (1953), 278-310, concentrates on Neolithic times. Robert M. Adams is more determinedly evolutionary in "Developmental Stages in Ancient Mesopotamia," in Julian H. Steward, ed., *Irrigation Civilizations: A Comparative Study,* Pan American Union, Social Science Monographs, no. 1, 1955. Georges Contenau, *Everyday Life in Babylon and Assyria,* trans. K. R. Maxwell-Hyslop and A. R. Maxwell-Hyslop (London, 1954) deals with the later Mesopotamian empires.

For more about Belt Cave see Carleton S. Coon, *The Seven Caves* (New York, 1957), chap. 4, and his *Cave Explorations in Iran,* 1949, University of Pennsylvania Museum Monographs, 1951. Alfred C. Moorhouse, *The Triumph of the Alphabet* (New York, 1953) describes the succession of innovations that led to phonetic writing. South Asian prehistory is reviewed in R. E. Mortimer Wheeler, *Early India and Pakistan to Ashoka* (London, 1959). Summaries of European prehistory are given in V. Gordon Childe, *Prehistory of European Society* (Harmondsworth, 1958). How important discoveries in European prehistory were made is the theme of Geoffrey Bibby's *The Testimony of the Spade* (New York, 1956). For a most readable summary of British culture growth see Jacquetta

Hawkes and Christopher Hawkes, *Prehistoric Britain*, rev. ed. (Harmondsworth, 1958). Stuart Piggott, *The Neolithic Cultures of the British Isles* (Cambridge, Eng., 1954) is concerned with the beginnings there of a new way of life. E. Vogt, "Swiss Pile-dwellings," *Antiquity*, 31 (1957), 68-72, contains up-to-date knowledge about an interesting phase of early Alpine culture. For more about "A Doctor's Grave of the Middle La Tène Period from Bavaria" see the article by J. M. de Navarro in *Proceedings of the Prehistoric Society*, 21 (1955), 231-248. A very pleasant book about Minoan civilization is Agnes Carr Vaughan, *The House of the Double Axe: The Palace at Knossos* (Garden City, N.Y., 1959). It is also worth looking at the lavishly illustrated *Crete and Mycenae* by Spyridon Marinatos (New York, 1960). Iron Age Greek civilization forms the subject of many books, including H. D. F. Kitto, *The Greeks* (Harmondsworth, 1951). This might be followed by R. H. Barrow, *The Romans* (Harmondsworth, 1949). In Michael Huxley, ed., *The Root of Europe* (London, 1952) several authors collaborate to trace the diffusion of Greek culture. In some respects a parallel work is R. E. Mortimer Wheeler, *Rome Beyond the Imperial Frontiers* (London, 1954). F. J. Haverfield describes *The Romanization of Roman Britain*, rev. George Macdonald, 4th ed. (Oxford, 1926), and R. W. Southern, *The Making of the Middle Ages* (London, 1953) continues European culture history beyond the fall of Rome.

Gordon R. Willey and Philip Phillips sketch New World prehistory schematically in *Method and Theory in American Archaeology* (Chicago, 1958). I have also found useful many parts of Louis A. Brennan's *No Stone Unturned* (New York, 1959). For the Clovis-Folsom period of Big Game Hunting I turned to E. H. Sellards, *Early Man in America* (Austin, Tex., 1952). Jesse D. Jennings provides a close-up view of some desert collectors 10,000 years ago living in *Danger Cave*, Memoirs of the Society for American Archaeology, no. 14, 1957). Harold S. Gladwin has written and richly illustrated *A History of the Ancient Southwest* (Portland, Me., 1957). Material on Nuclear American civilization is vast, though nothing is as well written as Eric R. Wolf, *Sons of the Shaking Earth* (Chicago, 1959). G. C. Vaillant in *The Aztecs of Mexico* (New York, 1944) gives an account that runs beyond their conquest but is partly out of date. J. Eric S. Thompson describes *The Rise and Fall of Maya Civilization* (Norman, Okla., 1954) and Paul Rivet *Maya Cities*, trans. Miriam and Lionel Kochan (New York, 1960). See also several articles in Julian H. Steward, ed., *Handbook of South American Indians*, Vol. 2, *The Andean Civilizations*, Bureau of American Ethnology, Bulletin 143, 1946. Donald Collier reviews the "Development of Civilization on the Coast of Peru," in Julian H. Steward, ed., *Irrigation Civilizations: A Comparative Study*, Pan American Union, Social Science Monographs, no. 1, 1955.

Two valuable summaries of world culture growth have appeared since I finished this chapter. *The Dawn of Civilization*, edited by Stuart Piggott (New York, 1961), is a beautifully produced, lavishly illustrated, and authoritative work written by experts. *Courses Toward Urban Life*, edited by Robert J. Braidwood and Gordon R. Willey, Viking Fund Publications in Anthropology, no. 32, 1962, isn't quite as much a pleasure to read. But it too utilizes authorities in examining cultural and other conditions under which full-fledged civilizatons emerged in some dozen world areas.

Index of Names

Index of Subjects

Nigeria, 89
Nikbi, 97
Nile River, 411–413
Nocturnal emissions, 275
Nomadism, see Pastoralism
Nonunilinear descent group, 98–99
North America, 280, 322, 429, 430
North American Indians, 262, 263, 376, 426–434, 435
North Pacific Coast, see Northwest Coast Indians
Northwest Coast Indians, 221, 316–318, 430
Northwest Territories, 242, 253
Notharctus, 383
Novels, use of, in understanding culture, 348
Nuclear America, 427, 430, 433, 434
Nuclear weapons, 328
Nuer, 188
Nupe, 60
Nursing, 260, 301, 302, 303
Nutrition, 292–293
Nyakyusa, 266–267

Obstetrics, see Reproduction
Oceania, 271, 321, 326
      See also Indonesia; Polynesia; Malaysia; Melanesia
Oder River, 393
Oedipus complex, 270, 304
Ohio, 430
Ohio River, 432
Old age, 278–279
Old Stone Age, see Paleolithic Age
Oldowan chopper, 384, 385, 386
Oligocene epoch, 378, 380
Omaha Indians, 208
Omens, 57–58
Oneida Colony, 354
Opera, 220
Opposition, between sexes, 178–179
      See also Radical opposition
Oracles, 57–58
      See also Divination
Oraibi, 69, 94, 107, 108, 109, 117, 118, 124, 177
Oral anxiety, 301
Oral gratification, 301
Oral zone, role of, in socialization, 301, 303
Ordeals, 192, 241
Ordovician period, 378
Oreopithecus, 381
Orestes, 419

Organism, human, as a source of culture, 322–324, 326
      See also Human nature
Organization, see International organization; Social organization
Organizational size, 125
Originality, 220
      See also Creativity
Origination, 47, 330–337
   simultaneous, 334–335
      See also Invention; Inventors
Orokaiva, 59
Ostracoderms, 377, 378–379
Oven, 402
Outcastes, see Untouchables
Ox, 35, 36

Pacific Ocean, 428
Painting, bark, 230–231
   Chinese, 228–230
Pakhtun, 133–136
Pakistan, 7–8, 35, 38, 39, 64, 66, 100, 134, 135, 136, 142, 149, 154, 157, 175, 180, 251, 269, 280, 322, 339, 392
   community development, 354–362, 367, 369
   prehistory, 399, 403, 408–411, 434
Palatalization, 149
Paleocene epoch, 378, 380
Paleolithic Age, 102, 158, 217, 279, 329, 374, 388–393, 396, 426, 430
Paleontology, 370–371
Paleozoic era, 371, 378
Papago Indians, 224
Paper, 338
Papyrus, 412
Parallelism, 335–336
Paranthropus crassidens, 382
Paranthropus robustus, 382
Parapsychology, 342
Parents, 56, 288
   role of, in socialization, 305
Parsi, 280
Passage ritual, see Ritual, passage
Passport, 141
Past, knowledge of, 28, 34, 38
   significance of, 194–196
Pastoralism, 42, 43, 44, 194
Pathans, 36, 38, 39, 64, 66, 68, 73, 95, 96, 97, 322
      See also Pakhtuns; Swat
Patriarchy, 101
Patrilineage, 95, 96, 110

Format by Jeanne Ray
Set in Linotype Fairfield
Composed by The Haddon Craftsmen, Inc.
Printed by The Murray Printing Company
Bound by The Haddon Craftsmen, Inc.
HARPER & ROW, PUBLISHERS, INCORPORATED